Creative
Action
in
Organizations

Creative Action in Organizations

Ivory Tower Visions & Real World Voices

Edited by

CAMERON M. FORD
DENNIS A. GIOIA

SAGE Publications
International Educational and Professional Publisher
Thousand Oaks   London   New Delhi

For information address:

SAGE Publications, Inc.
2455 Teller Road
Thousand Oaks, California 91320
E-mail: order@sagepub.com

SAGE Publications Ltd.
6 Bonhill Street
London EC2A 4PU
United Kingdom

SAGE Publications India Pvt. Ltd.
M-32 Market
Greater Kailash I
New Delhi 110 048 India

Printed in the United States of America

Library of Congress Cataloging-in-Publication Data

Main entry under title:

Creative action in organizations: Ivory tower visions and real world voices /
    edited by Cameron M. Ford, Dennis A. Gioia.
        p.   cm.
    Includes bibliographical references and index.
    ISBN 0-8039-5349-6. — ISBN 0-8039-5350-X (pbk.)
        1. Creative ability in business. 2. Organizational change.
    3. Organizational effectiveness. 4. Industrial management—Employee
    participation.   I. Ford, Cameron M.   II. Gioia, Dennis A., 1947- .
    HD53.C748   1995   95-8240
    658.4—dc20

This book is printed on acid-free paper.

95   96   97   98   99   10   9   8   7   6   5   4   3   2   1

Sage Production Editor: Astrid Virding
Sage Typesetter: Danielle Dillahunt

From the Research Community

TERESA M. AMABILE
*Professor of Business
Administration,
Harvard University*

JAMES R. BAILEY
*Assistant Professor of
Organization Management,
Rutgers University—
Faculty of Management*

DAG BJÖRKEGREN
*Associate Professor in
Organization and
Management Theory,
Stockholm School of Economics*

DANIEL J. BRASS
*Associate Professor of
Organizational Behavior, The
Pennsylvania State University*

JAY A. CONGER
*Professor of Organizational
Behavior, McGill University*

MIHALY CSIKSZENTMIHALYI
*Professor of Psychology,
University of Chicago*

FARIBORZ DAMANPOUR
*Associate Professor of
Organization Management,
Rutgers University—
Faculty of Management*

JAMES L. FARR
*Professor of Psychology,
The Pennsylvania State University*

CAMERON M. FORD
*Assistant Professor of
Organization Management,
Rutgers University—
Faculty of Management*

PETER J. FROST
*Edgar Kaiser Chair of
Organizational Behavior,
University of British Columbia*

CONNIE J. G. GERSICK
*Associate Professor of Human
Resources and Organizational
Behavior, University of California
at Los Angeles*

DENNIS A. GIOIA
*Professor of Organizational
Behavior, The Pennsylvania
State University*

NIGEL KING
*Lecturer in Psychology,
University of Huddersfield,
England*

SHELLEY A. KIRKPATRICK
*Research Analyst,
Pelavin Research Institute*

From the Management Community

F. E. BAILEY, CLU, CFP
President and CEO,
Bailey Financial Group, Inc.

ISAAC (ITZIK) R. BARPAL
Senior Vice President
and Chief Technology Officer,
Allied Signal, Inc., and
Former Vice President,
Science & Technology,
Westinghouse Electric Corporation

ROBERT MICHAEL BURNSIDE
Senior Research and
Applications Associate,
Center for Creative Leadership

ALAN G. CHYNOWETH
Vice President, Applied Research
(Retired), Bellcore

PEDRO CUATRECASAS, M.D.
President, Pharmaceutical
Research, Parke-Davis

JOHN ENGLER
The Governor of Michigan

NORMAN P. FINDLEY
Vice President, Domestic
and International Marketing,
Coca-Cola Enterprises

RUSSELL C. FORD
Senior Vice President,
Harristown Development
Corporation

C. JACKSON GRAY
Senior Vice President of Corporate
Planning and Development,
Woolworth Corporation

GEORGE HEARD
Vice President,
Engineering and Construction,
Coors Brewing Company

DELBERT H. JACOBS
Vice President & Center Manager,
Northrop Advanced Technology
and Design Center

NORMAN E. JOHNSON, Ph.D.
Senior Vice President,
Technology, Weyerhaeuser
Company

F. BEN JONES
Former Vice President,
Research and Development,
Phillips Petroleum Company

Dedication

Cameron would like to dedicate this book to his wife Gricel. Cameron and Gricel began dating, fell in love, and got married during the course of this project. This reinforced his belief in the importance of remaining open to opportunities and capitalizing on serendipity. Her disposition, which couples a flair for the whimsical and imaginative with steadfast pragmatism, embodies many of the paradoxes associated with creativity. She serves as a continuing inspiration in Cameron's life. Cameron would also like to thank his parents Donald and Carol, and his brothers Russell, Douglas, and Martin, all of whom have contributed important ideas and support.

Denny would like to dedicate this book to his daughters, Erin (13 years old) and Dana (12 years old), who live the experience of fantasy and creativity at every opportunity. Although the observation has been made many times before, it bears repeating that creativity is an everyday, and often every-moment, occurrence for a child. Creativity comes easily to every occasion and every location; there remains a lesson in that, perhaps especially as we try to organize ourselves for collective action.

Contents

Foreword

Creativity seems to be a topic of almost perennial fascination. Despite the wide scope of interest in the subject, however, our thinking about creativity has been rather narrowly focused. Historically, we have concentrated a great deal of energy on especially gifted individuals. We have tended to view these people as independent loners working at esoteric tasks or in artistic endeavors. In more recent times, however, there has been a kind of awakening and a realization that the focus of creativity should be broadened to include a wider population than near-geniuses. Conceptions of creativity also need to account for work in the more professional and perhaps prosaic domains of life. Given the practical importance of business and government, the study of creativity within the context of organizations should be an obvious target of attention. In the past it has not been. Relatively recently, however, interest has been on the rise. It has now become clear that work organizations are not merely places where creativity is needed, but settings where a distinctive brand of creativity might be bred, nurtured, and capitalized upon.

Over the past few decades the dialogues and debates about creativity have been framed and largely dominated by psychologists. Perhaps as a consequence, traditional approaches to the study of creativity have focused overwhelmingly on the individual as the main, and often only, contributor to creativity. Depictions of creativity have typically underplayed the influence of context and have devoted only minimal attention specifically to organizational contexts. Moreover, until recently, management scholars and management practitioners have been little more than background voices in the conversations regarding creativity.

In addition, most of the research into creativity has been conducted outside the boundaries of organizations, usually using children and students as subjects. These studies often have questionable relevance to the kinds of problems, issues, and activities common to organizations. Nonetheless, many writers and consultants continue to apply theories and findings from these removed domains (e.g., arts and education) in trying to improve creativity in organizations. The results have not been encouraging. Consequently, scholars and practicing managers have become disillusioned. They have questioned the usefulness of traditional approaches to understanding and managing creativity in organizations.

What we need is more thought and exploration that places the organizational context in the center of things so that we might frame conceptualizations and uncover findings that are specifically relevant to organizational settings. What we need are representative voices occupying the foreground of conversations about creativity in organizations, rather than the margins and backgrounds. What we also need is to have those who do research on organizational creativity talk along with those who practice and manage applied creative activity. As a result of this line of thinking, we as editors and representatives of the world of academe initiated a joint venture with our counterparts in the world of practice to produce this volume.

This book seeks to accomplish some of the above aims in its own creative fashion, by using a format that brings both academic and practitioner voices into the conversation together. It places the organizational context front and center in the discussion. It seeks to increase the relevance of academic work to practitioners and the relevance of pragmatic views to academicians. By now it is obvious that reflective practitioners can add valuable insights to scholarly efforts aimed at understanding and enhancing creativity and that action-oriented scholars can contribute to the production of practical wisdom at work.

This volume comprises an equal number of short, readable, to-the-point essays on creativity from representatives of both communities. Combining both perspectives generates a richer, more realistic and revealing view of the complex landscape that is creativity in organizations. By juxtaposing these two views from communities that too often talk past each other, we hope that this volume can make a useful contribution to a broad spectrum of people concerned with creativity in organizations. Overall, this book represents a rare attempt to incorporate views from the best traditions of the ivory tower with rich experiential lessons from the real world.

The central essays are intended to be lively, accessible, insightful, and relevant. They do not require work to read them; they instead encourage a spirit of fun. Creativity, after all, should have a lot more of the character of fun than of work. There is no law of the universe that dictates that learning should take the kind of effort that makes your head hurt. In principle, learning something useful can come easily. In this forum, it does.

We as editors have tried to make our own contributions. As a helpful prelude to the essays, we have provided a review chapter, also written in an accessible style, that articulates the key findings of the research that has gone before and assembles them into a distinctive, useful, and user-friendly framework for conceptualizing creativity in organizations. Following the essays, we have provided a chapter that captures the themes sounded in the contributors' writings in a way that highlights the shared points (and points of difference) between the two groups of authors; this chapter emphasizes some key dimensions that can help improve creativity at work. Finally, we have written a capstone chapter that attempts to integrate the preceding work with the essence of these essays to make a distinctive contribution to the literature on creativity.

There is some risk that the structure of our book might encourage readers to gravitate toward the writings of their own kindred spirits—practitioners might be inclined to read what other practitioners have written; academicians to read only what other scholars have written. We encourage you not to do that. One of the lessons from both sides of this house is that there are creative sparks available from seeing how the other side views the world. We are confident that you will find much in here that resonates with your way of seeing and your experience. We recognize, however, that you will not necessarily agree with everything. Although some views will ring true immediately, others might provoke your skepticism; still others might seem initially idealistic or, alternatively, perhaps even a bit too rooted in particulars. Little matter—so long as it stirs you to some fruitful reflection. Our intention here is as much to provoke as to inform.

Some of these essays are quite personal and relate rich descriptions of the "Aha!" or "Shazzam!" experience. Others are surprisingly candid in admitting to disappointments along the road. Both approaches point out in vivid terms that creativity is not a dispassionate or impersonal process. Furthermore, they also point out that creativity not only involves play and playfulness, it also involves a good dose of hard work and occasionally putting your neck on the line. Finally, they demonstrate that creativity in organizational settings consists of multidimensional processes that not only diverge in some fashion from the usual way of thinking, but also later converge on collective actions before coming to fruition (an observation that we have attempted to capture symbolically with the pair of divergent and convergent arrows on the cover.)

We suggest that you put this book on your desk, with the title visible to you throughout the day, and let it beckon to you. Read an essay in 10 minutes or less; muse on it for another 5. It doesn't take long for inspiration to strike if you're in the mood for a little vicarious wisdom. Consider an essay's possible relevance to your problems and your surroundings; apply a touch of your own brand of creativity; make the connection between your experience and those of the author. All these essays contain little pearls of wisdom for your consideration. Choose an essay; let it plant a seed that you can work with. Above all, have a good time learning a little something new or revisiting something you thought you already knew.

—Cameron M. Ford
—Dennis A. Gioia

Contemplating Creative Action in Organizations

1 Multiple Visions and Multiple Voices
Academic and Practitioner Conceptions of Creativity in Organizations

CAMERON M. FORD *Rutgers University*

DENNIS A. GIOIA *The Pennsylvania State University*

———————

*The real voyage of discovery
consists not in seeing new landscapes,
but in having new eyes.*
                              M. Proust

*It's new! Novel! Different!
Great!
Does it work!*
                              J. Mansfield

$\mathscr{C}$reativity is one of the most intriguing and elusive topics associated with human performance. It just might be the most seductive topic in the management of modern organizations, thus leading to the present day "romance with creativity." Everyone, it seems, is smitten by the idea. And yet, it also seems that we do not have a clear conception of just what constitutes creativity in organizations. What is this sometimes mystical enterprise that is associated with our most

3

admired people and organizations? And why this continuing fascination with a subject that, by most assessments, has had little new said about it for quite a few years?

Perhaps the reason for the continued romanticism associated with creativity, especially as applied to organizations, is the enduring belief that creativity enhances organizational effectiveness, and even survivability, particularly in times of accelerated or turbulent change. Creativity has been associated with all that is good: individual fulfillment, better group productivity, the development of successful business ventures, and even more grandiosely, the improvement of national economic well-being.

Therefore, we could probably justify our interest in producing this book by appealing to such worthy goals as trying to improve competitive advantage in business, providing organization members with an opportunity to realize their talents, or simply keeping up with the rapid pace of change in today's business environment. Such rationales are tried and true. We would like to offer what we think is an even more compelling rationale, however: Creativity is now a core necessity for success in a profoundly changing organizational world. Creativity is simply essential, because organizations and their environments are both changing so fundamentally.

The intertwined reasons for these changes are well known: increased availability of information technologies, further globalization of business activities, and moves away from hierarchies toward markets as a means of getting things done, among others. These changes are not causing organizations simply to do more or do less of what they have done in the past; they reflect qualitative changes that require new approaches.

The shift we are now experiencing from industrial to postindustrial society is on the same order of importance as the last major shift from craft to industrial society. It is a different kind of shift—not one merely of pace, but of character. It is a shift that is also paradoxical: It depends on creativity to fuel it, and also to cope with it. Creativity has been simultaneously the generator, facilitator, and (hopefully) savior of an intimidatingly ambiguous new world for people and organizations. Rather than being merely an enchanting concept cavalierly applied to off-beat problems, creativity has now become central to managing in this new world. In the process it has helped change the nature of the modern organization in that world.

The organization of the future, for instance, often will be based on transient teams of employees, vendors, and independent contractors. Members of these teams will be much more oriented toward the overall project success than coverage of "job responsibilities." Roles will be less specified and, therefore, functional expertise will be less valued than industry expertise. "Modular corporations" and "network organizations" will come to the fore.

Careers of the future will be based much less on progressing through an organization's hierarchy (after all, there won't be many hierarchies left), but rather on progressing through many different project assignments that develop an individual's marketable skills. The contract between individuals and organizations also is changing—focusing less on security and more on personal skill development. Success often will be measured by involvements in successful new projects. Rewards will go not to those with the ability to make "rational" choices in the face of uncertainty, but to those with the ability to take creative action in the face of ambiguity and to learn from the consequences of those actions. In this environment, intellectual capital is the most important resource for sustained effectiveness, and creativity stands out as the best way to leverage intellectual capital. Thus, in the new world of work and organization, creativity is paramount to project success and to career mobility.

THE ORIGINS OF THIS VOLUME

This book has been driven not only by the above observations about the nature of organizations and careers, but also by several key observations concerning the present state of creativity theory, research, teaching, and practice. First, most of the existing work on creativity has only minimal direct applicability to organizations. As a result, despite the thousands of writings on the subject, academics still have relatively little confidence in offering recommendations to organizational people struggling to develop creative solutions to "real-life" problems.

Second, in spite of all the recent interest in creativity by the practitioner community, organizational researchers have not taken up the research challenge in significant numbers. Why? Isaksen and Murdock (1993) have speculated that there are four reasons why "serious" researchers do not study creativity: that it is often construed as mysterious; that it is frequently treated as something magical; that it is occasionally associated with some form of madness; and perhaps most damaging, that it is sometimes perceived to be a "frivolous" topic by the academic community. There is something to be said for retaining some sense of the enchantment in the idea of creativity, so the first two reasons seem fairly harmless. The third reason comes from too many fanciful depictions of the creative process in popular writing. The final reason, however, is misguided and inhibits needed research in a rich area of immense practical importance.

Third, despite the relative lack of empirical research on creativity in organizations, much of what passes for common wisdom about managing creativity is drawn from research from non-organizational domains (e.g., the fine and performing arts, education, the history of science, child development, etc.). As intriguing as those studies are, there is either a force-fit or a wishful-thinking quality to many of the suggestions that derive from extrapolating that work to organizations. It is not at all clear that generalizing such findings is warranted. Indeed, there is suggestive evidence that the processes and outcomes in other fields might be fundamentally different. The factors that (for instance) help children produce better finger paintings are likely to be very different from the factors that help scientists to secure patents; the factors that help student research subjects develop more uses for a brick probably are rather different from the factors that help executives develop creative solutions to business problems. As self-evident as those observations might be, the implications of these differences have not been adequately taken into account by those who dispense advice regarding creativity in organizations.

The typical tactic of trying to generalize ideas from other domains to work contexts is risky. Teresa Amabile in 1982 sensitized creativity researchers to the virtual absence of consideration of context in the general creativity literature when she noted that a review of nearly 7,000 papers on creativity produced only 138 that examined social or contextual variables. Only a precious few of these 138 specifically considered organizational contexts.

Another tactic we sometimes resort to is gleaning research findings from studies on topics like group dynamics, decision making, and innovation, and inferring that these results hold for creativity, too (on the apparent assumption that creativity is directly related to each of these topics). Although some of these generalizations might have merit, we are nonetheless left with a shaky foundation upon which to base our prescriptions for improving creativity. Given this spotty history, it is not surprising that business leaders have come to be rather dismissive of academic descriptions and recommendations.

Overall, then, an examination of the existing writings on creativity suggests that many of them are frustratingly deficient in their usefulness in applied settings—and work organizations are arguably the ultimate applied setting. The worst fault of some of these writings is that they simply come across as superficial to experienced organizational hands and therefore lack credibility. For others, a greater fault is that their suggestions are deceptively inappropriate to organizational settings; these are of more concern to those who are trying to "manage" creativity, because they represent expensive dead ends that sap energy without producing results. One of the reasons for the dissatisfactions of practitioners is that we seem to have jumped to premature prescriptions for fostering creativity before we have acquired adequate descriptions of the distinctive nature of creativity in organizations.

THE UNIQUE CHARACTER
OF ORGANIZATIONS

Organizational contexts impose a special set of conditions on creativity. A partial list of obvious factors that are likely to be influential include: interaction patterns among employees; the degree of trust among team members; the design of incentive, appraisal, and reward systems; political issues involved in creative or innovative decisions; the availability of (and competition for) resources; the history and culture of the organization; means versus ends orientations; and internally driven versus customer-driven philosophies. All of these topics are key to understanding creativity in organizations, yet none of them has been studied adequately with a focus on their implications for creativity.

Organizations constitute a distinctive context within which creativity might be fostered or stifled. The organizational context needs to be recognized as an important realm associated with creative endeavor. The modern world can now appropriately be viewed as a world of organizations, perhaps more than as a world of individuals. As a consequence, the character of human achievement is now most often seen in the light of organizational sponsorship rather than individual accomplishment. The essentially organizational character of modern society makes the creative conduct of organizational life a first-order imperative for those of us who study and manage organizations.

These observations constitute another set of reasons why we have chosen to produce this book in this unusual form. Our intention is to construct a richer, more multidimensional, and more relevant view of creativity at work by using first-hand knowledge supplied directly by those concerned with understanding and implementing it.

SHEPHERDING THE CREATIVE PROCESS

We have played the role of shepherd in creating this volume of original essays on creativity in organizations. We had the good sense and good fortune to invite cooperative, creative people to join us. Half of these essays are from prominent scholars in the academic community and half are from leading executives from both private and public organizations. We asked all the authors to reflect on their experiences and/or concerns with creativity and write a short, pithy, engaging essay containing some distinctive observations about the creative process and its outcomes.

Our only (minor) howls of protest came as a result of our essay length guidelines (mainly from the academic side of the house, who wanted more space . . . we tend to be a long-winded lot, given half a chance). Despite the pleas, we held firm. Consequently, these essays are only one third the length of a usual book chapter; we wanted the authors to say what they thought was most important in short order—to get in and get out; to produce a focused, to-the-point position statement that interested readers could pick up, read quickly, and learn something useful or insightful from in just a few minutes. We think that particular goal has been achieved admirably.

The authors from the practitioner community are all recognized contributors to their industries or constituencies. We suggested that they offer thoughts on just what constitutes creativity, what they considered to be the most critical factors influencing the development of creative solutions in organizations, and what organizations could or should do to promote and improve the creativity of employees. Similarly, the contributors from academia are all recognized researchers and writers on organizational creativity who have been asked to reflect on their thinking and on their research programs dealing with creativity in organizations and to offer their most enlightening and useful commentary.

This volume tries to look at creativity in organizations in a different light. It tries to lower the boundaries between the academics and practitioners as it crosses the boundaries between scholarly and popular professional writing. Overall, the main contributions of the book derive from (a) its diverse contributors and their multiple perspectives, (b) its grounding in experience, and (c) its potential to generate a revised view of creativity in organizational contexts. We hope that this collection of insights, presented in an eminently readable format, might do more to help rethink creativity than one more intellectual treatise on the subject.

A BRIEF TOUR OF THE BOOK

To kick off the volume we have provided a different sort of review chapter to give the reflective reader an initial framework for thinking about creativity as she or he peruses the succeeding essays. Despite its substantive content and its grounding in empirical research, it is written in a fashion intended to engage all readers in a research-based exploration of what we think we know about creativity in organizations. We realize that reading a literature review often can feel a lot like wading through molasses, so we have attempted to capture the key findings of this research via the rich metaphor of creativity as mystery-to-be-solved. Don't let the writing style fool you, however. We based this chapter on the most comprehensive review of the empirical studies on creativity in professional and organizational contexts to date. We provide tabular displays of these studies to capture their contributions for interested readers. In this chapter we try to balance academic rigor with accessibility. We hope, and hope to demonstrate, that these ends are not mutually exclusive.

The review chapter is followed by the raison d'être for the volume, the contributors' essays. First come the essays from the academic writers, followed immediately by the essays from the practitioner authors. Each leads off with a short excerpt that captures a key idea contained within the ensuing essay. As will soon be apparent, the essays can certainly stand on their own as distinctive contributions. We elected to go a step further with them, however. We decided to treat the essays not only as a series of insightful observations, but also as "data" that we could use to search for themes that might enhance our overall understanding of creativity in organizations (in keeping with our incorrigible outlook as empiricists). Therefore, we content-analyzed the essays to produce a follow-on chapter that presents a look at the most significant themes underlying the essays, as well as a look at some of the enlightening differences between academic and practitioner views. This chapter is intended to extract the collective wisdom from the essays that readers might use in their own work settings. One of the overarching themes emerging from this meta-view is that fostering creativity in organizations involves not only the well-recognized notion of encouraging "divergent" thinking and act-ing, but also a less-recognized focus on subsequent "convergent" processes to bring it all together. As noted in the Foreword, this important idea is represented symbolically via the diverging and converging arrows on the cover of this volume.

The final, capstone chapter attempts to assimilate and synthesize, or at least reconcile, the themes and lessons from these essays with the main findings of the previous 45 years of research on creativity, as represented in the review chapter. We employ both sources to fashion a revised, and more relevant, framework for conceptualizing creativity in organizations. Such a framework should help to revitalize ways of understanding, researching, and managing creativity. Once again we have attempted to present this framework in a readable fashion, so that the scholarly analytical effort is user-friendly.

As the introductory epigrams encourage us to do, this book seeks to look at creativity in organizations with new eyes (Proust) while keeping our feet firmly rooted in practicalities (Mansfield). Our foremost goal for this volume is to employ multiple visions and multiple voices to make a bona fide contribution to the knowledge about, and the practice of, creativity in organizations. Our corollary goal is to offer a series of informative, insightful, and accessible essays on creativity from knowledgeable contributors. Those essays equally represent visions and voices from a thoughtful academic community and from a reflective practitioner community. Ultimately, we hope that this book can play some small role in redirecting the ways that we think about and act upon creativity in the context of organizations.

REFERENCES

Amabile, T. M. (1982). *The social psychology of creativity.* New York: Springer.

Isaksen, S. G., & Murdock, M. C. (1993). The emergence of a discipline: Issues and approaches to the study of creativity. In S. G. Isaksen, M. C. Murdock, R. L. Firestien, & D. J. Treffinger (Eds.), *Understanding and recognizing creativity: The emergence of a discipline* (pp. 13-47). Norwood, NJ: Ablex.

2 Creativity Is a Mystery
Clues From the
Investigators' Notebooks

CAMERON M. FORD *Rutgers University*

$\mathscr{C}$onsider the following scenario:

> Ladies and gentlemen, you may be wondering why I have invited you
> here today. Unfortunately, the occasion is not a pleasant one. A
> heinous crime has been committed—and I have been charged with
> conducting the investigation. Of course, my first step will be to develop
> an exhaustive description of the act in question. Once I establish the
> nature of the crime, I will direct my efforts toward uncovering three
> basic facts. I must first discover the culprit's motive for the crime.
> Then I must prove that the suspect had both the necessary means and
> the opportunity to commit the act. Only after I turn up all three of
> these clues will I be able to build a case for the suspect's guilt beyond
> a reasonable doubt. If I cannot forge compelling evidence regarding
> each of these elements of the crime, a jury will certainly set the suspect
> free.

Anyone who enjoys reading mystery novels or watching detective
dramas has probably read or seen countless scenes such as this one.
Almost every mystery concludes with an intricate description of the
motive, means, and opportunity necessary to gain a conviction.
Now, instead of directing our attention to an act of crime, suppose

we instead consider looking into acts of creativity. I propose that understanding an act of creativity requires a similar investigative approach. In the case of a criminal act, the investigator must first decide whether the act in question meets the criteria defining the crime in question. Once it has been established that a crime has, in fact, occurred, the investigator proceeds by developing a theory that accounts for the motive(s) of the actor(s), the means used to carry out the act, and the opportunity(ies) that facilitated the occurrence of the act. The establishment of the crime and the discovery of each of these three clues are all necessary and important for a complete depiction of the deed.

Similarly, an investigator of a creative act must first determine whether a particular act meets the criteria that define creativity (e.g., novelty, value, etc.). Once this is done, the detective must continue to work until a complete case can be presented. As is true in a criminal investigation, evidence that a creative act occurred and proof related to motive, means, and opportunity are necessary to a complete explanation that can lead to a verdict.

The jury is in on the current state of creativity research and the verdict is—*case dismissed for lack of evidence.* Creativity researchers have not only failed to define clearly the nature of the crime, they have also failed to develop a clear, comprehensive case that a jury can translate into a sentence for enhancing creativity. The reason for this state of affairs is simple to discern from even a cursory glance at the research literature on the subject—creativity investigators have focused on too narrow a range of clues; they also have lost sight of solving the case at hand. Consequently, they have failed to present an adequate explanation that describes the configuration of elements necessary to build their case. It is not surprising, therefore, that these investigations have failed to stir the imaginations or actions of interested practitioners of the act.

I do not use this analogy to suggest that the state of creativity research is criminal. Rather, it reveals some serious limitations to the approaches employed by previous investigations of creativity and suggests avenues for enriching future efforts. Researchers and practitioners are both generally frustrated by the state of our understanding of creativity. And practitioners are not the only ones who put little stock in this research. For example, Howard Gardner, an eminent creativity researcher at Harvard University, launched a research program under the label "Project Zero" to signify his belief that no firm knowledge has been developed in the field. The feeling I have after reading much of the research on the topic is similar to when I miss the last 10 minutes of a detective show or can't stay awake long enough to finish a mystery novel. My head is littered with potentially useful clues, but I can't formulate a theory that puts the pieces together. I am utterly dependent on Miss Marple, Perry Mason, Columbo, Jim Rockford, Ellery Queen, Sam Spade, Thomas Magnum, and others to spin the tale that ties the motive, weapon, and opportunity into a clever package. Unfortunately, in this case we cannot rely on some omnipotent detective to formulate a theory that can explain and guide creative acts. We are on our own.

This, however, is not cause for despair. Think of it instead as a challenge. There are many clues for us to examine. My purpose in this chapter is to provide some of these clues by presenting the empirical facts created from more than 40 years of empirical research on creativity in organizational and professional settings. These clues will establish a grounding in "what we know" that will help underscore the distinctive insights offered by the ensuing essays. Armed with ideas offered by previous research and those posed by our contributors, there should be enough clues for you to formulate your own view that solves this creativity mystery. Of course, we will offer our own theory that attempts to reconcile the facts in this case at the end of this volume. But, as when reading an Agatha Christie novel or watching a good detective drama, it is always more fun to see if you can solve the case on your own.

LET THE INVESTIGATION BEGIN!

So where do we start? Do we have any leads? To answer these questions one needs to understand a little about the investigators who conduct creativity research. Creativity was actually a relatively inconspicuous research topic until J. P. Guilford delivered a landmark speech to the American Psychological Association in 1950. In this speech Guilford argued that a primary mission of the psychology field should be to investigate creativity. Other psychologists listened, and the modern era of creativity research was under way. From then until now psychologists of various stripes have dominated the study of creativity. The most common approaches were based on psychometric (test measurement) methodologies and cognitive psychology. A critically important limitation of these approaches, however, is that they focus solely on identifying individual differences related to creativity. Although this research is unquestionably valuable, it ignores the impact of real-life contexts on creativity. Most important for our purposes is that few of these studies were done in organizations, used organization members as subjects, or otherwise considered how work environments influence creative acts. This lack of diversity has severely and sadly limited the accumulated impact of this large body of work. Many psychologists interested in creativity have taken stock of the state of their art, have judged it to be unsatisfying, and have suggested that new voices be added to the dialogue (see Isaksen, Murdock, Firestien, & Treffinger [1993] for several interesting commentaries on this point). Important and distinctive contributions have already emerged from the efforts of several psychologists who have employed alternative investigative approaches (e.g., Amabile, Csikszentmihalyi, Gardner, Gruber, Simonton).

During the 1950s the field of management was trying to establish itself as a legitimate "scientific" discipline. It borrowed ideas liberally from the fields of psychology, sociology, economics, political science, anthropology, history, engineering, and others in an effort to establish its scholarly roots. This intellectual diversity eventually paid off as original contributions developed that spurred the growth of the field. Management researchers have seldom made creativity research a priority, however. The relatively few studies that have been done are on the whole not widely known or well integrated into the management discipline. And the trend is not encouraging. The importance of creativity to management scholars seems to have eroded to dismal levels. For example, out of approximately 1,100 papers presented at the 1994 Academy of Management Meeting, 0 empirical studies of creativity were presented. None. Given its frequent mention in the popular press and its "buzz word" status, it is hard to imagine that efforts to pursue creativity as a distinct topic of inquiry are so rare among management scholars.

This would seem to leave investigators with two dubious tactics for unearthing clues to organizational creativity. We can import them from research produced in fields of inquiry that turn a blind eye toward organizational dynamics, or use management research that doesn't explicitly examine creativity per se and hope that the results hold for creativity as well. Neither of these options is particularly attractive. Most previous research on creativity pays no attention to organizational or professional concerns. Therefore, I provide only limited mention of these works in this review. Instead, I am going to focus on the studies that *do* exist that specifically examine creativity *in organizational and professional settings*. There are not as many as one might hope given the volume of research conducted since the early fifties. Nevertheless, a body of work exists that can provide a useful starting point for our initial fact-finding related to this case.

INVESTIGATIVE TECHNIQUE

The first step in my investigation was to narrow the field so that my questioning could be more precise. I decided to define the domain of this review to include empirical studies of creativity appearing in English-language journals since 1950 that included organization members or professionals as subjects. Therefore, I excluded conceptual papers and studies using students or other non-organizational participants. I also excluded most of the research on innovation because, perhaps surprisingly, most studies do not explicitly discuss or measure creativity. Innovation is generally conceived and measured as the adoption (not creation) of some new product or technology (see Rogers & Shoemaker, 1971; Zaltman, Duncan, & Holbek, 1973). Overall, the innovation literature limits itself to describing processes that influence the utilization, but not the development, of new ideas, products, and technologies. Reviewing these studies together would be like comparing apples and oranges. Rather than present you with fruit salad, I opted to focus only on studies of creativity per se. As a result, the conclusions presented by investigation should be clearer and more useful toward the goal of enhancing creativity in organizations.

Next, I rounded up the usual suspects and grilled them until I got what I was looking for. As a scholar this meant searching through a variety of resources to find papers that met my criteria. I included several existing databases in my hunt including *Psychological Abstracts, Social Sciences Index, Business Periodicals Index, ABI/Inform,* and the *Research Library Information Network.* These databases cover books held by major research libraries as well as more than 10,000 periodicals. Other important sources include Rothenberg and Greenberg's (1976) bibliography of approximately 7,000 creativity studies dating to 1974, the most current listing (1981) of the Institute of Personality Assessment and Research's listing of creativity publications, and the bibliographies of several recent, noteworthy reviews such as those conducted by Barron and Harrington (1981), Amabile (1983b, 1988), Mumford and Gustafson (1988), King (1990), and Woodman, Sawyer, and Griffin (1993). In addition, I examined the bibliographies of articles identified through these sources to see if I could find any additional works. I'm sure a few relevant studies slipped through my net. Nevertheless, I believe that this is the most comprehensive review of this literature to date.

JUST THE FACTS, PLEASE: DEFINING THE CRIME

As noted, the first step in an investigation is to establish that a crime has occurred. So, how do we decide that a creative act has taken place? It is not as simple as it first appears. Researchers seem to agree that creativity refers to something that is both *novel* and in some sense *valuable.* Deciding what to evaluate, however (i.e., a person, a process, a product) and who should evaluate (i.e., the creator, a researcher, expert judges, etc.) has generated heated debate among the detectives. Given our purposes, we can skip the boring details of this little squabble. Suffice it to say that leading researchers on the topic seem to be moving toward some consensus regarding key aspects of defining creative acts. Following this trend, I define *creativity* as *a context-specific, subjective judgment of the novelty and value of an outcome of an individual's or a collective's behavior.*

Odd as it may seem, this definition has a lot in common with the way in which criminal acts are defined. For example, definitions of "crimes" are socially constructed. Acts are often not inherently criminal; governing agents make judgment regarding the legality of various behaviors and develop laws accordingly. As a result, definitions of criminal acts often vary dramatically from government to government. Also, acts that are judged as criminal at one time may be seen as acceptable later and vice versa. Even the perpetrator's motives influence judgments regarding criminal acts. For example, a person who kills can be considered a murderer or a hero depending on the motives underlying the act. Laws also recognize different levels of a particular crime based on the seriousness of the consequences of an act. Thus, definitions of criminal acts can best be thought of as context-sensitive, subjective judgments of individual or collective behaviors that are codified into laws and further interpreted by the courts.

Given these similarities, let us go back and scrutinize the definition of creativity further. *Creativity is a context-specific judgment.* This means that evaluations of creativity can vary from one group, one organization, and one culture to the next. They may also change over time. Judgments of creativity could be considered at the level of a person, group, organization, industry, profession, or beyond. In principle this means that anything could be seen as creative as long as one person believes it so, or that nothing could be considered as creative unless everyone believes it so. It is therefore important for the detective to specify the context that will supply the most meaningful evaluations given his or her purposes. Our concern is with professional creativity in organizational settings. Completely personal evaluations are not likely to be meaningful in this context. Creative ideas in organizations are going to have to go public at some level if anything is to become of them. Nor does it seem appropriate to expand the scope of evaluations beyond the context that we are investigating. Therefore, given the aims of this book, assessments of creativity are best made by those within an organization or profession where a creative act occurs.

Creativity is a subjective judgment of novelty and value. This means that creativity is not an inherent quality that can be measured in the same manner as weight or height. Rather, it is an assessment that people make, typically based on whether they believe something is both novel and valuable. Whereas the previous concern focused on identifying who should judge creative acts, the concern here centers on the level of agreement among those judges regarding the presence or absence of the defining attributes of creative acts. As a rule, assessments of creativity are more meaningful when they are shared by others, regardless of the context. Yet, judgments of creativity can be biased and contested, just like judgments of guilt or innocence. In a criminal trial the jury selection process is oriented toward selecting favorable and rejecting negative biases that are likely to build agreement favorable to one's case. Some say that trials are often won or lost during this process. Similarly, one can influence the judging of a creative act by selectively employing the services of different jurists. Thus, in addition to defining creativity in terms of judgments made by those who are familiar with a particular organization or profession, I would add that higher levels of agreement among judges make evaluations of creative acts more meaningful.

Creativity refers to an outcome produced by an actor. This means that the jury has to have something to see, touch, or hear in order to make a judgment as to its novelty and value. Researchers call this a "product" definition because the judgment refers to some public outcome rather than to a process or a specific person. The logic in this is fairly straightforward. People are generally considered creative only when they come up with creative products (be these ideas, services, prototypes, artwork, etc.) on a fairly regular basis. Further, a process is considered creative only when it delivers a creative product (although a process could be judged as an end itself; in this case a "process" could be judged as an "outcome" and assessed as creative). Thus the concept of "creative product" should be thought of in broad terms. Anything that people can examine and judge, including communicated ideas, can be thought of as a product.

So what does all this concern with the definition of creativity mean to us? Simply that one must recognize that acts of creativity, like criminal acts, are often difficult to assess. Perhaps if evaluations of creativity held the same consequences as evaluations of crimes we would have a more rigorous system for classifying creative acts of different levels, in different contexts, produced by different intentions and states of mind. These difficulties have made it hard for researchers to fashion meaningful studies. The studies reviewed in this chapter use many different measures of creativity that often make findings difficult to compare. However, understanding the challenges underlying the definition of a creative act is more than an academic exercise. It is critically important to organizations that wish to promote and reward people based in part on the creativity of their work.

One last thing before we begin our search for clues. Other aspects of work performance can also be considered as context-specific, social judgments. More common types of performance may seem more "objective," but that is only because we have come to greater agreement about the use of certain measures. I believe that judgments of creativity are likely to be biased by many of the same influences that bias other performance measures. For example, the work of a man may be more likely to be viewed as creative than the work of a woman. Older workers may have trouble getting others to see their work as creative. The creativity of individuals working in stereotypically creative jobs (e.g., advertising, architecture, R&D) may be overestimated relative to those laboring in fields less typically thought of as "creative." Well-networked individuals may even be able to influence others' evaluations of creativity.

However, the bias that perhaps most blinds us to achieving a comprehensive view of the influences on creativity is one that researchers have labeled as "The Fundamental Attribution Error." The concept is simple: We tend to believe that people cause events, as we overestimate the actual influence that people have over events and underestimate the impact of situational factors. The implication is that we assume too quickly that personal characteristics are the causes of things. The adversarial process in the legal system helps courts avoid the effects of this bias. The prosecuting attorney is in charge of presenting evidence that a defendant is responsible for a crime while the defending attorney emphasizes other possible causes. This process forces the judge and jury to consider a broad range of possible causes underlying an occurrence.

Unfortunately, no such safeguard protects us from relying on simplistic explanations for creative behavior. For instance, when we try to explain creativity, we generally think of personal qualities like intelligence, divergent thinking skills, tireless dedication, and other heroic qualities. However, we typically ignore the context within which a creative product emerged. Researchers suffer from this problem as well (after all, we are people too). People tend to ascribe incredible powers to leaders and hold them exclusively responsible for results that occur under their stewardships. We seem to have a "romance with leadership" that comforts us because it provides us with simple explanations for events (Meindl, Ehrlich, & Dukerich, 1985). This bias tends to keep us from developing more realistic and useful explanations of leaders and leadership.

Creativity researchers, and lay people as well, seem to suffer from a similar love affair. Call it a "romance with creativity." Almost all the general research on creativity has attempted to identify personal characteristics of individuals that lead them to creative productivity. Most of us know a few wondrous tales of heroic individuals who have defied the odds to produce incredible creative works. The problem is that most of these popular stories are creative indeed—they grossly underestimate the influence that circumstances had on the emergence of famous creative products (see Robert W. Weisberg's book, *Creativity, Genius, and Other Myths* [1986] for an enlightening debunking of many popular tales associated with creativity). I do not mean to slight the importance of the motivations and talents of our creative legends. I believe, though, that this love affair with creators has led researcher to focus too narrowly on characteristics of individuals that lead them to commit creative acts. They have almost ignored the search for opportunities *when and where* creative acts are most likely to occur. This approach has certainly reduced the impact of creativity research in real-world settings. In organizational settings, this oversight is almost crippling. Organizations need not look so intently for heroes. Instead, we need to provide talented and motivated individuals with opportunities to enact creative solutions.

Having specified the nature of the crime and identified potential biases that might influence our judgments, I now turn attention toward presenting clues that will help build a viable case that explains acts of creativity. The following sections describe empirical facts regarding the motives, means, and opportunities associated with creativity in organizational and professional settings. I should warn the reader that the evidence is rather skewed toward understanding the creative individual, even though this review ostensibly features organizational contexts. This reflects the orientations of previous research approaches noted earlier. On the bright side, the specific clues I offer have good support from empirical research.

EXPLAINING THE ACT

The Motives for the Act. When we seek explanations for attention-getting acts, whether they be criminal or creative, we often look first for motives. Perhaps reflecting this tendency, research has probably discovered more about the motivations behind creative acts than we know about any other contributing factor. The motives that emerge from my review of the organizational creativity literature are similar to those mentioned in more general reviews of creativity in other domains (e.g., Barron & Harrington, 1981).

The portrait drawn here in some ways runs counter to the popular notion that creative individuals are ill-adapted to organizational life. Creative people are on average more professionally oriented and interested in attaining status and power than their less creative counterparts. On the basis of these preferences, one might expect them to fare well in traditional hierarchical organizations. Yet, the desires to realize creativity, variety, and independence are at odds with the core ideologies of bureaucratic organization and scientific management: job specialization, hierarchical coordination and control, and separation of planning from operations. Overall, the array of goals described in Table 2.1 suggests that creative individuals are likely to feel ambivalent about organizational life.

Tables 2.2 and 2.3 list influences on motivation beside personal goals. These influences fall into two categories. Expectations regarding personal capabilities make up the first category. For example, employees may often like to present creative solutions to problems. Yet, despite their desire, they are likely to sit by quietly if they harbor doubts regarding their own creative talent or personal competence. Negative expectations such as these can crush one's motivation to seek out even the most wished-for dreams. Emotions represent the second category of influences on motivation. They provide us with feedback regarding our moment-to-moment behaviors and help to regulate the energy we have available for future endeavors. Some emotions, such as depression and boredom, reduce energy levels and lead people to avoid certain activities. On the other hand, satisfaction, interest, and even anger can produce arousal and persistent effort toward one's goals.

TABLE 2.1 Primary Motives Associated With Creative Acts

Motives	Description	Supporting Empirical Research
Creativity	Interested in doing creative or novel things, curious, playful, adventurous, and appreciates esthetics	Morrison, Owens, Glennon, & Albright (1962); MacKinnon (1962); Jones (1964); Barron & Egan (1968); MacKinnon (1970); Udell, Baker, & Albaum (1976); Kirton (1976); Keller & Holland (1978); Kirton (1980); Kirton & Pender (1982); Amabile (1984); Kirton (1989); Foxall (1990); Tegano (1990)
Variety	Maintains broad interests, enjoys variety, and is open to new experiences	Buel (1960); MacKinnon (1960); Jones & Arnold (1962); MacKinnon (1962); Buel (1965); Barron (1966); Pelz (1967); MacKinnon (1970); Burke (1983)
Independence	Desires independence, autonomy, self-determination, and solitude	Sprecher (1959); Buel (1960); MacKinnon (1960); MacKinnon (1962); MacKinnon (1963); Buel (1965); McDermid (1965); Barron (1966); Pelz (1967); Barron & Egan (1968); Helson & Crutchfield (1970); MacKinnon (1970); Albaum (1976); Payne (1987); Kirton (1989)
Achievement	Seeks achievement and professional accomplishment	MacKinnon (1959); Morrison, Owens, Glennon, & Albright (1962); MacKinnon (1962); MacKinnon (1963); Chambers (1964); Jones (1964); Buel (1965); Barron (1966); Cline, Tucker, & Anderson (1966); Barron & Egan (1968); MacKinnon (1970); Ekvall (1976); Koberg & Chusmir (1987); Gardner (1993)
Superiority	Seeks dominance and has a high need for power	MacKinnon (1959); Buel (1960); MacKinnon (1963); Chambers (1964); McDermid (1965); Barron & Egan (1968); MacKinnon (1970); Andrews (1975); Koberg & Chusmir (1987)

TABLE 2.2 Expectations That Facilitate Motives Associated With Creative Acts

Expectations	Description	Supporting Empirical Research
Creative Self-Image	Views self as "creative" and possessing creative talent	MacKinnon (1962); MacKinnon (1970); Bergum (1973); Bergum (1975); Kirton (1989)
Self-Confidence	Has broad confidence in skills and abilities	Buel (1960); Smith, Albright, Glennon, & Owens (1961); MacKinnon (1962); Morrison, Owens, Glennon, & Albright (1962); Andrews (1965); Buel (1965); Cline, Tucker, & Anderson (1966); Taylor & Ellison (1967); Pelz (1967); MacKinnon (1970); James, Chen, & Goldberg (1992); Gardner (1993)
Tolerant of Ambiguity	Feels comfortable when facing situations that are ill-defined	MacKinnon (1960); MacKinnon (1970); Albaum (1976); Tegano (1990)

The influences related to expectations and emotions are again consistent with the broader creativity literature's findings. Creative individuals see themselves as "creative," are generally self-confident, and are comfortable with ambiguous situations. They are also more emotionally expressive and energetic than less creative individuals. Taken as a whole these characteristics tend to support persistent effort, even in the face of significant obstacles. Obviously, this is important given the considerable challenges that the pursuit of creativity can inflict.

Considering the positive attributes that characterize creative individuals it seems odd that organizations are commonly assumed to be hostile to creativity. The profile that emerges from prior research on creative individuals is that of an ambitious, achievement-oriented person who is capable of self-management and who enjoys learning from new challenges and approaches. On top of this, he or she is self-confident, comfortable in ambiguous situations, and energetic. Rather than sounding like the common stereotype of a creative person

TABLE 2.3	Emotions That Facilitate Motives Associated With Creative Acts	
Emotions	*Description*	*Supporting Empirical Research*
Emotionally Expressive	Are open to experiencing and expressing emotions	MacKinnon (1962); Dauw (1968a, 1968b); MacKinnon (1970); Kanner (1976); Udell, Baker, & Albaum (1976)
Energetic	Have vast amounts of physical energy	MacKinnon (1959); MacKinnon (1962); Buel (1965)

as an unstable, iconoclastic, malcontent, this sounds like a "Most Wanted" poster from a corporate recruiting office!

The conflict between creative individuals and bureaucratic organizations is, nevertheless, real. Interest in creativity leads people to avoid narrow, structured, rigid jobs (Kirton & Pender, 1982). Also, people with longer tenures tend to have less interest in creativity, suggesting that creatively motivated employees either leave or become socialized to have more pedestrian interests (Hayward & Everett, 1983; Holland, 1987). To the extent that organizations assign creative people narrow job responsibilities, reward and promote based on existing norms and procedures, and direct efforts up and down hierarchies rather than toward customer and client problems, creative individuals will be out of place.

Still, the research summarized in Tables 2.1, 2.2, and 2.3 may actually exaggerate the severity of the creativity-organization conflict. A look at the dates of the supporting studies listed in these tables finds few studies conducted within the past 20 years. Most of these earlier studies emerged, or were heavily influenced by, a single psychological research center, the Institute for Personality Assessment Research (IPAR). This fact raises two suspicions. First, although organizations might still be wary of creativity, they are probably less hostile to it than they were in the sixties. Second, by focusing solely on personal influences on creativity, early research on creative professionals unwittingly set up organizational contexts as the most obvious explanation for failure. This one-sided view may have overstated the extent to which organizations actively block creativity. Real conflicts that exist may abate as organizations continue to downsize, network with other companies, focus on customers, and empower employees. One could argue that organizational forms based on project assignments, self-management, and empowerment are almost ideally suited to the profile of a creative individual presented here.

As a final motivational note, exceptional cases of creative achievement such as Freud, Picasso, and Stravinsky can be described as intensified versions of this profile. In these instances, less positive terms like self-absorbed, egotistic, self-promoting, and insensitive to others may be more appropriate (Gardner, 1993). "Serial creators," in a fashion similar to unrepentant thieves and serial killers, represent a dramatic extreme that has probably had an undue influence on our stereotypes of creative individuals. Stereotypes based on otherworldly examples may, again, overstate the incompatibility between organizations and creative individuals. The profile that emerges here is that of a highly motivated person who is well suited for the challenges facing modern organizations.

How confident can we be in these clues? Overall, these are fairly robust findings that have emerged from a variety of settings. Certainly, there are methodological problems and biases reflective of the limited scope of most of the studies listed here. For example, many of these clues were discovered by surveying people working in "creative professions" such as writing, painting, architecture, research, and mathematics. In many of these studies, creativity was measured as achievement in these (creative) fields. This makes one wonder whether the personality traits identified by this research lead to creativity, or simply professional achievement. It also raises questions about whether the traits identified apply to other types of professions that are more deeply embedded in the organizational milieu. Writers, painters, architects, researchers, and mathematicians can hardly be considered representative of the majority of organizational actors.

But, a more vexing problem with this body of research is that it is almost devoid of theory. In a prototypical study, a sample of eminent professionals working in a "creative field" filled out a plethora of personality measures. Researchers then reported questionnaire items that eminent achievers answered differently from less successful colleagues. Most of the findings listed in Tables 2.1-2.3 are derived from studies that identify personality traits associated with creativity in this manner. As interesting as the results of these studies may be, they provide little explanation of *how* individual differences influence creativity. At worst, this research can be characterized as useless dustbowl empiricism; at best it represents a collection of puzzle pieces waiting to be assembled into a coherent picture. Based on the more favorable of these two interpretations, I have taken the liberty of trying to assemble these pieces into conceptual categories that are meaningful to both academics and practitioners (i.e., personal goals, expectations, emotions). The clues, as presented by this literature, are not organized in this fashion.

To sum up, it simply is not particularly useful to know that eminent professionals are more self-confident than their less successful colleagues. What are we to do with this piece of information? Viewing self-confidence as an influence on motivation, however, places the finding within a theoretical perspective that can focus our attention on fruitful questions and actions. For example, does self-confidence predict creative achievement, or does creative achievement enhance self-confidence? Is the self-confidence of creatives merely an accurate belief in their superior creative talents? Do supportive organizational climates enhance creativity because they improve peoples' self-confidence, or are self-confident people more likely to interpret their situations as favorable? Answers to these questions would allow researchers to address seemingly straightforward questions—such as "Are empowerment programs likely to enhance creativity?"—with greater confidence. Just as a correlation between skirt lengths and stock prices does little to help us understand economics, listings of personality traits offer little guidance to those who wish to understand and influence creativity.

The Means for Carrying Out the Act. What skills, tools, and weapons do those who commit creative acts possess? Are they hard to come by, or can anyone pick them up? The detectives that provide our clues to these questions are in many cases the same ones who provided clues regarding the creative actors' motives. Thus, for the most part, the criticisms offered of those investigations apply to this set of findings as well.

The evidence regarding talents that lead to creativity in organizational and professional settings is surprisingly sparse. This is especially true for the cognitive skills that are widely believed to produce creative ideas. The problem is not that we lack reliable tests of creative ability. Rather, it is that there is little evidence that these tests predict creativity at work. In other words, these tests have not been demonstrated to be valid (this particular discussion focuses on what researchers refer to as "criterion-related validity"—the criterion in this case being creative work achievement). But, what does it mean to say that a creativity test is valid? Traditionally, those who study organizational or professional creativity judge the validity of creativity tests by their ability to correlate highly with creative performance as judged by peers and/or supervisors. But, do low correlations between tests of ability and creative performance evaluations necessarily mean that these tests are invalid?

Placed into a broader investigative framework, one would expect creativity skills to relate to creative achievements only under specific circumstances. For instance, individuals should be motivated to accomplish creative ends. Without motivation, skills are irrelevant. Organizational factors also can intervene between motivation, creative ability, and realized creative performance. Further, evaluations of creativity, or any other type of work performance for that matter, are not likely to correspond perfectly to "true" achievement. Therefore, I believe that it is misguided to seek ability tests that try to fully predict creative achievement. Rather, currently popular creativity tests should be interpreted as measures of specific cognitive abilities that may or may not be related to creativity, depending on the nature of the task and the presence of other motivational and situational influences.

The utility of this logic regarding the convoluted relationship between creative ability and creative performance was revealed in a series of classic studies conducted by Frank Andrews, Donald Pelz, and their colleagues (Andrews, 1965; Andrews & Gordon, 1970; Pelz & Andrews, 1966). In these studies they consistently found no relationship between creative ability and creative performance in R&D organizations. Most researchers would conclude at this point that their test of creative ability was invalid. Closer examination, however, showed that creative ability was positively related to creative performance in favorable work environments and negatively related in poor work environments. In one particularly striking example, the correlation between creative ability and creative achievement was +.55 in favorable work settings, but –.97 in unfavorable work settings! The implications of this finding are compelling. Andrews (1965) summarized it best when he said, "High creative ability might be likened to a hardy seed, which yields blossoms when sown on fertile ground, but only thorns when falling on infertile ground" (p. 150). In other words, creative people in unfavorable situations may actually perform worse than their less talented co-workers. Although interesting, this is not an uncontested finding. Others exploring this relationship have found that creative ability enhances creative performance regardless of the circumstances (e.g., Owens, 1969). I tend to give more credence to Pelz's and Andrews's findings because they looked at important aspects of the R&D environment, used measures of "real" creative work performance, and were able to replicate their findings. Regardless of one's conclusions, these findings point out the critical importance of examining clues related to motive, means, *and* opportunity. Investigations that focus too narrowly on only one or two of these sources of evidence are bound to be inconclusive or suspect.

One more comment regarding common creative ability tests is in order. Despite the general agreement that creativity involves generating novel *and* valuable solutions, traditional tests of creative ability focus almost exclusively on novel production. By focusing exclusively on divergent thinking and remote association abilities, and ignoring abilities to separate more from less valuable solutions, these tests may be too narrow to predict creative achievement effectively. This may be especially true in organizational contexts where the value of creative solutions is especially salient.

Notwithstanding these concerns, a handful of studies have indicated that tests of creative ability are able to predict creative performance, at least to a modest degree. Additional clues have been unearthed regarding a handful of other talents utilized by those who commit acts of creativity. The findings that relate personal skills and abilities to creative acts are presented in Table 2.4.

The main findings from this research are that the ability to conjure up alternatives (divergent thinking skills—e.g., How many uses can you describe for a brick?), and the ability to find associations (associationistic skills—e.g., How is investigating creativity like investigating a crime?) help produce creative acts. Creative performance also

TABLE 2.4 Means That Contribute to the Occurrence of Creative Acts

Means	Description	Supporting Empirical Evidence
Creative Ability	Possesses divergent thinking skills, ideational fluency, and remote association skills	MacKinnon (1959); Datta (1964); Jones (1964); Barron (1966); Barron & Egan (1968); Gordon (1972); Tan-Willman (1974); Ekvall (1976); Roberts & Peters (1982); Amabile (1984)
Intelligence and Education	Compares favorably on traditional notions of intelligence as well as extensiveness of education	Van Zelst & Kerr (1951); Meer & Stein (1955); MacKinnon (1959); Smith, Albright, Glennon, & Owens (1961); MacKinnon (1962); Jones (1964); Antley (1966); Barron (1966); Barron & Egan (1968); MacKinnon (1970); Keller & Holland (1978); Simonton (1983)
Intuition	Prefers intuitive impressions to direct sensory perceptions	Barron & Egan (1968); MacKinnon (1970); Gotz & Gotz (1979); Gardner (1993)
Social Competence	Is capable of effective behavior in social circumstances	Barron & Egan (1968); MacKinnon (1970); Gotz & Gotz (1979); Gardner (1993)

increases with intelligence, but only up to an IQ of around 120. Perhaps surprisingly, intelligence beyond this level does little to enhance creative ability further. Education also helps, which may be a reflection of the need for expertise in a domain (see Amabile, 1983b; Simon, 1986). Too much education, however, may actually hinder creativity. Simonton (1983) found that education gradually led to higher creativity as people progressed through the attainment of a master's degree. Those who received Ph.D.s became less creative, though; probably because they became more dogmatic (this can't be good news for the academic contributors to this volume!). Another characteristic that I classified as a talent is a preference for intuition as a means of collecting information. This finding is not unequivocally supported by research, but it is consistent with the notion that creativity is facilitated by the ability to use abstract concepts in addition to sensory images. Abstract concepts allow one to imagine, intuit, and otherwise "play" with ideas, rather than be restricted to the here-and-now, objective quality of direct perceptions. Finally, social competence has been noted by a few researchers. This seems odd at first, given that making friends is not a core goal of creative individuals. Gardner (1993) explains this finding by arguing that highly creative individuals use their social skills to charm those who can further their creative goals, thus connoting some degree of Machiavellianism. They are not interested in socializing as an end in itself. Not surprisingly, the eminent creators Gardner studied made lousy friends. They tended to toss people aside after they had outlived their usefulness.

There is one additional finding not listed in any of the previous tables. Creative production appears to peak when people are relatively young, around 35, and gradually decline thereafter. This finding has been replicated on several occasions (Lehman, 1958, 1966; Simonton, 1977, 1991). Why does this happen? Probably two reasons. The cognitive skills that contribute to creativity may diminish throughout peoples' careers (see Simonton, 1991), and individuals' goals become more stability oriented as they grow older (see Mumford & Gustafson, 1988). Thus, aging may adversely affect both creative motivation and creative talent. However, an alternative explanation for this finding may be that it is an artifact of the gradual decline in productivity that has been noted in scientific and artistic careers (where these findings have been established).

This section has specified the means that individuals use to realize creative acts. None of these findings, however, sheds light on the extent to which creativity can be trained. Managers clearly have little faith in creativity training, often dismissing it out of hand. In one survey, 91% of the managers questioned said they believed that creativity cannot be trained or developed (Whiting, 1971). One could interpret this as a cop-out, freeing these managers of accountability for creativity (92% also said that creativity was the responsibility of their subordinates). Research has shown that creativity can be enhanced through training in some cases (Hall Rose & Lin, 1984). Other research, however, has called into question the effectiveness of creativity training in organizational settings (Rickards, 1975; Rickards &

Freedman, 1978). It does seem that peoples' attitudes toward utilizing creativity techniques can be improved through training (Basadur & Finkbeiner, 1985; Basadur, Graen, & Scandura, 1986; Basadur, Wakabayashi, & Graen, 1990). Other studies demonstrated that these new attitudes led to changes in decision-making behavior (Basadur, Graen, & Green, 1982; Basadur & Thompson, 1986). However, direct evidence that creativity training positively affects creative productivity in organizational settings is sparse at best. It thus appears that managerial skepticism regarding creativity training is well justified.

So, to the motivation-related clues presented in Tables 2.1, 2.2, and 2.3, we need to add creatively talented, intelligent, intuitive, and socially competent to the profile. Combining all of these characteristics makes the creative person sound more than a bit superhuman—which is why I tend to think of this profile as representing an idealistic prototype of the eminent creator. Given the opportunity, individuals who closely match this profile are likely to focus their efforts tirelessly on creative endeavors regardless of the circumstances. Those who possess only some of these characteristics, however, or possess them to a modest degree, are still capable of impressive creative achievements in facilitative environments.

Our investigation now turns toward uncovering clues related to opportunities that support the commitment of creative acts.

The Opportunities That Encourage the Act. Just as "extenuating circumstances" can lead otherwise law-abiding citizens to engage in criminal acts, organizational environments can serve to draw out the creative proclivities of even those who seldom undertake creative acts at work. A few situational contributors to creativity have received wide empirical support. Several others have been noted often enough to supplement these primary contributions. The best supported findings are that effective leadership, discretion, and extensive communication networks provide fertile ground for creative acts to flourish. Other likely contributing factors include change-oriented management, a nurturing organizational culture, an effective reward system, adequate resources, and instructions to "be creative." These findings are summarized in Table 2.5.

"Effective leadership" is a rather broad notion. The leadership behaviors that have been found to aid creative acts include setting clear expectations about what is to be accomplished and supporting subordinate's choices regarding means toward these goals. Leaders who lead by example or serve as role models were also noted in several studies. Overall, these behaviors reflect an empowerment-oriented leadership style. One potential limitation of these findings, however, is that they emerged from a limited array of professional settings. In these particular contexts, engineers, scientists, architects, and similar others would probably consider managerial efforts to dictate work methods to be highly inappropriate. This leaves one to wonder if the same leader behaviors would facilitate creativity in situations where directive, task-oriented leadership approaches are suitable.

The finding that discretion gives rise to creative acts seems to be closely related to the practice of unobtrusive, participative leadership. Professionals also noted in some studies that they were more creative when they could choose among different project assignments or could start projects on their own. Of course, taking action based on this finding requires a leap of faith for most managers. It requires trust—pure and simple. Well, maybe not so simple. Four varieties of trust are essential: management's trust in their employees' competence; management's trust in their employees' motives; employees' trust in management's competence; and employees' trust in management's motives. If any one of these links is missing, the atmosphere of mutual respect necessary for discretion-oriented management to succeed will be absent. Unfortunately, the trends here are not encouraging. Employees have grown more cynical of management based on the fallout of years of restructuring and downsizing, and management has become more wary of employees' commitment to their organizations. Discretionary behaviors, and creative acts in particular, may be especially vulnerable to untrusting environments. In these climates people regress to complying with the immediate, well-specified expectations of their jobs and avoid straying beyond the boundaries of their positions.

Another finding running counter to the stereotype of the solitary genius inventor is that creativity has been associated with frequent communication with others, especially those in other disciplines. However, the networks identified in these studies were distinctly professional rather than social networks. This is consistent with the notion that creative individuals seek to enhance their work by build-

TABLE 2.5 Opportunities That Encourage the Occurrence of
Creative Acts

Opportunity	Description	Supporting Empirical Research
Effective Leadership and Mentoring	Empowerment-oriented leadership that is supportive, participative, unobtrusive, outcome oriented with clear direction, where the leader serves as a role model	Pelz (1956); Raudsepp (1958); Fiedler (1962); Andrews & Farris (1967); Pelz (1967); Owens (1969); Andrews & Gordon (1970); Owens (1972); Andrews (1975); Torrance (1983); Amabile (1984); Bailyn (1985); Ekvall & Tangeberg-Anderson (1986); Ranftl (1986); Amabile & Gryskiewicz (1987); Payne (1987); Plunkett (1988); Orpen (1990); Redmond, Mumford, & Teach (1993)
Discretion	Tasks have limited structure and individuals are given choice over work methods	Andrews (1967); Pelz (1967); Andrews & Gordon (1970); Parmenter & Garber (1971); Hage & Dewar (1973); Andrew (1975); Cummings, Hinton, & Gobdel (1975); Paolillo & Brown (1978); Langer, Duncan, & Rassen (1980); Amabile (1984); Bailyn (1985); Ranftl (1986); Amabile & Gryskiewicz (1987); Payne (1987); West & Savage (1987); Plunkett (1990)
Effective Communication Networks	Frequent contact with interdisciplinary networks of people at different levels of an organization	Pelz (1956); Raudsepp (1958); Andrews (1965); Andrews (1967); Pelz (1967); Parmenter & Garber (1971); Paolillo & Brown (1978); Simonton (1984)

ing relationships with those who can contribute to their efforts, even if these relationships are likely to wither when they are no longer needed to support work. Unfortunately, none of the cited studies were conducted recently enough to consider the impact of advanced information technologies on networking. The availability of improved communication technologies almost certainly makes this influence

TABLE 2.5 *continued*

Opportunity	Description	Supporting Empirical Research
Change-Oriented Management	Organization's management is receptive to creativity and change efforts	Parmenter & Garber (1971); Gordon (1972); Hage & Dewar (1973); Abbey & Dickson (1983); Amabile & Gryskiewicz (1987); Orpen (1990)
Nurturing Organizational Culture	Organization culture is characterized by cooperation, collaboration, and concern for employee well-being	Raudsepp (1958); Siegal & Kaemmerer (1978); Amabile & Gryskiewicz (1987); Eisenberger, Fasolo, & Davis-LaMastro (1990)
Effective Reward System	Rewards are outcome oriented, equitable, and related to status	Van Zelst & Kerr (1951); Raudsepp (1958); Parmenter & Garber (1971); Paolillo & Brown (1978); Abbey & Dickson (1983); Amabile & Gryskiewicz (1987)
Adequate Resources	Organization supplies necessary funds, facilities, time, and personnel to support creative efforts	Amabile (1984); Moriarty & Vandenbergh (1984); Amabile & Gryskiewicz (1987); West & Savage (1987)
Directions to "Be Creative"	Leader suggests that employees seek creative solutions to a problem	Datta (1963); Cummings, Hinton, & Gobdel (1975); Fontenot (1993)

easier to realize. One could even speculate that participating in intra- and inter-organizational computer mediated interactions would be associated with creative performance.

A change-oriented management mind-set also encourages creative acts. This probably reflects the influence of goal alignment between workers' personal desires to do creative things and management's desire to realize the creative talents of their employees. A nurturing organizational culture probably helps creativity because it reduces the extent to which people feel threatened when they air new ideas. By minimizing the anxiety associated with creative acts, nurturing organizations may have more varied ideas from which to choose. Effective reward systems may improve creativity by contingently rewarding professionally oriented, generally talented employees. To the extent that creative individuals' motivations and talents are above average, especially in professional, project-oriented work settings, one would expect them to be relatively high performers. If this is true, they would clearly prefer compensation systems that reward based on merit.

Similar to the findings related to motives and skills, the research presented here is largely atheoretical. Without a comprehensive theory to work from, these explanations are little more than informed speculation. However, a less speculative finding related to the affect of reward systems is the intrinsic motivation principle of creativity (Amabile, 1983a). This principle states that people are most creative when they feel motivated by the interest, enjoyment, and challenge associated with a particular task. External pressures, such as direct rewards or evaluations, tend to block creativity. In short, creativity can be derailed with money and review procedures. Obviously this has important implications for well-meaning organizations who would like to reward people for creative achievements. Why would rewards and evaluations of creative attempts hinder creative achievement? My hypothesis is that creativity is a fairly marginal goal for most people most of the time. This is especially true at work. By introducing external reviews or contracted-for rewards, personal goals that potentially conflict with creativity become more salient (e.g., making money, avoiding embarrassment, pleasing others, etc.). But, perhaps the greatest conflict created by task specific, highly visible external influences is with peoples' desire to be self-determining (see Deci, 1980). When people feel that they are working on a task because "they have to," the goal to create is quickly snuffed. When this happens, they are markedly less likely to complete the task creatively. Amabile (1988) provides support for this explanation. She reports that individuals for whom creativity is important, rather than marginal, are less susceptible to these extrinsic influences. Overall, creativity results from acts of free will in supportive environments, not from compliance to organizational reward systems and controls. As a practical matter, one should assume that most peoples' interest in creativity is fragile and requires careful nurturing to avoid having it wilt under the pressure of conflicting demands.

Not surprisingly, adequate resources such as money, facilities, and time help creative efforts (and other efforts as well!). Unfortunately, these resources are increasingly tough to come by, especially for more speculative enterprises. Businesses are more frequently turning to joint ventures and other cooperative forms of organizing as a means of spreading risk and bringing together necessary resources to support creative projects. Another approach to providing resources to creative gambles is to put small amounts of funding into a broad array of projects or options until their potential can be more realistically assessed.

Taken together, change-oriented management, a nurturing culture, an effective reward system, and adequate resources may speak to a higher truth: managerial credibility. Management that ignores change, shows little concern for employees, maintains inequitable reward systems, and fails to supply necessary resources is bound to breed cynical employees. Again this harkens back to the notion of trust. Employees will be skeptical about what they are told. They will question the competence of their managers. Even legitimate initiatives are likely to be looked upon warily. When credibility is low, management will have their hands tied when it comes to enhancing creativity. Creativity involves faith, patience, and trust among an organization's members. Threatening environments that fail to support and recognize worthwhile efforts are creativity graveyards.

Finally, asking people to develop a creative solution may, in fact, lead them to develop a creative solution. Ask and ye shall receive. This finding is especially intriguing because it seems so obvious, yet is seldom acted on. It may not be that simple, however. For example, people who are insecure about their creative abilities may feel anxious about recurring directives to "be creative!" They may also fear having their work evaluated against such a lofty standard. These requests might, consequently, activate personal goals that conflict with creativity. Also, if management's credibility is low, solicitations such as this are likely to be ignored. Yet, in a trustworthy environment, those who fit the creative person profile should be happy to attempt creative acts on request. They may even find it liberating.

One thing you might notice by comparing the citations from Table 2.5 on "opportunities" to those in the previous tables on "motives" (Table 2.1) and "means" (Table 2.4) is that there is almost no overlap. The detectives who study creative individuals rarely consider situational influences; those who study situational influences rarely

consider individual differences. In many cases, they seem only re-
motely aware that there is more than one cop on the beat. The
narrowness of these investigations makes it impossible to offer
confident insights regarding the interactions among various personal
characteristics or between personal characteristics and work environments. I have offered a few informed speculations of my own. But,
without more varied approaches in future research, the case for
creative acts is destined to remain open.

CONCLUSION

We now have an idea of what the usual suspects look like and the
hangouts that they like to frequent. The profile of the highly creative
individual is that of a self-confident, professional, achievement-
oriented person who enjoys creativity, variety, and independence.
This individual is also creatively talented, intelligent, well educated,
and intuitive. Given the positive character of these assorted traits, this
portrait looks like someone we might have suspected all along. In fact,
someone possessing all of these traits in good measure would likely be
a serial creator, driven to creative acts throughout an entire lifetime.

The opportunities that facilitate the commission of creative acts
are a bit more revealing. They include effective leadership coupled with
discretion, effective professional networks, change-oriented management, nurturing culture, effective rewards, adequate resources, and
appeals to be creative. Put most simply, capable people in effective
organizations are more likely to engage in acts deemed creative. That
simple homily does not provide much guidance, however. It does
imply that highly productive employees are more likely to engage in
creative acts. Research supports this notion. Evidence shows that
creative acts occur as a constant proportion of a person's overall
productive output (Simonton, 1977, 1991). Highly productive people
are therefore more likely to come up with creative ideas periodically.
Eminently creative individuals, for example, have been well known
for their prolific output. Thus, when it comes to creativity, if one takes
more shots, one scores more goals.

Should detectives direct their investigations toward identifying
serial creators or toward identifying extenuating circumstances that

would lead any reasonable person to commit an act of creativity? Put another way, can anyone commit a creative act, or are creative acts the exclusive domain of a gifted few? On the basis of this review, I suggest that individuals who closely match the profile I have constructed in Tables 2.1-2.4 will be more consistently creative in a variety of circumstances. They will seek opportunities to commit creative acts and will more often display creative acts even in less supportive contexts. Extreme cases, representing what we commonly think of as the creatively gifted, are probably destined to commit creative acts regardless of the circumstances. On the other hand, deviations from this profile do not doom creativity. They simply make its emergence more fragile, thus demanding more attentiveness and managerial tact. Perhaps even those who deviate significantly from the creative person's profile can offer occasional acts of creativity, but the situation would have to be just right. Realistically, though, there are those whose motivations and skills are such that perpetrating a creative act is highly unlikely. Nonetheless, the overall sentiment offered here suggests that the majority of those working in modern organizations are capable of creative acts.

In summary, prototypical "creative individuals" are low maintenance—they will commit creative acts even in the face of significant obstacles. These creative masters continue to hold the fascination of interested lay people and topflight investigators as well. Of course, the detective reports of these cases are likely to feature the personal characteristics these geniuses possess. And given the rarefied sample being investigated, this focus would be well founded. As mesmerizing as these creators can be, I believe that our interest in organizational creativity would be better served by a less elitist approach to thinking about and studying creativity. It seems overwhelmingly clear that otherwise well-motivated and bright individuals are capable of creative acts. However, they will require more tender loving care if their creativity is to blossom. It is this more broadly distributed capacity for creativity upon which organizations must pin their hopes and direct their efforts. Those interested in investigating and influencing creativity in organizational settings must realize that the interaction between the creative person and creative circumstances is most consequential for this population brimming with creative "potential." This view need not be unrealistically egalitarian. Those whose motivations are largely extrinsic (e.g., money, security, and so on) and otherwise easily distracted, and whose overall talent and knowledge is marginal, are unlikely to act creatively in any case. I believe that investigating creativity among the majority who are moderately predisposed toward creativity and, therefore, more susceptible to outside influences, is likely to produce more useful insights than either an elitist or a purely egalitarian view of creativity. The clues presented by this approach can further our understanding of the complex interplay among motives, means, and opportunities that contribute to creative acts.

Have we solved our mystery? Certainly not—but at least we have established the background of the case so that we can be more discerning as we look for more clues. We have some idea of *what* leads to creativity, but we still know little about *how* these factors collectively contribute to creativity. There is much detective work to be done. We need to try to understand how different influences interact, build on each other, or cancel each other out. Without a more comprehensive understanding of creative acts, our ability to influence creativity in organizational settings will be as limited as it has been in the past.

Now it is time to hand this investigation over to the top detectives we have summoned to help us break this case. They each provide their own clues, derived from a wide assortment of orientations and investigative approaches. Some of these detectives are from the psychological school; they have the most experience with this case and provide well-grounded insights into creativity at work. Others are management researchers who offer their views of how organizational arenas influence creative acts. Practicing detectives also get to have their say. Their contributions provide rare and invaluable pearls of wisdom regarding the pragmatic challenges associated with fostering creative acts in organizations. Gathering a legion of such diverse and talented detectives is a rare occasion indeed. Read on!

REFERENCES

Abbey, A., & Dickson, J. W. (1983). R&D work climate and innovation in semiconductors. *Academy of Management Journal, 26,* 362-368.

Albaum, G. (1976). Selecting specialized creators: The independent inventor. *Psychological Reports, 39,* 175-179.

Albert, R. S. (1969). Genius: Present-day status of the concept and its implications for the study of creativity and giftedness. *American Psychologist, 42,* 743-753.

Amabile, T. M. (1983a). *The social psychology of creativity.* New York: Springer.

Amabile, T. M. (1983b). The social psychology of creativity: A componential conceptualization. *Journal of Personality and Social Psychology, 45,* 357-376.

Amabile, T. M. (1984, August). *Creativity motivation in research and development.* Paper presented at the annual meeting of the American Psychological Association, Toronto.

Amabile, T. M. (1988). A model of creativity and innovation in organizations. *Research in Organizational Behavior, 10,* 123-167.

Amabile, T. M., & Gryskiewicz, S. S. (1987). *Creativity in the R&D laboratory.* Greensboro, NC: Center for Creative Leadership.

Andrews, F. M. (1965). Factors affecting the manifestation of creative ability by scientists. *Journal of Personality, 33,* 140-152.

Andrews, F. M. (1967). Creative ability, the laboratory environment, and scientific performance. *IEEE Transactions on Engineering Management, EM-14,* 276-282.

Andrews, F. M. (1975). Social and psychological factors which influence the creative process. In I. A. Taylor & J. W. Getzels (Eds.), *Perspectives in creativity* (pp. 117-145). Chicago: Aldine.

Andrews, F. M., & Farris, G. P. (1967). Supervisory practices and innovation in scientific teams. *Personnel Psychology, 20,* 497-516.

Andrews, F. M., & Gordon, G. (1970). Social and organizational factors affecting innovation in research. *Proceedings of the 78th Annual Convention of the American Psychological Association* (pp. 589-590). Washington, DC: American Psychological Association.

Antley, E. M. (1966). Creativity in educational administration. *Journal of Experimental Education, 34,* 421-427.

Barron, F. (1966). The psychology of the creative writer. *Theory Into Practice, 5,* 157-159.

Barron, F., & Egan, D. (1968, February). Leaders and innovators in Irish management. *Journal of Management Studies,* pp. 41-60.

Barron, F., & Harrington, D. M. (1981). Creativity, intelligence and personality. *Annual Review of Psychology, 32,* 439-476.

Basadur, M., & Finkbeiner, C. T. (1985). Measuring preference for ideation in creative problem-solving training. *The Journal of Applied Behavioral Science, 21,* 37-49.

Basadur, M., Graen, G. B., & Green, S. G. (1982). Training in creative problem solving: Effect on ideation and problem finding and solving in an industrial research organization. *Organizational Behavior and Human Performance, 30,* 41-70.

Basadur, M., Graen, G. B., & Scandura, T. A. (1986). Training effects on attitudes toward divergent thinking among manufacturing engineers. *Journal of Applied Psychology, 71,* 612-617.

Basadur, M., & Thompson, R. (1986). Usefulness of the ideation principle of extended effort in real world professional and managerial creative problem solving. *Journal of Creative Behavior, 20,* 123-134.

Basadur, M., Wakabayashi, M., & Graen, G. B. (1990). Individual problem-solving styles and attitudes toward divergent thinking before and after training. *Creativity Research Journal, 3,* 22-32.

Bailyn, L. (1985). Autonomy in the industrial R&D lab. *Human Resource Management, 24*, 129-146.

Bergum, B. O. (1973). Selection of specialized creators. *Psychological Reports, 33*, 635-639.

Bergum, B. O. (1975). Self-perceptions of creativity among academic inventors and non-inventors. *Perceptual and Motor Skills, 40*, 78.

Buel, W. D. (1960). The validity of behavioral rating scale items for the assessment of individual creativity. *Journal of Applied Psychology, 44*, 407-412.

Buel, W. D. (1965). Biographical data and the identification of creative research personnel. *Journal of Applied Psychology, 49*, 318-321.

Burke, R. J. (1983). Career orientations of type A individuals. *Psychological Reports, 53*, 979-989.

Chambers, J. A. (1964). Relating personality and biographical factors to scientific creativity. *Psychological Monographs: General and Applied, 78*, 1-20.

Cline, V. B., Tucker, M. F., & Anderson, D. R. (1966). Psychology of the scientist: XX. Cross-validation of biographical information predictor keys across diverse samples of scientists. *Psychological Reports, 19*, 951-954.

Cummings, L. L., Hinton, B. L., & Gobdel, B. C. (1975). Creative behavior as a function of task environment: Impact of objectives, procedures, and controls. *Academy of Management Journal, 18*, 489-499.

Datta, L. E. (1963). Test instructions and identification of creative scientific talent. *Psychological Reports, 13*, 495-500.

Datta, L. E. (1964). Remote associates test as a predictor of creativity in engineers. *Journal of Applied Psychology, 48*, 31-83.

Dauw, D. C. (1968a). Creativity and vocational needs of clerical personnel. *Personnel Journal, 47*, 870-876.

Dauw, D. C. (1968b). Creativity research on actuaries. *Journal of Creative Behavior, 24*, 274-280.

Deci, E. L. (1980). *The psychology of self-determination*. Lexington, MA: Lexington Books.

Eisenberger, R., Fasolo, P., & Davis-LaMastro, V. (1990). Perceived organizational support and employee diligence, commitment, and innovation. *Journal of Applied Psychology, 75*, 151-159.

Ekvall, G. (1976). Creativity at the place of work: Studies of suggestors and suggestion systems in industry. *Journal of Creative Behavior, 10*, 152-154.

Ekvall, G., & Tangeberg-Anderson, Y. (1986). Working climate and creativity: A study of an innovative newspaper office. *Journal of Creative Behavior, 20*, 215-225.

Fiedler, F. E. (1962). Leader attitudes, group climate, and group creativity. *Journal of Abnormal and Social Psychology, 65*, 308-318.

Fontenot, N. A. (1993). Effects of training in creativity and creative problem finding upon business people. *The Journal of Social Psychology, 133*, 11-22.

Foxall, G. R. (1990). An empirical analysis of mid-career managers' adaptive-innovative cognitive styles and task orientations in three countries. *Psychological Reports, 66*, 1115-1124.

Gardner, H. (1993). *Creating minds*. New York: Basic Books.

Gordon, G. (1972). The identification and use of creative abilities in scientific organizations. In C. W. Taylor (Ed.), *Climate for creativity: Report of the 7th National Research Conference on Creativity* (pp. 109-124). Elmsford, NY: Pergamon.

Gotz, K. O., & Gotz, K. (1979). Personality characteristics of successful artists. *Perceptual and Motor Skills, 49,* 919-924.

Guilford, J. P. (1950). Creativity. *American Psychologist, 5,* 444-454.

Hage, J., & Dewar, R. (1973). Elite values versus organizational structure in predicting innovation. *Administrative Science Quarterly, 18,* 279-290.

Hall Rose, L., & Lin, H. (1984). A meta-analysis of long-term creativity training programs. *The Journal of Creative Behavior, 18,* 11-22.

Hayward, G., & Everett, C. (1983). Adaptors and innovators: Data for the Kirton Adaptor-Innovator Inventory in a local authority setting. *Journal of Occupational Psychology, 56,* 339-342.

Helson, R., & Crutchfield, R. S. (1970). Creative types in mathematics. *Journal of Personality, 38,* 177-197.

Holland, P. A. (1987). Adaptors and innovators: Application of the Kirton Adaption-Innovation Inventory to bank employees. *Psychological Reports, 60,* 263-270.

Isaksen, S. G., Murdock, M. C., Firestien, R. L., & Treffinger, D. J. (Eds.). (1993). *Understanding and recognizing creativity: The emergence of a discipline.* Norwood, NJ: Ablex.

James, K., Chen, J., & Goldberg, C. (1992). Organizational conflict and individual creativity. *Journal of Applied Social Psychology, 22,* 545-566.

Jones, F. E. (1964). Predictor variable for creativity in industrial science. *Journal of Applied Psychology, 48,* 134-136.

Jones, S. L., & Arnold, J. E. (1962). The creative individual in industry research. *IRE Transactions on Engineering Management, 9,* 51-55.

Kanner, A. D. (1976). Femininity and masculinity: Their relationships to creativity in male architects and their independence from each other. *Journal of Consulting and Clinical Psychology, 44,* 802-805.

Keller, R. T., & Holland, W. E. (1978). Individual characteristics of innovativeness and communication in research and development organizations. *Journal of Applied Psychology, 63,* 759-762.

King, N. (1990). Innovation at work: The research literature. In M. A. West & J. L. Farr (Eds.), *Innovation and creativity at work* (pp. 15-59). Chichester, England: John Wiley.

Kirton, M. J. (1976). Adaptors and innovators: A description and measure. *Journal of Applied Psychology, 61,* 622-629.

Kirton, M. J. (1980). Adaptors and innovators in organizations. *Human Relations, 33,* 213-224.

Kirton, M. J. (1989). Adaptors and innovators at work. In M. J. Kirton (Ed.), *Adaptors and innovators: Styles of creativity and problem solving* (pp. 56-78). New York: Routledge.

Kirton, M. J., & Pender, S. (1982). The adaption-innovation continuum, occupational type, and course selection. *Psychological Reports, 51,* 883-886.

Koberg, C. S., & Chusmir, L. H. (1987). Organizational culture relationships with creativity and other job-related variables. *Journal of Business Research, 15,* 397-409.

Langer, P., Duncan, E., & Rassen, R. L. (1980). Factors contributing to large-scale instructional development. *Psychological Reports, 47,* 147-154.

Lehman, H. C. (1958). The chemist's most creative years. *Science, 127,* 1213-1222.

Lehman, H. C. (1966). The most creative years of engineers and other technologists. *Journal of Genetic Psychology, 10,* 263-277.

MacKinnon, D. W. (1959). The creative worker in engineering. *Proceedings: Eleventh Annual Industrial Engineering Institute*, pp. 88-96.

MacKinnon, D. W. (1960, September). Genus architectus creator varietas Americanus. *AIA Journal*, pp. 31-35.

MacKinnon, D. W. (1962). The nature and nurture of creative talent. *American Psychologist*, 17, 484-495.

MacKinnon, D. W. (1963). The creativity of architects. In *Widening horizons in creativity: The Proceedings of the 5th Utah Creativity Research Conference* (pp. 359-378). New York: John Wiley.

MacKinnon, D. W. (1970). The personality correlates of creativity: A study of American architects. In P. E. Vernon (Ed.), *Creativity: Selected readings* (pp. 289-311). New York: Penguin Books.

McDermid, C. D. (1965). Some correlates of creativity in engineering personnel. *Journal of Applied Psychology*, 49, 114-119.

Meer, B., & Stein, M. I. (1955). Measures of intelligence and creativity. *Journal of Psychology*, 39, 117-126.

Meindl, J. R., Ehrlich, S. B., & Dukerich, J. M. (1985). The romance of leadership. *Administrative Science Quarterly*, 30, 78-102.

Moriarty, S. E., & Vandenbergh, B. G. (1984). Advertising creatives look at creativity. *The Journal of Creative Behavior*, 18, 162-174.

Morrison, R. F., Owens, W. A., Glennon, J. R., & Albright, L. E. (1962). Factored life history antecedents of industrial research performance. *Journal of Applied Psychology*, 4, 81-284.

Mumford, M., & Gustafson, S. (1988). Creativity syndrome: Integration, application, and innovation. *Psychological Bulletin*, 103, 27-43.

Orpen, C. (1990). Measuring support for organizational innovation: A validity study. *Psychological Reports*, 67, 417-418.

Owens, W. A. (1969). Cognitive, noncognitive, and environmental correlates of mechanical ingenuity. *Journal of Applied Psychology*, 53, 199-208.

Owens, W. A. (1972). Intellective, non-intellective, and environmental correlates of mechanical ingenuity. In C. W. Taylor (Ed.), *Climate for creativity: Report on the 7th National Research Conference on Creativity* (pp. 253-268). Elmsford, NY: Pergamon.

Paolillo, J. G., & Brown, W. B. (1978, March). How organizational factors affect R&D innovation. *Research Management*, pp. 12-15.

Parmenter, S. M., & Garber, J. D. (1971). Creative scientists rate creativity factors. *Research Management*, 14, 65-70.

Payne, R. (1987). Individual difference and performance amongst R&D personnel: Some implications for management development. *R&D Management*, 17, 153-166.

Pelz, D. C. (1956). Some social factors related to performance in a research organization. *Administrative Science Quarterly*, 1, 310-325.

Pelz, D. C. (1967). Creative tensions in the research and development climate. *Science*, 15, 160-165.

Pelz, D. C., & Andrews, F. M. (1966). *Scientists in organizations: Productive climates for research and development*. New York: John Wiley.

Plunkett, D. (1988). Intervention for creativity: An OD approach. *Training and Development Journal*, 8, 68-71.

Plunkett, D. (1990). The creative organization: An empirical investigation of the importance of participation in decision-making. *The Journal of Creative Behavior, 24,* 140-148.

Ranftl, R. M. (1986, September-October). Seven keys to high productivity. *Research Management,* pp. 11-18.

Raudsepp, E. (1958). An opinion study of 105 experts: The industrial climate for creativity. *Management Review, 47,* 70-75.

Redmond, M. R., Mumford, M. D., & Teach, R. (1993). Putting creativity to work: Effects of leader behavior on subordinate creativity. *Organizational Behavior and Human Decision Processes, 55,* 120-151.

Rickards, T. (1975). Brainstorming: An examination of idea production rate and level of speculation in real managerial situations. *R&D Management, 6,* 11-14.

Rickards, T., & Freedman, B. L. (1978). Procedures for managers in idea deficient situations: A note on perceptions of brainstorming users obtained from a cross-cultural pilot study. *Journal of Management Studies, 15,* 347-349.

Roberts, E. B., & Peters, D. H. (1982, May). Commercial innovation from university faculty. *Research Management,* pp. 24-30.

Rogers, E. M., & Shoemaker, F. F. (1971). *Communication of innovation.* New York: Free Press.

Rothenberg, A., & Greenberg, B. (1976). *The index of scientific writings on creativity: General, 1566-1974.* Hamden, CT: Archon Books.

Siegel, S. M., & Kaemmerer, W. F. (1978). Measuring the perceived support for innovation in organizations. *Journal of Applied Psychology, 63,* 553-562.

Simon, H. A. (1986, March). How managers express their creativity. *Across the Board,* pp. 11-16.

Simonton, D. K. (1977). Creative productivity, age, and stress: A biographical time-series analysis of 10 classical composers. *Journal of Personality and Social Psychology, 35,* 791-804.

Simonton, D. K. (1983). Formal education, eminence and dogmatism: The curvilinear relationship. *Journal of Creative Behavior, 17,* 149-162.

Simonton, D. K. (1984). Artistic creativity and interpersonal relationships across and within generations. *Journal of Personality and Social Psychology, 46,* 1273-1286.

Simonton, D. K. (1991). Career landmarks in science: Individual differences and interdisciplinary contrasts. *Developmental Psychology, 27,* 119-130.

Smith, W. J., Albright, L. E., Glennon, J. R., & Owens, W. A. (1961). The prediction of research competence and creativity from personal history. *Journal of Applied Psychology, 45,* 59-62.

Sprecher, T. B. (1959). A study of engineers' criteria for creativity. *Journal of Applied Psychology, 43,* 141-148.

Tan-Willman, C. (1974). Assessment and prediction of creativity in teaching. *Psychological Reports, 35,* 393-394.

Taylor, C. W., & Ellison, R. L. (1967). Biographical predictors of scientific performance. *Science, 15,* 1075-1080.

Tegano, D. W. (1990). Relationship of tolerance of ambiguity and playfulness to creativity. *Psychological Reports, 66,* 1047-1056.

Torrance, E. P. (1983). Role of mentors in creative achievement. *The Creative Child and Adult Quarterly, 8,* 8-18.

Udell, G. G., Baker, K. G., & Albaum, G. S. (1976). Creativity: Necessary, but not sufficient. *Journal of Creative Behavior, 10,* 92-103.

Van Zelst, R. H., & Kerr, W. A. (1951). Some correlates of technical and scientific productivity. *Journal of Abnormal and Social Psychology, 46,* 470-475.

Weisberg, R. W. (1986). *Creativity: Genius and other myths.* New York: Freeman.

West, M. A., & Savage, Y. (1987, April). *Innovation among health care professionals.* Paper presented at the Third West European Congress on the Psychology of Work and Organization, Antwerp.

Whiting, B. G. (1971). Manager opinions on creativity. *Journal of Creative Behavior, 5,* 166-168.

Woodman, R. W., Sawyer, J. E., & Griffin, R. W. (1993). Toward a theory of organizational creativity. *Academy of Management Review, 18,* 293-321.

Zaltman, G., Duncan R., & Holbeck, J. (1973). *Innovations and organizations.* London: John Wiley.

ADDITIONAL EMPIRICAL STUDIES OF ORGANIZATIONAL OR PROFESSIONAL CREATIVITY

Albert, R. S. (1969). Genius: Present-day status of the concept and its implications for the study of creativity and giftedness. *American Psychologist, 42,* 743-753.

Amabile, T. M., & Gryskiewicz, N. D. (1989). The creative environment scales: Work environment inventory. *Creativity Research Journal, 2,* 231-253.

Amabile, T. M., & Sensabaugh, S. J. (1985). *Some factors affecting organizational creativity: A brief report.* Paper presented at the Creativity, Innovation & Entrepreneurship Symposium, The George Washington University, Washington, D.C.

Baldridge, J. V., & Burnham, R. A. (1975). Organizational innovation: Individual, organizational, and environmental impacts. *Administrative Science Quarterly, 20,* 165-176.

Basadur, M, Graen, G. B., & Wakabayashi, M. (1990). Identifying individual differences in creative problem solving style. *The Journal of Creative Behavior, 24,* 111-131.

Bigoness, W. J., & Perreault, W. D., Jr. (1981). A conceptual paradigm and approach for the study of innovators. *Academy of Management Journal, 24,* 168-182.

Buel, W. D., Albright, L. E., & Glennon, J. R. (1966). A note on the generality and cross-validity of personal history for identifying creative research scientists. *Journal of Applied Psychology, 50,* 217-219.

Burstiner, I. (1977). Creative management training for department store middle managers: An evaluation. *Journal of Creative Behavior, 11,* 105-108.

Chusmir, L. H., & Koberg, C. S. (1986). Creativity differences among managers. *Journal of Vocational Behavior, 29,* 240-253.

Clapp, R. G., & De Ciantis, S. M. (1989). Adaptors and innovators in large organizations: Does cognitive style characterize actual behavior of employees at work? An exploratory study. *Psychological Reports, 65,* 503-513.

Cole, S. (1979). Age and scientific performance. *American Journal of Sociology, 84,* 958-977.

Dauw, D. C. (1967). Vocational interests of highly creative computer personnel. *Personnel Journal, 46,* 653-659.

Dudek, S. Z., & Hall, W. B. (1978). Design philosophy and personal style in architecture. *Altered States of Consciousness, 41,* 83-91.

Feist, G. J., & Runco, M. A. (1993). Trends in the creativity literature: An analysis of research in the "Journal of Creative Behavior." *Creativity Research Journal, 6,* 2271-2286.

Fischer, W. A., & Farr, C. M. (1985). Dimensions of innovative climate in Chinese R&D units. *R&D Management, 15,* 183-190.

Ganesan, V., & Subramanian, S. (1982). Creative process and innovative performance among scientists. *Psychological Reports, 50,* 1172.

Gough, H. G. (1975). A new scientific uses test and its relationship to creativity in research. *Journal of Creative Behavior, 9,* 245-252.

Gough, H. G. (1985). Free response measures and their relationship to scientific creativity. *Journal of Creative Behavior, 19,* 229-240.

Gough, H. G., & Woodworth, D. G. (1960). Stylistic variations among professional research scientists. *Journal of Psychology, 49,* 87-98.

Gryskiewicz, S. S. (1988). Trial by fire in an industrial setting: A practical evaluation of three creative problem-solving techniques. In K. Gronhaug & G. Kaufmann (Eds.), *Innovation: A cross-disciplinary perspective* (pp. 205-231). Oslo: Norwegian University Press.

Hall, W. B., & MacKinnon, D. W. (1969). Personality inventory correlates of creativity among architects. *Journal of Applied Psychology, 53,* 322-326.

Helson, R. (1978). Psychological dimensions and patterns in writings of critics. *Journal of Personality, 46,* 348-361.

Jacoby, J. (1968). Creative ability of task-oriented versus person-oriented leaders. *Journal of Creative Behavior, 24,* 249-253.

James, L. R., & Ellison, R. L. (1973). Criterion composites for scientific creativity. *Personnel Psychology, 26,* 147-161.

Kasperson, C. J. (1978). Psychology of the scientist: XXXVII. Scientific creativity: A relationship with information channels. *Psychological Reports, 42,* 691-694.

Katz, A. N. (1984). Creative styles: Relating tests of creativity to the work patterns of scientists. *Personality and Individual Differences, 53,* 281-292.

Kavolis, V. (1966). Community dynamics and artistic creativity. *American Sociological Review, 31,* 208-217.

Kirton, M. J. (1989). A theory of cognitive style. In M. J. Kirton (Ed.), *Adaptors and innovators: Styles of creativity and problem solving* (pp. 1-36). New York: Routledge.

Kirton, M. J., & De Ciantis, S. (1989). Cognitive styles in organizational climate. In M. J. Kirton (Ed.), *Adaptors and innovators: Styles of creativity and problem solving* (pp. 79-96). New York, NY: Routledge.

Kirton, M. J., & McCarthy, R. M. (1988). Cognitive climate in organizations. *Journal of Occupational Psychology, 61,* 175-184.

Lacey, L. A., & Erickson, C. E. (1974). Psychology of scientist: XXXI. Discriminability of a creativity scale for the Adjective Check List among scientists and engineers. *Psychological Reports, 34,* 755-758.

Livingstone, L. P., Nelson, D. L., & White, M. A. (1992, August). *Person-environment fit on the dimension of creativity: Relationships with strain, job satisfaction and performance*. Paper presented at the annual meeting of the Academy of Management, Las Vegas, NV.

Livingstone, L. P., Nelson, D. L., & Jennings, D. F. (1993, August). *Dimensions of creativity fit as they relate to dimensions of job satisfaction*. Paper presented at the annual meeting of the Academy of Management, Atlanta, GA.

Lovelace, R. F. (1986). Stimulating creativity through managerial intervention. *R&D Management, 16*, 161-174.

Ludwig, A. M. (1992). The creative achievement scale. *Creativity Research Journal, 5*, 109-124.

MacKinnon, D. W. (1961a). Creativity in architects. In *Proceedings: Conference on the Creative Person* (pp. 1-24). Institute of Personality Assessment and Research, University of California, Berkeley.

MacKinnon, D. W. (1961b). Fostering creativity in students of engineering. *Journal of Engineering Education, 52*, 129-141.

Maier, N.R.F., & Hoffman, L. R. (1961). Organization and creative problem solving. *Journal of Applied Psychology, 45*, 277-280.

McPherson, J. H. (1972). Assessing the relationships between the industrial climate and the creative process. In C. W. Taylor (Ed.), *Climate for creativity: Report of the 7th National Research Conference on Creativity* (pp. 97-108). Elmsford, NY: Pergamon.

Mullins, C. J. (1960). Selection of creative personnel. *Personnel Journal, 39*, 12-13.

Owens, W. A. (1961). The prediction of research competence and creativity from personal history. *Journal of Applied Psychology, 45*(1), 59-62.

Pelz, D. C. (1975). Relationships between measures of scientific performance and other variables. In C. W. Taylor & F. Barron (Eds.), *Scientific creativity: Its recognition and development* (pp. 228-250). Huntington, NY: Robert E. Krieger.

Pelz, D. C., & Munson, F. C. (1982). Originality level and the innovating process in organizations. *Human Systems Management, 3*, 173-187.

Rickards, T., & Bessant, J. (1980). The creativity audit: Introduction of a new research measure during programmes for facilitating organizational change. *R&D Management, 10*, 267-275.

Robertson, T. S., & Wind, Y. (1983). Organizational cosmopolitanism and innovativeness. *Academy of Management Journal, 26*, 332-338.

Roe, A. (1951). A study of imagery in research scientists. *Journal of Personality, 19*, 459-470.

Roe, A. (1965). Changes in scientific activities with age. *Science, 15*, 313-318.

Schroder, H. M. (1989). Managerial competence and style. In M. J. Kirton (Ed.), *Adaptors and innovators: Styles of creativity and problem solving* (pp. 97-124). New York: Routledge.

Simonton, D. K. (1975). Sociocultural context of individual creativity: A transhistorical time-series analysis. *Journal of Personality and Social Psychology, 32*, 1119-1133.

Simonton, D. K. (1979). Multiple discovery and invention: Zeitgeist, genius, or chance? *Journal of Personality and Social Psychology, 37*, 1603-1616.

Simonton, D. K. (1988). Age and outstanding achievement: What do we know after a century of research. *Psychological Bulletin, 104*, 251-267.

Simonton, D. K. (1992). Leaders of American psychology, 1979-1967: Career development, creative output, and professional achievement. *Journal of Personality and Social Psychology, 62,* 5-17.

Slevin, D. P. (1971). The innovation boundary: A specific model and some empirical results. *Administrative Science Quarterly, 16,* 515-531.

Slivinski, L. W., & Chagnon, G. J. (1973). Creativity and occupational membership. *Studies in Personnel Psychology, 52,* 49-65.

Stein, M. I., Heinze, S. J., & Rodgers, R. R. (1955). Creativity and/or success: A study in value conflict. In C. W. Taylor (Ed.), *The identification of scientific talent* (pp. 201-232). Salt Lake City: University of Utah Press.

Taylor, D. W. (1975). Variables related to creativity and productivity among men in two research laboratories. In C. W. Taylor & F. Barron (Eds.), *Scientific creativity: Its recognition and development* (pp. 228-250). Huntington, NY: Robert E. Krieger.

Thamia, S., & Woods, M. F. (1984). A systematic small group approach to creativity and innovation: A case study. *R&D Management, 14,* 25-35.

Tucker, M. F., Cline, V. B., & Schmitt, J. R. (1967). Prediction of creativity and other performance measures from biographical information among pharmaceutical scientists. *Journal of Applied Psychology, 51,* 131-138.

PART II

Ivory Tower Visions

3 Boogie Down Wonderland
Creativity and Visionary Leadership

JAY A. CONGER *Professor of Organizational Behavior,*
McGill University

Great curiosity [needs to be] bounded by a sense of purpose.
Guided by curiosity and intent, visionary creativity is in part
an ability to synthesize diverse information, weeding out the
irrelevant, and conceptualizing what appears useful into a
coherent picture that helps formulate the vision.

For, you see, so many out-of-way things had happened
lately, Alice had begun to think that very few things indeed
were really impossible.

Lewis Carroll,
Alice's Adventures in Wonderland (1982)

$\mathcal{A}$s you will recall from Lewis Carroll's *Alice in Wonderland*, Alice was a terribly inquisitive young lady who had a remarkable adventure one afternoon. It is hard to imagine that out of all the river banks in the world, she would choose the very one that had a rabbit running by with a pocket watch. Serendipity was the starting point for her adventure. You might also recall that Alice's sister—sitting right beside her—failed even to notice the rabbit. Alice was clearly paying more attention. She choose not to ignore such an interesting opportunity. Instead she literally jumped on it, hoping it might answer her curiosity. Sensing that the rabbit was unique, Alice was determined to discover more. So, intent on her adventure, she seemed oblivious to any risks.

Quite remarkably, these very qualities of Alice's are similar to those of creative and visionary business leaders. For surprisingly, although Carroll meant for his story to be both a children's book and a satire on the politics of the day, he was inadvertently describing the creative process and one of the keys to creative leadership. This essay will explore these qualities and tie them directly to highly creative business leaders whom I have known and studied. Specifically, I will focus on one element of their creativity—their ability to be visionary. I have chosen to open with Alice so I can be a bit creative myself and at the same time illustrate a particular element of visionaries—their ability to see parallels. Now on to my leaders.

I have long been fascinated by business leaders who are able to detect strategic opportunities for their organizations that other leaders simply never see. It is what we might call *creative insight* or the more popular term, *vision*. Edwin Land of Polaroid, Steven Jobs of Apple Computer, Fred Smith of Federal Express, and Mary Kay Ash of Mary Kay Cosmetics all come to mind as examples of such visionary leaders. Edwin Land, for instance, realized early on that individuals wanted the instant pleasure of seeing their just-snapped photographs. Steven Jobs sensed that computing power would move away from highly centralized mainframes to much smaller, individual systems for the office, school, and home. Fred Smith foresaw that the Information Age would bring a desire for instant delivery of important information and hence the need for inexpensive overnight delivery services. And Mary Kay envisioned a new organization devoted to providing entrepreneurial opportunities for a growing class of women who were seeking careers and financial security, but not wishing to sacrifice their family life.

All of these leaders possessed a seemingly uncanny ability to foresee future market and social trends in their various worlds. Just as important, they were able to capitalize on them by devising revolutionary new products, services, or organizations. In this sense, they are extremely creative individuals. Their creativity comes from a unique ability to see opportunities before they are apparent to anyone else and then to devise a vision that promotes their realization. With this focus in mind, let us now turn to how they do it. And though research on visionaries is still scanty, we can draw some tentative but powerful conclusions as to their creativity.

THE CREATIVE PROCESS ITSELF

As mortals ourselves, we might imagine that visionary leaders possess a clear sense of their visions right from the start. Theirs is a superhuman ability to foresee future events. In reality, their creativity is not the magic lightbulb appearing over one's head. Nor is it the step-by-step planning process we normally think of when we talk about a company's planning department. Instead, it is a much more fragmented and intuitive process, and much of it has to do with an orientation toward information. Although it also depends on external events over which the leader may have no control, and therefore on a great degree of opportunism and luck, visionary leadership uses information as its tool to be opportunistic. Essentially, information and the leader's own perceptiveness are what allow him or her to see the often less apparent or odd opportunities in a given situation. For example, Steven Jobs had a close friend nicknamed the Woz. The Woz was a tinkerer at heart—an electronic tinkerer. He had been experimenting with a small box with a memory chip in it. As the box played games and performed complex calculations, Jobs spotted the opportunity. He realized the hidden potential of that box to become the personal computer and to one day supplant the mainframe. He knew that educational institutions were clamoring for computers but that the prices of mainframes kept them out of students' reach. The solution was to devise an inexpensive, less brainy version of the mainframe.

Now to be an opportunist, a visionary leader has to be paying attention—attention to marketplace needs that might not be apparent at first glance. After all, chance favors the prepared mind, Louis Pasteur once remarked. Fred Smith describes a related process:

Pogo, the cartoon character, pointed out one time that the way to be a greater leader is to see a parade and run like hell to get in front of it. And there's a lot of truth to that. I don't know of many innovations where somebody sort of just dreamed up an idea out of the clear blue and went off. I mean, there are usually some fairly discernible trends available for a long time indicating a demand for a product or service. And the time to act on that—to get to the front of the parade, if you will—is when that demand, and the technology needed to meet it, begin to converge. (quoted in Tucker, 1986, p. 35)

To "pay attention," visionary leaders must normally be great information collectors but with a difference—they use multiple and sometimes apparently unrelated sources of information. Again Smith's comments are insightful:

> Mostly, I think it [visioning] is the ability to assimilate information from a lot of different disciplines all at once, particularly information about change, because from change comes opportunity. So you might be reading something about the cultural history of the United States, and come to some realization about where the country is headed demographically. The common trait of people who supposedly have vision is that they spend a lot of time reading and gathering information, and then synthesize it until they come up with an idea. (quoted in Tucker, 1986, p. 48)

One executive I studied so personified this stereotype that he would awake at 3:00 a.m. and read a wide range of books until 6:30 a.m., when his day started. Together we often discussed his interests in philosophy, oriental art, and spirituality while talking about business issues. Colleagues would say, "You'll be constantly amazed by his breadth of knowledge." His behavior was driven by a great curiosity, but one bounded more often by a sense of purpose.

Purpose is critical because it serves as the organizing and weeding-out principle among the many diverse sources of information and insight that a creative person can generate. My executive friend reading in bed every morning was searching for opportunities tied to the world of telecommunications—he was testing and exploring the viability of his new-found bits of information in helping him see emerging opportunities for his company. His ultimate goal was to revolutionize the telecommunications industry by matching the next wave of technology to societal and market changes.

Guided, then, by curiosity and intent, visionary creativity is in part an ability to synthesize diverse information, weeding out the irrelevant and conceptualizing what appears useful into a coherent picture that helps formulate the vision. In addition, part of the information-collecting process often involves the ability to see parallels outside of one's industry. For instance, the delivery network of Federal Express's

North American operation is designed around an airport hub in Tennessee. All packages are shipped directly to the hub before being cleared and shipped to their respective destinations. This might seem silly—a package going from New York to Miami has to pass through Tennessee! But in reality, it is the most efficient network system possible because it dramatically simplifies what would otherwise be a nightmare of flight schedules. The idea for this centralized hub was borrowed from a business that long ago faced the same dilemma and resolved it in the most efficient manner—the banking industry. For example, banks daily face the overwhelming problem of clearing everyone's checks—literally millions of checks received from and going to thousands of banks all over the continent. To facilitate the exchange, all checks are cleared through centralized clearing houses operated by the Federal Reserve. Bank A does not send Bank B's checks directly to Bank B. Instead, all banks send their received checks into a clearing house that sorts them and distributes the cashed checks to their original issuing bank, which minimizes what would be enormous coordination efforts and expenses for individual banks. Fred Smith saw this parallel and applied it to his fledgling vision of overnight package delivery.

BACKGROUND EXPERIENCES THAT HELP THE CREATIVE PROCESS

But how does one know what information could be important? And how does one know which opportunities are worth pursuing or experimenting with? Certain background characteristics may favor the ability to see the relevant and weed out the irrelevant. For instance, it would appear that the visionary leaders I have studied often share the following characteristics (see Conger, 1989):

1. *Broad exposure to a product/service and industry during their early and mid-career:* The earlier career years of many visionary leaders are frequently characterized by a breadth of exposure to markets or products or organizational functions that provide them

with a relatively comprehensive understanding of an industry and, as a result, a unique vantage point to detect shortcomings and emerging opportunities and to assess their viability.

2. *Exposure to and experimentation with innovative ideas, tactics, and strategies:* It is a mistake to think that leaders are the sole creative geniuses behind their ideas. Often times, their creativity comes from being open to the creativity of others and understanding the practical implications. Steven Jobs's idea for the MacIntosh computer came from a visit to Xerox's corporate research center where he saw a prototype model. Mary Kay Ash is credited with pioneering the "home party" for selling cosmetics. In reality, the idea came from her earlier career experiences as a sales person for Stanley Home Products, which sold home cleaning products directly to its customers through "house parties."

3. *Personal experiences that heighten sensitivity to constituents and markets:* Personal work experiences in the marketplace show the way to market opportunities. Ross Perot, the legendary founder of Electronic Data Systems (EDS), began his career selling computers for IBM. In his job, he observed that many of his customers could not use their computers effectively because of inadequate software provided by the company.

At the same time, he sensed a tremendous but unfulfilled demand for software to process state and federal medical claims. These insights would form the core service of his venture, EDS. Mary Kay's strong employee orientation was the by-product of her own personal experiences. Because of an invalid father, she had served as the family housekeeper while her mother worked to support the family financially. Later, Mary Kay would marry, have three children, and then divorce. The divorce led to a financial crisis and to a job as a sales person for Stanley Home Products. She then discovered that the company's house-party selling approach allowed her to tend to her family while also providing a steady income. These experiences of struggling while also striving to be supportive of her family were the genesis behind her vision of a company devoted to helping women prosper.

4. *Enjoyment of and the search for the difficult challenge:* Creativity for many visionary leaders is often the result of their attempts to do something difficult. "Unreasonable demands often force invention, by excluding conventional solutions and requiring the maker to search beyond them" (Perkins, 1981, p. 100). Visionary individuals think of possibilities, not impossibilities. Risk taking is clearly an element of the process, and for many visionary leaders, sheer enjoyment. Like Alice in Wonderland, the risk becomes an adventure.

CONCLUSION

As with Alice and her rabbit, creativity in leadership demands a unique ability to see what others do not see. Whether it is the rabbit with the pocket watch or the need for low-cost, user-friendly computing power, opportunities are always presenting themselves. The issue is whether our immersion in the status quo and in our worldview will preclude the "eyes" we need to detect these chance and remarkably important opportunities. Visionary creativity can only come about when we realize that we must encourage managers to be greater information-seekers, to seek out broad marketplace experiences, to experiment with innovation, to get closer to constituents, and then for organizations to reward them for seeking out difficult challenges and taking risks. ▨

REFERENCES

Carroll, L. (1982). *Alice in Wonderland.* New York: Oxford University Press.
Conger, J. A. (1989). *The charismatic leader.* San Francisco: Jossey-Bass.
Perkins, D. N. (1981). *The mind's best work.* Cambridge, MA: Harvard University Press.
Tucker, R. B. (1986, October). Federal Express' Fred Smith. *Inc.*

4 Managing Creativity

RICHARD W. WOODMAN *Clayton Professor of*
Business Administration and Professor of Management,
Texas A&M University

I have no wish to oversimplify the complex mosaic of forces at
play in work settings that impact creative behaviors, processes,
and outcomes. We cannot directly manage creativity because we
really do not directly manage either creative persons or processes.
Indeed, to attempt to do so is likely to be counterproductive. What
we can manage is aspects of the situation that impact creative
behavior and outcomes. The high-payoff strategy is to understand
and identify contextual aspects that evoke and nurture creative acts.

$\mathcal{I}$ have been interested in creativity in organizations, first as an industrial engineer, then as a manager, and finally as a behavioral scientist, for a number of years. My interest has been consistent, but over the years my perspectives on organizational creativity have changed. As an engineer I thought more about innovation—the process whereby an organization develops and implements changes in products and services. Over time, I came to believe that organizations were often inept at fostering needed innovation and began to wonder why. Organizations seemed to do best what they had done before; they were weaker at doing anything for the first time.

As a manager, my perspective changed but my conclusions were similar. My experience indicated that we knew surprisingly little about managing creative employees, understanding creative processes, or fostering creative outcomes. As a behavioral scientist I do not really know a great deal more about creativity than I did when I was an engineer. I think I have a better handle on what we don't know, however, and which questions we need to be asking. I also have a more useful framework to think about organizational creativity. This framework can potentially provide avenues for both managerial action and scientific inquiry.

Despite the title of this essay, I do not believe that we can actually manage creativity—at least not directly. Let me explain. *Organizational creativity* can be defined as the creation of a valuable, useful new product, service, idea, procedure, or process by individuals working within a complex social organization. In some respects, organizational creativity is a very "special case" of organizational change. Managing change is always difficult, but managing for creative outcomes in organizations is an especially tricky business. It requires some understanding of creative persons, the creative processes involved in producing desired creative outcomes, and the "creative situation" or context within which the creative behavior and process take place. My argument that we cannot directly manage creativity stems from the observation that we really do not directly manage either creative persons or processes. Indeed, to attempt to do so is likely to be counterproductive. What we can manage is aspects of the situation that impact creative behavior and outcomes. Therefore, I particularly want to focus on this creative situation, because the context is the key to the manager's influence on the creative process.

The best we can hope for is to increase the probability of creative behavior by (a) adding things to the situation that enhance creativity and (b) removing things from the situation that serve as barriers to creativity. Organizational research supports the notion that many of the factors influencing creative behavior and creative outcomes in organizations can be meaningfully discussed in terms of characteristics of the work setting that either enhance or reduce the probability of creativity. In a very real sense, it is these characteristics that we manage, not creativity per se.

AN INTERACTIONIST
PERSPECTIVE ON CREATIVITY

It is useful to take an interactionist perspective on creativity. From this perspective, creative behavior (indeed, all behavior) is an interaction of person and situation. We must examine both the person and the situation in which the person is behaving in order to fully understand and explain the individual's behavior. Thus understanding creative persons is important, but this is only part of the behavioral puzzle. The person—with his or her cognitive skills, personality, and other attributes having a bearing on creativity—is a "given" in our management equation. That is, once the human resource management decisions regarding selection have been made (this could easily be the subject of another essay) and the creative person is a member of our organization, then management's task is one of managing context to enhance the creative potential of employees. Management's task is not one of changing the person in the person-situation interaction. At the risk of seeming to slip something by the careful reader, let me point out how controversial the previous statement is. One implication of my position would seem to be to suggest that creativity training is not particularly valuable. To my view, there is little hard evidence that creativity training in organizations meaningfully increases the probability of organizational creativity. I don't believe that it does much harm (except for the opportunity costs of choosing to utilize training resources that could be more effectively employed in other ways); however, creativity training is not where the action is in terms of high-payoff managerial behavior.

THREE PROPOSITIONS CONCERNING ORGANIZATIONAL CREATIVITY

My work on organizational creativity has led to the development of three propositions that summarize (at least a portion of) our knowledge regarding creativity in complex organizations. These propositions suggest relationships between the work setting and individual, group, and organizational creative performance.

Proposition 1. The creative performance of individuals in an organization depends on (1) characteristics possessed by these individuals (who are a "given" in a managerial sense as argued above), (2) social influences that enhance or constrain individual creativity, and (3) contextual influences that enhance or constrain individual creativity.

An example of important social influences impacting creative behavior is found in group norms. Studies indicate that norms supporting open sharing of information will enhance creativity. Similarly, norms and work cultures that support risk-taking behavior will enhance creativity. Conversely, there is considerable evidence that creativity is reduced by rigid norms that create high conformity. I mention these only as examples. The point is that, even though our information is very incomplete, we do nevertheless know some things about how social influences (manifested as norms and culture) impact creativity. Importantly, aspects of these social influences can be managed. They can be understood, measured, and changed if need be.

An example of the contextual influences referred to in Proposition 1 is the reward system. The relationship between rewards and creativity is a complex one. In general, any behavior can be positively reinforced. Evidence suggests, however, that extrinsic rewards may actually constrain some creativity, whereas intrinsic motivations and rewards—those internal to the person—may foster creativity. This creates an interesting challenge for performance appraisal and reward systems that focus on creative processes and behaviors. My point is not to be prescriptive in terms of what such appraisal and reward systems should look like (frankly, I don't have a clue), but rather to suggest that here again is an opportunity to manage context.

Proposition 2. The creative performance of groups in a complex organization depends on (a) the creative performance of group members (naturally) as well as (b) aspects of the group that enhance or constrain creativity and (c) contextual influences that enhance or constrain the group's creativity.

An example of group characteristics that are associated with creativity would be group composition. Evidence suggests that diversity increases group creativity while homogeneity serves as a constraint. Similarly, highly participative structures and cultures seem to increase group creative performance, whereas autocratic leadership, rigid structure, and the like tend to suppress it. Again, many group characteristics, as well as the context within which the group functions, lend themselves to managerial action. Work groups—their characteristics and context—can be understood, measured, and changed.

Proposition 3. The creative performance of the organization depends on the creative performance of the groups of which it is composed as well as other aspects of the organization that enhance or constrain creativity.

Among the organizational characteristics that seem to have a strong impact on creativity are communication channels and information flows. Evidence suggests that there is a logical and predictable relationship between information and creativity. Restrictions on information availability both within the organization and between the organization and its environment tend to hinder creativity. Creativity is enhanced by unfettered communication and information exchanges. Organizational design and structure provide another good example. In general, adaptive organizational forms (such as matrix, networks, collateral or parallel structures) increase the odds for creativity. Bureaucratic, mechanistic, or rigid structures decrease the probability of organizational creativity. Redesigning systems and structures is never easy. Nevertheless, no one would argue that these things should be left to chance. Organizational design characteristics provide another arena where managerial action can impact the probability of creativity.

I have no wish to oversimplify the complex mosaic of forces at play in work settings that impact creative behaviors, processes, and outcomes. The challenges are great, and there is much that we do not yet know about the complexities of creativity. Yet, neither of these observations provide a rationale for managerial inaction. We do know some things about how aspects of the work setting interact with human behavior to determine creative outcomes. In contrast to the human being, none of the aspects of the work setting are genetic. With regard to managing creativity, the high-payoff strategy is to understand and identify contextual aspects that evoke and nurture creative acts, as well as factors that constrain creativity. These are the things that need to be designed into and/or out of the situation. These are the things that we manage. ▨

5 Creativity and Entrepreneurship

HARRY NYSTROM *Professor of Marketing
and Organization, Institute of Economics, Uppsala, Sweden*

*The need for constructive vagueness—to be flexible and open for
future change, yet maintain a clear sense of direction—makes the
creative process a difficult balancing act, with seemingly conflicting
demands. There is a need to be open minded and determined,
flexible and unveering, both withholding judgment and jumping to
conclusions. The timing and balancing of risk creation and risk
reduction is the hallmark of the successful entrepreneur. Here,
then, is the bridge between creativity and entrepreneurship—the
ability to handle such counteracting tendencies successfully.*

❦have always been intrigued by two seemingly different worldviews
found in society. They seem to coexist peaceably enough but are
seldom explicitly recognized as interrelated or brought into close contact with each other. The first is the analytical world of the bureaucrat
or social engineer, emphasizing plans and structural limitations; the
second is the innovative world of the artist or entrepreneur, stressing
new ideas and open possibilities. Traditionally, economic theory and
management theory have been based largely on the first worldview
and have neglected the second. To bring these two views together in
constructive dialogue concerning the creative management of organizations, we need to consider the creative process itself and the role of
the entrepreneur in envisioning and enacting innovation.

To achieve novelty in thought and action we need to go beyond
the idea of highly directed thought, as assumed in most psychological
approaches to decision making, and highly directed action, which is
the basis for economic theory and traditional approaches to management. This intellectual heritage of the Western world has helped to
create efficient institutions and companies, but has tended to make
us forget a fundamental issue that requires creativity: the purpose for

which these organizations are designed and how to change them for the better.

IMAGE AND INNOVATION

Image and innovation are central concepts related to creativity and entrepreneurship. Both challenge our imagination and existing way of doing things and thereby help to open new possibilities for looking at the world. They point to the future more than they reflect the past and stress the desirable more than the immediately achievable. Managing image and innovation is the essence of creative leadership.

Images may be defined as subjective knowledge structures. They therefore influence how things are perceived. In the static sense, image may be seen as closely related to impression management—how to make people favorably inclined toward existing conditions. In a more dynamic sense, however, images may be viewed as open and flexible mind-sets, which help people to "go beyond the information given" (Bruner, 1974).

Innovation, on the other hand, may be defined as the result and implementation of creativity. It is the process of bringing new ideas into use. As Drucker (1985) has aptly observed, it is the "tool of entrepreneurship." With the exception of Schumpeter (1934), economists have not paid much attention to innovation and entrepreneurship, viewed in this dynamic light. They evidently find it difficult to handle within their accepted analytical frameworks, which stress predictability and continuous change. Similarly, most psychologists have avoided dealing with the dynamics of image and creativity, because these phenomena are elusive and difficult to define and measure.

A notable exception is Arieti (1976), who emphasizes the dynamic importance of images for the creative process and argues that "the image, by not faithfully reproducing reality is an innovation, a state of becoming, and a force of transcendence" (p. 49). The creative process therefore may be seen as the individually guided and balanced unfolding and converging of experience, the constructive way in which our view of the world may achieve both novelty and focus. The early stages of this process imply first a widening and then a condensing of information in an ongoing interaction with the environment. This process opens up new vistas to the mind and, if successful, leads to the constructive combining of previously unrelated images and ideas. The need for constructive vagueness—to be flexible and open for future change, yet maintain a clear sense of direction—makes the creative process a difficult balancing act, with seemingly conflicting demands. There is a need to be open minded and determined, flexible and unveering, both withholding judgment and jumping to conclusions.

In a static, analytical approach to decision making, evident in many traditional approaches to management, these are clearly contradictory and impossible demands. By its very nature, however, creativity can only be viewed as a dynamic process, a flow of activities rather than a fixed activity. The early stages of the creative process are ideally characterized by fuzzy and implicit ideas, allowing for many degrees of intellectual freedom to make room for divergent thinking and wide-ranging inspiration from diverse sources. At this stage there is a pronounced need for tolerating ambiguity, experimentation, and rethinking. The later stages, on the other hand, are more analytical and characterized by more convergent thinking and formalization. Highly focused and explicit thought processes are essential for more precision and to evaluate and communicate the solutions envisioned during the earlier stages. Although being precise and consistent may be a disadvantage during the earlier stages (by prematurely closing off consideration of critical but as yet uncrystallized ideas), they may aid the later stages of the creative process.

ENTREPRENEURSHIP

In contrast to the above notions, *entrepreneurship* may be defined as the visualization and realization of new ideas by insightful individuals, who are able to use information and mobilize resources to implement their visions. This view does not require entrepreneurs to be highly skilled in generating new ideas, but instead emphasizes the promotion and implementation of radical change. Although entrepreneurs who excel in this endeavor often are highly creative, they just as often base their entrepreneurship on the ideas of others. At the same time, entrepreneurs with original ideas of their own are usually highly motivated to succeed, but whether they do so depends on their ability to market their ideas, as well as their sensitivity and openness to other peoples' viewpoints. Although some successful entrepreneurs are also creative inventors, this need not be and often is not the case. Many inventors, on the other hand, lack the entrepreneurial skills necessary to evaluate and promote their ideas. The entrepreneur is a visionary activist who excels in the creation of opportunities and the active handling of risks and uncertainties. He or she initially increases business risks by searching for new opportunities and experimenting to see if they are worthwhile. Simultaneously, and later on, entrepreneurs are strongly engaged in reducing risk, by actively changing prevailing conditions.

This proactive dualism and switch in behavior is difficult to capture in conventional economic models, which usually assume a continuous process of information gathering and risk reduction. This sequential broadening and narrowing of experience and risk, however, is an essential aspect of the creative process and of entrepreneurship. The timing and balancing of risk creation and risk reduction is the hallmark of the successful entrepreneur. Here, then, is the bridge between creativity and entrepreneurship—the ability to handle such counteracting tendencies successfully. Creativity and entrepreneurship are therefore two essential and complementary aspects of image and innovation management. They are both necessary to achieve added value in thought and action by generating and implementing new knowledge. Together they make up the elusive but decisive ability to break out of existing patterns of thought and action to find new ways of looking at and handling reality.

IMPLICATIONS OF THE PARADOX

How, then, may we achieve breakthroughs, if we accept that intentional thoughts and action usually follow conventional paths and patterns? Paradoxically, we often find that the more effort we use to try to be original, the more we get locked into existing ways of thinking and behaving. We need external stimuli to escape from our own conceptualizations, and the more unrelated these stimuli are to the problem at hand, the more likely that they will provide original solutions. This is why we often find that chance and accident are the basis for striking originality in art or business. But someone has to notice and use these gifts from the unknown, and that is the role of creativity and entrepreneurship in both art and business.

Jackson Pollock, for instance, revolutionized the art world and inspired a new art movement, Abstract Expressionism, by spontaneously dripping paint on a canvas and then interpreting and manipulating the results of the chaos he had intentionally created. Chance and creative genius make a potent elixir, not only in the art world but also in the world of business. Pharmacia, for example, a world-leading Swedish company in pharmaceuticals and medical diagnostics, owes its original success largely to the accidental discovery that a contamination in sugar proved to be an ideal substitute for blood plasma. It also developed several other major new products from accidental discoveries (e.g., Debrisan, a new sore treatment, which originated from the accidental spilling of a chemical substance by a doctor on a patient). However, Pharmacia also organized itself to gain maximum benefit from such unplanable events. By building and maintaining a challenging and creative company culture and a strong corporate image of technological leadership, as well as openness and fairness in dealing with outside sources of ideas, it has been able to attract and develop unique ideas from within and also from outside researchers and inventors.

I would like to conclude this essay with an anecdote. A few years ago I visited China in connection with a research project that focused on differences in business culture between the East and West and on the marketing strategies Swedish firms should use when entering the Chinese market. We wanted to visit the Business Fair in Canton to interview Chinese businesspeople, and had engaged a Chinese guide as translator and introducer. He was quite disturbed that we were academic researchers, not businesspeople, and was afraid that we would spoil his reputation, because only serious businesspeople were allowed to visit the Fair. He tried to instruct us in how to behave so that we would be taken as legitimate businesspeople and ushered us in through a back door. He simply could not understand why anyone would pay a visit to China merely to gain academic knowledge and not be directly involved in useful business transactions. In a final desperate attempt to understand the purpose of our visit, he asked if we owned the university, because we then might be trying to sell it or some of its services. When the answer was no, he just shook his head and said, "Funny business."

From a conventional standpoint, creativity and entrepreneurship, either in academia or business, may often appear to be "funny business," too. Yet, if we want to gain new insight and find new opportunities in a changing world, that might be just what we need. As management researchers we need to be more open in our search for knowledge and more serious in studying the creative process and its implications for product and company development. This is not necessarily—as much of the traditional management literature implies and our Chinese guide seemed to believe—a contradiction in terms or a waste of time. From an image and innovation management point of view we must learn to understand better the conditions for individual and company creativity and entrepreneurship and to develop new management models that build on our knowledge of how successful creative artists as well as successful business people view and handle reality. ▧

REFERENCES

Arieti, S. (1976). *Creativity: The magic synthesis*. New York: Basic Books.
Bruner, J. S. (1974). *Beyond the information given. Studies in the psychology of knowledge*. London: George Allen & Unwin.
Drucker, P. (1985). *Innovation and entrepreneurship*. London: Heinemann.
Schumpeter, J. (1934). *The theory of economic development*. Cambridge, MA: Harvard University Press.

6 Creative Values and Creative Visions in Teams at Work

MICHAEL A. WEST *Professor of Work and Organizational Psychology, University of Sheffield, England*

Creativity in organizations is associated with uncertainty, ambiguity, conflict, and risk. Developing a negotiated, shared, and evolving vision means accepting uncertainty over time and encouraging, not minimizing, change. It also involves giving up some control to enable team members to develop their own vision, which may well be at variance with that of other teams in the organization. This is the stuff of creativity.

⸺⊱◈⊰⸺

*H*uman ingenuity in a value-free context expresses itself in myriad ways that can be constructive, destructive, political, acquisitive, abusive, or nurturing. In organizational settings we have examples of how human ingenuity has been used to develop means of mass destruction; ways of exploiting others; ways of addicting people so that they squander their resources unwisely; and methods of deceit that attack fundamental principles of human relationships. Organizations are not necessarily benign agents in which we should unthinkingly foster ingenuity or creativity. Ingenuity in a value-free context can be as much a threat as a benefit to society.

Team creativity from this point of view involves the shared development and application of ideas that help society in adaptive ways. Whereas ingenuity can be merely an arid search for novel combinations of disparate conceptual elements, team creativity has a deeper reality—the discovery of meaning through new ways of seeing patterns in the world. Innovation is then the application of that team creativity in ways that are beneficial in society.

As organizations become increasingly complex in response to environments that grow ever more changeable in their social, political, and economic character, the actions of individuals within organizations become decreasingly influential. Organizations have responded to environmental changeability by making the team the necessary functional unit. Individuals rarely bring about change within organizations; teams more often do. Teams have the resilience, range of skills, abilities, and experience to ensure that creative ideas are put into innovative practice. Societal changes, too, are often initiated through the activities of small groups of committed, persistent individuals whose values may well lie outside the acceptable social range. What factors determine whether a team is likely to be effective in bringing about creative change? Much of what follows is based on research evidence I and my colleagues have gathered from teams in a wide variety of organizational settings.

TEAM VISIONS

For a team to be creative it must have vision to give focus and direction to creative energies. This is not some empty mission statement espousing motherhood and apple pie and hiding a poverty of orientation in action. Vision for a team should be a clear, shared, negotiated, attainable, and evolving ideal of some valued future outcomes. To a primary health care team it might be enabling patients to take responsibility for their health by giving them a sense of power and control over their own physical health outcomes.

Vision Clarity. There are a number of dimensions along which the vision of a team can be understood. The first is clarity. Many teams do not take time to explore and articulate their objectives and to attempt to encapsulate these into a vision statement. In other cases the vision may be quite appropriately implicit rather than explicit. Bona fide implicit visions influence creativity far more than explicit but artificially fashioned mission statement.

Shared Vision. If team members do not share a team vision, their individual creativity cannot be pooled to produce creative team outcomes. This implies that visions are also negotiated, because members of teams do not come together with identical values and visions. When the team leader or organizational hierarchy determine rather than influence the "vision" for a team, the vision is unlikely to be shared and will have little influence upon creativity. Where there is a strong shared sense of valued goals or orientations within a team, it is much more likely that commitment and creativity will be engendered and employed. Visions must therefore be negotiated by team members coming together, working through their differences to find a consensual sense of their valued orientation.

Evolving Visions. The foregoing necessarily implies that a vision should be evolving. Visions are reflections of human values, interests, expectancies, and beliefs. Because people develop and change and because teams develop and change, the vision itself must evolve over time. A vision that is not reviewed and modified as part of team development becomes merely a marker of their past.

TEAM PARTICIPATION

All of the foregoing requires that teams be participative. Participation is a means to reduce resistance to change, encourage commitment, and produce a more human-oriented "culture." It incorporates three fundamental concepts: influence over decision making, information sharing, and interaction.

Influence Over Decision Making. Where team members have influence over decision making, they are more likely to contribute their creative ideas. Indeed, all team members should take responsibility for aspects of team functioning, rather than assuming that the team leader is responsible for objectives, strategies, and processes. There are times, however, when it is inappropriate for all members to make a decision. True team participation occurs when the processes of decision making are collectively determined, but where particular decisions are placed in the hands of individuals. Decision making in this way does not become a paralysis of action. It is not a process of empty consultation designed to placate the members of the group. Such participation ensures that the views, experience, and abilities of all within the team are added to the pallet of ideas with which the team will paint the future.

Information Sharing. Unless people within teams communicate and share information in an openhearted and generous way, the team can miss opportunities to generate creative new ways of doing things. But information sharing, too, holds its disadvantages if team members simply overwhelm one another with e-mail messages or written memoranda. Richness of information is determined by the medium through which the information is channeled. E-mail messages and written memoranda are impoverished media for information sharing. The richest form of information sharing is face-to-face communication. Thus, teams should encourage face-to-face communication and use written media only for simple messages.

Interaction Frequency. Frequency of interaction of team members will necessarily determine the extent to which they exchange ideas, information, and conflicting views, and will therefore enrich their collective bank of knowledge and creative opportunities. When team members avoid one another to avoid conflict, they are essentially avoiding opportunities for creativity and creative consensus.

Safety. Creativity is about things new and different: the untried and untested; things that may fail; things that may generate resistance and conflict. Creativity is about taking risks. Team members are only willing to try out new ideas—and to risk appearing foolish—if they feel safe from ridicule or attack. In so many areas of human behavior the same phenomenon is found. The patient who feels a sense of safety, warmth, and empathy from the psychotherapist is more likely to risk giving voice to denied or repressed experiences. Similarly, we are likely to play with new and different ideas to the extent that we find that our team provides a sense of safety and support in the expression of those ideas.

TASK ORIENTATION

High task orientation, which is critically necessary to team creativity, is characterized by reflexivity, constructive controversy, tolerance of minority ideas, and commitment to excellence.

Reflexivity. Reflexivity is fundamentally important in ensuring the appropriateness of team strategies and processes and task outcomes. The more that teams take time to reflect critically upon their objectives, strategies, and processes and then, crucially, modify them, the more creative and effective are they likely to be. Many teams argue that they are too overwhelmed by demands to take time for such reflection; yet there is abundant evidence that doing so leads to more effective and creative outcomes. Such reflexivity, however, carries with it risks that more uncertainty rather than less may be created, that existing processes and strategies of the team may be challenged, that new ones may have to be sought. Yet, it is the ability to live with uncertainty and ambiguity and readily adapt chameleon-like in the face of changing demands, while sticking firmly to the evolving vision, that characterizes creative, effective teams.

Constructive Controversy. In the teams that practice these principles, there is a high level of "constructive controversy" where team members feel their competence is affirmed rather than attacked, where there is a climate of cooperation and trust rather than a climate of competition and distrust, and where critical review is seen as a constructive process rather than a destructive, aggressive conflict. In such teams there is a concern with excellence of outcomes and not with the individualistic ambitions of team members.

Minority Influence. The extent to which a team can tolerate within its membership a minority who adopt differing views is an important determinant of creativity. Much, if not all, creativity is applied in practice via conflict—that is, by overcoming resistance to change in others. The team itself may be a minority within an organization, not just encouraging new and improved ways of doing things, but, by its stands, encouraging independent and creative thinking and acting more widely within the organization. Minorities influence others through processes of conversion and conflict, which enable other minorities to express their differing creative views. All of which is of great importance in organizations that seek to adapt to the ever-changing and increasingly complex world we are creating. How a team manages a minority within its membership is an important indicator of its ability to be a creative adaptive social unit.

SUPPORT FOR INNOVATION

I and my colleagues have repeatedly found that support for innovation emerges as the most significant predictor of the innovation and creativity of teams. But support has two distinct elements: espoused support and active support. In many teams support for innovation is espoused, but when the practicalities of support are examined, it is rare for team members or top management to give time, resources, and cooperation for the development of new ideas. Yet, it is precisely these activities that determine the extent to which creativity within teams occurs. If new ideas are accepted and encouraged verbally but team members do not provide the necessary practical support, the platitudes of verbal encouragement soon lose their currency.

CONCLUSIONS

One theme characterizing this essay is that creativity in organizations is associated with uncertainty, ambiguity, conflict, and risk. The ideas offered here are not some easy remedy for teamwork without danger or difficulty. Developing a negotiated, shared, and evolving vision means accepting uncertainty over time and encouraging, not minimizing, change. It also involves giving up some control to enable team members to develop their own vision, which may well be at variance with that of other teams in the organization. This is the stuff of creativity. There are risks and opportunities in participation, with team members taking, rather than avoiding, responsibility for decision making and maximizing rich means of communication. Such participation enables the group to become a vital, evolving social unit, the creative energies of which are released, but with unpredictable outcomes. Reflexivity involves challenge to existing ways of doing things. This may mean encouraging uncertainty in the face of rapid change, rather than attempting to minimize it, which is often our natural reaction. But our world is changing by our own making and old ways of responding to changing circumstances are no longer helpful. The creative response to change is to work with, rather than against, the forces of change.

Ultimately, a team that is truly creative and evolving should have the level of reflexivity and courage to recognize when its own useful life span has reached its end. A team does not necessarily go on being creative or effective year after year in the face of changing circumstances and changing developmental patterns within its members. For a team to exist in the knowledge that it may self-determine its own demise is the ultimate creative challenge, reflecting an ability to deal with uncertainty and ambiguity and a level of reflexivity that overcomes the self-serving nature of so many social organizations at the expense of the broader society. So, too, within organizations should teams have the power to dissolve and for team members to be reincarnated in new and different forms with new and different visions based on both their shared and differing values. ▧

7 Discovering the Unknowable, Managing the Unmanageable

TERESA M. AMABILE *Professor of Business Administration, Harvard University*

The highest levels of creativity are likely to occur when knowledgeable, cognitively flexible people, who really care about the work they do, are working in an atmosphere that challenges their skills, supports their autonomy, and encourages their risk taking.

⊷━━━●◈●━━━➤

A few years ago, during a seminar for managers from different companies, I mentioned the importance of risk taking to the creative process. One manager raised his hand and, to the amusement of others in the audience, earnestly remarked, "In my company we pride ourselves on encouraging people to take risks. We really do. [pause] We don't want them to make mistakes, but we do want them to take risks."

Anyone who invests time in reading this book is taking the risk that this somewhat suspect topic of creativity can hold some value for rigorous organizational research or profitable organizational practice. Isn't creativity really about the arts, or about personal eccentricity, or about impracticality? No. But creativity is about risk—not the flaky, crazy, no-ties-to-reality risk that many people associate with it, but the passionate, thoughtful, adventuresome risk of the great inventors, great leaders, and great artists in history.

An idea or product is creative if it is a novel and appropriate solution to an open-ended problem. It has to be different from what's been done before, but it can't be merely bizarre; it must be somehow appropriate to the problem—correct, useful, meaningful, or valuable. And the problem must be open-ended—whether it's a scientific problem, a management problem, or a problem in artistic expression. If someone tells you how something is to be done, there is obviously no room for creativity.

Organizations need creative solutions to many problems because, in fact, no one knows the best way to solve those problems. In that sense, creative solutions are unknowable in advance and, thus, the exact way to manage the creative process cannot be specified. You might say that creativity research is about discovering the unknowable and that fostering creativity in organizations is about managing the unmanageable.

RESEARCH ON CREATIVITY: DISCOVERING THE UNKNOWABLE

In our 20 years of research on creativity, my students, colleagues, and I have progressed from carefully controlled (but artificial) laboratory experiments to ecologically valid (but only loosely controlled) studies of creativity in real-world organizations. The early experiments gave us a clear view of social factors that can kill creativity: expected evaluation of one's work, surveillance while working, contracted-for reward, competition, and constrained choice. As we continued with our work, however, we learned why many creativity researchers never venture outside their laboratories: It's a jungle out there. It's difficult to gain access to research sites, it's difficult to formulate workable methodologies and comprehensive measures, and it's nearly impossible to conclude anything about causality from nonexperimental research results.

But, for two main reasons, we believed that it was imperative to venture beyond the confines of our laboratory. First, we realized that the variables we'd studied experimentally might operate very differently on committed, expert professionals who are trying to be creative in their jobs every day. Second, we had no way of knowing if the variables we had chosen to study in our laboratory carried much weight in real-world creativity.

We began our organizational research by doing semi-structured interviews in collaboration with colleagues at the Center for Creative Leadership. Focusing initially on R&D scientists in organizations, we asked for detailed descriptions of high-creativity and low-creativity events in their work experience. Detailed content analyses of the transcripts of dozens of interviews revealed striking patterns. Over and over again, the same factors showed up in the high-creativity stories; we called these Environmental Stimulants to Creativity. And a different set of factors showed up repeatedly in the low-creativity stories; we called these Environmental Obstacles to Creativity.

Identifying these two sets of factors from our interview analyses led to the development of The Work Environment Inventory, a questionnaire that assesses these work environment factors related to creativity. This instrument has proved tremendously useful in our recent work with organizations—for example, in a study we just completed with a company we call High Tech Electronics International. Projects that were rated by experts as high in creativity differed on several environment dimensions from those that were rated as low in creativity. The high-creativity projects were characterized by: (a) organizational encouragement and support for creativity, including fair judgment of new ideas, recognition for creative work, and encouragement to take risks; (b) supervisory encouragement, which combines clear overall goal-setting with openness to new ideas; (c) work group supports, which stem from open, trusting communication within a challenging, committed group of skilled co-workers; (d) sufficient resources, including facilities, money, and information; (e) challenging work that is perceived as important; and (f) freedom in deciding how to do one's work. The low-creativity projects were higher on: (a) organizational impediments to creativity, including political problems, excessive criticism of new ideas, destructive competition, and an emphasis on maintaining the status quo; and (b) workload pressure—having too much to do in too little time.

Although all of these work environment features distinguished high- from low-creativity projects, some clearly carried more weight than others. The strongest contributors to creativity were work group supports, challenging work, and organizational encouragement. The weakest contributors were workload pressure and sufficient resources. The remaining factors—organizational impediments, freedom, and supervisory encouragement—had a moderate impact. These findings have begun to give us a sense not only of what influences creativity in organizations, but also of where most of the "action" is.

All of the work we have done to this point—the experimental studies, the interviews, the questionnaire studies—has led to a basic conclusion. Creativity is complex, and complexly determined. It depends on features of the persons doing the work, on features of the environments in which they find themselves, and on interactions between persons and their work environments. The highest levels of creativity are likely to occur when knowledgeable, cognitively flexible people, who really care about the work they do, are working in an atmosphere that challenges their skills, supports their autonomy, and encourages their risk taking.

Of course, with every question about organizational creativity that we begin to answer, at least three or four new questions rear their nagging heads. Here are just some of the open questions that currently intrigue us—we hope other researchers will join us in their pursuit: Are some types of people more likely to view their work environments as favorable to creativity, while other types of people will view the same environments less favorably? As new people enter a work group, or new supervisors, how does the work environment change? Which kind of change is more likely to have a strong impact on people's perceptions of their work environment for creativity; change at the level of the overall organization or change at the more local, departmental level? What is the impact of specific kinds of organizational change on the environment for creativity and on organizational creativity itself? We are beginning to pursue this last question with a study of the impact of downsizing in a large technical organization.

APPLICATIONS OF CREATIVITY RESEARCH: MANAGING THE UNMANAGEABLE

When seeking suggestions on how to implement research findings about creativity, some managers assume that we wouldn't want to foster creativity throughout an organization. They assume that some areas should be targeted for creativity, and others should be left safely uncreative. I concede that I do not want the pilot flying my plane to be creative when I go on a routine flight. However, I do want him to be capable of creativity should a crisis arise. Similarly, even though we may view "creative accounting" with suspicion, I would argue that accountants need to think creatively about their practices in the face of improved information technologies and flatter organizational structures. Although we may be more concerned about achieving high levels of creativity in some areas than in others, no area of an organization should be relegated to creative wasteland status.

Based on what we now know about creativity, this is what managers should do to foster creativity in organizations. First, they should work to eliminate the environmental obstacles—the turf battles, the caustic reactions to new ideas, the lack of commitment to innovation. Second, they should create an environment where the stimulants are richly, redundantly present: an orientation toward innovation and risk taking, from the highest levels of top management on down; strategic direction for projects, coupled with procedural autonomy for those doing the projects; work that people perceive as challenging, interesting, and important; rewards and recognition for creativity; frequent, work-focused feedback; stimulating, diverse work teams; open communication and collaboration across the organization; and commitment of adequate resources and time for projects.

EPILOGUE:
MARRYING THE UNMARRIAGEABLE

Finally, let me urge a partnership that might seem like a marriage of the unmarriageable. Creativity researchers and managers have often viewed each other as hostile parties—or, at least, irrelevant. So often it happens that researchers are off trying to discover the unknowable, while practitioners are off trying to manage the unmanageable, both toiling in uninformed isolation. But it doesn't have to be this way and, in fact, it shouldn't be; their union is a marriage of necessity.

Researchers and managers can form profitable alliances, if both are willing to do a little thought reform. Practitioners have to accept that researchers don't have all the answers and will never be to able to get those answers unless they gain active cooperation and collaboration for their research. Researchers have to admit that they have a lot to learn about organizational practice, about creativity as it's needed in everyday work, and about complex multiple influences on the creative process. Like any marriage, it involves risk. Both have to realize that there's no such thing as taking risks without making mistakes. ▨

8 Individual Creativity and Organizational Innovation
An Uncertain Link

NIGEL KING Lecturer in Psychology,
University of Huddersfield, England

Individual creativity and organizational innovation, as commonly defined, are overlapping concepts. They are not interchangeable, and the link between the two is not straightforward and linear. Encouraging creativity will not always lead to more or better organizational innovation. Striving for innovation will not always help satisfy the needs for creativity of individual organizational members.

In this essay I want to discuss the relationship between individual creativity and innovation in work organizations, and to suggest that the link between the two is more complex than is often assumed. Inevitably, I must start by addressing the issue of definition, though I do so with the knowledge that the debate over what is meant by the terms *creativity* and *innovation* could fill the space I have available twice over and still reach no firm conclusion.

For the purposes of this essay I will, therefore, propose working definitions that reflect the way the two concepts are commonly utilized within work and organizational psychology. *Work creativity* is seen as the process by which an individual produces a novel and appropriate solution to a work-related problem. The problem may be presented to the individual to solve (e.g., a Managing Director asking her Marketing Director, "How can we increase the market share of product X?"), or it may be identified by individuals themselves ("How can I get this team to function more effectively?"). *Organizational innovation* is generally defined as the sequence of activities by which a new element is introduced into an organization with the intention of changing or challenging the status quo. Implicit within most definitions of organizational innovation is that it aims to be beneficial. As Michael West, Jim Farr, and others have pointed out, however, the benefit need not be directed at the organization as a whole. Rather, it may be beneficial only for certain groups or units within the organization, or for elements of society outside the organization.

The concepts of work creativity and innovation as defined above differ in three main ways. First, they differ in the type of novelty required. Creativity requires that the product be novel to the creator; innovation requires that the product be novel to its organizational setting. Thus a manager changing companies and introducing a practice that was routine in his or her previous organization but is novel in the new one could not be considered creative, but would be considered innovative. Second, innovation is essentially public; it aims to make a positive change to the status quo and to have an effect on people other than the initiator of the innovation. Creativity too may be public, but it does not have to be so. An individual may engage in creative activities purely for his or her own benefit with no aim of having an impact on other people. Finally, creativity is seen principally as a cognitive process—a special type of mental activity used in problem solving—although the importance of motivational and emotional factors is increasingly recognized. Innovation is a social process; it does not presuppose the involvement of any specific mental attributes or activities.

Despite these differences, innovation and creativity within the work setting are clearly associated and at times overlapping concepts. Frequently, where we identify individuals as being innovative in their work, we feel quite comfortable in also describing them as creative (and vice versa). It is somewhat surprising, then, how little attention has been paid to the ways in which the processes of creativity and innovation relate to each other in organizations. As a practical matter, people usually assume an intimate relationship between these two processes; some even use the terms interchangeably. Yet, if one accepts the definitions I just proposed, the relationship between creativity and innovation becomes less obvious, and perhaps problematic.

On the academic side, the reason this relationship has been overlooked is that the individual-level and organizational-level research literatures have tended to develop separately. Individual-level research has concentrated on such questions as: How can we identify creative individuals? What types of motivating factors help or hinder individual creative performance? Do opportunities for creative expression lead to feelings of mastery, job commitment, and job satisfaction? On the other hand, organizational-level research has been dominated by attempts to identify factors associated with the adoption of innovations, with particular emphasis on: leader characteristics, organizational structure, size and resources, organizational strategy, organizational climate and culture.

What we are missing is an answer to the question; "Are the conditions favorable to organizational innovation also favorable to individual creativity?" The absence of direct empirical evidence has not stopped academic and popular writers from making assumptions about the nature of the creativity-innovation link. This is particularly true in training programs aimed at increasing innovation. Here it is often taken for granted that facilitating individual creativity will make organizations more innovative and that innovative organizations will encourage individual creative expression. Such a proposition makes intuitive sense, and certainly the literature suggests that the kinds of organizations that are highly non-innovative—hierarchical, centralized, and with a culture intolerant of risk—are also antipathetic toward individual creativity. It does not necessarily follow that the opposite holds true, however; that the most highly innovative organizations are the most supportive of individual creativity. In a study of four divisions of a large Swedish chemical company, Harry Nystrom found that the division whose climate was most favorable toward creativity was not the most successful in terms of innovation. The most innovative division showed characteristics generally found to inhibit individual creativity; conflict, disharmony, and lack of trust. I suspect most of us could think of examples from our own experience of organizations where the encouragement of creativity is not matched by high levels of successful innovation.

What I want to consider now is why there might sometimes be a mismatch between the expression of individual creativity and innovative performance in work organizations. The research literature offers a number of explanations that may lead to practical suggestions. Turning first to personality research, some of the traits found to be associated with creativity could be problematic for organizational innovative performance. For instance, creative people tend to show a strong need for autonomy and independence, and a disregard for social norms. Although they produce excellent new ideas, they may not be good at communicating them to others in a nonthreatening manner. Effective innovation very often requires a change agent or idea champion who is highly skilled socially and able to understand the perspectives of organizational members affected by the innovation.

Research into the motivational basis of creativity (particularly that of Teresa Amabile and her colleagues) also helps to make sense of creativity-innovation mismatches. A large body of laboratory and field research has shown that creativity is generally facilitated by a state of intrinsic motivation—engaging in the activity for its own sake—and inhibited by a state of extrinsic motivation—engaging in the activity in order to gain rewards or avoid punishments. At the organizational level, however, the motivations for innovation are, in the main, quite clearly extrinsic; to increase productivity and profitability, to overcome competition, or to respond to some unanticipated threat or crisis. Of course, in some circumstances extrinsically motivated organizational innovation may be achieved through individuals engaging in intrinsically motivated creative activities. A motor manufacturer may be stimulated to develop an innovative new model because of growing competition with Far Eastern rivals, while the engineers responsible for the project respond creatively because they find the task intrinsically rewarding. No organization, however, can guarantee that it will only introduce innovations that all affected members find intrinsically motivating. For most people, even those in roles recognized as "creative," innovation will sometimes require the undertaking of tasks not found satisfying in and of themselves.

So far my discussion of work creativity-innovation mismatches has focused on two levels of analysis; the individual and the organization. There is, however, a third level that is of great relevance to this area: the work group. Groups commonly play key roles in the process of organizational innovation. A single innovation may involve such diverse groups as an R&D team, a marketing team, a group of top managers, and a board of directors. Depending on the nature of the innovation and the stage of the innovation process, the group characteristics that help facilitate progress of the innovation might conflict with those conducive to individual creativity. For instance, it is generally held that a democratic, participative leadership style aids creative performance among group members. Authoritarian leadership is not viewed as conducive to creativity. But democratic group leadership may actually make it harder to turn creative ideas into actual implemented innovations. I saw an example of this in a study I carried out in residential homes for elderly people. In one home, a member of the care staff proposed the adoption of a new shift system, whereby instead of having separate day and night care staff, all care staff were combined into a single group that would rotate through three 8-hour shifts. After a trial period the majority of care staff were willing to adopt the innovation. However, because the management had insisted that the change must receive unanimous backing in order to proceed, and this was not achieved, the new rotation was abandoned. If the management had taken a less participative approach to innovation decision making, the change (which they favored) could have gone ahead—albeit with the risk of losing the loyalty and commitment of the minority of staff members who were strongly opposed to it.

I have argued here that individual creativity and organizational innovation, as commonly defined, are overlapping concepts. They are not interchangeable, and the link between the two is not straightforward and linear. Encouraging creativity will not always lead to more or better organizational innovation. Striving for innovation will not always help satisfy the needs for creativity of individual organizational members. If this argument is valid (and as any academic would tell you, there is clearly the need for further research before we tell whether or not it is), two conclusions can be drawn for the management of organizations. First, if an organization feels it is underachieving in the sphere of innovation, it should not automatically and exclusively turn to the enhancement of individual creativity as a solution. Buying some creativity training may look like an easy answer, but it may be answering the wrong question. Second, we need to develop a broader understanding of the function of creativity in organizations. It is not simply a means to the end of increasing levels of innovation. Perhaps the most important outcome of maximizing opportunities for creativity is the personal growth and development of organizational members, and their job satisfaction and commitment to the organization. ▨

9 Creativity as Heroic
Risk, Success, Failure, and Acclaim

DEAN KEITH SIMONTON *Professor of Psychology,*
University of California, Davis

Quality of output seems to be a mere probabilistic function of
quantity of output. Putting it in different terms, creativity is a
consequence of sheer productivity. If a creator wants to increase
the production of hits, he or she must do so by risking a parallel
increase in the production of misses. Creative geniuses stumble,
they trip, they make horrible mistakes. The most successful
creators tend to be those with the most failures!

~~~~~~~~~~~~~

$\mathcal{O}$ne of the oldest archetypes in human culture is that of the hero.
The hero clashes with the Fates at tremendous personal risk. This
archetype is richly portrayed in the mythology of ancient Greece: the
legendary exploits of Perseus, the Twelve Labors of Hercules, Jason's
quest for the Golden Fleece, the far-reaching wanderings and adventures of Odysseus. Other cultural traditions depict the same basic
ideal: Gilgamesh of the Sumerians, Samson of the Hebrews, Siegfried
of the Germanic peoples, or Ilya Muromets of the Russians. As
popular immortals, these idols become the centerpieces of heroic
literature: *Iliad, Aeneid, Beowulf, Chanson de Roland,* and *Poema del*
Mio Cid. These are Western examples, but exemplars also populate
the Japanese *Heike monogatari,* the Chinese *San Guo zhi yan-i,* the
Sanskrit *Mahabharata,* the Persian *Shah-nameh,* and the Swahili epic
poems *Muhamadi* and *Herekali.*

In the modern era, the archetype remains alive and well. Only these
days the classic hero shows up on the silver screen and picture tube
in contemporary or futuristic attire. The archetype assumes the form
of Indiana Jones in *Raiders of the Lost Ark* or Luke Skywalker in *Star*
Wars. Many movie stars have carved out their careers as the living

image of the primordial type: Charles Bronson, Clint Eastwood, Chuck Norris, Arnold Schwarzenegger, Sylvester Stallone, and John Wayne.

The fictional nature of the epics and flicks should not blind us to the fact that many heroic stories are fanciful embellishments of the lives of real historic figures. El Cid was a genuine (if opportunistic) champion in the medieval wars between Christian and Moslem Spain. More importantly, history is replete with examples of genuine heroes. Alexander the Great, Julius Caesar, Saladin, Gustavus Adolphus, Charles XII, Frederick the Great, Washington, Nelson, and Napoleon all showed enormous personal courage in times of intense physical danger. By their acts of heroism, these soldiers proved themselves worthy of apotheosis as contemporary manifestations of the classic archetype. Thus, we see Washington in his own day styled the American Cincinnatus.

I wish to focus on a more subtle form of heroism, however. The world of creative achievements is also a realm of heroic acts. These actions may spill no blood, but that does not make them less courageous. Great creators are great risk takers in their own fashion. We often do not fully appreciate this reality, owing to a widely circulated myth about the creative genius. Too often we conceive of these luminaries as paragons of perfection: They conjure up magical creations with a "stroke of genius"—whether by a flash of insight or an exercise of an uncanny intellectual brilliance. We too frequently see geniuses as infallible agents, as if they had some direct conduit to truth or beauty. This commonplace image is pure myth. Creative geniuses stumble, they trip, they make horrible mistakes. Their highest and most acclaimed successes are constructed on the low rubble of humiliating failures.

Research on the careers of notable creators has unearthed an important principle that illustrates this reality: the equal-odds rule. Take some deceased creator and compile a chronological list of all works he or she produced over the life span. These products might entail scientific papers, patents, poems, paintings, compositions—whatever, for it doesn't really matter. Now, divide these works into two groups, hits and misses. The hits are contributions that were successful in some appropriate way, such as scientific articles that are cited widely by fellow scientists, patents that support products that made millions, poems that crop up in anthology after anthology, and so forth. The misses are failed attempts, wasted efforts that received no such endorsements from the world at large. Next, count the number of hits and misses that occur in consecutive periods of the creator's career, such as successive decades or half decades. Finally, analyze these data two ways. First, calculate the correlation between the two sets of observations. In the overwhelming number of cases, you will obtain a positive association. In other words, on the average, those segments of a creator's career when the most hits emerge will usually be the same periods that see the most misses as well. Hits and misses fluctuate roughly in tandem, rather than in opposition. Second, for each career period divide the number of hits by the number of total attempts (hits plus misses). This yields a "quality ratio," or success rate, across the career. Then plot how this hit rate changes over the course of the career. Typically, the quality ratio neither increases nor decreases as the creator gains more experience or maturity. Rather, this ratio more or less fluctuates randomly across the career.

Hence, we arrive at the equal-odds rule: Quality of output seems to be a mere probabilistic function of quantity of output. Putting it in different terms, creativity is a consequence of sheer productivity. If a creator wants to increase the production of hits, he or she must do so by risking a parallel increase in the production of misses. The creator apparently does not improve the odds of success through accumulated experience or expertise. Not only does this principle apply to fluctuations in output with the career of a single creative individual, it also applies to contrasts across creative careers. Those individuals who produce the most total output will, on the average, produce the most acclaimed contributions as well.

I know that this statement may elicit some skepticism. Aren't there mass-producers who generate piece after piece of worthless trash? And aren't there also perfectionists who manage to offer the world nothing but polished gems? Yes, no doubt there are such people. Yet, they only appear every once in a while; they are the exceptions rather than the rule. For example, American Nobel laureates publish twice as many scientific papers as other scientists still worthy enough to make it into *American Men and Women of Science*. The number of citations that a scientist received in the work of fellow scientists is strongly associated with the total output of publications. In fact, the total number of publications predicts the amount of citations received by a scientist's three most acclaimed works. Moreover, this correspondence between quantity and quality holds over the long haul. For instance, the total length of the bibliography of a 19th-century scientist predicts how famous he or she is today. Thus, a scientist who was then in the top 10% of the most productive elite has a 50-50 chance of earning an entry in a recent edition of the *Encyclopedia Britannica*. In contrast, their less prolific colleagues only have 3 chances out of 100 of earning that distinction. Riemann could make a lasting impact on science with only 19 publications, Mendel with only a half dozen, but instances like these do not occur frequently enough to overthrow the equal-odds principle.

And from this principle we can also make this startling inference: The most successful creators tend to be those with the most failures! Because the quality ratio is not proportionately higher for the most prolific, the supreme geniuses must have strewn their careers with mistakes and fiascoes. American poet W. H. Auden put it well when he noted: "The chances are that, in the course of his lifetime, the major poet will write more bad poems than the minor." Why? Because major poets "write a lot." This observation holds for major creators in other domains, as well.

Take Albert Einstein as a case in point. In his crusade to overthrow quantum physics, he often made embarrassing booboos. Once, after a long exchange with Niels Bohr, Einstein composed an elaborate argument that he thought would destroy the central thesis of Bohr's Copenhagen school. Bohr found a fatal flaw, however: Einstein had neglected to account for his own theory of relativity! Yet Einstein pressed on. He continued his search for a unified theory that ignored some essential tenets of quantum physics. He even could defend his hopeless situation with the maxim, "Science can progress on the basis of error as long as it is not trivial." Einstein was willing to sacrifice his reputation in the quest for his scientific Holy Grail.

The boldness of extraordinary genius often produces more than a few miscarried experiments. This trait is responsible also for some rather sensational scenes in intellectual or aesthetic history. These episodes may not be as monumental as the military hero risking all on the battlefield, but they are dramatic nonetheless. Think, for example, of the audience at the first performance of Igor Stravinsky's *Le Sacre du Printemps* in 1913. There was such an uproar of shouting, catcalls, and feet stamping, followed by fist fights and spitting, that the music was soon submerged in the pandemonium. Shortly after excerpts of James Joyce's *Ulysses* began to appear in an American literary journal in 1918, it was banned as pornography. And contemplate the hostile response of those attending the notorious Armory Show of 1913. Marcel Duchamp's "Nude Descending a Staircase" was denounced as "an explosion in a shingle factory"; Henri Matisse and Constantin Brancusi were hanged in effigy. Yet Stravinsky, Joyce, Duchamp, and the rest were undaunted by all the ruckus. They continued to take chances in pursuing their unique visions. Hence, the willingness to take creative risks often brings with it a special knack for alienating the public. The upshot is sometimes eventful scandal and protest.

The need to risk failure to gain success manifests itself beyond artistic endeavor. Not all of Thomas Edison's 1,093 patents protected money-making contraptions. In fact, the money he lost trying to devise a new method for extracting iron ore cost him all of his profits from the electric lightbulb. Henry Ford, Walt Disney, and Colonel Sanders each faced bankruptcy one or more times before becoming millionaires. Elvis Presley's first performance at the Grand Ole Opry got him fired. And what about the most praised American presidents? Jefferson's first attempt to win the presidency was a failure, as was Jackson's. Franklin Roosevelt previously lost as a vice-presidential candidate; before Lincoln emerged victorious in the presidential election of 1860, he had lost more campaigns than he had won. Examples like these amply illustrate the rule, "nothing ventured, nothing gained." This willingness to take the hard knocks and punches on the road to success implies a good deal more about how to make the big time. You obviously must exhibit a rare self-confidence. To avoid discouragement, you need the ego-strength of an Achilles or a Siegfried. In addition, you must display an awesome persistence. When at first you don't succeed, you must try, try again.

As Winston Churchill once put it, "Never give up. Never. Never. Never. Never. Never. Never."

By thus looking at the entire configuration of qualities that belong to these notable risk takers, it is reasonable to view as heroes these people who echo the legendary ancients. If we accept this analogy, then an irksome issue raises its ugly head: How do such figures fit with the big corporations that dominate modern industrial societies? Can large organizations make room for the daredevil ventures of these excessive risk takers? Well, yes, in a way. Often these wild spirits manage to found their own companies and design their entire business to reflect their idiosyncrasies and shenanigans. Thomas Edison, Henry Ford, and Edwin Land are classic examples. Too often, however, the institutions these innovators found undergo a process akin to Max Weber's notion of the "ritualization of charisma." Good business sense replaces high-wire acts in three-ring circuses. At times, this structural change in the organization occurs fast enough to lead to the founder's excommunication or ostracism. Steve Jobs's fate at Apple Computer typifies this ironic course of events. To be sure, some corporations work mightily at trying to maintain the proper amount of creative craziness to keep themselves at the leading edge. The old Bell Labs, Sony, and most recently, Intel, may offer examples. Nonetheless, it may be that the weight of the profit margin always makes it difficult to preserve the ambiance required for gutsy creativity. As companies become more and more risk averse, they frequently spend more time avoiding failures than seeking successes. They too often ignore Henry Ford's advice, that "Failure is the opportunity to begin again more intelligently."

I cannot offer a solution; I only present the problem. Especially in our fast-moving high-tech industries, the task is to identify the creative heroes, clothe them in the armor of their trade, open up the drawbridges, and send them out to do battle, to conquer unknown worlds. Most missions will find these knights errant returning battered and wounded. But that is the price for the fewer times that they return in splendor from their adventures, all trumpets blaring and grand trophies in tow. ▨

10 Creativity
It's All in Your Social Network

DANIEL J. BRASS *Associate Professor of Organizational Behavior, The Pennsylvania State University*

The "strength of weak ties" lies in the fact that such ties often act as bridges between different groups. As such, these weak relationships often are a key source of novel, divergent, nonredundant information.

⌀t is difficult to be creative, particularly about creativity, when sitting alone in an office staring at a computer screen. That observation is not an apology for the following. Rather, that is the point of this essay. No one is creative alone. You and I are only as creative as our social networks.

This idea didn't come to me as I was sitting at my computer. It was the result of a fortuitous interaction in the mail room. Two of my colleagues, who happen to be the editors, were discussing this book. As is often the case in our department, colleagues view all problems or questions from their individual research perspectives. We like to jokingly tell each other, "It's all ____ (fill in your favorite research perspective)." The same is true in most organizations; marketing managers view problems from a marketing perspective, production managers see the same problems from a production perspective.

Thus, as Cameron Ford and Denny Gioia were discussing creativity, I flippantly interjected, "Creativity—it's all in your social network!" All three of us laughed, but this offhand comment was then reinforced by another colleague, Martin Kilduff, who is also interested in social networks and who entered the mail room just as we were laughing. None of us took this idea seriously, but I later found myself playing around with applications of a social network perspective to creativity. A couple of days later, I proposed the idea to the editors, and the result is this essay.

Now, I should explain that I don't do research on creativity, and the editors are not very interested in social networks. I know as much about cognitive schemas as they know about weak network links— very little. Thus, although we are social friends, we don't often discuss our research with each other. Each of us has a closely interconnected set of professional colleagues who are interested in similar research questions and with whom we exchange ideas and papers. In the case of social network researchers and creativity researchers, few interconnections exist.

Therefore, the logic of my assertion that creativity is a social process may not be immediately apparent to those interested in the study of creativity. Most of the writing on creativity, whether academic or practitioner oriented, has been decidedly psychological in nature. The almost exclusive focus has been on individual traits and cognitive processes. We seem to be fascinated by the biographies of Thomas Edisons. We have an insatiable need to understand how the minds of such creative people work. This is the "romance of creativity." We seem to believe that if we could only understand the mental processes of Thomas Edison, we could somehow train our own minds to be creative. It's a romantic notion, but let me venture out on a limb and suggest that it's also a myth. Creativity is not "all in your mind."

It is our minds, in fact, that prevent us from being creative. As we seek to make sense of the world around us, we are constrained by our cognitive abilities. We perceptually attend to relatively few, familiar stimuli, and organize them into simplifying patterns consistent with our previous experience. Consistency and commitment are the "hobgoblins of the mind" (Cialdini, 1989). Processing information automatically is the only way we can function in everyday life, but that very necessity also limits our ability to be creative.

Thus, we are constrained by our own previous experiences. To break out of this rigid consistency, many creativity exercises, focusing on the individual, provide "tricks" on rearranging, or recombining, our understanding of these previous experiences. Therefore, to generate original, valuable ideas, we can (a) rely on our own bounded memories, complete with filters, biases, and other hobgoblins; or, we can (b) seek out new knowledge and information from other sources. It is this second opportunity, specifically the use of our social networks, that has been largely ignored in the study of creativity and the search for innovation in organizations.

An individual's social network consists of a set of nodes (people) and the presence or absence of links (relationships) among these people. Figure 10.1 illustrates two such social networks. The links might represent a number of possible relationships, such as communication, friendship, advice, or workflow in an organization. For purposes of illustration, let's assume that they represent work-related interaction in an organization. A line connecting two nodes indicates that the two people interact with each other; the absence of a link indicates no interaction.

These social network links can be further characterized as weak ties or strong ties (Granovetter, 1973, 1982). A strong tie is a frequent, repeated, perhaps important interaction, often containing a positive affective component. A weak tie is an infrequent interaction containing little or no affect. For example, two people linked by a strong tie might be close friends within the same department, whereas a weak tie might connect two acquaintances across different departments.

The principle of transitivity can be applied to strong ties. We are not likely to be friends with two people who dislike each other. Friends of an individual are likely also to be friends. That is, others who are linked to an individual via a strong tie are likely also to be linked by a strong tie. Several people linked by strong ties might be considered a clique, or a highly cohesive work group. Figure 10.1A illustrates the transitivity of strong ties. Person A is linked to several others who are themselves linked to each other. This pattern of strong ties is not unusual in functionally differentiated departments in organizations.

Conversely, people who are linked to another via weak ties are not likely to be linked themselves. An individual's acquaintances are much less likely to be linked than an individual's friends, just as workers in different departments are less likely to be linked than workers in the same department. Figure 10.1B illustrates a network of weak ties. Person B is weakly linked to several others who are not themselves linked.

The "strength of weak ties" (Granovetter, 1973, 1982) lies in the fact that such ties often act as bridges between different groups. As such, these weak relationships often are a key source of novel, divergent, nonredundant information. Two people linked by a weak

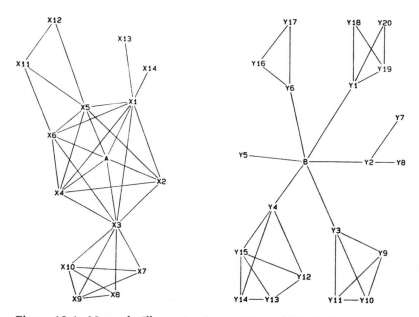

Figure 10.1. Networks Illustrating Strong Ties and Weak Ties

tie are likely to travel in different social circles. On the other hand, two friends are likely to be in the same social circle (your own clique) and subject to the same information that is available to you.

An example may help illustrate the strength of weak ties. Suppose Persons A and B in Figure 10.1 are both looking for new jobs. Person A relies upon his strong ties, and obtains the same, redundant job openings from his or her group of close-knit friends. Person B contacts his or her weakly connected acquaintances, and obtains a number of different and diverse job openings. We might predict that Person B is more likely to find the more satisfying job. Studies have confirmed that successful job hunters are more likely to use weak ties than strong ties (Granovetter, 1973, 1982).

Similarly, research has shown that two randomly selected people can "reach" each other through a surprisingly few number of links if these "paths" are composed of weak links. These findings have become known as the "small world" phenomenon (Travers & Milgram, 1969). Likewise, the diffusion of ideas or innovations is accomplished more effectively through the use of weak ties (Rogers, 1983). Now, suppose that Managers A and B are each asked to generate a novel, creative solution to an organizational problem. Each can ponder the problem, attempting to counteract their own hobgoblins. Or, each could rely upon his or her social network contacts. Based upon studies that show groups superior to individuals in solving unstructured problems, I would predict that using the social network will produce more creative solutions. And, based upon the above examples, I would predict that Manager B's weakly linked social network will generate more creative solutions that Manager A's strongly connected network.

Here's a simple test of this prediction. Select an article or technical report that you judge as creative, and check the references cited. Do the referenced articles cite each other? Compare that with a noncreative article. I'd venture that you'll find more cross-references among these cited articles.

Before abandoning your friends and building a network of acquaintances, let me stress that *friend* and *acquaintance* are only surrogates for strong and weak ties. The key difference is whether your connections are themselves connected—whether there are "structural holes" (Burt, 1992) in your network. As mentioned in the original example, the editors are friends of mine, but our professional networks do not intersect. They represent strong ties in my friendship network, but are weak ties in my professional network.

Although strong ties are not likely to provide novel, nonredundant information, they do have some advantages over weak ties. Strong ties may be more credible, trusted sources of information; more motivated to provide the information; and more readily available. Obviously, strong ties also provide social and emotional support. For example, mentoring relationships in organizations would involve strong ties. Thus, some balance between strong and weak ties is advisable.

In organizations, as in other settings, similarity breeds attraction, and interaction breeds similarity. In addition, the division of labor and formation of horizontally and vertically differentiated groups creates additional barriers to interaction. Employees in functionally differentiated work groups develop strong ties within such groups, with few links crossing group boundaries. Thus, we should not be surprised when these homogenized groups fail to provide creative solutions to organizational problems. Faced with an ever-changing environment and the need to innovate, organizations can foster weak ties by creating cross-functional, heterogeneous task forces and project teams, particularly in areas such as research and development. Employees can be encouraged to build "acquaintances" across departments by creating temporary cross-functional teams in both formal (e.g., training programs) and informal (e.g., softball teams) activities. This networking activity is especially important for managers in their roles as "linking pins" throughout the organization (Likert, 1961).

Having argued that creativity is a social network process, let me conclude by inching back off my self-created limb. Social interaction, especially weak links, provides the novel input for creative problem solving in organizations. We must still fight the hobgoblins of our minds, however. Alexander Fleming had to recognize the possibility that the bacteria growing in a spoiled agar plate might eventually lead to a useful solution (i.e., penicillin). Similarly, we must be mentally open to novelty and diversity of information obtained through weak links. We must suspend our need to dismiss inconsistency as dumb or trivial. Further, we must cognitively integrate this information so as to arrive at a creative solution. Thus, I cannot totally dismiss the cognitive research of my friends. Nor did they dismiss my offhand comment, "Creativity—it's all in your social network!" ▨

REFERENCES

Burt, R. S. (1992). *Structural holes: The social structure of competition.* Cambridge, MA: Harvard University Press.

Cialdini, R. B. (1989). Commitment and consistency: Hobgoblins of the mind. In H. J. Leavitt, L. R. Pondy, & D. M. Boje (Eds.), *Readings in managerial psychology* (4th ed.) (pp. 145-182). Chicago: University of Chicago Press.

Granovetter, M. S. (1973). The strength of weak ties. *American Journal of Sociology, 78,* 1360-1380.

Granovetter, M. S. (1982). The strength of weak ties: A network theory revisited. In P. V. Marsden & N. Lin (Eds.), *Social structure and network analysis* (pp. 105-130). Beverly Hills, CA: Sage.

Likert, R. (1961). *New patterns of management.* New York: McGraw-Hill.

Rogers, E. M. (1983). *Diffusion of innovations.* New York: Free Press.

Travers, J., & Milgram, S. (1969). An experimental study of the "small-world" problem. *Sociometry, 32,* 425-443.

11 The Role of Collaboration in Creativity

NIRMAL K. SETHIA *Associate Professor of Mangement and Human Resources, California State Polytechnic University*

Individual creators need communication and interaction with their professional community to keep abreast of its knowledge frontiers and to "persuade" it about the significance of their own new contributions. Collaboration is an obvious medium of building professional bonds and links. Believers are necessary at the minimum to validate one's novel ideas, but often they are also needed to "spread the message," and possibly even take up leads that may have to be pursued to fulfill the real promise of one's breakthroughs.

⟶⟶◆⟵⟵

$\mathscr{A}$s creativity becomes an increasingly important element in organizational performance, a new understanding of creativity is needed to take us beyond the currently dominant—but sadly stagnant—intrapersonal, trait-centered perspective. In the organizational-managerial context, creativity can be best defined quite simply as contributions, or work accomplishments, that are original and useful. Recent creativity studies have made some progress toward examining the organizational determinants of creativity. But this progress does not signal a real breakthrough because creativity continues to be viewed as essentially an individual-level phenomenon. Although the guiding question in the traditional approaches to creativity has been, "What distinguishes a creative individual?" the organizational perspective asks—"What should managers do to make individuals more creative?" Significant progress in understanding and managing creativity can be made by focusing our inquiries on creative work rather than on creative individuals. After all, the interest in someone as a creative individual arises from the work this individual has produced. Consider the instance of Andrew Wiles, who has emerged as the latest instant creative celebrity. Why? Because, he proved "Fermat's Last Theorem" and thereby solved a 350-year-old problem in mathematics.

100

I would propose that our guiding question should be, "How does creative work get accomplished?" rather than, "What distinguishes a creative person?" One important fact immediately appreciated by focusing on creative work is that, notwithstanding the popular myth, creativity is a highly collaborative or collective endeavor. As Zuckerman (1977) in her study of science Nobel laureates observes: "Quite contrary to the twin stereotypes that scientists, especially the better ones, are loners and that important scientific contributions are the products of individual imagination . . . , the majority of investigations honored by Nobel awards have involved collaboration" (p. 176). It is indisputable that individual talent and motivation are germane to creativity, but the contacts, relationships, and interdependencies that evoke and nurture creativity are also of equal significance in bringing creative work to fruition.

OF CREATIVITY AND COLLABORATION

Zuckerman's study reveals many facets of collaboration in the highest levels of creative scientific work. Some more recent works have explored many varied examples of creativity in artistic and technological as well as scientific domains, where collaboration or mutually supportive relationships have been highly important (Becker, 1982; Briggs, 1988; Hughes, 1989; Westrum, 1989; Schrage, 1990). However, none of these works examine creativity or its collaborative dimensions from a management perspective. This essay has three aims: first, to provide a general framework for analyzing the modes of collaborative interaction in creative work; second, to discuss the outcomes of collaboration; and third, to point out some key issues in "managing" creative collaborations.

Collaboration in the present context refers to professionally valuable interpersonal interactions within dyads, triads, or larger groups engaged in the pursuit of a single common goal or a shared general purpose with interdependent goals. Some of the more common modes of creative interaction—which frequently overlap—are as follows.

Co-Creation or Shared Creation. Co-creation or shared creation may be regarded as the only "true form" of collaboration. Co-discoverers, co-inventors, and co-authors engage in this form of collaboration. As example is the discovery of the double helix structure of the DNA molecule by Watson and Crick. Of importance here is the question about the relative contributions by the involved individuals. In some instances, usually rare, the answer may be simply a matter of how much someone has contributed, but often the situation is more complex and requires a judgment of the worth of different contributions. For this purpose, Westrum (1989) postulates a spectrum ranging from "calculative" (e.g., technical assistance) to "generative" (e.g., intellectual collaboration). Schrage (1990), on the other hand, proposes a 2 × 2 matrix based on low versus high levels of "conceptual" and "technical" contributions.

Complementary Roles. Such criteria of relative worth are relevant also to complementary roles. In many cases a creative achievement can become a reality only when people with different professional skills and different professional roles combine their efforts. The "idea generator" and the "idea champion" constitute a well-know example of such roles. Other examples are: inventors and model-builders (Hughes, 1989); artists, art dealers, and art critics (Assouline, 1990; Becker, 1982); authors and editors and their publishers (Schrage, 1990); and film actors and directors (Briggs, 1988).

Master-Apprentice. Zuckerman (1977) provides several very illuminating case histories of master-apprentice networks and their importance to the scientific enterprise. This type of interaction is obviously important to the "apprentice" in that it offers the ideal setting for what Bandura (1986) calls creative modeling:

> In most creative endeavors, the requisite knowledge and skills are learned by example and by practice through some form of apprenticeship. Innovators do not cease to be observational learners simply because they have gained some mastery of their craft. They continue to learn things from others that might add dimensions to their own creative work. (p. 104)

As Zuckerman (1977) argues, however, some of the "masters" also would not have made the same level of impact on science and achieved the same level of eminence without their intellectual progeny.

Pace-Setters and Followers. Some individuals, through their referent power, exercise a magnetic influence on others in their field. These pace-setters cause their "followers" to move voluntarily in a certain direction and self-impose certain standards of creative achievement. Consider what was said of the "father" of the discipline of molecular biology, Max Delbruck, by his one-time colleague Gunther Stent: "Delbruck managed to become a kind of Gandhi of biology who, without possessing any temporal power at all, was an ever-present and sometimes irksome spiritual force. 'What will Max think of it?' became the central question of molecular biological psyche" (quoted in Zuckerman, 1977, p. 126).

Professional Community-Community Member. Most professionals function as members of a formal or informal professional community. Their own work is viewed as creative only to the extent that it extends the horizons of their community and is so acknowledged by it. The individual creators therefore need communication and interaction with their professional community to keep abreast of its knowledge frontiers and to "persuade" it about the significance of their own new contributions (see Kuhn, 1970; Simonton, 1988).

OUTCOMES OF
COLLABORATIVE INTERACTIONS

In the course of creative work, an individual may engage in all of the above types of collaborations. A few of these collaborations may last for a long time, most others come to an end before too long. Irrespective of their durations, productive collaborations leave lasting imprints on the collaborators. These imprints arise from the following types of basic outcomes of collaborations.

Process Outcomes. One major category of benefits accrues through the experience itself—which includes the knowledge and techniques one learns from others. Even more valuable, however, may be the learning that takes place in terms of acquiring taste and temperament, and modes of thought and action (Zuckerman, 1977). Another benefit can be a strengthening of one's sense of self-efficacy (Bandura, 1986), which is very critical in creative work.

Product Outcomes. Through collaborative effort people do achieve ends they otherwise may not be able to achieve. Reasons for this include the sheer amount of effort required, the range of expertise needed, and even the motivational influence of others. The last aspect is evident from how Robert O. Wilson, the founding director of Fermi Lab, described his experience working with J. Robert Oppenheimer: "Oppenheimer stretched me. His style, the poetic vision of what we were doing, of life, of a relationship to people, inflamed me. In his presence, I became more intelligent, more vocal, more intense, more prescient, more poetic myself" (quoted in Hilts, 1982, p. 71).

Professional Outcomes. Collaboration is an obvious medium for building professional bonds and links. These bonds and links are useful in creating a critical mass of "believers" in one's own cause. Such believers are necessary at the minimum to validate one's novel ideas, but often they are also needed to "spread the message," and possibly even take up leads that may have to be pursued to fulfill the real promise of one's breakthroughs (see Hughes, 1989).

MANAGERIAL IMPLICATIONS

The course that collaborative attempts ultimately take is greatly influenced by organizational practices and processes, which may need significant alterations before today's organizations can become truly conducive to collaboration. Top leaders in an organization serve as role models and also shape the organization's culture; unfortunately, they often appear to value "zero-sum" competition more than synergistic collaboration. The prevalent reward systems in most organizations place greater emphasis on individual achievement than on collaborative accomplishments. Typical organizational structures and career systems also exhibit little flexibility and sensitivity toward collaborative behaviors. Interactionist models of human thought and behavior are applauded by most organizational scholars, but we tend to forget that the most significant interactions could be human interactions. Maybe it is time to revisit, in the specific context of creative work, Douglas McGregor, who said, "Fads will come and go. The fundamental fact of a man's capacity to collaborate with his fellows in face-to-face groups will survive the fads and one day be recognized" (McGregor, 1960, p. 242). Organizations must take up this challenge to encourage and reward collaborators. This probably provides our best avenue for improving creativity in organizations. ▨

REFERENCES

Assouline, P. (1990). *An artfull life: A biography of D. H. Kahnweiler.* New York: Grove Weidenfeld.

Bandura, A. (1986). *Social foundations of thought and action: A social cognitive theory.* Englewood Cliffs, NJ: Prentice Hall.

Becker, H. S. (1982). *Art worlds.* Berkeley: University of California Press.

Briggs, J. (1988). *Fire in the crucible: The alchemy of creative genius.* New York: St. Martin's.

Hilts, P. (1982). *Scientific temperaments.* New York: Simon & Schuster.

Hughes, T. P. (1989). *American genesis.* New York: Viking.

Kuhn, T. S. (1970). *The structure of scientific revolutions.* Chicago: University of Chicago Press.

McGregor, D. (1990). *The human side of enterprise.* New York: McGraw-Hill.

Schrage, M. (1990). *Shared minds: The new technologies of collaboration.* New York: Random House.

Simonton, D. K. (1988). *Scientific genius: A psychology of science.* New York: Cambridge University Press.

Westrum, R. (1989). The psychology of scientific dialogues. In B. Gholson, W. R. Sadish, Jr., R. A. Neimeyer, & A. C. Houts (Eds.), *Psychology of science* (pp. 370-382). New York: Cambridge University Press.

Zuckerman, H. (1977). *Scientific elite.* New York: Free Press.

12 How Organizations Channel Creativity

WILLIAM H. STARBUCK *ITT Professor of Creative Management, New York University*

Top managers are especially prone to resist changes—their promotions and high statuses persuade them that they have more expertise than other people. They have strong vested interests. Reorientations threaten their dominance, and they believe they will catch the blame if current practices, strategies, and goals prove wrong. Also, organizational properties that support some goals conflict with the properties that support others, so organizations must take conflicting actions, and every "solution" creates a new problem.

⟨*O*⟩rganizations cannot obtain creativity merely by hiring creative people. Most organizations have many members who come up with creative ideas, but all organizations ignore or suppress some forms of creativity, and organizational creations often reflect the contributions of diverse individuals.

The following story shows how contrasting value systems and different skills interacted to produce two important inventions (Hounshell & Smith, 1988). In December 1926, Charles Stine, the Director of DuPont's Chemical Department, wrote a memorandum advocating that his company should undertake "pure science work." He listed four reasons, the last and least important of which was practical applications. Three months later, after Stine had relabeled his proposal "fundamental research," DuPont's Executive Committee gave him money for a new building and a budget for 25 scientists.

By the beginning of 1928, Stine had hired only nine scientists, including just one organic chemist. The organic chemist, Wallace Hume Carothers, moved to DuPont because it had offered him almost twice the $3,200 he had been making at Harvard. Soon after moving, Carothers told a friend:

A week of the industrial slavery has already elapsed without breaking my proud spirit. Already I am so accustomed to the shackles that I scarcely notice them. Like the child laborers in the spinning factories and the coal mines, I arise before dawn and prepare myself a meager breakfast. Then off to the terrific grind arriving at 8 just as the birds are beginning to wake up. Harvard was never like this. (Hounshell & Smith, 1988, p. 231)

Carothers espoused the then-radical views that polymeric molecules were true molecules and that they could be incredibly large. He set out to create such molecules by aggregating smaller molecules. Within a year, he published a landmark paper proving his case. By the end of 1929, he was supervising eight men.

During April 1930, two members of Carothers's group made important discoveries. Arthur Collins produced the first neoprene rubber, and Julian Hill made the first lab-synthesized fiber. The neoprene was an accidental by-product of efforts to purify another polymer, and it took DuPont little time to turn neoprene into a commercial product. Carothers's group, however, played no part in this development, for Carothers was pursuing the implications of the synthesized fiber. This too had happened by accident, a by-product of efforts to produce larger and larger molecules. While removing hot polymer from some apparatus, Hill observed that molten polymer could be drawn into filaments that turned into very strong yet very elastic fibers if they were stretched after cooling. Carothers's and Hill's efforts to produce useful fibers went nowhere at that time, however, and Carothers turned to other interests.

In June 1930, Stine was replaced by a new chemical director, Elmer Bolton, who believed that fundamental research ought to yield "practical applications." When Carothers was looking for new research topics in 1933, Bolton encouraged him to take another look at synthetic fibers. Carothers did so, but concluded after a time that the problem was inherently unsolvable. The goal was to produce a fiber with a high melting point and low solubility, and Carothers reasoned that these properties would make spinning impossible.

Bolton, however, kept synthetic fibers at the top of his personal priority list. In March 1934, he persuaded Carothers to make yet another stab. Carothers suggested to Donald Coffman that he try to make a fiber from an aminononanoic ester. Five weeks later, Coffman stuck a cold stirring rod into a molten polymer and observed a fine, tough, lustrous fiber adhering to the rod when he pulled it out. This was the first nylon.

All members of Carothers's group turned their efforts toward nylon. They began to repeat Coffman's work using variations of the chemicals he had used. Over the summer, they tried 81 chemicals, 5 of which looked promising. In February 1935, the U.S. Government granted a patent for nylon to Gerald J. Berchet, a member of the team.

DuPont mounted a crash program to bring nylon into commercial production. This effort, which took 5 years, did not involve Carothers's group. The development team was headed by Crawford H. Greenewalt. The researchers working on it envisioned nylon replacing cellophane, leather, photographic film, and wool. But DuPont's executives decided that development would progress faster if it focused on a single use. They chose women's stockings.

POLITICS AND UNDERSTANDING
FAVOR VARIATIONS

Normann (1971) observed that organizations react quite differently to two types of change proposals: variations and reorientations. Variations would modify organizations' domains only incrementally, whereas reorientations would redefine those domains. Variations exploit organizations' experience, preserve existing distributions of power, and more easily win approval from partially conflicting interests. Reorientations take organizations outside familiar domains and redistribute power to people who understand the new markets, technologies, and methods. Reorientation proposals thus meet resistance from those top managers who stand to lose power because their expertise would become obsolete.

For example, for many years NCR Corporation defined its domain as cash registers, adding machines, and accounting machines, all of which were electro-mechanical. It built a homogeneous group of top managers having expertise in this domain. In 1953, NCR bought a small computer company; and in 1959, this subsidiary developed the first solid-state computer in the world. But NCR's home-office managers acted as if the computer subsidiary was a threat. They warned that the rapid expansion of computer leasing would lower corporate earnings. Product-oriented sales managers told their sales staff, "Don't waste your time on computers. Sell posting machines." By 1968, NCR's computer hardware was lagging roughly 4 years behind IBM's. "NCR's late entry is opportune," NCR's Chairman assured its stock-holders. "Our timing is perfect." By 1971, the computer revolution had overtaken NCR. Wall Street analysts predicted that NCR could no longer compete in the computer age. NCR's top managers could not plot, let alone produce, a reorientation. Bankruptcy loomed, investors revolted, and NCR's directors finally had to replace the president (Meyer & Starbuck, 1993).

Watzlawick, Weakland, and Fisch (1974) emphasized the relativity of perception. They remarked that reorientations seem illogical be-cause they violate basic tenets of a current cognitive framework, whereas variations make sense because they modify actions or ide-ologies incrementally within an accepted overarching framework. The action proposals that look sensible are ones that follow prece-dents, harmonize with current actions, resemble the practices in other organizations, use resources that are going to waste, fit with top managers' values, or reinforce power holders (Starbuck & Milliken, 1988; Staw & Ross, 1978).

Managerial ideologies cherish variations. Managers believe organi-zations should grow incrementally at their margins. According to Peters (1980), the firms that managers regard as being well run "tend to be tinkerers rather than inventors, making small steps of progress rather than conceiving sweeping new concepts" (p. 196). Variations are often programmatic: Research departments generate opportuni-ties for complementary actions; sales personnel report on competi-tors' actions within current domains.

Emphasizing variations may be essential in normal situations because of gross perceptual errors. Several studies suggest that most people hold highly erroneous beliefs about their organizations and about the organizations' environments (Tosi, Aldag, & Storey, 1973; Downey, Hellriegel, & Slocum, 1975; Grinyer & Norburn, 1975; Payne & Pugh, 1976). Because mis-representations and inadvertent biases permeate formal reports (Hopwood, 1972; Altheide & Johnson, 1980), the organizations that take formal reports seriously either get into trouble or perform ineffectively (Grinyer & Norburn, 1975; Starbuck, Greve, & Hedberg, 1978). Variations mitigate the effects of perceptual errors by keeping actions close to those that have worked in the past; incremental actions are likely to produce expected results even when the actors thoroughly misunderstand their environments.

However, variations are also inadequate (Miller, 1990). Because people choose variations and interpret results within the frameworks of their current beliefs and vested interests, perceptual errors both persist and accumulate. Because organizations create programs to repeat their successes, they try to choose variations that will halt social and technological changes. Such variations can succeed only to small degrees and only briefly, of course. Organizations that stop innovating may not only find themselves confronting crises, they may lose the capacity to innovate (Hedberg, Nystrom, & Starbuck, 1976).

HIERARCHIES
OFTEN IMPEDE INNOVATION

Hierarchies amplify these tendencies. Porter and Roberts (1976) reviewed research showing that people in hierarchies talk upward and listen upward. They send more messages upward then downward, they pay more attention to messages from their supervisors than to ones from their subordinates, and they try harder to establish rapport with supervisors than with subordinates. People also bias their upward messages to enhance good news and to suppress bad news (Janis, 1972). This bias becomes problematic because problems are much more likely than opportunities to motivate organizations to attempt changes (Hedberg, 1981).

These communications biases seem to be stronger in some firms, with one result being an increased propensity to run into serious trouble. After studying 20 firms that were facing crises, Dunbar and Goldberg (1978) concluded that the chief executives in these troubled firms generally surrounded themselves with yes-sayers who voiced no criticisms. Worse yet, the yes-sayers deliberately filtered out warnings from middle managers who saw correctly that their firms were out of touch with market realities; many of these middle managers resigned—other were fired for disloyalty.

Top managers' perceptual errors and self-deceptions are especially potent because top managers can block actions proposed by their subordinates. Yet, top managers are also especially prone to perceive events erroneously and to resist changes—their promotions and high statuses persuade them that they have more expertise than other people. Their expertise tends to be out of date, however, because their personal experiences with clients, customers, technologies, and low-level personnel lie in the past. They have strong vested interests. Reorientations threaten their dominance, and they believe they will catch the blame if current practices, strategies, and goals prove wrong. They exacerbate their misperceptions by socializing with other top managers, who face similar pressures.

Organizations therefore tend to behave similarly to Marx's (1859/1904) observations about societies. Marx said elites try to retain their favored positions by blocking social changes. Technological changes, which elites cannot halt, make technologies increasingly inconsistent with social structures, until the elites can no longer control their societies. For organizations, however, the issues are somewhat different: Top managers can block both social and technological changes within their organizations, but they have little influence over technological or social changes outside their organizations.

Marx further said that when elites can no longer control a society, a revolution transforms the social structure. This observation also generalizes only partly to organizations. Reorientations do punctuate sequences of variations (Tushman & Romanelli, 1985), and reorientations also activate and broaden political activities. But, few reorientations transform organizational structures dramatically (Normann, 1971; Rhenman, 1973; Jonsson & Lundin, 1977). Indeed, in organizations, changing just a few top managers can produce sweeping behavioral and ideological changes (Starbuck, 1989).

CREATIVE SOLUTIONS
TO UNSOLVABLE PROBLEMS

Organizations' members regularly devote creativity to trying to solve unsolvable problems (Starbuck, 1994). Because societies promote inconsistent values, organizations' members try to pursue inconsistent goals. Also, some of organizations' overall goals encompass inconsistent subgoals. Organizational properties that support some goals conflict with the properties that support others, so organizations must take conflicting actions, and every "solution" creates a new problem.

Hierarchical dominance makes a pointed example. Western societies say hierarchical control, unity, and efficiency are good, but they also say democracy and equality are good. These societies' citizens expect organizations to use hierarchical structures to coordinate actions and to eliminate waste even though hierarchical control is undemocratic and unequal. Thus subordinates should refuse to follow superiors' commands and organizations should oppose such insubordination. One result is that organizations' members try to create "solutions" that conceal hierarchical controls or that bring subordinates' goals into line with superiors' goals. These efforts have produced an interesting historical progression in organizations.

During the late 1940s, the solution was "democratic" management. Then after a time, many subordinates surmised that this was feigned democracy and many managers learned that democratic choices are not always profitable. During the early 1950s, the solution became for managers to show "consideration" while also controlling task activities. Then after a time, many subordinates surmised that their superiors' consideration was illusory. During the late 1950s, the solution became "management-by-objectives," in which superiors and subordinates were to negotiate mutually agreed goals for the subordinates to pursue. Then after a time, many subordinates surmised that they had little say about their goals. During the 1960s, the solution became "participative management," in which workers' representatives were to participate in managerial boards. Then after a time, many workers surmised that managers were exerting strong influence within these boards and that the workers' representatives were gaining personal benefits from belonging to these boards. During the early 1980s, the solution became "organizational culture," by which organizations were to develop agreement about values, goals, and methods. Then many workers resisted homogenization and after a time, many managers learned that general solidarity did not translate into operational goals and methods. During the late 1980s, the solution became "quality circles," which broadened during the 1990s into "total quality management." Then after a time . . .

Profit maximization offers another example. Firms try simultaneously to bring in as much revenue as possible and to keep costs as low as possible. To maximize revenues, the marketing personnel ask firms to produce customized products that are just what the customers want and to make these products available just when the customers want them. To minimize costs, the production personnel seek to minimize inventories and machine downtime, so they would like to deliver the same product to every customer, or at least to produce different products in optimal quantities on efficient schedules. Thus, marketing and production personnel conflict about what to do and when to do it. Seeing unpleasant conflicts, managers try to "resolve" them. These efforts can only ease short-run symptoms, however, because the conflicts are intrinsic to the goal of maximizing profit.

Such unsolvable problems evoke frustration, of course, but they also present opportunities for genuine creativity. For one thing, inconsistent goals reflect the fact that people create organizations to carry out complicated, difficult, but important tasks. These tasks justify creative effort. For another thing, it occasionally happens that someone finds a way to solve an unsolvable problem—as when Carothers's group discovered nylon. These surprising solutions are a major reason creativity fascinates and rewards us. ▨

REFERENCES

Altheide, D. L., & Johnson, J. M. (1980). *Bureaucratic propaganda.* Boston: Allyn & Bacon.

Downey, H. K., Hellriegel, D., & Slocum, J. W., Jr. (1975). Environmental uncertainty: The construct and its application. *Administrative Science Quarterly, 20,* 613-629.

Dunbar, R.L.M., & Goldberg, W. H. (1978). Crisis development and strategic response in European corporations. *Journal of Business Administration, 9,* 139-149.

Grinyer, P. H., & Norburn, D. (1975). Planning for existing markets: Perceptions of executives and financial performance. *Journal of the Royal Statistical Society, Series A, 138,* 70-97.

Hedberg, B.L.T. (1981). How organizations learn and unlearn. In P. C. Nystrom & W. H. Starbuck (Eds.), *Handbook of organizational design* (pp. 3-27). New York: Oxford University Press.

Hedberg, B.L.T., Nystrom, P. C., & Starbuck, W. H. (1976). Camping on seesaws: Prescriptions for a self-designing organization. *Administrative Science Quarterly, 21,* 41-65.

Hopwood, A. G. (1972). An empirical study of the role of accounting data in performance evaluation. *Empirical Research in Accounting: Selected Studies* (suppl. to *Journal of Accounting Research, 10)*, 156-182.

Hounshell, D. A., & Smith, J. K., Jr. (1988). *Science and corporate strategy: DuPont R&D 1902-1980*. New York: Cambridge University Press.

Janis, I. L. (1972). *Victims of groupthink*. Boston: Houghton Mifflin.

Jonsson, S. A., & Lundin, R. A. (1977). Myths and wishful thinking as management tools. In P. C. Nystrom & W. H. Starbuck (Eds.), *Prescriptive models of organizations* (pp. 157-170). Amsterdam: North-Holland.

Marx, K. (1904). *A contribution to the critique of political economy*. Chicago: Kerr. (Original work published 1859)

Meyer, A. D., & Starbuck, W. H. (1993). Interactions between politics and ideologies in strategy formation. In K. Roberts (Ed.), *New challenges to understanding organizations* (pp. 99-116). New York: Macmillan.

Miller, D. (1990). *The Icarus paradox*. New York: Harper Collins.

Normann, R. (1971). Organizational innovativeness: Product variation and reorientation. *Administrative Science Quarterly, 16,* 203-215.

Payne, R. L., & Pugh, D. S. (1976). Organizational structure and climate. In M. D. Dunnette (Ed.), *Handbook of industrial and organizational psychology* (pp. 1125-1173). Chicago: Rand McNally.

Peters, T. J. (1980, July 21). Putting excellence into management. *Business Week, 2646,* pp. 196-197, 200, 205.

Porter, L. W., & Roberts, K. H. (1976). Communication in organizations. In M. D. Dunnette (Ed.), *Handbook of industrial and organizational psychology* (pp. 1553-1589). Chicago: Rand McNally.

Rhenman, E. (1973). *Organization theory for long-range planning*. London: John Wiley.

Starbuck, W. H. (1989). Why organizations run into crises . . . and sometimes survive them. In K. C. Laudon & J. Turner (Eds.), *Information technology and management strategy* (pp. 11-33). Englewood Cliffs, NJ: Prentice Hall.

Starbuck, W. H. (1994). On behalf of naivete. In J.A.C. Baum & J. V. Singh (Eds.), *Evolutionary dynamics of organizations* (pp. 205-220). New York: Oxford University Press.

Starbuck, W. H., Greve, A., & Hedberg, B.L.T. (1978). Responding to crises. *Journal of Business Administration, 9,* 111-137.

Starbuck, W. H., & Milliken, F. J. (1988). Executives' perceptual filters: What they notice and how they make sense. In D. C. Hambrick (Ed.), *The executive effect: Concepts and methods for studying top managers* (pp. 35-65). Greenwich, CT: JAI Press.

Staw, B. M., & Ross, J. (1978). Commitment to a policy decision: A multi-theoretical perspective. *Administrative Science Quarterly, 23,* 40-64.

Tosi, H., Aldag, R., & Storey, R. (1973). On the measurement of the environment: An assessment of the Lawrence and Lorsch environmental uncertainty subscale. *Administrative Science Quarterly, 18,* 27-36.

Tushman, M. L., & Romanelli, E. (1985). *Research in organizational behavior: Vol. 7. Organizational evolution: A metamorphosis model of convergence and reorientation*. Greenwich, CT: JAI Press.

Watzlawick, P., Weakland, J. H., & Fisch, R. (1974). *Change*. New York: Norton.

13 Promoting Creativity in Organizations

EDWIN A. LOCKE Chair of the Management Faculty,
University of Maryland

SHELLEY A. KIRKPATRICK Research Analyst,
Pelavin Research Institute

*The uncreative person memorizes facts; the creative person
constantly tries to make connections between facts. The uncreative
person takes facts as given; the creative person tries to rearrange
them in new ways. The uncreative person carefully regulates what
the subconscious is allowed to feed the conscious mind; the
creative person allows a free flow between the conscious and the
subconscious. The uncreative person holds to fixed assumptions;
the creative person constantly challenges assumptions. The
uncreative person reacts to new discoveries in conventional ways;
the creative person looks for unconventional applications.*

$\mathcal{T}$he first author's favorite philosopher, Ayn Rand, speaks of creativity as "the power to bring into existence an arrangement (or combination or integration) of natural elements that had not existed before.
(This is true of any human product, scientific or esthetic: man's
imagination is nothing more than the ability to rearrange the things
he has observed in reality)" (quoted in Binswanger, 1986, p. 109).

The key implication of this definition is that to be creative, one
first needs to study reality. A scientist in a drug company who wants
to find a cure for AIDS, for example, must first master an enormous
amount of factual knowledge (e.g., advanced chemistry, the nature of
the AIDS virus, the nature of the immune system, the interaction
between different elements of the immune system and the virus, etc.).

Much of the creative process is just plain hard work. Thomas
Edison, for example, tried out more than 10,000 substances before
finding a suitable filament for the lightbulb. Creative discoveries,

then, do not emerge full-blown, divorced from any prior knowledge, through mystical insights or causeless intuitions. They certainly do not emerge from fictional mental entities such as the "id." (As to modern sculptors who weld pieces of scrap metal together at random, claiming inspiration from an ineffable unconscious, it is best to identify exactly what the products of their labor are: piles of junk).

This is not to deny that the subconscious plays an important role in creativity. But to put it in its proper context, the subconscious plays a crucial role in almost everything one does. The conscious mind cannot hold more than about seven disparate objects or disconnected elements in focal awareness at once (as psychologist George Miller has shown). The rest of what one knows is stored in the subconscious; we define the subconscious as that which is in consciousness but not in focal awareness. In fact, one could not even do something as simple as read a magazine without relying on one's subconscious. If the meanings of the words one read were not already automatized and stored, one would not be able to grasp the meaning of the first sentence except by looking up every word in a dictionary, and this would only work if those words were defined in terms of other words one had previously stored. One's subconscious is, therefore, useful in proportion to what one has put into it. The computer cliché, "garbage in, garbage out" applies similarly to computers and to the subconscious mind. One cannot be creative if one has stored no relevant knowledge or if one has stored chaotic jumbles of half-digested concepts, random disconnected facts, and arbitrary opinions.

On the other hand, there is no guarantee that people with large stores of knowledge will actually be creative. Knowledge is a necessary but not sufficient condition for creativity. People with high intelligence have the capacity to grasp more complex abstractions and therefore the ability to acquire more knowledge and more complex knowledge than less intelligent people. This ability gives people with high intelligence more creative potential than those with low intelligence. Psychologist Arthur Jensen has noted that there has never been a creative genius who was not highly intelligent. But, as in the case of knowledge, high intelligence does not inevitably lead to high creativity. What, then, differentiates the creative from the uncreative person, if both possess equal knowledge and intelligence?

Our belief is that it involves differences in their methods of thinking (what Ayn Rand calls "psycho-epistemology"). We are indebted to J. P. Guilford and Russell Ackoff for some of the ideas that follow: The uncreative person memorizes facts; the creative person constantly tries to make connections between facts, including those not obviously related. The uncreative person takes facts as given; the creative person tries to rearrange them in new ways. The uncreative person carefully regulates what the subconscious is allowed to feed the conscious mind ("it's never been done that way"). The creative person allows a free flow between the conscious and the subconscious; new and unusual connections are not censored but encouraged and explored. The uncreative person holds to fixed assumptions ("banks are places where people save and borrow money"); the creative person constantly challenges assumptions ("why couldn't banks sell insurance, manage investments, and sponsor credit cards?"). The uncreative person reacts to new discoveries in conventional ways ("the microwave oven is a nice way to heat food"); the creative person looks for unconventional applications ("could microwaves be used to wash clothes or cars or to send telephone messages?").

THE TRANSLATION TO ORGANIZATIONS

The implications of the foregoing for creativity in organizations are fairly straightforward. In the realm of selection, organizations should hire people who are knowledgeable, intelligent, creative in their thinking processes, and willing to work tenaciously (like Edison) to attain a goal (these traits can be measured, in part, by tests, interviews, and past behavior). With respect to training, the acquisition of new knowledge can be encouraged by numerous means, including outside courses on both content issues and creative thinking, in-house seminars, and professional meetings. However, the selection and training of suitable people is most beneficial if it occurs in the context of other organizational policies and practices that facilitate creativity.

A key factor, we believe, is *organizational culture*. We define organizational culture as the values of the organization as manifested in action, especially the actions of the leader and top executives. Values imply norms or expected ways of acting. Culture affects the extent to which creative solutions are encouraged, supported, and implemented. A culture supportive of creativity encourages innovative ways of representing problems and finding solutions, regards creativity as both desirable and normal, and favors innovators as models to be emulated. An example is 3M, where employees are not only expected to develop new innovations, but are also expected to find new ways to finance the initial phases of their projects. At Hewlett-Packard, new employees "are nothing" until they have been part of a successful product development team. The cultures at both these companies highly value creativity and innovation.

In addition, creativity must be supported by specific goals for creative behavior, combined with explicit time limits. An example is the bank president who simply asked his officers to come up with "big savings without layoffs" in 2 hours (from Peters, 1987, p. 309). Some might assume that such a direct procedure might not work because the officers would resist a direct order or would lack the knowledge to cut costs. The result, however, was that a significant share of the ideas were implementable. 3M actually has a requirement that 25% of revenue comes from products that did not exist 5 years ago. HP, it is said, routinely turns out eight new products a week.

Creativity must also be rewarded. HP gives out "gold stars" to recognize creative achievement. On the other hand, Tom Peters (1987) stresses that innovative companies are not afraid to allow failure—as a means of achieving ultimate success. Their employees learn by doing and are not punished when a solution does not work perfectly the first time.

DESIGNING ORGANIZATIONS
FOR CREATIVITY

Structures in creative organizations tend to be flexible, with few rules and regulations, loose job descriptions, and high autonomy. Open communication is encouraged. At 3M, employees are organized into cross-functional teams to facilitate the exchange of ideas. Open communication includes questioning others' ideas and disagreeing in a constructive manner. For example, Motorola encourages constructive conflicts—even to the point of loud and heated arguments—to get to the best solution.

So, how does one develop a creative culture? We believe that the prime responsibility rests with the CEO. The process begins with the leader's vision (e.g., "Our company will innovate endlessly to create new and valuable products and services and to improve our methods of producing them."). A vision is a transcendent goal that represents shared values, has moral overtones, and provides meaning; it reflects what the organization's future could and should be. The leader may stress the importance of major creative breakthroughs and new products, constant incremental improvements, or the discovery of creative ways to attain goals. (On the latter, see the history of Wal-Mart.)

Leaders must communicate the vision relentlessly through a variety of media and through formal and informal channels (Nanus, 1992), and they must constantly "sell" the vision to employees (Kouzes & Posner, 1987). The vision can be communicated in many ways. For example, leaders can simply tell employees what the vision is in speeches, impromptu talks, videos, booklets, newsletters, and annual reports. Further, the leader can model vision-appropriate behavior in his or her own actions. The leader must abide by all aspects of the vision, even in informal settings, because every action is observed and interpreted by subordinates. The leader also can use dramatic gestures to make a point. For example, the chief executive officer of Corning, Arthur Houghton, wanted to move Corning away from the decorative glass business and toward higher technology. He went down to the warehouse containing some of the most beautiful glass that Corning ever produced and, using a lead pipe, proceeded to smash hundreds of dollars' worth of the glass into smithereens (from Peters & Austin, 1985).

Once communicated, the leader must act to ensure that the vision, which initially represents only a dream, is implemented in reality. Some specific steps must be taken to do so (see Locke & Associates, 1991); these steps include the procedures noted above: selection, training, goal setting, communicating, structuring, and rewarding.

In summary, then, creativity in organizations is best achieved by the following means:

1. The leader must formulate a vision that emphasizes the importance of creativity and must communicate this vision continually to all employees.
2. A creative culture must be developed though specific steps taken to implement the vision. These include:
   a. The selection of people who are intelligent, knowledgeable, and tenacious and who use creative thinking processes;
   b. Continual training to update knowledge and teach creative thinking skills;
   c. The setting of specific, quantitative, and time-bound goals for creative products;
   d. The encouragement of frequent and even heated discussion and communication among team members, among teams, and among all employees;
   e. The use of organizational structures that are flexible and give high responsibility (in line with ability) at every level;
   f. The rewarding of creative achievement but not the punishing of initial failure. ☒

REFERENCES

Binswanger, H. (1986). *The Ayn Rand lexicon.* New York: New American Library.
Kouzes, J., & Posner, B. (1987). *The leadership challenge: How to get extraordinary things done in organizations.* San Francisco: Jossey-Bass.
Locke, E. A., & Associates. (1991). *The essence of leadership.* New York: Lexington/Macmillan.
Nanus, B. (1992). *Visionary leadership.* San Francisco: Jossey-Bass.
Peters, T. (1987). *Thriving on chaos.* New York: Harper & Row.
Peters, T., & Austin, N. (1985). *A passion for excellence.* New York: Random House.

14 The Many Facets of Creativity

PETER J. FROST *Edgar Kaiser Chair*
of Organizational Behavior,
University of British Columbia

Product innovations do not sell themselves; new ideas and
inventions need novel organizational responses to help them move
through terrains not automatically designed to recognize and
appreciate novelty. Organizations need managers and professionals
who are trained to be effective politically in their activities.

In the 1960s Spence Silver, a researcher for 3M company, came up with an odd glue that did not stick permanently; he did so as a result of noticing certain novel properties and reactions when he experimented with one of a family of monomers without following the prescribed procedure for the experiment (see Nayak & Ketteringham, 1986). Although there was little immediate interest in his discovery, he kept it alive for years within the 3M organization, presenting it at in-house seminars whenever the possibility arose. In 1974, Art Fry, another member of 3M, had the inspiration that connected a need for a bookmark for a church hymnal that would stick to a page temporarily and Spence Silver's strange glue compound. The idea for Post-it Notes was born.

Fry coupled this creative insight with several subsequent actions, both persistent and inventive, that moved the idea to a usable product. Post-it Notes became a viable product in the company through the political acumen of Geoff Nicholson, Fry's manager. He created a strategy designed to get the attention and support of the 3M Marketing Department for this product that did not conform to the stated 3M goal of devising products that "stick better" than any that competitors can produce. Nicholson was able to get enthusiastic support for the notes from secretaries of senior executives. Managers and secretaries became "hooked" on the notes and Nicholson was then able to demonstrate firsthand to the general sales manager, Joe Ramey, the value of the products. He needed further ingenious efforts to get the marketing managers to engage customers in ways that showcased the product.

Several lessons about creativity emerge from this story. (Many aspects of the story are replicated in other product creation cases. See Frost & Egri, 1991.)

1. For every creative act (one that involves original, novel connections between ideas, events, actions) that produces a technical idea or product, there is likely to be a need for a corresponding creative act that produces a social form or arrangement that enables the technical idea or product to move successfully through the organization. (Geoff Nicholson's inspired use of the informal political network within 3M is one such example.)

2. For every case of a creative individual in an organization, there is likely to be involvement of other creative people without whom the product would not likely survive. Such key people might not be noticed or rewarded in the chronicling of the creative event.

3. Creative technical and social inventions are more likely to emerge and survive in organizations in which there is a culture that allows individuals and groups to experiment, and that permits ideas and people to "hang around" until a context emerges for which the ideas and the inventors become salient and find applications. (We may be talking months or even years in some cases.)

4. When creativity is unleashed it will likely spark controversy and engender resistance from those with vested interests in a current idea, product, or social arrangement. Taking creative ideas and products from birth to maturity will usually involve some political activity and support if they are to survive. Someone or some group will need the political will and skill to tackle the hurdles of resistance and threat if a creativity is to come to fruition. Some ideas and their champions might not survive this process.

5. The path from idea generation to final resolution is likely to be nonlinear and full of surprises or "accidents." Idea champions need to be watchful for disjunctures in the path to resolution and be ready to take advantage of opportunities that present themselves along the way (e.g., Fry's insight presented opportunities for Silver). Nicholson's

sensitivity to opportunity was evident in his convincing a key player, general sales manager Joe Ramey, to accompany him to watch people react to Post-it Notes at a time when the drive to market the product was in trouble; Ramey became convinced of the value of the produce as a result of this experience and became a crucial supporter of the project (Nayak & Ketteringham, 1986).

6. Creative acts are acts of courage. First, because the creator of a technical or social innovation is entering uncharted waters and will likely receive mixed reviews about the value of the fledgling idea. Second, because the creator will likely encounter ridicule and hostility when the idea is presented and as it flows through the system. Third, because at points along the path to possible acceptance of an idea, the creator will have to invest a great deal of himself or herself in the process of getting the innovation accepted. Fourth, because creative acts pursued can fail and sometimes threaten the careers of their originators.

7. Some groups have traditionally been less supported and recognized for their creative abilities in organizations. Women and ethnic minorities in North American organizations come to mind.

What might organizations do to enhance the practice and products of creativity among individuals and work groups? Providing the time, opportunity, and encouragement for creative acts to emerge and to live long enough to be tested and evaluated are important actions that can make a significant difference. Organizations need to give as much attention to the creativity of the social organization as they do to the creativity of technical accomplishments. Product innovations do not sell themselves; new ideas and inventions need novel organizational responses to help them move through terrains not automatically designed to recognize and appreciate novelty. Organizations need managers and professionals who are trained to be politically effective in their activities. If there are no individuals who have the will and the skill to use power in ways that can persuade, influence, remove roadblocks, and in other ways mobilize resources around a new idea, product, or social arrangement, the vitality of the organization is likely to diminish. Organizations need to use creativity and political will to identify blocks to innovative thought and action, perhaps especially among women's and minority groups, which typically have been discounted and overlooked as creative contributors in the past.

For the future, to understand and work with the special dynamics of creativity within the context of organizations, we need to learn more about the linkages between power and creativity. What are the processes that facilitate and legitimate creativity in organizations? Are there systematic biases in organizations, or in institutions generally, that prevent or discount the creative contributions of women? Of ethnic minorities? Of different occupational groups? We need to understand the factors that influence successful and unsuccessful transfers of creative ideas/products from their creators to others and to whole systems. What characteristics, processes, techniques made a difference? Why does creativity flourish in some organizations and not in others? Are there generalizable forms of social organization that can most reliably enhance the likelihood of success for innovations?

I have emphasized three major themes in this brief essay. One is the role that political activity plays in enhancing or diminishing the creative process. The second is the role of collaboration in the journey from the birth of an idea to its acceptance in a realm beyond its creator. The third is the notion that creativity in organizations needs to be thought of systemically and culturally. We have neglected to attend sufficiently to each of these phenomena. We have assumed that creative ideas will survive if they are "good enough," that the fittest innovations will be the ones that endure, thus overlooking the way in which the uses of power may bias the outcome. We have discounted the contributions of several people rather than the single "hero" in our descriptions of successful creations, thus overlooking the many ways that different people make a creative idea viable. We have failed to notice the impact that the values and interdependencies that exist in organizations can have on specific creative ideas, thus overlooking the ways that they can inhibit or enhance the probability of creativity. We have lost the opportunity, in each case, to learn the lessons needed to make future innovations successful. My hope is that in redressing these blind spots we will be able to enhance the impact of creativity in an era in which we are sorely in need of inspiration and new ways of seeing, doing, and being. ▨

REFERENCES

Frost, O. J., & Egri, C. P. (1991). The political process of innovation. *Research in Organizational Behavior, 13,* 229-295.

Nayak, P., & Ketteringham, J. (1986). *Breakthroughs.* New York: Arthur D. Little.

15 Is Your Creative Organization Innovative?

FARIBORZ DAMANPOUR *Associate Professor*
of Organization Management, Rutgers University

*The characteristics of what we call "creative" organizations
today will be necessary conditions for the typical organizations
of tomorrow. Innovation will no longer be a strategic choice,
and internal flexibility, freedom, self-control, and trust will all be
required organizational characteristics necessary for organizational
survival. Assuming that the qualities of individuals that promote or
inhibit creativity will not change much over time, then what must
change is the structuring of organizations.*

---

*A*n entrepreneur not fully happy with his job takes on market
opportunity and forms a new company with several colleagues. The
company has a distinctive approach to organizing and a unique
human resources philosophy. The structure is flat, hierarchy and
formal communication are minimal, jobs are enriched and secure,
and the company is committed to the growth of the employees. Every
employee is an owner-manager, receives higher compensations than
rival firms, and participates in profit-sharing plans and stock options.
The workforce is kept small and challenged, teamwork is emphasized,
and employees are organized into self-selected, self-managed teams.
Staffing is very selective, managers are not to supervise but to
motivate and train employees. These qualities are all said to facilitate and foster creativity in organizations. The company is successful in its early years. The entrepreneur is praised for this humanistic approach. He is noted as a new-wave capitalist, and his
company is cited as a reinvention of the American corporation. The
company goes out of business in less than 6 years. It is People's
Express Airlines.

What follows is an examination of the ways in which researchers and practitioners currently represent, and misrepresent, organizational creativity and innovation. Although I touch on many factors that influence creativity, my aim is not to redefine familiar terms but to suggest a more comprehensive and systematic approach to the study of organizational creativity. I focus primarily on the harnessing of creativity for organizational innovation, on the assumption that this is a strategic imperative facing many organizations in today's dynamic business environment. My approach emphasizes issues that have emerged from previous academic research. I believe, however, that my discussion provides valuable practical insights concerning the frequent ineffectiveness of popular creativity and innovation interventions.

CREATIVITY, INNOVATION, AND ENTREPRENEURSHIP

In order to understand, and to facilitate, creativity in organizations, we have to begin by putting it in context. Indeed, creativity cannot be seen as an end in itself; it must be defined in terms of the larger goals of an organization. Take, for instance, the relationship between creativity and organizational innovation. Innovative organizations are those that introduce new technologies or management techniques pertaining to products, services, and production and administration processes earlier and more often than their competitors. These new products and services arise from the innovation process itself, which involves the generation, adoption, development, and implementation of new ideas. Creative individuals and teams influence all stages of the innovation process, but organizational innovation requires more than simply fostering creativity. Hence the following important distinction: Whereas creativity is a function of an individual or a small team, innovation is the product of an organization. That is, innovation's success or failure depends on many factors both within and outside of an organization, from employee relations to market and regulatory forces. Facilitating creativity is a necessary, but not sufficient, condition for organizational innovation.

Likewise, innovation is only useful if it contributes to the performance, the effectiveness, or even the survival of the organization.

Although innovation may be the sole reason for the existence of an organization or a unit (an R&D lab, or a product-development unit), it need not be the primary aim of the organization as a whole in all situations. Thus creativity and innovation should be understood by organizations as distinct, though related, potential goals. Encouraging either, or both, is a strategic choice.

From these observations follows another essential distinction, between innovative and entrepreneurial organizations. An entrepreneur is typically a creative individual who develops an original idea into a product or service and launches an organization to market that product or service. Such an organization is small, uni-product, and dominated by the entrepreneur, and it typically does not survive for long. If it does survive, it may or may not evolve into an innovative organization. An established organization with a commitment to innovation, on the other hand, usually offers several products or services and possesses a wider array of decision makers. Innovation is a relatively simple process in an entrepreneurial organization, but in an established organization it is more complex. The management of innovation is not similar in the two types of organizations.

Current literature often assumes that the factors that support organizational creativity are universally applicable. Clearly, any discussion of these factors should take contrasts between creativity and organizational innovation, and entrepreneurial and innovative organizations, into account.

FACTORS INFLUENCING CREATIVITY

Generally, the factors that influence creativity can be divided into two groups: Individual or team attributes, such as personality, synergy, cognitive ability, and experience; and organizational attributes, such as flexibility, reward systems, resources, and climate. If individual attributes have their greatest effect on entrepreneurial firms, organizational characteristics are prime determinants in innovative organizations. For the purposes of this essay I will limit my analysis of the relationship between these factors and creativity to two organizational characteristics—flexibility and bureaucratic control, really opposite ends of one continuum.

Most researchers and practitioners assume that giving workers autonomy, freedom, and control over accomplishing their tasks facilitates workers' creativity. Conversely, excessive formalization, red tape, and managerial control are thought to discourage such behavior. In this schema, creativity is expected to flourish within organizations that have flexible, open structures and to be inhibited in those with rigid, bureaucratic systems. The former group of organizations is thus expected to be more innovative than the latter.

When I reviewed the empirical research on organizational innovation, however, I did not find consistent support for this line of reasoning. In fact, the cumulation of findings of past research shows only a modest positive association between participation in decision making and innovation, and no significant associations between both degree of formalization and extent of hierarchy and innovation. How can we explain these inconsistent findings and abate practitioners' frustration with the unreliability of these interventions? Again, a closer look at these factors reveals that certain assumptions about organizational creativity we take for granted may be ill advised.

TYPES OF ORGANIZATIONS
AND CREATIVITY

These surprising results are partly explained when a distinction is made between types of organizations, whether market types (industrial or consumer) or product technology types (good-producing or service-producing). Compare, for example, the effects of flexibility and bureaucratic control on creativity in manufacturing and service organizations. In manufacturing organizations, outputs are tangible, standardized, and can be stored for later use, while in service organizations, outputs are intangible, customized, and the producer interacts with the clients or customers to complete delivery of the services. Because of the nature of their activities, service workers need more flexibility and less bureaucratic control to deliver their services effectively. Accordingly, the negative effect of formalization and hierarchical control on both creativity and innovation is more pronounced in service organizations. These results suggest that organizational facilitators and inhibitors of creativity and innovation differ from one industry or sector to the next.

In fact, other distinctions between types of organizations may be even more crucial for determining predictors of creativity. In recent years the application of information and computer technologies such as computer integrated manufacturing and flexible automation in manufacturing has lessened the contrast between service and manufacturing organizations. For the purposes of influencing creativity, it may be more useful to distinguish organizations based on considerations such as technological intensity and industry-wide competition. For instance, members of organizations that employ complex, intensive, or customized technologies and operate in very competitive environments must engage continually in the generation of new ideas and creative problem solving. Consequently, such organizations require both a flexible structure and a climate conducive to innovation; self- and peer control replace hierarchical control. On the contrary, organizations that use simple, routine technologies within less competitive environments can operate effectively with more bureaucratic control and less flexibility and remain, within their own industries, innovative. Unfortunately, most academic research on creativity and innovation fails to recognize the importance of distinguishing between different organizational contexts when studying determinants of creativity and innovation. Taking these distinctions into account would allow creativity and innovation researchers to offer more definitive advise to interested practitioners.

CREATIVITY AND
ORGANIZATIONS OF THE FUTURE

If we agree with the predictions of our trendsetters and futurists, the positive characteristics of what we call the "creative" organizations of today will be necessary conditions for the typical organizations of tomorrow. Innovation will no longer be a strategic choice, and internal flexibility, freedom, self-control, and trust will all be required organizational characteristics necessary for organizational survival. Assuming that the qualities of individuals that promote or inhibit creativity will not change much over time, then what must change is the structuring of organizations. These changes must enable them to be sufficiently creative to cope with increasingly complex technologies and competitive environments.

Certainly, organizations of tomorrow will have more fluid boundaries than do the organizations of today. Communication and cross-fertilization of ideas among various functional units of one organization are already deemed conducive to innovation; in tomorrow's organizations, innovation will require further cooperation among teams of people from different organizations. These individuals and teams will represent a variety of organizational cultures and will work in different geographical locations, perhaps even different countries. Their cooperation will be temporary, team members will often communicate through computer networks, and—most likely—will speak different languages. Current theories of organizational creativity must become more comprehensive in both assumptions and scope if they are to facilitate the management of such complex, cooperative efforts in organizations operating in a fluid environment.

To be effective, the organization of the future needs to be both creative and efficient, entrepreneurial and innovative. It must manage creativity and innovation, not only within its own boundaries but in relation to other organizations with very different goals and cultures. As such, the effective organization of the future defies the dualities we customarily use when we study the facilitators and inhibitors of creativity in organizations. Determining all of the contexts, characteristics, and conditions that foster organizational creativity is thus a pressing challenge facing practitioners and academics alike. ▧

16 Training Creativity in the Corporation
The View From the Psychological Laboratory

ROBERT W. WEISBERG *Professor of Psychology,*
Temple University

Pessimism is in order regarding attempts to transfer creativity from the domain of an artist to that of an employee. There are probably no general principles that can be extracted from the work of a painter that will spontaneously transfer to work in designing circuits for portable telephones, or designing a method for increasing consumers' interest in a new savings instrument. Furthermore, even if employees are explicitly made aware of the expected value to be obtained from the art-exposure programs, any information gleaned from an artist is likely to be so general in nature as to be of little practical help to a worker.

◄━━━◆◆◆◆◆◆━━━►

"Now let's have the 'chicken cheer,' " says the session leader. A dozen managers shed their jackets and stand up. A vice president from a Midwestern industrial giant glances uneasily around the room, his cheeks glowing pink. The leader starts. One by one, others join in. They flap their arms and scratch at the floor with their feet. Finally, the room fills with crowing sounds a rooster would envy. Strange as it may seem, such sessions are becoming a way of business in the United States. With the intensity of itinerant evangelists, "creativity consultants" are roaming the corporate landscape preaching an appealing gospel to managers: You can learn to be creative. And business is listening. . . . Participants learn a variety of exercises intended to get their creative juices flowing. Using devices ranging from the "chicken cheer" to the flying of kites, creativity consultants try to break down rigid thinking that blocks new ideas. (Smith, 1985, p. 80; copyright © 1985, Business Week; reprinted by permission)

$\mathscr{T}$here is, as the above example makes clear, a healthy business in training creative thinking. An important assumption underlying many such programs, including the one discussed above, is that, if we are not creative, it is because of some sort of block. The purpose of the chicken cheer and other exercises is to break down blocks and to facilitate unconventional thinking. This same assumption underlies the very influential "brainstorming" method developed 50 years ago by Alex Osborn, which put a premium on generating wild ideas without judging their value. Related approaches for overcoming mental blocks include Guilford's notion of divergent thinking and deBono's lateral thinking (see Weisberg, 1993, for a review). However, despite the popularity of the idea that fostering creativity requires fostering production of unconventional ideas, there are several reasons for questioning the value of such training programs.

First, individuals engaged in work that demands creative thinking (e.g., research scientists) do not believe that free associative (or divergent, or lateral) thinking plays an important role in their work: They report that they use conventional thinking and problem solving. Second, laboratory studies of groups and individuals have indicated that problems are solved most efficiently when the individuals are informed from the very beginning about the constraints under which they are working. This violates the axiom at the core of "creative thinking" interventions, that is, that constraints and blocks should be ignored during the idea-generation process.

Having seen little return on their investments in brainstorming and chicken cheers, many corporations have tried new methods aimed at increasing their employees' creativity. For example, some large businesses have tried to improve their employees' ability to find fresh solutions to old problems by exposing them to artists and works of art. Programs such as this are based on the assumption that a set of "creativity skills" exists that is relevant to all situations that require creative thinking. Thus, a research scientist can learn how to think more creatively by talking to an artist. This assumption is questionable, however, based on much recent psychological research in the area of "transfer of knowledge."

Knowledge transfer occurs when an individual learns something in one context and applies it in another. In studies of knowledge transfer, experimental participants (usually college students) are exposed to some "critical" or "base" information from one context and then given a "target" problem to solve in another context. The object of these studies is to see if exposure to base information facilitates the participants' subsequent problem-solving efforts. Results from these research efforts lead to the rather dispiriting conclusion that knowledge is seldom transferred across contexts. Corporate art-exposure programs could be looked upon as unfounded exercises in this kind of transfer. Based on a review of controlled laboratory studies, as well as case studies of the development of significant creative works, there is little reason to believe that employees' exposure to art will have a positive effect on their creativity at work (Weisberg, 1993).

Even so, the news isn't all bad. Studies of transfer have found more encouraging results when they take the degree of similarity between base information and a targeted problem into account. Researchers often differentiate between *surface* and *underlying* similarities. Surface similarities include resemblances in such things as the location, context, physical objects present, and so on, between base information and a target problem. Underlying similarities refer to more abstract, general principles drawn from the base information and applied to a target problem. With this is mind, consider the three problems presented in Table 16.1. The Radiation Problem has been used as a target problem in many investigations of knowledge transfer. The General's and the Lightbulb stories in Table 16.1 have an underlying similarity to the Radiation Problem, because all three have the same "simultaneous convergence" structure: The force must first be broken into parts, which are then recombined at the goal.

The Radiation Problem is also similar to the Lightbulb story, because lasers and rays are similar. The General's story is different from the other two in this respect. Thus, although all three situations in Table 16.1 are similar in "underlying" structure (i.e., the principle involved), they are different as regards "surface" structure (i.e., the physical objects that embody that principle). One could expect that knowledge would be transferred more easily from the Radiation Problem to the Lightbulb Problem, because they share both underlying and surface similarities. The General's story, on the other hand, is more "remote" from the other problems because it does not share surface similarities.

Controlled laboratory studies have demonstrated that individuals exposed to the Lightbulb story solve the Radiation Problem more frequently than do naive individuals. Those exposed to the General's

TABLE 16.1 Materials Used in Studies of Transfer

The Radiation Problem: Suppose you are a doctor faced with a patient who has an inoperable malignant tumor in his stomach. There is a kind of ray that can be used to destroy the tumor. If the rays are directed at the tumor at a sufficiently high intensity the tumor will be destroyed. Unfortunately, at this intensity the healthy tissue that the rays pass through on the way to the tumor will also be destroyed. At lower intensities the rays are harmless to the healthy tissue but they will not affect the tumor, either. What type of procedure might be used to destroy the tumor with the rays, and at the same time avoid destroying the healthy tissue? (Solution: Take two weak bundles of rays and direct them at the tumor from different angles, so that they converge at the tumor.)

The Lightbulb Problem: In a physics lab at a major university, a very expensive lightbulb, which would emit precisely controlled quantities of light, was being used in some experiments. The lightbulb overheated, and the filament inside the bulb broke into two parts. The surrounding glass bulb was completely sealed, so there was no way to open it. The lightbulb could be repaired if a brief, high intensity laser beam could be used to fuse the two parts of the filament into one. Furthermore the lab had the necessary equipment to do the job. However, a high-intensity laser beam would also break the fragile glass surrounding the filament. At lower intensities, the laser would not break the glass, but neither would it fuse the filament. How could you use the laser to repair the filament without breaking the bulb? (Solution: Use two weak lasers and combine them just at the filament.)

The General's Problem: A general was trying to destroy a fortress that was situated at the center of a country with roads leading in to it, by using his army. He needed to use his army as a complete group in order to destroy the fortress. He could not march his army down a road to the fortress, however, because the roads were mined to explode when large groups of men passed over them. How could the General successfully attack the fortress? (Solution: Divide his army into small groups of men and send them simultaneously from a number of different directions.)

story, however, do not transfer knowledge gained by solving the Radiation Problem—they perform the same as people with no experience. In order to facilitate transfer from the General's story, one must explicitly tell people that the story is relevant to the Radiation Problem; no "spontaneous" transfer occurs when the only similarity between the critical material and the target problem involves underlying structure. It is generally believed that in order for spontaneous transfer to occur, there must be both surface similarity (so that presentation of the target problem will "remind" the problem solver of the critical material) and underlying similarity (so that the critical material can be used to guide solution of the target).

Similar conclusions have been drawn from case studies of creative thinking in many domains: Even in the case of the most creative thinkers, only "near" spontaneous transfer occurs. A nonsystematic sampling of cases is presented below (for further discussion see Weisberg, 1993).

1. The "wing-warping" control system developed by the Wright brothers for their Flyer, the first successful powered airplane, controlled the plane's orientation by raising and lowering the rear edges of the tips of the wings. The Wrights had observed birds controlling their orientation in the air by adjusting the tips of their wings.

2. After Thomas Edison invented the lightbulb, he developed a system to bring electricity to homes so that the lights could be used. This system was based on the already in-place system used to deliver natural gas to residences for lighting.

3. James Watson and Francis Crick used Linus Pauling's work on the helical structure of protein as one source for their development of the double-helix model of DNA.

4. Charles Darwin's knowledge of the use of "artificial selection" by farmers was one of the factors contributing to his theory of natural selection.

5. Johannes Gutenberg is reported to have developed the first printing press by analogy to the wine press, a machine that applied a force over a large surface, which is what Gutenberg needed.

It now becomes clear why pessimism is in order regarding attempts to transfer creativity from the domain of an artist to that of an employee. There are probably no general principles that can be extracted from the work of a painter that will spontaneously transfer to work in designing circuits for portable telephones, or designing a method for increasing consumers' interest in a new savings instrument. Furthermore, even if employees are explicitly made aware of the expected value to be obtained from the art-exposure programs, any information gleaned from an artist is likely to be so general in nature as to be of little practical help to a worker. As an example, one executive expressed hope that seeing artists "trying new things" would help corporate workers in solving their problems. "Try something new" is surely of little help, however, when a person is faced with a resistant problem. As well, one company brought in a string quartet to demonstrate the importance of teamwork. Again, that message is of such a general nature as to be of little practical assistance.

Is the situation hopeless? Is there nothing that businesses can do to improve the creativity of their employees? The answer to improving creativity training is based on maximizing the transfer of critical information, thereby increasing employees' problem-solving capacities. Transfer occurs most readily when the base and target have both surface and underlying similarities in common, which means that the base and target are from the same domain. One should therefore provide employees with as much information as possible about the domains in which they work; that is, one should encourage broad-based expertise. Remote transfer may also be made possible if employees can be taught to take advantage of underlying similarities between situations that have no surface elements in common. Although this will not occur spontaneously, it could be facilitated if a problem is analyzed at an abstract level in hopes of discovering other potentially relevant situations. Thus, a more potent creativity training technique might provide employees with a database of potentially useful situations, organized in terms of their underlying structure, that could be searched using a new problem as a probe in order to see if any structural matches could be found. The problem solvers could be taught ways of analyzing new problems that would facilitate their attempts to search the database.

There are a number of ways in which creative thinking might be facilitated, but they involve solid preparation, effective problem solving, and hard work. No chicken cheers, please, and leave your kite at home. ▨

REFERENCES

Smith, E. (1985, September 30). Are you creative? *Business Week*, p. 80.
Weisberg, R. W. (1993). *Creativity: Beyond the myth of genius*. New York: Freeman.

17 Q: Does Feedback Enhance or Inhibit Creativity in Organizations? *A: Yes!*

JAMES L. FARR *Professor of Psychology,*
The Pennsylvania State University

All employees have the potential to be creative or innovative in performing their jobs, and their creativity and innovativeness are affected by the feedback they receive. Providing feedback that stresses learning and mastery by employees, that encourages employees to be creative, and that strengthens employees' beliefs about success is congruent with contemporary organizational thought that emphasizes the need for employees to be empowered in their work, to be committed to the organization, and to feel ownership in the tasks they perform.

Feedback about work performance has powerful and complex effects on people. Yet these effects often lead to paradoxical responses. In most organizations employees crave more feedback than they currently receive. At the same time many employees complain that the only feedback they get is either about what they've done wrong or what they've failed to do. Although few people really want more bad news about their performance, many fear that the alternative to negative feedback is no feedback at all! The simplistic solution to this dilemma is somehow to encourage managers in organizations to provide more positive feedback to their employees. In general, more positive feedback probably would be a good thing, but the issue is a bit a more involved than that. Besides, getting managers to give their employees more positive, and less negative, feedback is just not that easy to do.

Before complicating the apparently straightforward issue of feedback even further, I should explain why I think feedback is relevant to creativity in organizations. To me, creativity in work settings is not limited just to the creation of something new and valuable for the

137

world at large, but also includes the notion of innovation for local benefit; that is, the introduction and application in a specific work setting of something that is new to the adopting unit (whether it be a product, process, procedure, or idea), and that has intended value for a person, organizational unit, or the wider society. I also believe that in an effective organization all employees have the potential to be creative or innovative in performing their jobs, and that their creativity and innovativeness are affected by the feedback they receive.

FEEDBACK AND
WORK PERFORMANCE

With this definition of creativity and my associated belief about the ubiquitous need for it among employees, feedback becomes key to enhancing organizational creativity in a number of different ways: First, by communicating to employees that creativity and innovation are expected to be a normal part of their jobs; second, by informing employees about occasions when the status quo just isn't good enough or soon won't be—that is, encouraging the identification of "performance gaps"; third, by suggesting the parameters that surround problem-solving situations (e.g., time, resource availability, or other constraints); and fourth, by motivating individuals by providing both recognition for past creative efforts and incentives for engaging in future efforts.

As suggested in the introduction to this essay, however, the feedback that most of us experience in our work organizations often does not seem to encourage our creativity (except perhaps in creatively figuring out how to avoid feedback we don't want to hear or how to twist the feedback we do receive until it better fits what we'd like to hear). Much of the feedback given in organizations is negative in tone. Negative feedback discourages creativity, especially if it is directed at the person rather than the task at hand, or if it compares the recipient's performance with the performance of others. Creativity is discouraged in these situations because such feedback makes the person defensive about his or her performance. That is, it motivates or orients a person toward demonstrating to others (usually one's superiors in the organization) that he or she can perform the job without making mistakes. Such an orientation leads people to play safe: to take on tasks they know they can perform, to avoid challenging or stretching assignments, and to continue to use procedures they have used many times in the past. These tendencies are all exactly the opposite of the ones that facilitate creativity in employees.

Even feedback that is positive in tone can discourage creativity if it focuses strictly on bottom-line, comparative (with other employees) statements about short-term performance outcomes. Such feedback, whether it is positive or negative, is likely to foster a motivational or goal orientation that matches the message sent; that is, a straightforward concern for demonstrating one's competence to others. Although positive feedback that tells employees that they are performing their jobs better than others might not make those employees defensive, such feedback still recognizes and rewards these individuals primarily for the efficient performance of the job, as currently defined and structured.

I am not about to say that efficient job performance is a bad thing, but I will say that it is not the only goal for an organization and certainly not the main concern for an organization that wants to encourage creativity in employees. This call for a reduced focus on efficiency concerns has gained considerable support with the increasing emphasis on the concept of continuous improvement in many organizations. Continuous improvement means that a part of each employee's job is to figure out how to make the organization more effective in meeting its strategic objectives. Although more efficient performance of tasks might be a part of this process, more significant improvements usually involve fundamental shifts in how the organization does its tasks and its business; that is, continuous improvement calls for more creative and innovative approaches.

FEEDBACK AND MASTERY

If the usual kind of feedback reinforces the status quo, what kind of feedback will enhance creativity and innovation? One answer to this question is based on the observation of Teresa Amabile and others that one of the foundations of creativity is the possession of skill or competence in knowledge domain(s) that are relevant to one's work. Feedback that encourages a person to develop mastery in the relevant knowledge domain clearly would help to encourage creativity. Feedback that stresses improvements in abilities that an individual has demonstrated, or increases knowledge or skill levels, would encourage mastery efforts. Mastery efforts might include taking on difficult or novel tasks, developing new approaches for dealing with existing problems, and setting higher standards for personal performance. Feedback that indicates how far one has come, rather than how far one has to go, encourages learning or mastery and decreases defensive reactions to feedback. Focusing on changes within the person, rather than making external comparisons to other employees, directs the energy of the person toward self-improvement, not toward "beating the other person." Thus, a possible, positive side effect of such feedback might be increased cooperation and collaboration among employees and decreased competition and conflict.

FEEDBACK AND FAILURE

Feedback to encourage creativity also must reinforce the important belief on the part of the employee that he or she can be creative. A particularly vexing aspect of trying to encourage creativity is that many creative or innovative efforts will not fully succeed, so that "easy to give" positive feedback might not be feasible or credible. How does one couch feedback about an unsuccessful creative effort so that it does not deter future creative attempts? A major deterrent to accomplishing a challenging goal, such as developing an innovative approach to a problem, is the belief or expectation that failure is likely (what Albert Bandura would label as a low self-efficacy belief). An expectation of failure can easily become a self-fulfilling prophecy—I don't expect to succeed so I don't try very hard; lack of effort leads to failure, which reinforces and strengthens my prior expectation of failure; I then see even less likelihood of success so I give up and don't attempt the task at all.

To prevent this snowballing effect of ever stronger beliefs about failure, feedback should include statements about the expectation that future creative efforts will be successful, that the employee has the abilities and skills to be creative, and that continuing to apply those abilities and skills will increase the odds of future success. In addition, related to the earlier point about learning and mastery, feedback should emphasize the learning that occurred from the failed attempt. Using failure as a learning opportunity strengthens the employee's orientation toward task mastery and reduces the likelihood of defensive reactions that thwart creativity.

There also is a natural tendency for people to look for factors in their work environment that can explain why their performance was not fully successful or why a new program failed to achieve its goals. Managers should not treat all of these factors as mere "excuses" for poor performance. Some are likely to be valid and might offer good opportunities for reducing constraints on future attempts at innovation. Managers also should be aware that evaluators of another's performance have a tendency to place undue weight on the individual as a cause of success and, especially, as a cause of failure. Edward Deming has argued that organizational systems account for much more variability in performance than we usually realize. Managers should therefore restrain themselves from too quickly placing "blame" on individual employees for unsuccessful innovation attempts.

I would like to emphasize that changing the way that managers provide feedback to their employees is not a simple thing to do. We often provide negative feedback, without even realizing it, by our nonverbal behavior—those sighs, grimaces, rolling eyes, and shaking heads can undo a lot of positive comments! Also, many organizations have become so bottom-line oriented in these times of severe competition that it might seem heretical or overly idealistic not to focus feedback just on performance outcomes and employee comparisons. It will undoubtedly require a major organizational effort to develop managers who can provide feedback of the type described in this brief essay.

I believe, however, that providing feedback that stresses learning and mastery by employees, that encourages employees to be creative, and that strengthens employees' beliefs about success is congruent with contemporary organizational thought that emphasizes the need for employees to be empowered in their work, to be committed to the organization, and to feel ownership in the tasks they perform. ▨

18 Everything New Under the Gun
Creativity and Deadlines

CONNIE J. G. GERSICK *Associate Professor*
of Human Resources and Organizational Behavior,
University of California at Los Angeles

*With varying degrees of panic, teams pull up short when someone
voices the perception, "We're running out of time!" At that point,
successful groups quickly complete or drop agendas. They cast
around for fresh ideas, often with the newly sought input of outside
stakeholders. They come up with novel ways to approach their
work and new insights on material they had already generated.*

---

*The whole business of having a deadline and a time schedule
imposed is the ongoing largest single challenge of creativity within
a corporate context. "Dead" is the operative word in "deadline."*
From an interview with Gerald Hirshberg,
Vice President, Nissan Design International

$\mathscr{S}$ome of the contributors to this volume, having been asked to
define *creativity*, may have looked up the word in the dictionary. I
looked up a different word. Webster's (1978) first entry for *deadline* is:
"Originally, a line around a prison beyond which a prisoner could go only
at the risk of being shot by a guard." Deadlines place strong psychological
boundaries around us; they restrict us to a pre-dictated area, and threaten
nasty consequences if we step outside it. Creativity implies just the
opposite: freedom of imagination, spontaneity, the new and unpredictable. How is it that people (from the award-winning artists at
Nissan Design International to students doing homework) can be
creative by a deadline? How do deadlines affect the creative process?

My interest in this issue began with my research on task forces—
teams brought together specifically to do creative projects in limited
time periods. I wanted to know what such groups did to produce novel

work by appointed times. The dominant existing model, based mainly on laboratory and therapy groups, makes the process sound logical. It is built on the paradigm of development as a universal sequence of incremental steps. The core concept is that all teams begin by exploring the situation, then debate over and choose plans, and finally, with this solid preparation, get down to work (Tuckman [1965] offers the classic summary). When I set out to observe "real" project groups in the field (Gersick, 1988), I expected to see some variant of that model.

The eight groups I watched from start to finish—bank executives designing a new account, hospital administrators planning a management retreat, psychiatrists reorganizing a mental health center, and others—surprised me. They did not all proceed the same way, and they did not work in deliberate stages. They worked in punctuated equilibria, alternating short bursts of quantum progress (the creation of work patterns) with relatively long periods of momentum (work within those patterns).

More specifically, team development looked like this: Groups started off in a variety of ways. For example, one decided what to do immediately and got right to work; one was stumped; one began by fighting its assignment. No matter how they began, each group continued on its chosen path for considerable time. Then each group reached a crisis. With varying degrees of panic, every team pulled up short when someone voiced the perception, "We're running out of time!" At that point, the seven successful groups all quickly completed or dropped agendas they had been pursuing since they started. They cast around for fresh ideas, often with the newly sought input of outside stakeholders. They came up with novel ways to approach their work and new insights on material they had already generated. This set them on a second period of momentum, which carried every team to its 11th hour, when each one finished in a final burst of effort.

There are several interesting features here. First is the rapidity with which groups formed assumptions on what their tasks were about and where they were in the work process (rank beginners, sure what to do, resistant to the task, etc.). One group expressed the whole outline of its work in seemingly offhand conversation within 30 seconds of convening; all groups set basic patterns by the end of their initial meetings. A second notable feature is the tenacity with which groups held onto these patterns during momentum periods. Even groups who were frustrated and unhappy with what they were doing kept doing it. Third, and possibly most remarkable, is the regularity of the crisis through which every successful group leaped forward on its task. Even though teams' time limits varied from several days to several months, and even though they had made varying progress on their tasks, every group enacted its "punctuation" exactly halfway between its beginning and its deadline.

TEAMS, TIME, AND CREATIVITY

This portrayal suggests some intriguing observations about creativity. On one hand, it justifies our intuition that creativity is chancy and nonrational. Significant elements of our choices about how to approach a piece of work are not the result of step-by-step deliberation. Many of the fundamental perspectives that direct any search for creative ideas are adopted and "closed for consideration" swiftly, implicitly, and tenaciously. On the other hand, and contrary to intuition, the muse can be amazingly punctual. The regular midpoint occurrence of productive insight in one team after another seems almost uncanny.

A second study of project teams (Gersick, 1989) replicated the patterns outlined above and provided clues to understanding them. Teams of management students, given 1 hour to create a radio advertisement, were videotaped while they worked. I then played back selected portions of the tape, so I could ask team members "What were you thinking then?" or "Why did you do that?" Midpoint transitions emerged reliably within 2 minutes of the half-hour. Transcripts of meetings and interviews show that midpoint inspiration springs from teams' pacing themselves, somewhat like runners pacing a race. This involves setting work speed and intensity, and perhaps more importantly, dividing the total time into sections that are treated differently. With varying degrees of awareness, teams allow themselves half their time (sometimes other divisions are used) to pursue their initial tracks. At the appointed milestone, a self-imposed mental alarm clock goes off. The alarm reminds them of the deadline, signals the end of the first era of work, and orders a shift into the home stretch.

How can this pattern of activity foster creativity in organizations? Mednick (1962) proposed that creativity is the power to see existing facts freshly and to combine existing ideas in new ways. At the half-way mark, a reasonably functional team will have built a stock of ideas, information, and opinions about its task. Transitions foster inspiration by simultaneously interrupting teams' momentum on that work and jolting them to move ahead. Research on a cognitive phenomenon called the Einstellung effect (Luchins, 1940) helps explain. It shows that people deliberately stick with problem-solving strategies as long as they feel they are working on items in a series. Bracketing problems into separate sets helps break the spell, facilitating strategic rethinking. By segmenting time into separate eras, the midpoint alarm clock seems to halt teams' train of thought, providing them an opportunity to look at the "old" materials they have generated in new ways.

The emotions typical of midpoint transitions aid in this process. Fear ("half our time is gone!") helps shake teams into finishing those sub-tasks they can complete and dropping approaches that aren't working. Optimism ("We still have half our time left!"), combined with a new-found eagerness to appreciate promising ideas and make them work, helps encourage teams that it's not too late to take a new tack. My evidence to date suggests that, with some exceptions, earlier times inspire insufficient fear and later times inspire insufficient optimism to spark the special achievements possible at the midpoint.

No one I have ever interviewed has expressed a priori awareness of the regularities described above. People who often work with deadlines, however, sense the ironic predictability of the unpredictability they experience. In response to Mr. Hirshberg's fervor about deadlines, I asked if he broke them. His reply: "No, we always make deadlines. We've never missed! And we do it in ways that make their hair turn grey. Because it doesn't look like we're ever gonna finish."

FACILITATING DEADLINED CREATIVITY

There are several good reasons for anxiety and corporate challenge around creative work under deadline. Although inspiration may behave more lawfully than most people would imagine, it cannot be fully tamed. The transition is a special opportunity for insight, but it does not guarantee that ideas will come or that what comes will be good. To make matters more difficult, the path of creative progress is distinctly uneven. Even teams who later find excellent use for their ideas may work for significant stretches of time without feeling they have much to show. "It doesn't look like we're ever gonna finish."

This roller coaster can indeed make both project workers' and their bosses' hair turn gray. "Corporate types," looking (literally or figuratively) over employees' shoulders, worry about resources and opportunities slipping by. "Creatives" worry that inspiration won't come, especially in the face of such pressure. The accompanying emotions can be intense despite any number of past successes. As one top Nissan designer said about a current project, "We'll end up—I guarantee it—with everybody loving what we've done. . . . But there will be all kinds of heartache and pain before we get to that point!"

A part of the excitement and fun of creative work undoubtedly comes from the very unpredictability that makes it painful at times (Konner [1982] wrote that human joy is predicated on overcoming fear). A project structured to guarantee high-quality output, achieved in comfort, would call for much more routine than inventiveness. Even though we can't "make" creativity happen, there are some things we can do to facilitate it.

Getting Started. The way a task assignment is presented, right from the start, can heavily influence the path people take as they begin a piece of work. Hackman and Walton (1986) provide an excellent discussion of the art of framing tasks. They stress the need to set goals that are directive enough to energize people, but open-ended enough to challenge them to be inventive.

First Period of Momentum. A key task in a project's first period of momentum is to build up the repertoire of material that a group subsequently will draw upon. Because major progress can be made very swiftly later (during the transition), it might be more important at this time to collect information and generate ideas than to make firm decisions about exactly what the end product will look like.

Uncertainty is uncomfortable, and people might be anxious to settle on choices as soon as they can. They might make better choices, however, if they delay a while. At Nissan, designers are told not to start drawing until they have spent time in research and brainstorming sessions especially invented to "inform intuition."

The Midpoint. There is a limit on how long it is good to keep options open: It is the midpoint. The critical feature of a successful transition is the formation of choices that provide a foundation for the next phase of work (of two teams I observed who passed their midpoint without having made these choices, one was dismantled on the spot, and one did not finish its task). Some commonalities among successful teams suggest ways to make the most of this fleeting opportunity. Reviewing "where we are" and "where we need to be" helps move people's sights off the trees and onto the forest. Midpoint contact with outsiders—for example, with the client or the manager who assigned the task—can help teams settle disputes, clarify requirements, or find new approaches to the work. A change in routine might even be helpful. Dedicating more time to a midpoint meeting is an obvious way to encourage progress, but teams may also benefit from gathering in a new location or at a different time of day than they have before.

Setting Stable Deadlines. People hearing about midpoint transitions sometimes draw the mistaken conclusion that groups don't really get down to work until the midpoint. They react by suggesting: "You could just move the deadline up, and then the transition will happen faster!" Sometimes moving deadlines is unavoidable, and sometimes such a jolt might have a positive effect. Moving deadlines creates at least three problems, however: First, people use the amount of time allotted as a rough indicator of how ambitious a project can be. Shortening the time sends a message by reducing the room available to generate and execute ideas. Second, the midpoint is embedded within an overall pace. Moving a deadline after a group has started can cut off preparation the group had been counting on. Finally, ambiguous deadlines undermine people's ability to synchronize their work—and to set up developmental transitions in the first place. People cannot easily pace themselves in unison or get motivated by a midpoint when they have learned that the "real" deadline is anyone's guess.

I have no doubt that most of the readers (and writers) of this book have felt the power of deadlines. Despite the pervasiveness of the phenomenon, we have little research on how time and time limits affect creativity. The findings reported here raise interesting questions for the future: What kinds of tasks are best done without deadlines? How do people from cultures with different concepts of time pace their work? What happens when people whose work, temperament, or values make them time-conscious need to cooperate with people whose work, temperament, or values make them forget the time? In short, the specific patterns explicated here are probably not universal, and we have a lot to gain by learning more.

A final thought follows from one last quotation from a designer, who said creative work requires a "leap of faith." For better or for worse, deadlines give us one of the most forceful ways we have to command ourselves: "Jump!"   ▨

REFERENCES

Gersick, C.J.G. (1988). Time and transition in work teams: Toward a new model of group development. *Academy of Management Journal, 31*, 9-41.

Gersick, C.J.G. (1989). Marking time: Predictable transitions in task groups. *Academy of Management Journal, 32*, 274-309.

Hackman, J. R., & Walton, R. E. (1986). Leading groups in organizations. In P. S. Goodman & Associates (Eds.), *Designing effective work groups* (pp. 72-119). San Francisco: Jossey-Bass.

Konner, M. (1982). *The tangled wing.* New York: Harper Colophon.

Luchins, A. S. (1940). Mechanization in problem solving: The effect of Einstellung. *Psychological Monographs, 54*, 248.

Mednick, S. A. (1962). The associative basis of the creative process. *Psychological Review, 69*, 220-232.

Tuckman, B. (1965). Developmental sequence in small groups. *Psychological Bulletin, 63*, 384-399.

Webster's new world dictionary (2nd college ed.). (1978). Cleveland, OH: William Collins-World Publishing.

19 Creativity Training and Hemispheric Function
Bringing the Left Brain Back In

CRAIG C. LUNDBERG *Blanchard Professor of Human Resource Management, Cornell University*

The right brain is often viewed as intuitive and holistic; the left verbal, rational, linear, and logical. Creativity, then, has become strongly associated with the right hemisphere. But, creativity is a discovery process that starts with what one can already do well. What we do well, especially in the West, is use our left brains. If we are to enhance creativity in our lives and in our organizations, we should concentrate on developing the creative possibilities of the left brain, rather than on trying to perform some unnatural convolutions that emphasize the right brain.

◆━━━◆◇◈◇◆━━━▶

I learned very early in my psychological career to regard with a good deal of skepticism current theories explaining creativity.
—Rollo May

PROLOGUE

Several years ago a local accounting organization asked me to speak at a dinner meeting. They wanted something non-accounting, contemporary, and entertaining. I agreed to speak on creativity and submitted a title that emphasized conventional thinking—that is, creativity associated with the right hemisphere of the brain. On the appointed evening a large crowd had gathered. My host, presumably pleased with the turnout, turned to me during the dinner that preceded my talk and showed me his brochure. Startled, I noted that I was to speak on creativity using the "left" brain. Rationalizing that the assembled accountants really wished to be entertained and wouldn't know the basis for my remarks, I decided, playfully, to talk

149

to the misprinted title—surprising myself during the next hour that it seemed to make sense. That evening prompted the research that is summarized below.

ON CREATIVITY IN GENERAL

Interest in creativity has existed for centuries (Rothenberg & Hausman, 1976), with a major resurgence beginning in the 1960s. From the time of Ornstein's (1972) influential book, much attention has been focused on the differences between the two hemispheres of the brain and the implications of these differences. Creativity training especially has been based on the conception of the so-called split-brain approach. This essay will argue first that contemporary training for creativity has become unrealistically focused on right hemisphere operations; second, that this focus is unwarranted in light of brain research; and third, that creativity training might appropriately refocus on the left hemisphere. My thesis is this: If contemporary creativity training is based upon better tapping the brain's right hemisphere, and if the attribution of hemispheric specialization is not true, then creativity training is misdirected and perhaps should be reconceptualized based upon a dual hemisphere or left hemisphere model.

The line of thinking pursued here is significant in two ways. With a better understanding of hemispheric functioning, the acknowledged difficulties of implementing creativity training might be clarified. That is, if the model underlying the majority of creativity training efforts is improperly focused, then organizational creativity training will continue to fail regardless of the effort devoted to it. Furthermore, with an alternative model upon which to base creativity training, new training practices might be discovered or invented. An alternative model would also encourage the comparative testing of models, which would eventually enhance creativity training and practice.

The literature on creativity is both elusive and broad. A wide assortment of fields and disciplines have contributed—literature, philosophy, art, psychology, counseling, and linguistics, for example. Many attempts have been made to distill knowledge and focus our understanding. Hallman (1963) points out that creative acts are multifaceted and include psychological, environmental, cultural, physical, and intellectual aspects. He proposes

> that the creative act can be analyzed into five major components: (1) it is a whole act, a unitary instance of behavior; (2) it terminates in the production of objects or of forms of living that are distinctive; (3) it evolves out of certain mental processes; (4) it co-varies with specific personality transformations; and (5) it occurs within a particular kind of environment. (p. 221)

MacKinnon (1962) sums up the issue of the meaning of creativity:

> Many are the meanings of creativity. Perhaps for most it denotes the ability to bring something new into existence, while for others it is not an ability but the psychological processes by which novel and valuable products are fashioned. For still others, creativity is not the process but the product. Definitions of creativity range all the way from the notion that creativity is simple problem solving to conceiving it as the realization and expression of all of an individual's unique potentialities. (p. 19)

CREATIVITY AND THE BRAIN

Although the origins of the idea of two hemispheres in the brain go back at least as far as 1844 to the British anatomist Wigan, it was the 20-some years of work by Drs. Roger Sperry, J. E. Brogan, and M. Gazzaniga, among others, researching the physiology of the brain, who discovered two different kinds of consciousness, perception and thought (each associated with the right or left hemisphere, respectively). This line of work was given visibility and popularity after the publication of Ornstein's *The Psychology of Consciousness* (1972). The conventional view of the two hemispheres and their functioning is one of contrast and specialization.

Early psychological sophisticates such as Ornstein (1972) and Watzlawick (1978) contrast hemispheric functioning, that is, the right is intuitive and holistic, the left verbal, rational, linear, and logical. Much of the contemporary creativity literature can be traced back to these two authorities. Creativity, then, has become strongly associated with the right hemisphere. Gazzaniga and LeDoux (1978) neatly characterize the shift of thinking about creativity as well as prick the myth that has evolved:

> Then in the late 1960s and early 1970s, the basic claims concerning hemispheric functioning underwent a radical change. There arose a barrage of popular and overdramatized accounts of the uniqueness of mind left and right. These representations of the implications of the split-brain observations gave rise to a cult-like following and were largely written by people who had never seen a patient, but they were fed, in part, by new studies carried out by those directly involved in the experimental exercise. We believe that these "pop" versions of hemisphere function are in error. (p. 6)

CONVENTIONAL TRAINING FOR CREATIVITY

Creativity training for organizational members today appears to be based on one of two closely related assumptions as to the locus of creativity, each with its corresponding model for enhancing creativeness. One line of reasoning is: The right hemisphere is the creative one and creativity is therefore enhanced by developing it. It is argued that in Western societies educational systems are "heavily dominated by the verbal-analytical model" (Ornstein, 1972, p. 163). That is, we tend to concentrate on the verbal and intellectual (i.e., science and logic) as major sources of knowing in the West. The second line of reasoning is only slightly different: The right hemisphere is again the intuitive, holistic, creative one, but it is already adequate; therefore creativity enhancement merely requires more or better access to it. Most creativity training techniques, however, are not explicit as to which model is assumed. The second one probably is predominant in that creativity training techniques tend to use a sequence of steps that more or less follow the classical ones outlined by Wallas (1926): preparation, incubation, illumination, and verification (e.g., "Synectics," which is a system of practices that induces a climate conductive to the alternative identification of problems and use of analogies and striking images).

TOWARD AN ALTERNATIVE MODEL
OF ENHANCING CREATIVITY

Now let me argue, in two ways, for a model of creativity training that refocuses attention to the left hemisphere. The first argument is essentially a logical one. My point of departure is the so-called personal style hypothesis (Morris, 1972), which states that more is to be gained from attempts to apply natural enhancements to a person's style than from equivalent efforts to remake or reformulate that person's style in the image of some unfamiliar or pseudo-logical one. If it is true that in the West most people are right-handed (left hemisphere dominant), the personal style hypothesis suggests that creativity might be enhanced by working further or in new ways with the left hemisphere. This of course goes against our conventional views of the function of the two hemispheres. Yet it has been asserted and seems widely believed that creative genius is 99% perspiration and that creativity actually boils down to a fresh way of seeing and making sense of things. If this line of reasoning holds at all, then the left hemisphere is essential for creativity, and perhaps what is required is more or different attention to the very processes in which the left hemisphere supposedly excels. This assertion is not unreasonable when we note certain neurophysiological findings: first, that the two hemispheres are connected by the corpus callosum, which coordinates their mutual functioning; and second, that the right hemisphere silently monitors and, if necessary, corrects the utterances and decisions of the left.

Studies of the cerebral commissures (the fibers of the corpus callosum), brain lesion work, sodium amytral experiments, and hemisphere anesthetization of animals and humans (both brain damaged and normals) provides an understanding of intra- and inter-hemisphere function at variance to the "pop" view noted previously. Gazzaniga (1970) and Gazzaniga and LeDoux (1978) describe a great number of the relevant studies whose major findings include: (a) lost functions due to damage, surgery, or anesthetization return with time, even when the hemispheres are sectioned; (b) such midsagittal sectioning produces a state of mental duplicity, that is, two separate conscious spheres coexist within one cranium; (c) when the brain is intact, the commissural system provides each hemisphere with a copy of the sensory world directly observable by the other hemisphere; thus (d) hemispheric lateralization is not specialization—with the exception of language, which is usually in the left hemisphere. The implications of this work strongly dispel the view of the two hemispheres as contrasting and specialized in function.

The two arguments just outlined, individually and in combination, give credence to the feasibility of creativity enhancement by focusing training efforts on the left hemisphere. In other words, because each hemisphere duplicates the other (except for linguistic functioning) and is coordinated/integrated with the other, creativity training, which is dependent on language, most usefully should exploit existing left hemispheric dominance.

IMPLICATIONS FOR
CREATIVITY TRAINING

Although the implications for creativity training of the model just presented are no doubt several, we can note some essential, perhaps prototypical features. Regardless of the claims made, most creativity techniques are highly language-dependent and are examples of intentional search processes—in other words, they are conscious, rational devices for more or less playfully extending or manipulating what is already known. These features, that is, language manipulation and intentional search, are almost always prominent. These techniques are usually demarcated by either a "meta message" condoning or encouraging combinatorial flexibility (repetition, reordering, exaggeration, reframing: all suggestive of a looser temporal organization), or a patterned, voluntary elaboration or complication of process.

The net effect of these observations is simply this: The time has come when our thinking about creativity should be scrutinized with more care. Creativity is a discovery process that starts with what one can already do well. What we do well, especially in the West, is use our left brains. If we are to enhance creativity in our lives and in our organizations, we should concentrate on developing the creative possibilities of the left brain, rather than trying to perform some unnatural convolutions that emphasize the right brain. ▧

REFERENCES

Gazzaniga, M. (1970). *The bisected brain.* New York: Appleton-Century-Crofts.

Gazzaniga, M., & LeDoux, J. (1978). *The integrated mind.* New York: Plenum.

Hallman, R. J. (1963, Spring). The necessary and sufficient conditions of creativity. *Journal of Humanistic Psychology, 3,* 14-27.

MacKinnon, D. W. (1962). The personality correlates of creativity: A study of American architects. In G. S. Nielson (Ed.), *Proceedings of the SIV International Congress of Applied Psychology, 2,* 11-39.

Morris, W. T. (1972). Matching decision aids with intuitive styles. In H. S. Brinkers (Ed.), *Decision making: Creativity, judgment and systems.* Columbus: Ohio State University Press.

Ornstein, R. (1972). *The psychology of consciousness.* New York: Freeman.

Rothenberg, A., & Hausman, C. R. (1976). *The creativity question.* Durham, NC: Duke University Press.

Wallas, G. (1926). *The art of thought.* New York: Harcourt Brace Jovanovich.

Watzlawick, P. (1978). *The language of change.* New York: Basic Books.

20 Management of Cultural Innovations

DAG BJÖRKEGREN *Associate Professor in Organization and Management Theory, Stockholm School of Economics*

Instead of going to work between 8 and 5, the romantic artist was expected to live a Bohemian life and create unique works of art that revealed the deeper truths about the world. This artistic ideal, however, makes a poor fit with industry's need for commercial artists who design industrial commodities during regular office hours.

$\mathcal{W}$here but in the arts might one gain knowledge about creativity? And where but in the activities of art-producing organizations might one gain some sense of unusual creativity in organizations? The production of cultural commodities is inherently innovative, with expectations that each art product should be unique. The latest hit record might be a wonder of musical triviality, but the technical and social production processes necessary to generate it are not quite so simple. This essay explores the phenomenon of cultural innovation in pop music as a way of seeking insight into creativity in modern organizations. It particularly highlights the importance of marketing if creative work is to result in valuable new products, not merely interesting new creations.

FROM LORD BYRON
TO THE ROLLING STONES

Pop music is industrialized music in the sense that production and product are so integrated that the final outcome (the pop record) consists of technical, commercial, and musical considerations that cannot be separated from each other (Frith, 1988). The 20th century's popular music is a genuine industry product, produced by the record industry, but its roots are in the British art schools of the 19th century (Frith & Horne, 1987) that first steered artistic knowledge in such a direction that it could be used for design of industrial commodities.

One problem for the art schools and their students was Romanticism's artist ideal. In feudal society, works of art were central to cultural life. It had been customary that paintings and poems were ordered in the same way as houses. A poem or a painting should have certain motifs, be painted and written in a certain style, and be of a specific size, all decided by the buyer. Who wrote or painted was of less importance as long as the person in question was in possession of the necessary skills (Wolff, 1987). During the romantic era the artist became the center of attention as a chosen and divinely gifted person. The notion of the artist as the lonely genius, set above the rules of the rest of the society, originates from this time. Creativity was mostly a matter of emotion and intuition. Either one had the gift or one did not. The romantic ideal embraced the artist as the chosen genius, floating high above the demands and trivialities of everyday life. Instead of going to work between 8 and 5, the romantic artist was expected to live a Bohemian life and create unique works of art that revealed the deeper truths about the world.

This artistic ideal made a poor fit, however, with the British industry's need for commercial artists who design industrial commodities during regular office hours. In the eyes of artists, to work as a commercial artist was seen as a career failure, yet very few art school students could support themselves on their art. Most people instead found their aesthetic pleasure in the emerging popular culture industry's products (movies, records, comic strips, advertisements, postcards, photographs, etc.) rather than in art galleries. Although art school students spent less and less time on their artistic endeavors, they remained ambiguous about becoming commercial artists because that entailed a betrayal of Romanticism's artistic ideal. Perhaps unexpectedly, the 1960s pop music industry became a solution to this dilemma.

During the 1950s, future pop musicians like John Lennon (the Beatles) and Keith Richards (the Rolling Stones) were art school students. That time's intellectual music and clothing were jazz and a duffel coat, but working-class music and clothing were rock and black leather. Both Lennon and Richards rebelled against the intellectual, art school style by dressing in black leather clothing, combing their hair like Elvis Presley, and listening to rock instead of jazz. The famous Beatles' mop-top was an art school hair-cut that proved to be an excellent attention-getting device. The Rolling Stones' rebel-look originated from Keith Richards's street style. Such individualism rendered commercial potential to art student musicians. They turned art ideals into a commodity that sold music. Personal originality thus became a commercial asset. The music itself initially posed a problem, however. Rock was seen as genuine music, made on the artist's terms, not artificially fabricated music on the market's terms, like pop music. Rock music should therefore be performed as close to the original as possible, but this restriction proved impractical. Soon, *original* was redefined to mean new variation instead of faithful reproduction. In this way the music also was transformed into original art. Not only the form (the musicians' personalities and appearance) but also the content (the music) became original, especially when rock musicians began to write their own music.

This art-influenced music became a commercial success. The commodity that was offered emphasized difference (different music and clothing). By consuming this commodity, teenagers were given a chance to be a little bit different and original themselves. The Rolling Stones became packaged rebellion for mass consumption, and the Beatles "just were the Zany Foursome they were sold to be" (Frith & Horne, 1987, p. 102). The English art school students who became pop musicians had invented a new business concept that sold lifestyles in commodity form for mass consumption. At the same time they preserved Romanticism's ideals since that was the lifestyle being sold, albeit in a mass-produced form.

It became difficult, however, to uphold any original artistry in the face of commercial mass exploitation (musician Frank Zappa's wife, for instance, could not understand how her husband could think he was up to anything serious when his audience mainly consisted of screaming teenagers). One approach to this problem was for the artists to assume artistic control over their work in the studio, which allowed them to be original even though their art was mass produced. The other solution, which gained full force during the 1980s, had its roots in 1960s pop art and its aesthetic ideology.

BUSINESS ART

Pop artists, such as Andy Warhol, tried to highlight the aesthetic qualities of ordinary consumer goods in their art. Andy Warhol, however, pushed this ideology further. According to Warhol, all art was commercial. High art only used different marketing techniques. Because all art was commercial, the best art must be the most popular art; therefore, the best measurement for judging aesthetic quality was . . . money. Because all art was commercialized, artists might just as well take advantage of it and turn commerce into art:

> Business art is the step that comes after Art. . . . Being good in business is the most fascinating kind of art. During the hippie era people put

down the idea of business—they'd say "Money is bad," and "Working is bad," but making money is art and working is art and good business is the best art. (Warhol, 1975, p. 92)

This aesthetic ideology made the packaging of the music more important than the music itself, a trend that soon gave rise to the punk movement. Punk was subversive pop art that aimed at exposing instead of praising modern consumer society's functioning. Malcolm McLaren, one of the originators of punk, was an art school student who wanted to expose the record industry's mechanisms "by burrowing into the money-making core of the pop machine, to be both blatantly commercial (and thus resist the traditional labels of art and Bohemia) and deliberately troublesome (so that the usually smooth, hidden, gears of commerce were always on noisy display)" (Frith & Horne, 1987, p. 132).

He accomplished this aim by creating the Sex Pistols, who became famous for gross and indecent behavior, especially in their dealings with record companies. Punk directed attention not only to the record industry's functioning but also to its own and society's artificial and constructed character. Punk ended up in the same way as art rock—in a new market segment. Out of punk's doubts that there existed anything genuine and natural, a new romanticism transpired in the 1980s. Revolt was turned into style and rock into fashion. If there didn't exist anything genuine, the packaging of the music was more interesting than the music. If personality had sold music in the 1960s, image sold the music in the 1980s.

This subversive packaging style became just another marketing concept because "co-option has always been the name of the commodity game" (Frith & Horne, 1987, p. 179). The culture industry further developed this marketing concept by turning the act of consumption itself into an art form. In such a vein, judging the aesthetic qualities of different brands of toilet paper was seen as just as much an aesthetic activity as judging a painting's aesthetic qualities. This development was facilitated by the pop art argument that expendable art was no less serious than permanent art (Alloway, 1966/1988). Through creative consumption of the "right" commodities, consumers could signal their own creativity and originality: their "art." And the artists could become super-consumers, setting fashion trends through innovative consumer behavior. Through the British art schools' influence on the production of popular music and culture, the consumption of commodities became the dominating art form in England at the end of the 1980s. Everyone had become creative; everyone was a pop artist.

This brief look at cultural innovation in the art world has some implications for creativity and innovation more generally in organizations. It in particular underlines the importance of not only discovering but also realizing the commercial potential of new creations, if creative work is to result in innovative products that create new markets. The Beatles' commercial potential, for instance, was realized first when they met their manager Brian Epstein, who dressed them up in tailored suits and black boots, stressed their mop-top look, and got them a record deal with EMI in 1962. Before that, The Beatles had mainly been playing in seedy rock clubs in Hamburg and Liverpool, with a rough teddy boy look, and without any record contract.

The way the production of pop music has evolved since the 1960s, the importance of clever marketing to turning new musical styles into valuable new products, has increased rather than decreased. One explanation for this development might be that the general noise level in the media has become so high that only very loud signals can be heard. Thus it no longer seems enough for a product simply to be "new" if it hopes to find a market. It must also break through the general noise level in media and become a media event. ▨

REFERENCES

Alloway, L. (1988). The development of British pop. In L. Lippard (Ed.), *Pop art* (pp. 27-68). Toledo: Thames & Hudson. [Original work published 1966]

Frith, S. (1988). *Music for pleasure*. Surrey, UK: Polity Press.

Frith, S., & Horne, H. (1987). *Art into pop*. Suffolk, UK: Methuen.

Warhol, A. (1975). *The philosophy of Andy Warhol*. New York: Harvest/Harcourt Brace Jovanovich.

Wolff, J. (1987). *The social production of art*. Hong Kong: Macmillan.

Why No One Really Wants Creativity

BARRY M. STAW *Lorraine T. Mitchell Professor of Leadership and Communication, University of California, Berkeley*

Most people do not follow a life pattern similar to that of a creative, nor would they want to. The average person may become intrigued when the glories of successful creativity are hailed by the media. But when confronted with the bald truth that most scientists never come up with any earthshaking findings, most new businesses end in failure, and most whistle-blowers get demoted or fired, it is not surprising that people generally opt for a safer, more normal life than that followed by the creative.

For years I have been among the advocates of creativity—the usual set of academics who decry the status quo, argue the merits of being different, and push for organizational innovation. Well, I've had enough. The term *creativity* has a nice ring to it and nearly everyone thinks it is a good thing, but few people or organizations really want creativity. When they think it through, when the processes involved and their attendant costs are made clear, people and firms tend to back away from creativity, perhaps with just cause. Let me elaborate.

CELEBRATING THE VICTOR

It is very common in both the creativity literature and the organizational world to trot out the successful entrepreneur, inventor, or business venture to show off the benefits of creativity. We celebrate the victor—the person or organization that has pulled off the major coup or taken the market by storm. Interviews are given, biographies are written, and success stories printed. Copying the victor is also common practice. Self-help books proliferate on how to make us more creative, often modeled on characteristics of people known to be

161

creative. Consultants abound, selling programs designed to renew, reorient, revitalize, or reinvent organizations, usually modeled on the practices of firms that have recently experienced success with a major new product or service. There are, of course, serious questions about whether the correlates of creativity actually cause creativity and, for sure, much of the research on creative people and innovative firms has lacked adequate controls or methodological rigor. But even if we take these correlates at face value, assuming they are the real factors driving creativity, this still does not mean that people really want or need creativity. Would people, given the chance, make the choices and enact the behaviors necessary to become creative? I doubt it.

WHY INDIVIDUALS
REJECT CREATIVITY

Although there are a multitude of creativity theories, most researchers in this area do agree on a short list of characteristics shared by many of those who are creative. Creatives are risk takers. They are willing to take their chances on an unproven solution rather than go with the tried and true. Creatives are nonconformists. They are willing to defy convention and even authority to explore new ideas and to get to the truth. Creatives are persistent. They don't give up when they get frustrated or rebuffed by a problem, they keep at it. Creatives are flexible. They are able to reformulate a problem when facing failure rather than just give up or continue down the same path. Finally, creatives put in long, hard hours. They become totally absorbed in their work, often to the exclusion of their family or personal life.

The picture of the creative individual does not mesh well with the proclivities of the average person. For example, research on decision making has repeatedly found that people are risk averse, at least when it comes to possible gains. That is, when given a choice between a large but uncertain reward (e.g., 10% chance to win $10,000) and a smaller and certain payoff (e.g., 100% chance to win $1,000), people will generally choose the sure thing. Only when they are in losing situations have people reliably been shown to choose the riskier alternative. Likewise, when given a chance to follow the majority or minority point of view, most people opt for the prevailing view. This is, of course, an adaptive strategy in most situations. Yet, evidence shows that people often choose to follow others even when that means abandoning the truth, and this is especially the case when the conformist strategy is backed by an authority or someone who seems to be in charge.

In terms of decision style, most people also fall short of the creative ideal. They are satisficers rather than searchers for the optimal or most desirable solution. They follow a number of energy-saving heuristics that generally lead to a set of systematic biases or inaccuracies in processing information. And, unless they are held accountable for their decision-making strategies, they tend to find the easy way out—either by not engaging in very careful thinking or by modeling their choices on the preferences of those who will be evaluating them.

The overall picture does not favor creativity. Most people do not follow a life pattern similar to that of the creative, nor would they want to. The average person may become intrigued when the glories of successful creativity are hailed by the media. But when confronted with the bald truth that most scientists never come up with any earthshaking findings, most new businesses end in failure, and most whistle-blowers get demoted or fired, it is not surprising that people generally opt for a safer, more normal life than that followed by the creative.

In defending creativity one can, of course, argue that creative acts are not really rational decisions in terms of a full calculus of costs, benefits, and the probabilities of various outcomes. Perhaps creatives are altruists, people who accept personal risks and costs that will only benefit the larger collective, such as an organization or society. Perhaps creatives are slightly tilted individuals who don't really mind the endless nights nursing a laboratory experiment or the social isolation that comes with taking the minority viewpoint. For a few, taking the creative route is something they must do, something that makes inherent sense. For some, the creative act is a bit like falling in love. Creative people can become so smitten with a project or venture that the simple calculation of costs and benefits seems downright inappropriate. My own father is a little like this. He frequently asks others what they think about his latest business deal. But when others look at the numbers and ask how he will turn a profit, he simply crosses out the offending figures, replacing them with more "realistic" estimates that are 20% higher.

So my point is this. Most people admire creative individuals, at least in retrospect. They admire the successful entrepreneur, scientist, writer, or musician. But this does not mean that the typical person would make the same choices in life, given the odds of failure, nor would that person really want to follow a pattern of social behavior and decision making that mimics those who are known to be creative. We should therefore consider ourselves lucky that there are a few people out there willing to take the creative route. We need them.

WHY ORGANIZATIONS REJECT INNOVATION

Much of the same logic pertains to organizational innovation. Although there is practically a cottage industry devoted to celebrating successful innovations and touting their characteristics as the "new solution," few managers really want to pay the price for innovation. To most managers, being innovative means that they have to do everything wrong.

First, instead of the normal recruitment process in which people are brought in who have the skills needed by the firm and the values it admires, innovative companies must let down their barriers. They must accommodate those whose skills are more peripheral and whose goals are suspect.

Second, instead of socializing new members of the organization to absorb the values and culture of the firm, the innovative corporation must encourage people not to listen, at least not too hard. There is nothing that kills innovation like everyone speaking in the same voice, even if it is a well-trained voice.

Third, instead of issuing directives and policy statements and hoping that they will be obeyed, innovative firms must encourage disobedience. In fact, those in power should go so far as to encourage active opposition. Innovative organizations are those that harbor multiple perspectives and objectives, not simply a variety of views about how a particular product should be designed and produced.

Fourth, instead of striving for lower costs and efficiency, innovative companies must opt for adaptiveness. They need to have excess capacity and personnel devoted to seemingly meaningless ventures. Because innovation requires investing in losers as well as winners, adaptive firms must be prepared to follow several competing designs simultaneously, and move through a sequence of product alternatives before settling on a single course of action.

Finally, to be truly innovative, firms must be industry leaders rather than followers. They must stick their necks out on untried products and technologies, not knowing if they will be successes or failures. They can't wait for other firms to launch the first products, only to come in late, making some adjustments to reap the profits. They must pursue projects that often appear to be more folly than wisdom.

Naturally, most organizations and their managers would hesitate in adopting these suggestions. They might consider a few items on the list interesting or worth long-term consideration, but that is a far cry from taking concrete action to accomplish them.

From what we know about organizations, they work very hard to recruit and select employees who look and act like those already in the firm. For those who might have slipped into the organization without the proper skills and values, socialization is usually the answer. Creating clones of existing personnel is generally what management wants and gets. Those who deviate from the prevailing culture become dissatisfied and tend to leave the organization, leaving room for those who have been "properly socialized."

Research also shows that organizational power structures are difficult to change. Those in power set the agenda; they reward those who fall in line politically, who are willing to support the existing order. Power also begets power. Those who have power get the resources to maintain their positions, while others must struggle to survive. There are few known cases of those in power willingly giving up their influence or sharing it with the opposition.

Finally, almost by definition, the organizational world is populated by followers rather than leaders. Even the Japanese corporations currently touted as the world's most successful enterprises are not generally considered industry leaders. Though Japanese management is praised for its quality control techniques and novel inventory systems, little is made of the basic conservatism of Japanese industry. These companies generally let other firms do the innovating. Once a product has been developed and the market possibilities made clear, they enter the fray as efficient and effective producers.

In summary, organizations find it hard to see the logic of innovation. Being a creative organization may sound good, but when the details are described more fully, it is just not the path most corporations or their management want to take.

ASSESSING THE DAMAGE

Does the fact that few individuals or organizations really want creativity doom us to mediocrity, to a path without progress and hope? Certainly not. My point in writing this essay is simply to deflate the notion of creativity, to let the air out of some of the rhetoric usually seen in creativity manuals and texts. Creativity is not something we all strive to achieve, nor something we can all improve upon given proper effort and guidance. In my view, creativity suffers from a large case of false advertising. The popular press, along with the collusion of many consultants and academics, has sold us the notion that we can reap the rewards of a Galileo, Edison, or Picasso without paying the full price. Likewise, managers are told that they can convert their own organization into a slick Silicon Valley firm without losing something in the bargain. The reality is that only a few individuals and organizations really want to be creative, when all the details are known. We should appreciate the few takers of this questionable deal rather than scold the majority for its caution and common sense. ▧

22 Shifting the Focus From Individual to Organizational Creativity

MIHALY CSIKSZENTMIHALYI *Professor of Psychology, University of Chicago*

KEITH SAWYER *Consultant, Culpepper Consulting Group*

An organization may be internally creative, through the implementation of cost-saving technologies or new accounting procedures or the development of new technology in R&D. However, the biggest impact on profitability and market share most often derives from external creativity; novel responses to new legislation or radical market shifts. Creativity at the internal level is no guarantee of business success at the external level, but it is a prerequisite. The danger is that internal creativity can become isolated, feeding on itself in an incestuous fashion.

꧁꧂

𝒜ttempts to increase innovation in organizations have been based largely on the belief that by increasing individual creativity, and by identifying and removing fetters to individual creativity, organizations can increase their ability to respond to changes in the external environment. Many creativity researchers and consultants typically have treated creativity as an individual trait and have underestimated its social and organizational components. For instance, a 1993 *Technology Review* article surveyed a wide range of creativity consultants, almost all of whom focused on techniques to foster individual creativity. In contrast, we believe that organizational creativity, which emphasizes social and group creative processes, will be a key factor in corporate success in the future, particularly in industries with complex, changing business environments. After all, innovation is a trait of entire organizations, not of individuals, because it is the full organization that must invest in the development, manufacturing, and marketing of a new product. Although employees' creative insights are neces-

167

sary, they are a relatively minor factor in the overall innovativeness of the organization. There is no lack of good ideas, the problem is creating a system to manage the research and development.

A SYSTEMS APPROACH

In the early part of this century, Henri Poincaré described his own process of creative mathematical thought in terms of three stages: "this appearance of sudden illumination [is] a manifest sign of long, unconscious prior work . . . [this unconscious work] is possible, and of a certainty it is only fruitful if it is, on the one hand preceded, and on the other hand followed, by a period of conscious work" (Poincaré, 1913, p. 389). Expanding on this notion, psychologist Hadamard (1945) proposed a four-stage model of creative insight. In this model preparation is followed by an incubation stage during which the subconscious repeatedly attempts new combinations of mental elements until one becomes stable and coherent enough to emerge into consciousness, resulting in illumination, the subjective experience of insight; the final stage is verification, or the conscious evaluation and elaboration of the insight.

Our own research confirms the basic outline of the four-stage model. Insights often occur during "idle time" when a person is removed from the tight schedule and time demands of the usual office routine. Of course, idle time would not be productive without the periods of hard work that precede it; it would never lead to practical effect without development and refinement following the insight. Although such stage models are generally accurate, they must be expanded to address how social and contextual factors influence the creative process. When asked to describe a moment of insight, creative people often mention interpersonal contacts, strategic or political considerations, and a knowledge of what questions were "interesting" as defined by others in their sphere of activity. Although the insight often occurs in isolation, it is surrounded and contextualized within an ongoing experience that is fundamentally social, and it would be meaningless out of that context.

The systems view developed by Csikszentmihalyi (1988, 1990) proposed that creativity must be defined with respect to a system that includes individual, social, and cultural factors that influence the creative process and help to constitute a creative outcome. These influences are separated into the "field" (the group of gatekeepers who are entitled to select a novel idea or product for consideration) and the "domain" (the symbolic system of rules and procedures that define permissible action within its boundaries). Examples of domains are the "generally accepted accounting practices" invoked in every annual report or the production processes in place in a factory. Domains are presented to organization members as "given knowledge," the basic factors of the profession. In practice, however, most creativity involves identifying those points at which the domain can be changed for the better, without excessive cost. A novice treats the domain as unchangeable; an expert or virtuoso not only realizes what can or should be changed, but also how difficult such change will be. In the systems view, the creative process involves the generation of a novel creative product, the selection of the product by others in the field, and the retention of selected products that the field adds to the domain.

The "cycle of entrepreneurship" provides a good example of the application of the systems view to business—for instance: A researcher or executive independently develops a novel solution to a market need. The corporation's management, acting as the field, concludes that this novel, creative product is not suited to the domain of their business. The stymied individual then creates a new field and domain, in the form of a start-up corporation. This pattern has resulted in two methods of appropriating the entrepreneur's drive and initiative; either by becoming an investor in the start-up (thereby joining the new field) or initiating new corporate policy designed to encourage "intrapreneurship" (changing the field's selection process to be more receptive to innovation).

BRINGING IT TO BUSINESS

The view of creativity as a system process has strong implications for organizations. The "field" represents the other employees in the organization, and the "domain" represents the accepted body of practices, often inscribed in formal documentation. Just as physics and literature are different domains, accounting and operations also are different domains. These are examples of horizontally different domains. Similarly, product lines and market segments are vertically distinct domains. Businesses are usually organized either functionally, with fields (organizational units) corresponding to horizontal domains, or in market units, with fields corresponding to vertical domains.

In addition to these domains and fields, corporations must act within an external environment with its own domains and fields, such as market competition and government legislation. Today's increasingly activist consumers form yet another "field" that affects the organization's success. To integrate these multiple, intersecting forces, both within and without the organization, we propose a model that accounts for several levels at which "creativity" might be defined for an organization. In addition to the vertical and horizontal distinctions, both external and internal dimensions must be accounted for. These are distinct domains and fields both inside and outside the organization.

External forces acting on creativity include such domains of activity as market forces (number of products, cohesiveness of product lines, geographical diversity) and government legislation (regulatory constraints). These external forces also include external fields such as consumers (needs, degree of market segmentation), competitors (number of competitors, market share, brand loyalty), politicians, and suppliers (permanent relationships, degree of independence, second-source availability). Internal forces acting on creativity include such domains as technology (limitations, pace of new developments), organizational structure, finance, and product lines. Internal fields include the staff (receptiveness to novelty, degree of rigidity), the corporate culture/informal organization, the individual's location within the organization, major stockholders, and the board.

The relative complexity of this model, incorporating both internal and external systems, and vertical and horizontal levels, can help explain why "creativity" is so difficult to define. Creativity can occur within any one of these domains—and can be derailed by any one of these fields. Creativity means different things in different industries; an innovation in financial services may have very little in common with a manufacturing process innovation. Furthermore, creativity means different things in different organizational functions; a marketing innovation may have very different characteristics than a technical or accounting innovation. An organization may be internally creative, through the implementation of cost-saving technologies or new accounting procedures or the development of new technology in R&D. The biggest impact on profitability and market share, however, most often derives from external creativity; novel responses to new legislation or radical market shifts.

Creativity at the internal level is no guarantee of business success at the external level, but it is a prerequisite. The danger is that internal creativity can become isolated, feeding on itself in an incestuous fashion. The challenge for organizations is to create corporate cultures that direct internal creativity toward external creativity, resulting in increased market share and customer satisfaction. For example, internal R&D creativity that results in a product innovation must be linked with the more mundane creativity of implementation for the organization to become externally successful—a commonly noted failing of American business.

LESSONS FROM OUR RESEARCH

These ideas can be combined with findings from our research to generate several observations that are directly relevant to creativity in organizations. To recapitulate and integrate some of these findings:

1. The creative process is heavily dependent on social interaction, which takes the form of face-to-face encounters and of immersion in the symbolic system of one or more domains.

2. The most significant insights (e.g., those that lead to innovative new products or uses for new technology) are often characterized by a synthesis of information from multiple domains, which can be as far apart as chemistry is from social norms, or as close as neighboring branches of mathematics.

3. To achieve such a synthesis, there must be: (a) thorough knowledge of one or more domains; (b) thorough immersion in a field that practices the domain; (c) attention on a problematic area of the domain; (d) idle time for incubation that allows insights to emerge; (e) ability to recognize an insight as one that helps resolve the problematic situation; (f) evaluation and elaboration of the insight in ways that are valuable to the field or domain.

4. The most important individual characteristics are strong interest, curiosity, or intrinsic motivation that drive a person or group to commit attention to a problematic area in a domain, and beyond generally accepted boundaries of knowledge.

5. It is essential not to fill schedules with goal-directed, conscious, rational problem solving, so as to allow for the serendipitous combination of ideas.

6. It is important to provide opportunities for testing insights, to develop their consequences.

IMPLICATIONS FOR UNDERSTANDING ORGANIZATIONAL CREATIVITY

Our perspective generates several implications. First, that individuals are not the proper level of analysis. Creativity is a systems-level phenomenon defined internally by the corporate culture and externally by the business environment. Second, the multileveled systems view of the corporation suggests a difficulty in translating internal creativity into external creativity. Executives should analyze their organization's multiple domains and fields and attempt to understand how the various internal and external fields are related. Third, because so many key insights result from the combination of more than one domain, organizations should encourage cross-domain fertilization by establishing liaisons among different units. Fourth, creativity takes time; it will not emerge overnight. The more significant the creative insight, the longer the period likely to be required for preparation and incubation. Fifth, some rewards should be in the form of formal "idle time." Promising employees should be assigned to spend time in the library or the lab for a day every week or month, to refresh their patterns of thought. They also should be encouraged to take their allotted vacations and not work too many weekends.

Finally, the systems model of creativity implies that there must be a commitment from the top of the organization. Innovation is often opposed by entrenched political interests. Only strong support from top management will make it possible to overcome the inertia of the status quo. ▨

REFERENCES

Csikszentmihalyi, M. (1988). Society, culture, and person: A systems view of creativity. In R. J. Sternberg (Ed.), *The nature of creativity: Contemporary psychological perspectives* (pp. 325-339). New York: Cambridge University Press.

Csikszentmihalyi, M. (1990). The domain of creativity. In M. A. Runco & R. S. Albert (Eds.), *Theories of creativity* (pp. 190-212). Newbury Park, CA: Sage.

Hadamard, J. (1945). *An essay on the psychology of invention in the mathematical field.* New York: Dover, and Princeton, NJ: Princeton University Press.

Poincaré, H. (1913). *The foundations of science.* Garrison, NY: Science Press.

23 Ten Tips Toward Creativity in the Workplace

ROBERT J. STERNBERG *IBM Professor of Psychology and Education, Yale University*

TODD I. LUBART *Visiting Scholar, Ecole Supérieure de Commerce de Paris*

The price we pay for our short-term perspective is loss of competitiveness. Although major changes are needed, only minor changes are made. Where basic research is needed, only applied research is undertaken. Where major innovations are required, only minor ones are tolerated. Competing in a rapidly changing marketplace requires thinking strategically and not just tactically, and being proactive rather than reactive. Genuine creativity requires a broad time horizon, not a quick fix.

AUTHORS' NOTE: Research for this essay was supported under the Javits Act Program (Grant No. R206R00001) as administered by the Office of Educational Research of Improvement, U.S. Department of Education. Grantees undertaking such projects are encouraged to express freely their professional judgment. This essay, therefore, does not necessarily represent the positions or policies of the U.S. Government, and no official endorsement should be inferred.

$\mathcal{I}$t has escaped practically no one's notice that America has had to reassess its preeminence in the world marketplace. As is always true when a competitor slips in the rankings, people can generate multiple reasons for the loss of "the edge" or they can deny the phenomenon altogether. For example, there are those who like to view the United States as a "creative" country, in contrast to "imitative" countries such as Japan. But this face-saving mechanism is losing proponents as we import or jointly develop technological innovations from Japan and Europe, more now than ever. Others bemoan unfair "rules of the game" as they note that Japan closes many of its markets. But one country does not unilaterally make the rules, and all have to play by the rules of the international marketplace, whether they are agreeable to us or not.

One thing that almost everyone agrees on is that increasing the creativity and productivity of our workforce would help improve U.S. competitiveness in a global business environment. That process is not nearly so complicated as it might first seem. Toward this end, we propose 10 tips that we believe will help inspire creativity and productivity in the workplace. All have been successfully implemented—especially in cases where the organizational culture and context foster rather than inhibit creativity.

1. Reward Creativity in Those Who Display It. Perhaps the most obvious and least followed route to creative enterprise is to reward people who show it. Any number of managers say they want creative ideas and suggestions, only to ignore them or even actively punish employees when they are received. People will respond to what you do, not what you say. Thus, if you want creativity, you need concretely and visibly to reward people who show creative work.

Creativity needs to be rewarded down the line. If you reward creativity, but those above or below you do not, your possibilities for success will be limited. Employees will realize that your call for creativity is not being supported either by top management or by the immediate supervisor. If you are high in the chain of command, you can encourage your subordinates to reward creativity, and give them incentives for doing so. One of us recently suggested to a high-level executive that if he was having doubts about whether his next lower level of management was rewarding creativity, he should use a suggestion box so that employees could bypass traditional channels and convey creative suggestions directly to him. Employees would be assured that suggestions would be confidential, and they would receive cash incentives for those suggestions that were adopted. Also, there would be no penalties for "far out" or unused suggestions.

Don't assume immediately that you already reward creative work. Many people instinctively believe they do, but then would be hard pressed to show how they actually do it. Make a list of the concrete, visible things you do to reward creativity, and then lengthen the list. That will be the first step toward generating creative performance in your enterprise.

2. Take Sensible Risks. We call our approach to creativity the "investment theory of creativity," because we believe that creative people and enterprises, like good investors, "buy low and sell high" (Sternberg & Lubart, 1991). There are people who generate and fight for ideas that may sound strange or infeasible to other people, but eventually they convince others of the worth of these ideas. Creative people are thus like canny investors who buy unpopular stocks with low price-earning ratios, realizing that future value will be found in the best of these underappreciated stocks. Of course, not every stock with a low PE ratio is a potential winner, nor is every novel idea. To be truly creative, an idea needs not only to be novel, but appropriate for the task at hand and capable of leading to products of quality, as well. If you think of or hear about an idea that at first sounds untenable, give it another chance before dismissing it.

Good investors know that there can be no major returns on an investment without sensible risks. No one ever became rich by leaving their money in a 5% passbook savings account. Similarly, no one ever has a genuinely creative idea without taking risks, because creative ideas go against the grain of vested interests and established ways of doing things. Taking sensible risks, and letting others take them, too, also means being prepared for failure. Creative people inevitably make mistakes, but mistakes based on attempts to be creative need to be allowed, because they are the ones that can generate major long-run returns. At the same time, it is always important to balance risks with diversification. It's good to have a mix of creative possibilities, just as one has a mix of investments, to balance the impact of any particular investment that may not work out.

3. *Overcome Obstacles, Don't Let Them Overcome You.* As mentioned above, people who "buy low and sell high" inevitably confront obstacles. Similarly, creative people encounter obstacles by the very nature of what they are trying to do. The question is not whether they face obstacles; it is whether they have the perseverance and fortitude to overcome them.

Advancements in most firms take the form of a pyramid; fewer and fewer people make it to higher and higher levels. The more creative people are usually the ones who make it toward the top. They are the ones who recognize that creative endeavors tend to have long-term rewards, so they often trade short-term losses for long-term gains. It often seems that people doing the least thinking are the most rewarded in the short term. After all, such people are not threatening to anyone. They also stand little chance of making any significant contribution to long-term endeavors. Eventually, they just disappear into the woodwork.

Therefore, if you choose the creative path be prepared to fight for your beliefs. You will have to. You will need to convince others of the worth of your ideas, because, unfortunately, creative ideas rarely sell themselves. Be ready to hear objections that are both senseless and counterproductive. Moreover, these objections may be echoed by the multitude. When Copernicus first proposed that the Earth revolved around the sun, his idea was dismissed with scorn. People had only to look up into the sky to see that the opposite was true. He persevered; you will need to as well.

4. *Think for the Long Term.* We believe, as do many others, that the single greatest obstacle facing business and investments in our country is the short-term perspective of managers and investors. Immediate returns too often are emphasized. Stocks are now held for shorter periods in the United States than ever before, and for shorter periods than elsewhere in the world. People want an annual report that shows that this year, like every year, has been a "good year."

The price we pay for our short-term perspective is loss of competitiveness. Although major changes are needed, only minor changes are made. Where basic research is needed, only applied research is undertaken. Where major innovations are required, only minor ones are tolerated. Competing in a rapidly changing marketplace requires thinking strategically and not just tactically, and being proactive rather than reactive. Too often, we play catch-up with our competitors, trying to make money off established niches while they are already defining the next niche. Genuine creativity requires a broad time horizon, not a quick fix.

5. *Keep Growing.* Why is it that many of the successful companies of yesterday are the Chapter 11s of today? Why has their position in industry after industry slipped from number 1 to number 2, number 3, or lower, in the world marketplace? We believe it often is because an early success was followed by complacency and inertia. People were content to rest on the laurels of their predecessors rather than to seek laurels of their own. Virtually all creative ideas have a natural life cycle. We need to recognize when it is time to move on to the next idea. Creative people and organizations not only buy low, they sell high. Once an idea has had its success and generated its profits, it is time to move on. The canny investor knows not only when to buy, but when to sell. Similarly, we need to recognize when old ideas that once worked no longer do.

6. *Beware of the Dangers of Knowing Both Too Little and Too Much.* We all know the maxim that "a little bit of knowledge can be a dangerous thing." For example, we may have a creative idea, but if the competition has already tried it (even if it failed), ignorance will be costly. We need to know what has been done to avoid repeating past mistakes, and also to build upon past contributions. Ignorance is not bliss when it leads to costly mistakes.

Knowing too much, however, can be as dangerous as knowing too little. The problem here is not in knowledge, but in stereotypical and fixated patterns of behavior. Sometimes "self-experts" make the stupidest mistakes because they are unwilling to acknowledge that the best solutions may be ones they don't know about and never would have generated. They are so certain that what they have been doing is correct that they close themselves off to other possibilities. The cost of expertise can thus be rigidity and intolerance of change. When you hear people say things like, "That's not the way things are done around here" or "Of course that would never work," be on your guard. Existing knowledge may be hindering rather than helping a move toward creative decisions.

7. *Tolerate Ambiguity.* Although we like to think that creative ideas come in sudden bursts of inspiration, they seldom actually do. Rather, they develop slowly over time, piece by piece. Often, the pieces do not initially seem to fit together, or some of the pieces are simply wrong. At other times, we may feel like we are trying to solve a jigsaw puzzle, except that the puzzle is missing some pieces or even has some pieces that don't fit. The temptation is to quit with a half-finished puzzle, or simply to declare the puzzle unsolvable.

To be creative, people and organizations need to learn to tolerate the ambiguity of creative problem solving. There may well be long stretches of time in which things don't seem to make sense. During these stretches, there will be both external pressure (from the organization) and internal pressure (from within yourself) to close prematurely on the problem. Yet, the most creative solutions are the ones that are generated by people who are willing to wait—to tolerate ambiguity long enough to get to an optimal solution. It is hard to wait, but the results will often justify the frustration and ambiguity.

8. *Reconceptualize Unsolvable or Intractable Problems.* Sometimes a problem just doesn't seem to have a solution, or at least not a good one. The key to such a problem is often to reformulate it altogether. Many of our most creative inventions came about as result of such reformulations. For example, the very popular Post-it Notes, which can be put on paper and removed without leaving a mark, came about because someone formulated an adhesive that was weaker than the available ones, rather than stronger—despite the fact that he was being paid to formulate stronger adhesives and despite the fact that his supervisors initially saw no use for a new weak adhesive. In another instance, a friend solved the problem of having a terrible boss not by finding himself a new job, but by finding his boss a new job (unbeknownst

to the boss, of course). He then got his boss's job. The examples are endless, but the principle is simple. When you just can't seem to solve a problem, try to think of another way of posing the problem.

9. *Find What You Love to Do.* We know that people do their most creative work when they love doing what they're doing. There is no substitute for intrinsic motivation—the motivation that comes from within. Although intrinsic motivation does not guarantee creative work, dislike of or disinterest in one's work almost guarantees a lack of creativity. We have, on occasion, hired people to do one thing, only rapidly to switch them to another because we found that the other job was a better fit for their talents and interests. Sometimes the very same job can be redesigned to enhance its interest. This often means giving people greater responsibility for their contributions to a group product.

10. *Know When to Shape Environments, and When to Leave Them.* We began our essay with a discussion of the environment (see Tip No. 1) and we end with a discussion of the environment, because we believe that the beginning and end of creativity in organizations are in the work environments we provide for people. Suppose you are in an environment that does not reward creativity. What can you do? Try shaping the environment so that it better rewards what you value. The shaping may be a slow, sometimes arduous process. It may involve gradual, incremental changes that cumulatively have an important impact, even if no single change does. Each step you take toward implementing the 10 tips in this essay is one more step toward producing a creative environment. And perhaps the most creative challenge you face is creating an environment that fosters creativity.

At the same time, you need to recognize that sometimes change just can't be accomplished. If top management is so complacent or so scared that they nip creativity in the bud wherever they see it, you have to ask yourself whether you really want to stay in that environment. Too often, people stay with what they have because they fail even to consider other possibilities. Or they assume—without fully

---

TABLE 23.1 Ten Tips for Fostering Creativity

1. Reward creativity in those who display it.
2. Take sensible risks.
3. Overcome obstacles, don't let them overcome you.
4. Think for the long term.
5. Keep growing.
6. Be aware of the dangers of knowing both too little and too much.
7. Tolerate ambiguity.
8. Reconceptualize insoluble or intractable problems.
9. Find what you love to do.
10. Know when to shape environments, and when to leave them.

---

exploring options—that other options are closed to them. You need to know when to stay, but also when to leave. You may be able to find as yet unattained creativity, but not in your current environment.

We have presented 10 tips for fostering creativity in the workplace. These suggestions have been summarized in Table 23.1. It is up to you, however, to find the right work environment to realize your own creativity. If you find yourself saying, "It would be nice, but . . . ," then you have not committed yourself to creativity. Being creative requires a commitment—and it is not an easy commitment either to make or to realize. The one thing that is certain is that it is a commitment worth making. ▧

REFERENCE

Sternberg, R. J., & Lubart, T. I. (1991). An investment theory of creativity and its development. *Human Development, 34,* 1-31.

24 Creative Post-Processing
On Making Turbulence Valuable

KRISTIAN KREINER *Associate Professor of Organization Management, Copenhagen Business School*

MAJKEN SCHULTZ *Associate Professor of Organization Management, Copenhagen Business School*

Creativity may be sparked by rather mundane, routine events. But the sparks of creativity only ensue when mundane, routine events are successfully coupled to rather alien zones of experience. Perhaps we can begin to appreciate the challenge of creativity as the constructive use of new opportunities as they are haphazardly encountered. Creativity resides in the ability to redefine such deviance as a logical, or at least promising, next step in the collaborative venture.

$\rule{3cm}{0pt}$

$\mathcal{R}$ationality and creativity are a pair of celebrated labels that we frequently use in our appreciation of Western business practice. We celebrate behavior as rational when it is serious, devoted to chosen values, and aimed at achieving desired outcomes. In contrast, we celebrate behavior as creative when it is playful, reveals alternative ways of seeing, and leads to inspired, surprising, yet valuable consequences. On most occasions we use rationality and creativity as mutually exclusive labels; yet, both concepts describe behaviors that are oriented toward the future and attempt to achieve envisioned outcomes. Each approaches this goal differently, however. Rationality attempts to exploit proven conventions skillfully; creativity attempts skillfully to escape them.

Because actual future outcomes are always hard to predict in social worlds, what is being labeled as rational or creative are the attempts, rather than the outcomes. We expect that these attempts are designed intentionally, based on logics either of creativity or rationality. When such labeling is done after the fact (i.e., after outcomes are known), it is considered somehow to be "cheating." Such instances are often denigrated as mere post hoc rationalizations and are treated as self-serving attempts to claim intentionality and competence where it was not actually involved. Clearly the notion of "rationalizing" carries connotations far different than those of being rational. Furthermore, rationality, rationalization, and even the notion of post hoc processing about actions and outcomes, are not usually associated with creativity. Our research tell us, however, that they should be!

It is possible, and indeed fruitful, to consider creativity without intentionality. In fact, the post-processing of action might, under certain conditions, be the only source of creativity. This heretical view stems from our study of cross-national projects in the context of commercial product and technology development in Europe. We have studied the progress of such projects over the past 4 years and have witnessed many innovative achievements in the face of tremendously varied and turbulent environments. In the traditional sense, many of the outcomes easily qualify as creative. But the battles fought and won to achieve these innovations were not the expected ones, according to the usual view of creativity in organizations. The expected battles in organizational creativity or innovation are fought against conventions. As such, creativity usually is conceived as the successful departure from conventional, routine, expected paths. Such departures are battles because individual traits, organizational structures, and societal institutions all reward staying on a known path by reenacting conventions.

The functional rationale for creative solutions that depart from convention often resides in the belief that they may add variety to an organization's portfolio of possible alternative actions (which facilitates adaptation or competitive advantage, because new choices become possible). In highly complex, turbulent situations, however, the portfolio of alternatives is seldom narrow or limited; in fact, the possible alternatives are frequently overwhelming. Very often, extraordinary variety ensues just from mundane acts that happen to touch upon new and unprecedented environmental conditions. Thus this picture is not one of organizations struggling to create variety. Rather, it is one of organizations struggling to deal constructively with too much variety. These conditions still lead to a battle, and still give rise to playful, ingenious, and inspired performances, but these are not directed toward the enabling of action. Instead, they are directed toward making sense and use of previous action. Creativity thus occurs not at the stage of thought or action, but at the stage of post-processing the consequences of action.

In this situation of confronting actions and outcomes to be interpreted, we come to appreciate post-processing and its creative role in facilitating innovation. Manifest options and results need to be creatively linked to the vision and strategy of the organization. Creative post-processing thus involves a dynamic interplay between emergent options and the definition and redefinition of the project vision.

THE EUREKA EXPERIENCE

EUREKA is a pan-European program that facilitates a cross-national pooling of technological capabilities for commercial purposes. The intent of the program is to enhance the competitiveness of European firms and nations in the world market, and the projects that we base this essay on were very much dedicated to frontier R&D work. The "climate" was thus one of extreme uncertainty and competition; it also was one that demanded creativity and innovation.

EUREKA takes its name from Archimedes' exclamation of triumph at his discovery, while in his bath, that he could calculate density by measuring the volume of displaced water—a discovery that enabled him to complete his assigned task of determining whether the king's goldsmith was cheating on the amount of gold in the crown. Except for the exclamation, Archimedes and his time, place, and problem resemble the EUREKA projects and their contexts only vaguely. He was working on a very concrete task; he was working all by himself; he had no competitors; and he was working in seclusion from the world outside his village. The genius of Archimedes showed precisely in his ability to make a profound discovery in such barren circumstances. Water spilling over the edge of his bath represents well the mundane kinds of clues he had to operate on.

How different from the circumstances in modern EUREKA R&D projects, where tasks are ambiguous, collaboration is mandatory, competition is global, and change is constant. These circumstances understandably produced project behavior that would appear rather undisciplined. Research agendas changed, plans were altered or forgotten, collaboration drifted outside the project, new partners were engaged and former ones dropped. Few would expect much positive impact from such apparently haphazard occurrences; the usual managerial inclination would be to straighten these project partners out.

Close observation suggests, however, that the project behavior was not actually undisciplined. Rather, it was the environment in which they operated that was undisciplined! For example, no less than 80% of the successful projects in our study experienced one or more changes in ownership during our period of observation. Thus, such projects needed to adapt to a strategic context that changed substantially and continually. Projects had to realign themselves constantly to the explosion in scientific and technical knowledge. Each EUREKA partner also had to deal with local demands, account for new ideas and competencies, adjust to new collaborators, and more, all of which had to be balanced against the agreements and plans negotiated within the EUREKA project structure. To characterize their environment as "turbulent" is almost an understatement. In observing these circumstances, however, we came to appreciate the behavior of the EUREKA partners as rather "methodical" within the context of an undisciplined environment. There was a certain routine character to the way in which people pursued new leads and ideas, even when these took them off on a tangent. There was also a certain inertia in the patient monitoring of networks, conferences, and also in the preliminary investigation of ideas and opportunities, for example.

In one instance, we observed a EUREKA project manager who almost accidentally encountered a researcher at a conference who claimed to be able to conduct a certain kind of experiment that our project manager had failed to do. Within weeks, the manager brought experimental material to the researcher's laboratory and worked with him for some time. Although obviously a betrayal of the EUREKA project plans and partnership, it is hard to define the manager's behavior as undisciplined (or creative for that matter). Most managers worth their salt would pursue such a lead whenever possible. Our point is simply that when you approach a highly turbulent and undisciplined world in a methodical, rational way, variety in performance and experience will ensue.

CREATIVITY AS POST-PROCESSING
OF CONSEQUENCES

Post-processing means that events and consequences are fitted into a framework of intentions, values, strategies, agreements, and meanings that was not necessarily invoked before an action or outcome occurred. In the EUREKA projects, "post-processing" meant creating a legitimate link between the spoils of wandering off from projected paths into "foreign" territory, on the one hand, and the current beliefs about the nature of existing agreements concerning the EUREKA collaboration on the other. As would be expected, these wanderings did not always produce spoils to be reconciled. Many times there simply would be nothing to reconcile. Other times, the attempts to reconcile were unsuccessful, potentially disrupting to the collaboration itself. At still other times, the fresh inputs redefined research agendas and collaborative patterns within the projects.

However, the spoils seldom manifested themselves as unambiguous results and clear-cut inputs to the project partnership. Thus, whether spoils were recognized and whether they were successfully reconciled with the project efforts was at least as much dependent on the ingenuity and—we would claim—creativity of the actors as on the nature and variety of extra-collaborative experiences. The dividing line between the pedestrian and the creative projects did not run between what different actors did or saw, but between how creatively actors made something of what they had *already* done or seen. That "making something of" is actually the seedbed of innovation. Occasionally, it changed the course and success of the projects dramatically.

By insisting on reconciling the spoils of such explorations within the existing framework of EUREKA collaboration, the partnerships managed to regenerate and adapt continuously. In this sense, the post-processing tapped directly into the very dynamics of EUREKA projects.

CONCLUSION

The EUREKA context is perhaps a prototypical example for the turbulent, modern world of collaborative ventures. We contend that most organizational contexts produce ample amounts of variety that might be capitalized upon. When systems fail to capitalize on variety, the problem is often that variety is considered illegitimate and deviant. But if the deviance resides not in the collaboration or in individual actors, but in a turbulent environment itself, then the EUREKA experience reminds us that creativity may be sparked by rather mundane, routine events (like taking a bath). But the sparks of creativity only ensue when mundane, routine events are successfully coupled to rather alien zones of experience (like measuring the purity of gold). Perhaps we can begin to appreciate the challenge of creativity as the constructive use of new opportunities as they are haphazardly encountered. Creativity resides in the ability to redefine such deviance as a logical, or at least promising, next step in the collaborative venture—that is, as a form of continuity. Oftentimes, partners stand to lose little from willingly entertaining such interpretations. Occasionally, subsequent events graciously reward such willingness.

Viewing creativity as post-processing focuses our attention away from the usual concentration on overcoming mental and organizational barriers to the generation of novel alternatives (i.e., the production of variety). Instead, it encourages the development of productive ways of exploiting dynamic environments by linking haphazard opportunities to the evolving goals of the organization. Most important, post-processing repositions creativity into the mundane pragmatics of surviving in turbulent environments. ▨

25 Creativity and the Aesthetics of Imperfection

KARL E. WEICK *Rensis Likert Collegiate Professor*
of Organizational Behavior and Psychology
University of Michigan

An aesthetics of imperfection creates a different mind-set toward error. Errors now become viewed as experiments from which people can learn, as oddities to be incorporated or made normal, as items to be isolated from ongoing processes so their effects will be localized, as inevitable when personal activity rather than an impersonal product is being assessed, as potentially the right notes for some other song, as an excuse to say "let it pass," as evidence that involvement is high, as transient flaws that will make sense as events unfold.

Imagine T. S. Eliot giving nightly poetry readings at which, rather than reciting set pieces, he was expected to create impromptu poems—different ones each night, sometimes recited at a fast clip; imagine giving Hitchcock or Fellini a handheld motion picture camera and asking them to film something, anything—at that very moment, without the benefit of script, crew, editing or scoring; imagine Matisse or Dali giving nightly exhibitions of their skills—exhibitions at which paying audiences would watch them fill up canvas after canvas with paint, often with only two or three minutes devoted to each "masterpiece."

Gioia, *The Imperfect Art*, 1988, p. 52

Implausible as those performance pressures sound, they are part of everyday life for jazz musicians. And equivalent pressures are increasingly commonplace when managers try to innovate under pressure. The hallmark of jazz is improvisation, defined as "playing extemporaneously, i.e. without benefit of written music . . . composing on the spur of the moment" (Schuller, 1989, p. 378). Alec Wilder, a composer who labors over his compositions, finds himself astonished by what jazz musicians are able to do:

> I wish to god that some neurologists would sit down and figure out how the improviser's brain works, how he selects, out of hundreds of thousands of possibilities, the notes he does at the speed that he does—how in God's name, his mind works so damned fast! And why, when the notes come out right, they are right. . . . Composing is a slow, arduous, obvious, inch-by-inch process, whereas improvisation is a lightning mystery. In fact, it is the creative mystery of our age. (Suhor, 1986, p. 134)

Although much of what makes successful jazz improvisation does remain a creative mystery, some factors that may contribute to this success are becoming clearer. An important one is how improvising musicians react to failures, flawed execution, dissonant notes, and traps. Their reactions suggest a mind-set that may help others besides musicians when they also attempt to generate variations that are hard to justify.

I have labeled this mind-set "the aesthetics of imperfection," following Gioia (1988, p. 55). This mind-set is not an apology for failure nor a license to fail. Instead, it is meant to acknowledge and appreciate the fact that failures occur when people make a genuine, deep, committed effort to improvise. I am not talking about sloppy failures or lazy failures, but about failures of reach. How people react to failures of reach can have a decisive effect on their subsequent willingness to improvise.

An appropriate context to illustrate imperfections and creativity is Robert Graves's poem "In Broken Images," which I used in the second edition of *Social Psychology of Organizing* (Weick, 1979) to show tensions in organizational life surrounding plans, creativity, rationality, and other myths.

In Broken Images

He is quick, thinking in clear images;
I am slow, thinking in broken images.

He becomes dull, trusting to his clear images;
I become sharp, mistrusting my broken images.

Trusting his images, he assumes their relevance;
Mistrusting my images, I question their relevance.

Assuming their relevance, he assumes the fact;
Questioning their relevance, I question the fact.

When the fact fails him, he questions his senses;
When the fact fails me, I approve my senses.

He continues quick and dull in his clear images;
I continue slow and sharp in my broken images.

He in a new confusion of his understanding;
I in a new understanding of my confusion.

(Reprinted by permission from Carcanet Press)

I used to think the nouns in that poem were the key, reflecting the incompleteness, fragmentation, the bits and pieces we always have to work with. I now think that I paid too little attention to the verb *continues* that crops up over and over. That's where the drama lies. People *continue* despite the broken images. That's what happens when a jazz musician plays a sour note. That's what happens when a novelist rolls another sheet of paper into the typewriter, knowing full well that the novel is stuck and not working. That's what happens when one more attempt to design a circuit fails, or when an observer at a shuttle launch spots yet another hydrogen leak and the temptation is to ignore it. These interruptions are commonplace, they often are the prelude to innovation, and yet they are seldom recognized as an inherent feature of any process of improvisation. Failure may become accepted as an inevitable property of improvisation, if we can reframe its aesthetic qualities and reduce some of the stigma that goes along with failure. Only then will it be possible to encourage people to fail boldly, and mean it, and incur their trust.

Jazz, like any other creative act, has its haphazard moments.

> Errors will creep in, not only in form but also in execution; the improviser, if he sincerely attempts to be creative, will push himself into areas of expression which his techniques may be unable to handle. Too often the finished product will show moments of rare beauty intermixed with technical mistakes and aimless passages. (Gioia, 1988, p. 66)

But if we label jazz as haphazard art, the question remains, "Haphazard relative to what?" The answer is, haphazard relative to the planned, methodical carefully crafted world of products that are symmetrical, balanced, well formed, perfect. The aesthetics of perfection require that products be evaluated separately from their makers. This is not appropriate for evaluating spontaneous, creative activities that are inseparable from their producers.

So, we need to articulate a different set of standards that take more account of the raw materials at hand, the context, the situation the person had available to work with when the improvisation unfolded. This is where we find the aesthetics of imperfection.

An aesthetics of imperfection yields judgments like this:

1. given what she started with, this isn't bad;
2. given the opportunities and problems that she set up for herself, this is a clever resolution;
3. given the melody she had to work with, these notes have significantly enlarged that melody;
4. given the temptation toward clichés and busyness that are set up by that melody line, this person consistently avoided those traps.

An aesthetics of imperfection involves judgments made in the context of retrospective blueprints. For example, success is judged against what the person started with, namely the melody, the chords, the co-workers, and what the person did with those elements.

An aesthetics of imperfection also involves appreciating what people do with imperfections once they occur. For example, given that sour note, was its effect localized, was it blended, was it normalized, was it transformed into a plausible next step?

An aesthetics of imperfection also involves a more refined inter-pretation of errors themselves. Sample judgments might include: Of all of the errors you could have made under these conditions, were the ones you actually made novel, were they errors of excessive reach, were they untypical for you, were they effortful, were they original, could they have been made by someone who is lazy or distracted?

David Sudnow (1979) has done a marvelous job of summarizing the small imperfections that signal true improvisation. He focuses on those errors that should appear among jazz pianists, unless the performance was worked out earlier and simply memorized.

> Look especially for the [presence] of those little false starts being forever turned into the music as the improvisational hand aligns and realigns itself. Look for [much] in the way of things being said—I mean placed—for things being placed and then placed again, and then again, before a longer burst of venturing movements. Look for the [appear-ance] of those clear mistakes that are then turned into parts of the music as the hand cycles back to pick up a sour-sounding note, doing it again for emphasis, making it of the music by elegantly integrating its harshness into a small digression. Watch out for the [appearance] of that special sort of developing tension that resolves with the sense of "Wow, he made it come off." Watch out for many imitations of that tension. And be especially cautious of the intricately fingered melody whose structuring for the hand strongly suggests a lot of prior work just to get that particular one learned. (pp. 43-44)

An aesthetics of imperfection creates a different mind-set toward error. Errors now become viewed as experiments from which people can learn, as oddities to be incorporated or made normal, as items to be isolated from ongoing processes so their effects will be localized, as inevitable when personal activity rather than an impersonal prod-uct is being assessed, as potentially the right notes for some other song, as an excuse to say "let it pass," as evidence that involvement is high, as transient flaws that will make sense as events unfold. These interpretations of error are not just excuses, although they may sound that way to some people. Instead, these are judgments that reflect the ways in which processes differ from products, and human activity differs from human intention. An aesthetics of imperfection does not use as its standard compliance with or deviation from some plan or ideal or blueprint. Instead, it uses as its standard some estimate of the degree of organization and form that could have been extracted retrospectively from the materials at hand, given that they were generated by a fallible human being acting publicly under time pressure, with fallible tools.

An aesthetics of imperfection treats errors as opportunities rather than threats. This aesthetic contains the implicit recognition that the word *error* is not even particularly meaningful when used to describe an activity that itself consists of playing everything BUT actual notes of the melody itself. Successful improvisation enriches a melody, but what is happening literally is that every one of those improvised notes is an error. Each improvised note is not the same note the composer wrote on the musical staff when the melody was first created. Thus, to talk about errors nested within an activity that is itself a celebration of error is to suggest the need for a different vocabulary and set of images than those associated with perfection.

An aesthetics of imperfection makes imperfection a personal signature of involvement rather than a public signature of failure. Error is not simply reframed as a virtue, but is seen instead as a sign of continuing struggle for virtue glimpsed in spur-of-the-moment improvisation. If an aesthetic of imperfection is shared, then people should be more willing to take the risks associated with innovation. It is the aesthetics of perfection, wrongly extrapolated from products isolated from their producers and the conditions of their production, that wreak havoc and inspire fear in those who are told to innovate by bosses blind to the human side of innovation. ∎

REFERENCES

Gioia, T. (1988). *The imperfect art.* New York: Oxford University Press.

Schuller, G. (1989). *The swing era.* New York: Oxford University Press.

Sudnow, D. (1979). *Talk's body.* New York: Knopf.

Suhor, C. (1986). Jazz improvisation and language performance: Parallel competencies. *Etc., 43,* 133-140.

Weick, K. E. (1979). *The social psychology of organizing* (2nd ed.). Reading, MA: Addison-Wesley.

Real World

PART III

Voices

The Changing Face of Creativity

F. BEN JONES *Former Vice President,*
Research and Development
Phillips Petroleum Company

Creativity in the context of business is inseparable from the concept of value. The basis chosen for assessing value (i.e., commercial, humanitarian, societal, artistic, etc.), defines the focus and objectives of creative effort. The idea of invention as the critical goal of the technical knowledge worker is being replaced by the realization that innovation (i.e., the useful application of invention in practice) is the ultimate value-related objective.

My convictions about creativity, how it might be defined, stimulated, and valued, have been formed during four decades in industry. During that time, I have been an industrial researcher, technology manager, and business executive. I offer my comments about creativity within the context of those experiences.

CREATIVITY AS CREATION OF VALUE

According to Webster, to be creative "is to exhibit the power or ability to create; to produce an original product of human invention or artistic imagination." To be applied effectively today in the arena of industrial R&D, I would reformulate that definition: "Creativity is the act of envisioning, demonstrating, and applying cost-effective methods to (a) eliminate recognized technical problems and (b) provide significant and profitable technology-based opportunities in targeted areas of business activity."

From the beginning of the industrial revolution, invention—as an act of contriving something previously unknown—has been a hallmark of creativity. In earlier times invention was largely a private effort supported by the resources of the individual or by an academic institution. Creativity was an individual rather than a group event. During this century, industry began to organize staffs of technically trained people whose purpose was collectively to create technology leading to business opportunity. Industrial R&D was born.

The evolution of industrial R&D activity that followed has brought about considerable change in perceptions concerning the value and proper focus of creative technical effort. Private inventors presumably saw their objective clearly enough to derive powerful creative stimulus. Would-be inventors in modern organizations are dependent on their leaders for guidance on direction and goals so they do not become out of touch with the needs of the enterprise. Today's business organizations must assure that creative technical activity is suitably aligned with corporate direction and objectives. Creativity in the context of organizations today is heavily influenced by the need to realize practical commercial value, which inevitably raises the issue of whether creative effort should be focused or allowed broad freedom to explore individual interests (which in turn has provoked a debate about whether the act of focusing in itself imposes any significant limitation on the creative process).

ASSESSING CREATIVITY

The emergence of the patent system in the late 18th century significantly affected the issue of creativity for industry. Establishing the patent as a form of legal right to protect the products of creative thought allowed inventions to be treated as intellectual property (i.e., as assets). Treating creative effort as a potentially asset-building enterprise quickly led to questions about value and evaluation. Perceptions about creativity and associated value can be quite different depending on whether the viewpoint is that of a knowledge worker or a resource allocator. Attempts to manage these perceptions have influenced how industry organizes, allocates resources, and measures and rewards efforts to create and apply worthwhile technology.

Measuring creative technical ability has long been of interest to the knowledge worker, technology manager, and business executive alike. Many approaches for doing so have been proposed and tried. Years ago, Phillips' R&D conducted a study of the then current techniques, aided by a group of behavioral scientists as consultants. The main conclusion at the time (early 1970s) was that the best assessment of an individual's creative ability and effort was likely to be given by the person's peers. Nonetheless, recorded and published evidence has long been used as the main means to quantify and recognize creativity (e.g., technical publications, reports, and—particularly within industry—the issuance of patents). Patents have the special benefit of deriving from a strict screening procedure for inventiveness, originality, and adequacy of description. Unfortunately, nothing in the processing of patent applications automatically deals with assessing business relevance and projected commercial value. Holding a large patent portfolio does not in itself assure significant value. That realization, and the rapidly rising cost of obtaining and maintaining patents, has prompted a movement toward a greater selectivity in patenting and in the underlying creative technical efforts.

MYTHS ABOUT
INDUSTRIAL CREATIVITY

There are some deeply ingrained beliefs about the commercial value of technical creativity that have come under challenge in recent years. Here are some examples: (a) If invention was the early foundation of much of the manufacturing industry, then ever-increasing efforts at invention should provide a sure path to future business growth and profitability. Therefore, larger and larger R&D organizations and facilities are called for. (b) If a singular technical accomplishment had been of value, then diversifying the scope of ongoing activity would surely add to the creative output—in other words, throw a bigger net and you will catch more fish. (c) If newness and uniqueness were evidence of creativity then a company should generate and develop as many new ideas as possible. Develop the idea first and find practical application afterward. If a development is unique, then practical value will certainly be found eventually. To all of these beliefs, the response is Not Necessarily! They are all myths in waiting.

During the 1980s, innovation as the practical application of ideas and a necessary extension of invention was being rediscovered. Focus began to shift toward refining skills needed for rapid and timely implementation of technology in order to realize value from creativity. Change began to accelerate in the world of industrial R&D. In the process of rethinking for the future, companies began more seriously to question and evaluate the business value of their efforts to create opportunity and competitive advantage through technology. Few questioned the basic belief that technical development could help business, but a growing number were uncomfortable and uncertain about the value of the gains made in relation to the resources expended. By the mid-1980s the introspection was pervasive. Technology managers and their business operations counterparts became involved with more elaborate efforts to understand the factors that controlled the realization of business value from creative technical effort. Belief in the inherent commercial value of invention was reshaped by the recognition that innovation was what really connected to the bottom-line performance of business. The fact that not all inventions make significant profit (less than 5%, in my experience) was rediscovered the hard way.

INDUSTRIAL CREATIVITY TODAY

Today, creative technical efforts by industry show signs of change. A much greater effort is being made to align the direction of corporate technology with the defined goals and objectives of the business. Open and effective communication is key to successful alignment. New tools for assessing risk and projecting the expected business impact of innovation are now being developed by more progressive organizations. Reward and recognition systems are being modified to highlight the importance of successful innovation that is needed to bring value from creative technical effort into business. Creative technical knowledge workers are strongly motivated by a desire to accomplish and contribute something of significance with their efforts. It is the obligation of the leadership of the organization to establish a culture that unambiguously defines the elements of winning behavior. Organizational change is occurring through streamlining of management, decentralization, and other configurations intended to facilitate more rapid movement from creative discovery to successful implementation of innovation. It is truly an exciting time.

Here are some experience-based observations about modern technical creativity:

• Technical creativity will remain of critical importance to society, but the practical definition of creativity will continue to evolve. Creativity in the context of business is inseparable from the concept of value. The basis chosen for assessing value (i.e., commercial, humanitarian, societal, artistic, etc.), defines the focus and objectives of creative effort.

• Introducing the requirement for practical value forces movement away from earlier benchmarks for assessing technical creativity. The idea of invention as the critical goal of the technical knowledge worker is being replaced by the realization that innovation (i.e., the useful application of invention in practice) is the ultimate value-related objective.

• Efforts to realign and focus the efforts of the technical knowledge worker in industry are challenging business and technology leaders alike to clarify and communicate the future direction of the enterprise and the value system that will be used in recognizing and rewarding creative accomplishment.

There is no effective substitute for knowing clearly the broad objectives and vision held by the very top corporate leadership. This strikes to the core question of how technical creativity is to be involved. In the early history of organized R&D effort at Phillips Petroleum Company some 65 years ago, the founder-chairman and his immediate successors indicated clearly what they wanted to accomplish in the business through technology. From this direction, the early R&D organization responded with a succession of inventions that became significant commercial innovations in the refining of petroleum and in the use of natural gas and gas liquids as transportable fuels and petrochemical feedstocks. When the creative technical personnel delivered the targeted innovations, there was little uncertainty as to whether corporate management was willing and ready to commit resources, and the corporation expanded profitably. Management was getting what it had already asked for. The practical definition of creativity was consistent and understood.

In later years, a much larger and more diverse Phillips R&D organization pursued a variety of creative efforts and produced an amazing record of invention across a broad front of synthetic and polymer chemistry, physics, geoscience, and bioscience. When introduced, the response to these inventions in many instances was that the corporation was unwilling or unable to make a serious attempt at commercial exploitation. Much creative effort was expended that produced little commercial value. The practical definition of creativity had diverged.

In more recent times, Phillips' management has worked much harder to clarify and communicate the vision, goals, and priorities of the corporation. The basis for defining the focus and value of creative technical effort for the current organization is being reestablished. We are relearning that creative effort can be inspired by clear knowledge of desired objectives and motivated by the sense of urgency conveyed by a demanding situation and a need to act. The challenge for technical management is now that of communicating the goals and assuring the knowledge worker that creativity, even in tightly focused areas of desired accomplishment, is still an essential ingredient for success. The wheel has come full circle. ▧

27 Corporate America
Creativity Held Hostage

PEDRO CUATRECASAS *President, Pharmaceutical Research,*
Parke-Davis

We talk about the importance of encouraging creativity without
realizing that the basic premises of corporations as currently
constituted are inimical to a creative way of life. The most serious
and alarming characteristic of these corporations is that their
dominating actions are directed primarily toward achieving
efficiencies, toward reducing costs and making profits, and toward
"control," not toward enhancing freedom and creating value. Top
management likes to talk about long-term innovation, yet it tries to
manage it (financially) on a quarterly basis.

***

*H*uman beings, unlike other animal species that are more geneti-
cally homogeneous, are endowed with a unique individuality that
seeks expression. This individuality, coupled with extraordinary intelligence, provides the basis for creative contributions by everyone.
Thus each person is a "creative" being, able to think and do things
differently than others.

Most people accept the notion that each individual is capable of
creativity, however defined. In fact, our educational systems are increasingly geared to developing and encouraging creative expression. That
is why our children are exposed to play and art in our schools. We
preach in both our secondary and advanced education that it is the
process of thinking, reasoning, and questioning, rather than memo-
rizing, that is important. We want people to think for themselves, to
pass their own judgments, to solve their own problems, and to find
their own ways in life for inner satisfaction and more.

Creativity is usually evident when people come up with questions
or suggestions or solutions that are not obvious or predictable. The
most creative actions are almost by definition unconventional in

201

some way. Such novel, innovative, or unique solutions can lead to valuable ideas or a potentially useful new product. Often they result in enrichment of the environment or inspiration to others, as artistic expressions might do.

Creativity usually emanates from a sense of curiosity or from an inner drive for asking questions and solving problems differently. To do this, people must have freedom to express individuality of thought or action. They must be able to engage in "playing" with ideas and abstractions, often with imagery and fantasy, and to draw from analogies with apparently unrelated experiences. Above all, people must feel that the problem-solving process is fun and provides them with a unique sense of identity and self-satisfaction.

However, a monumental contradiction exists between this type of thinking and what society does to people when they "grow up" and take jobs. All these enlightened rationales seem to go out of the window when it comes to managing people at work. Our culture has somehow created dehumanized monsters as workplaces. We talk about the importance of encouraging creativity without realizing that the basic premises of corporations as currently constituted are inimical to a creative way of life and personal innovation.

I would argue that corporations are organized to achieve conformity, control, and even regimentation. Because professional people spend most of their time at work, that means that creativity is left for weekend pastimes. Is that what we want? Of course not. Creativity in the workplace should be like creativity anywhere else. Although people sometimes do find ways—in spite of (not because of) the corporate culture—to be creative in their jobs, this is usually done surreptitiously or by "bucking the system." Our objective should be to create an organizational environment that encourages creativity at work, mainly by providing individuals with freedom and by avoiding unnecessary policies that demand conformity.

Do our current corporate structures and practices encourage, accommodate, or even tolerate such behavior from employees? Usually, they do not. It is amazing how unimaginatively similar different corporations are today with respect to organizational structures, policies, and operating principles. And it does not seem to matter if their histories or business objectives are different. All have now "modernized." Most have been guided by the conventional wisdom of modern business school teachings. As a result they have essentially copied each other; many even use the same consultant-gurus. Most also use the same slogans and employee-directed brain mashing techniques. One sees little imagination, innovation, or creativity in their structures and processes. Moving from one to the other is easy, but boring. The most serious and alarming characteristic of these corporations is that their dominating actions are directed primarily toward achieving efficiencies, toward reducing costs and making profits, and toward "control," not toward enhancing freedom and creating value. Management controls finances, external relations, hierarchical divisions, compensation, working hours, dress codes, ad nauseam. The tone is set by similarly minded lawyers, bean counters, and powerful human resource personnel who rule authoritatively over the professionals they are supposed to serve. Style and form have become more important than substance. *Compassion, humor, diversity*, and *creativity* are not in the vocabulary.

Managers are taught to control and manipulate people, to get them to do what they (and the corporation) want them to do. Executive comfort derives from order, stability, predictability, and focus—but the focus is on conformity, the conventional, and implicit intolerance for new ideas. "Focus" turns out to be myopic tunnel vision rather than clarity of thought, purpose, or vision. Predictably enough, behaviors become formalized, operations rigid, relationships autocratic, and vision shortsighted. Top management likes to talk about long-term innovation, yet it tries to manage it (financially) on a quarterly basis.

How can individuals express true creativity in such environments? The notions of standardization and routinized behavior are diametrically opposed to creativity. Yet, this is the way most companies are organized in order "to get things done, and fast." There is no time to be wasted by allowing people to experiment, to have fun, and to do things extemporaneously. One should not take chances; business people have to be tough minded and disciplined, so the reasoning goes. Never mind that company "output" or accomplishments might be mediocre or pedestrian. Efficiency rules. "If you're not with us, get off the train," is a common expression of top business executives.

Corporations tend to be authoritarian institutions run by a few people with enormous power who are survivors and products of the "system." They are thus not likely to be sensitive to its weaknesses, but rather committed to its preservation. They will simply do the same, but more of it and faster and better. Creativity-stifling systems are thus perpetuated.

There are a number of widely embraced business practices that underscore the fundamentally anticreative nature of most organizations. For example, the popular "benchmarking" asks people to copy what others are doing, not to come up with their own unique ways of doing things. "Management by objectives" predetermines the expected behavior or outcomes, thus sterilizing the future (taking the spontaneity and the beauty out of it), and sets a punitive tone for accomplishing "job duties." Basing bonuses on very specific and measurable accomplishments is insulting because it limits exploration into innovation. Compensation based on output puts the focus on the concrete, the quantitative, the predictable, and it discourages the softer and less tangible expressions needed for potentially creative actions. Formal "performance appraisals" are basically demeaning; they "create" an almighty judge (the supervisor), whose credentials are sometimes arbitrary and accidental, and they reinforce master-slave relationships. Presentations to management are preceded by lengthy "rehearsals" that replace spontaneity and personality with sterile polish. "Succession planning" exercises usually cause executives to identify (and sometimes to force-rank) the "high potential" employees who fit their preconceived notions, thus guaranteeing virtual clones and the perpetuation of mediocrity and the status quo. Slogans as popular tools for top executives to "create" an image are often unwittingly designed to achieve uniformity of thought and action. These words effectively enslave employees to existing or preconceived ways of doing things, rather than empower them to innovate (despite slogans to the contrary). The common use by top executives of external "experts" or consultants who often know less than internal professionals, tells employees that management does not believe in or respect their capabilities. Many corporations have "special programs" to promote creativity. This is, of course, an admission that creativity does not, or cannot, exist under normal conditions. For programs to work they must become part of the way of life or culture. All these common features in modern corporate life work against the creative life.

Is there no hope? Does the presence of these practices mean that creativity in the workplace is not possible? Of course not. Things can change. Because the current corporate structures were created by people, they can be undone or changed by people. Furthermore, creativity is an instinctive and enduring human quality. But before major changes can occur, it is necessary to appreciate that changes are necessary. Clearly, discussions should be focused less on "what can we do to promote creativity" and more on how we can remove those barriers that suppress the creative drive. If the institutionalized barriers begin to disappear, then it will be easier to establish systems and relationships that stimulate self-driven, genuinely challenging opportunities for people, and allow their natural creativity to emerge. Most people will be creative if you simply let them do it. There are no compelling reasons why corporations could not function in radically different ways. The long-term effectiveness of corporations would improve despite operating in greater apparent ambiguity. Those with the courage and vision to do things differently will be the survivors of tomorrow, the corporations of the future.

Some of the signs of change are already visible. The general malaise and decreased level of innovation of large companies have become more evident in recent years. Many groups within large companies fortunately are finding ways to avoid or escape the stultifying systems and are creating their own ways, often defiantly. Also, small, loosely organized, dynamic companies (e.g., in biotechnology) are springing up everywhere. This seems to be the rage these days. Is there a message there? Maybe the main message is not that "small" companies are the way to go, but that large corporations should be run more as if they were small companies. Why not? ▨

28 Coaching Your Way to Creativity

RUSSELL C. FORD *Senior Vice President,*
Harristown Development Corporation

*In my mind, creativity can be promoted by conscious efforts
to break the habitual processes people adopt in organizations.
Make sure that everyone gets involved regardless of their job
title or function. Make sure that different ways of thinking and
approaching problems are encouraged. Vary the availability of
resources. It also helps, in my judgment, to surprise people at
the outset with unexpected approaches to the situations they
are being asked to respond to. This helps a manager put a little
"walk" behind the "talk" associated with improving creativity.*

━━━━◆━━━━

I am the coach of a Little League baseball team. For 6 years I've
been managing 6- to 10-year-olds. I am also a senior executive and
CEO directing the development and construction of multi-million-
dollar commercial real estate projects. In the context of this book on
creativity there is no doubt in my mind that I should document my
credentials in this order. As "The Coach," my players surround me
with their enthusiasm and creativity, and make it all the easier for
me to be creative (which, if you have ever witnessed a T-ball game,
you will know is an extremely important coaching asset.) As "The
CEO," however, my project players are often too much the creatures
of habit to recognize the need for creativity.

Creativity is "the defeat of habit by originality," said George Lois.
I think this gets to the point very nicely. For in fact it is the originality
without habit that makes my baseball teams so creative, and the habit
without originality that eats away at the creativity demanded by my
projects. Fortunately, some of my coaching experience has served me
well in coaching my project teams, and in the end I am pleased to
report that creativity does indeed exist in the adult world. Exploring
analogies is one of the time-honored ways of improving creativity.

206

With this in mind, allow me to continue my comparison of management approaches.

EVERYBODY PLAYS!

The rules in my baseball league require that every kid play, and that no kid play more than two innings at any one position. Now I have players with ability and players with heart, and like every great manager I want to win (I tell the kids we are here just to have fun, but I would be lying if I told you I didn't keep score). Some of my players can throw and some can catch, some can hit and some can run, a few can even do two out of four. Unfortunately, baseball requires that they do all four. But a funny thing happens when everyone plays. Enthusiasm begins to make up for lack of ability and, guess what, enthusiasm breeds creativity, and creativity promotes success, albeit sometimes in ways unforeseen.

For example, one year I had a little girl who could run like the wind, and throw like . . . well, like a girl. With the bases loaded by the opposing team, this kid made an unassisted triple play by catching a pop fly and then running down two baserunners who had not tagged up. While Coach Ford was yelling, "THROW THE BALL!!!" she, recognizing her limits, talents, and the opportunity before her, created a surer and better way to get the job done.

In this day of specialization it is hard for us to envision making a place for everyone to play, and allowing people to play different positions, on our project teams. Yet, it is critical that we do. One of the first things I do in my real estate projects is to gather my team and tell them that we will all meet together on a regular basis throughout the entire project. I do this no matter what our agenda from meeting to meeting so that each individual on my team has the opportunity to understand the big picture and the unexpected ways in which they might contribute.

For example, I once hired a young women who was trained as a landscape architect. By virtue of her background, I involved her in a streetscape improvement project primarily so that I could be sure the right trees were selected. Her role was relatively minor in what was to be a 3-year project, but by attending all the project meetings she was able to see how the project players and pieces fit together. She got so enthusiastic about her involvement that I eventually made her my on-site manager. With little or no background in street and utility construction, she convinced both the state transportation department and my own project engineers to drop more than $500,000 worth of unnecessary highway manual requirements by continually showing them pictures of solutions utilized in other places (some of which these same people had previously approved!). I loved it, and it proves to me that it is important to make sure everybody plays.

AND NOW FOR
SOMETHING REALLY DIFFERENT!

Doing something different doesn't necessarily make it creative, but it is a great place to start. One practice, my "boys and girls of summer" just would not run fast around the bases. With the temperature hovering around 95 in the shade, I knew I needed a more creative approach. So, I lined them up on their hands and knees at home plate, told them they were horses in the Kentucky Derby, and that the fastest crawler around the bases would win. The resulting enthusiasm had them crawling around the bases faster then they had been running! After that I kidded them that they couldn't run as fast as they could crawl. With a collective, "Oh yeah, Coach!" they quickly responded to the challenge and proved their Coach wrong.

Similarly, I once had an architect design an overhanging floor at the top of a 15-story hotel I was building. Beautiful, right? Only he forgot about the problem I would have washing the windows on the floors below. A little background is necessary here. You see, windows in tall buildings are washed from a swing stage mounted on the roof and then dropped over the side (the little platform you see the window washer standing on outside your office window). With the overhanging top story, when the stage would be swung over the side, the window washer would be left swinging 10 feet out in front of the building. He would have a great view, but couldn't reach the windows. The project team met and eventually proposed a complicated $200,000 alternative based on their professional habit of turning to window washing companies for a solution. I was not happy! However, it so happened that I had just hired a young guy to head up the hotel's building maintenance department. I explained this problem to him, and in one of those moments when you slap your forehead and wonder why you didn't think of that, he said, "Why don't you just drill two small holes through the overhanging fifteenth floor and drop the swing stage ropes through there?" By the stunned look on my face he incorrectly concluded that he better make this sound more elaborate, so he added, "If you want to, we could make little brass plates to fit over the holes so it would look nice." Total cost for this approach from a different point of view—$575!

WHAT? MY THREE BEST PLAYERS ARE ON VACATION!

Little League baseball teams are, unfortunately, comprised of players with parents who want to take family summer vacations. This can put a severe dent in a coach's ability to field a complete team. Varying resources, however, can also promote creativity. I once played a game in which the other coach and I had a grand total of 12 players between us. We immediately jumped to the conclusion that we would have to reschedule the game. Our kids, however, saw no need for that, and simply proposed that 9 kids go out in the field and the other 3 would bat. After three outs another three would bat, and so on. This struck me as a very noncompetitive solution (remember I like to keep score), but the kids didn't see it as a big enough problem to justify postponing their baseball game.

My window-washing story also illustrates the relationship between creativity and resource availability. The design professionals dealing with my $42-million building didn't think in terms of solutions that cost less than six figures. My building maintenance guy, who had never seen a six-figure budget in his life, was geared to think in much smaller terms for a solution. I have found that adjusting the magnitude of resources available to solve a problem, while at the same time closing off habitual options, frequently promotes creative alternatives that I suspect would never have seen the light of day otherwise.

COACH SAYS LISTEN!

This phrase, used as a variation on Simon Says with my kids, is my way of getting 15 little kids to shut up for a few minutes. I am convinced that the only reason this works is because they think it is part of a game in which if they don't listen they lose. Another variation on this theme is when I tell them to say "not here" when I call the roster off. This backwards approach gets their attention the first time, and I only have to call role once.

With these examples in mind, let me sum up by saying, "Coach says listen!" In my mind creativity can be promoted by conscious efforts to break the habitual processes people adopt in organizations. Make sure there are opportunities for everyone to play, and play different positions, regardless of their job title or official function. Make sure that different ways of thinking about and approaching problems are encouraged. Vary the availability of resources. These are three important methods that I have found useful for facilitating creativity. It also helps, in my judgment, to surprise people at the outset with unexpected approaches to the situations they are being asked to respond to. This helps a manager put a little "walk" behind the "talk" associated with improving creativity.

As a coach of a kids' baseball team I look forward to the creative environment that emerges every season. As adults operating in organizational structures we seem to lose that environment, and the enthusiasm that goes with it. Therefore, we have to make a conscious effort to seek out and promote opportunities for creative action. If you want to know how good it feels to succeed in leading that effort, before you try it on for size at work, give me a call. I can always use an assistant coach!

29 Creating a Creativity Revolution

DELBERT H. JACOBS *Vice President & Center Manager, Northrop Advanced Technology and Design Center*

Emerging information technologies provide an avenue for utilizing the creative talent of individuals that, to a great extent, allow people to rise above the constraints of bureaucracy and time. The invention of the printing press, radio, TV, computers, and mass telecommunications have gradually quickened the pace and power of information. This remains the key path to creativity and societal progress.

It was easy last fall to make a commitment to provide this essay on Creativity with a due date months into the future. Too easy! St. Patrick's Day is past and Vernal Equinox is imminent. The editor threatens to "get ugly" if inflicted with further procrastination.

POINT 1:
"IT IS HARD TO COMMIT
CREATIVITY TO A SCHEDULE"

But what is creativity, and who says so, and what do "they" know anyway? I guess the shared frustration among both academics and practitioners with basic questions like these is what inspired the development of this book. Well, I'll define it my way, based on my observations and experience. *Creativity* is the accomplishment of a realistic new vision that often integrates elements of science, art, imagination, and practical usage. By this, I mean a synergy of ideas, natural laws, and past and present knowledge combined in new and exciting ways.

The personalities of creators vary to the extremes, but are almost always characterized by vision, enthusiasm, self-confidence, persist-

211

ence, brilliance, and sweat equity. From the Sistine Chapel of Michelangelo to the works of Mozart to the vaccines of Pasteur or Jonas Salk to lasers, micro-circuits, and Bill Gates's software genius of today, these characteristics seem to be nearly always present in creative people and teams.

Nevertheless, creators need creative environments. Given half a chance, they will leave structured comfort to focus on their visionary initiatives. Creative people exist in all cultures, environments, races, and stations of life. But, creativity does not flourish when rigid taboos (whether organizational or cultural) are present. The creative individual or team must be free to search, innovate, learn, fail, and rebound with positive energy. Some appreciation, mentor, or measure of success helps sustain creative energy in periods of adversity. Unfortunately, multiple layers of skeptical managers or worse—committees—wear down, stifle, and extinguish the creative spirit. Unfortunately, this is just what big organizations tend to do. They put a constraining bureaucratic net over the creators to be sure they won't stray too far from committee-derived norms. Of course, the creators don't stray, they just disappear—poof! Nevertheless, I believe creativity can reappear spontaneously when the bureaucratic heat is off, especially with mutual peer encouragement.

POINT 2:
"CREATIVITY IS VAPORIZED
WHEN FORCED TO CONFORM TO
BUREAUCRATIC PROCESSES AND BEHAVIOR"

Undoubtedly, over history, thousands of brilliant creations remained undiscovered and in obscurity for decades, maybe even centuries. I think, however, that the incredible explorative spirit of humankind eventually predominates and frees itself from myopic or totalitarian managements or governments. So how might we stimulate creativity in our increasingly complex and stressful society? What can we do to foster and stimulate our net creative potential? The absence of war? No. Unfortunately, history shows that war inspires creative technologies initially used in nefarious machines. Prosperity? Maybe. Yet, if we're all fat, dumb, and happy then the stress needed to produce sweat equity is unlikely. Education? Perhaps. But, is our school system, reward process, and teaching society capable and supportive of creativity? I score it a C+. Other nations score lower yet, but are working to improve education far harder than we are.

I have a powerful idea I want you to consider that would make it easier for individuals to circumvent the stifling effects of bureaucracies. The idea has been ricocheting through my mind for months, but a venture capitalist recently put it in focus the best. He said the United States needs to create a new "Library of Alexandria" where all the world's tangible knowledge is electronically networked in distributed storage and readily accessible to all in a user friendly environment. *User friendly* means simple access through voice, keyboard, visual, electronic, or tactile data manipulation in a quick, cheap, interesting way. Some kids' video games reflect this, as does the Apple Newton palmtop and many emerging devices. Of course, even if all the information is assembled and electronically available, there would be some ungodly number of specific topics. So, how do we make communication efficient? I think this is where artificial intelligence comes in. Our personal computers must artificially adapt to and anticipate the user's intellectual personality, so with some defining descriptions from us, they narrow and focus the search in the "Library of Alexandria," draw data and correlate information, and organize it into readily assimilable segments of increasing depth and perception. This proliferation of specific information could be sent to each user through millions of soon-to-be available fiber-optic channels and digital data links. This system linkage could responsively and interactively conduit individually tailored information from beyond organizational and national boundaries and place it into the home or office.

POINT 3:
"INFORMATION IS THE STUFF
FROM WHICH CREATIVE SOLUTIONS ARE BUILT"

If we can get the photons, electrons, and binary bits to be presentable, hopefully we could quickly provide necessary information to the creatively inclined. This is where other new technologies come in. Exciting high resolution 2-D flat panel picture displays—and better yet, interactive 3-D virtual image displays—will make the information world come alive to even the most skeptical driver on the information superhighway. Visualization, an important aspect of the creative process, will improve understanding and interest immensely. Also, computer interfaces that link stored information to a modern, global, home computer network are necessary. With this technology, people working at home computers could form, manipulate, examine, store, and modify information and ideas that are personally interesting. This way, information is generated, stored, and received nearest to its best point of origin or application.

My belief is that easy quick access to almost infinite data, as screened by artificially intelligent personal computers, combined with exciting interactive 2-D and 3-D display capability, will result in new levels of individual and team creativity through the synergy of information, talent, imagination, knowledge, inspiration, and needs of the participants.

POINT 4:
"EMERGING TECHNOLOGIES PROVIDE THE MEANS FOR TALENTED PEOPLE TO UTILIZE NEW AND DIVERSE IDEAS IN THEIR QUEST FOR CREATIVE SOLUTIONS"

Because of the magnitude of this modern "Library of Alexandria" venture, it would require champions from the ranks of enlightened individuals, scholars, technologists, businesses, governments, and the farseeing support and active participation of U.S. voters, teachers, students, and entrepreneurs. Alexander and his scholars found this necessary, too, in the society of their era. It is an Apollo Program or Manhattan Project for the nineties. It can and will be done—either soon by a creative U.S. project venture; or eventually and incrementally over time—maybe by Japan, Europe, India, Singapore, or wherever.

If knowledge is power, this accessible compilation of the world's knowledge would surely stimulate creativity at all levels of society. I believe grassroots inventions and innovation would flourish. Time and access barriers would be lifted. Individuals would be freed of many of the bureaucratic constraints that vanquish their creativity. The technology would provide the means, but the accessibility of ideas, knowledge, and information is what will ultimately energize the creative potential of our people and their institutions. Enhanced capital markets, enterprises, hardware and software products, services, recreation, entertainment, and educational breadth and quality would result.

Taken together, my four points argue that emerging information technologies provide an avenue for utilizing the creative talent of individuals that, to a great extent, allows people to rise above the constraints of bureaucracy and time. The invention of the printing press, radio, TV, computers, and mass telecommunications has gradually quickened the pace and power of information. This remains the key path to creativity and societal progress. We can accelerate and adapt it to the betterment of humankind. Let's get together and do it! ▨

30 Creativity in a Large Company
All You Have to Do Is Ask for It

ALEXANDER MacLACHLAN *Deputy Undersecretary for Technology Partnerships—U.S. Department of Energy, and Senior Vice President (Retired), DuPont Research & Development*

Set high expectations; have management that is supportive, especially when things go wrong; bet on committed people—and you get creativity and success. If you behave in the opposite manner by being restrictive, focusing on reducing risk to zero, excluding peripheral investigations by edict, you get what you deserve: stifled creativity and few commercial successes. And watch out for number-oriented zealots. They mean well, but they are deadly to creativity and they ruin businesses subject to change.

To me, creativity means commercial success. Perhaps the word that might be more appropriate for most of the organizational situations we face is *innovation*, but there is no doubt that outright creativity is frequently necessary. Yet, I have never felt a concern about creativity. Creativity always seems to be there when you need it if you have good people in place and if you create the right set of conditions.

In the pursuit of commercial success creativity is certainly key, but running dry on creativity is usually the fault of management, not the people who produce innovative ideas, products, and services. Let me use a few examples from my own experience to illustrate why I think this way. The first two show the negative side, but the second two show how easy it really is to get an organization to "go creative." My position is pretty simple: I believe creativity responds to sponsorship and that is management's job.

Some years ago we had an amazing technology that we expected to revolutionize the production of a major commodity chemical. It promised to save energy, produce purer products, and solve a major environmental problem. Prototypes were developed and potential customers were consulted. Although initial results were spectacular, we quickly discovered that reliability and lifetime-in-use were serious problems that stalled development for years. Suddenly, one of our customers suggested an apparent breakthrough. Our scientists were excited and wanted to investigate, but here is where the story turns sour. By this time our costs were high, progress had been slow, and consequently disillusionment had set in with management; they had reached the scapegoat-seeking phase. Not surprisingly, a directive came down: "Stick to products that got us the lead we have, and do not explore the new approach suggested by our customer."

Often in R&D such a directive would be largely ignored and some under-the-table work would be carried out just from curiosity, but in this case management was inexplicably adamant. They put the fear of God into everyone. So, we did not even run the normal scouting experiments. The implications were not insignificant. The technical people lost not only their curiosity but also their professional integrity. They became like mindless automatons, working harder and harder, even though they knew the route they pursued was fundamentally doomed. I need go no further. We wasted millions, ended up with horrendous patent problems, and burned out a lot of good people. There is a happy ending of sorts. Today it is a good (if mundane) business, but the lost opportunity is invisible, and the human toll is unknown.

My second negative example is similar. Here, we already had a great business, a business we invented . . . but the world was changing. New technology was coming forward, and the creative people in the business wanted to examine the new technology. But, the top guy could not forget how hard-won the current profitability had been, because this business had rough going in the early days. Furthermore, he had just come from a successful stint at closing down a real loser that had taken on a life of its own. He was determined to retain our earnings at their current high level and not repeat the lesson of his former business. Trouble was, he was not able to understand the difference. New technology was an enigma to him. It presented risks he could not deal with and threatened his theories of how to manage safely for the stockholders (in the short term). He could only see the potential for new risky research to damage the bottom line; he somehow could not envision success. His directive to the business was: "Do what you now know how to do and improve it." He insisted on proving the net present value contribution of new products to a degree that allowed no risk. Therefore, we took no risks, and in a matter of 5 years previously hardly noticed competition came to dominate this market. In that period, the market grew in double-digit figures annually and today, more than 10 years later, we are barely a contender in a break-even position.

These first two examples illustrate the power of strong, negative management who fear the unknown. In both cases these managers had generated wealth for DuPont by cleaning up messes. When they were given opportunities to deal with problems, but also to take advantage of change, they failed. Watch out for single-minded approaches! Watch out for number-oriented zealots! They mean well, but they are deadly to creativity and they ruin businesses subject to change.

My comments now turn to the positive. DuPont has much to be proud of as it certainly has benefited from an enormous and rich history of creativity. My two examples are drawn from just the past few years but illustrate the patterns that characterize our history of success and innovation. The conclusion I have drawn after years of being involved in creative enterprises is simply stated: If you want creativity, ask for creativity! Sounds easy, but for some reason it usually seems to be difficult, except when there is a crisis. When there is no other choice but to create or lose something you cannot afford to lose, then you get a crisis and creativity abounds. There is a powerful lesson in that observation.

The recent need to rapidly replace the chlorofluoro compounds with non ozone-depleting substitutes led to fast actions and fast success, so much success that we accelerated the replacement schedule. What happened? Why did this project go so well even though the risks and unknowns were monumental? First and foremost, our top management said, "Let's show the world what we can do. We want to lead in environmental initiatives and we will support you to the hilt. We also believe there is a real opportunity to prosper as a result of solving an environmental problem." We all knew time was short and competition was keen. Getting the right processes patented and running in high yield in an unprecedentedly short time was the crisis for us.

A daunting number of things had to be done fast. Task forces to look at all the current uses were formed. Their job was to identify which products should be pursued first and which ones could be delayed or even foregone. Other groups began to study how we might manufacture new compounds. In an incredibly short time we had creativity everywhere. Novel catalysts were designed; computer programs were invented to calculate physical properties of all the possible compounds to help select the best ones. We invented these computational techniques because we could not afford the wasted time to have all the new compounds made and tested. Groups all over the company came up with ideas and networked with the task forces. Existing pilot plants were commandeered, modified, or jury-rigged. The R&D budget skyrocketed. Crisis after crisis cropped up and was overcome. No one allowed discouragement. In less than 4 years we accomplished what any sane and experienced manager would have said should take a decade, if all went well. The jury on our solution is not yet in, however. It will be many years before we can call this project a commercial success. But, by any standard, it is a human success of admirable proportions and potentially of great benefit to our planet. By all rights, that should lead to commercial success as well.

My second and much briefer example of organizational creativity resulted in DuPont's lead manufacturing position for one of the major ingredients for nylon 6, 6. For years we had known that in principle one could make this ingredient much cheaper from a different set of raw materials. Unfortunately, the chemistry did not cooperate. The reaction we needed would have violated a chemistry law considered inviolable. One of the top executives of the company threw down the challenge to our basic research laboratory. Almost everyone scoffed and chalked up his challenge to one more example of high-level management's wishful thinking. One scientist, however, thought it could be done based on some chemistry he was investigating and, within a short period of time, he startled us all with an amazingly novel solution. He succeeded where many others failed and gave DuPont an elegant and profitable process advantage.

Over and over again I have seen the pattern repeated. Set high expectations; have management that is supportive, especially when things go wrong; bet on committed people, and you get creativity and success. If you behave in the opposite manner by being restrictive, focusing on reducing risk to zero, excluding peripheral investigations by edict, you get what you deserve: stifled creativity and few commercial successes.

So, to summarize: Creativity in large organizations is not a problem unless you make it one. All the gimmicks touted by consultants to expedite creativity are at best occasionally useful. They sometimes lead to success, but the tried-and-true way to accomplish really important things is to provide the atmosphere, sponsorship, and support to excellent, experienced people and get out of the way. Having or creating a crisis that inspires people is also helpful. Good management—with faith in people and ideas—knows how to do this. ▨

31 Creativity by Decree—A New Approach

ISAAC R. BARPAL *Senior Vice President and Chief Technology Officer, Allied Signal, Inc., and Former Vice President, Science & Technology, Westinghouse Electric Corporation*

Can creativity be decreed? Can you expect scientists and engineers to be creative in a business-like environment, such as a corporate science and technology center—as opposed to a university or a national lab? The answer is unequivocally YES. A business-driven technology enterprise, as part of a major corporation, is a do-able and even mandatory approach to modern research and development. Total quality is the only acceptable performance level and in today's world, no other behavior will do.

How do you measure the output of an R&D lab? Are you meeting your clients' expectations for generating usable innovations? What is the ultimate value of your efforts? Does the concept of quality apply to R&D labs? If so, is yours acceptable? Is a central (i.e., corporate) lab justified in today's world? Can we obtain the needed technology from the outside? Why doesn't the lab produce billion-dollar success stories? Why are R&D people not productive in the usual sense, like the rest of us?

Those and other similar questions were asked by my CEO on the day he asked me to become Westinghouse's Corporate Chief Technology Officer. My charge was to attempt to combine business and technology in a more productive way. His idea was to break the mold—for the first time to bring in a person who did not have a traditional R&D background—and make a bona fide effort to answer the questions above in a way that would benefit the company. In this essay I will discuss the first few of these questions as a way of taking a more general view of managing creativity and innovation in a business organization.

Our corporate R&D center was (and is) a magnificent facility where ideas are generated and then slowly, painfully, and with a lot of difficulty, translated into business unit needs. But the process was unnecessarily complex and sometimes even dysfunctional, primarily because of a mutual lack of understanding of expectations and needs between the inventors of innovations and the developers and appliers of those innovations.

Upon my arrival at the Center, an impressive multi-building complex with more than a million square feet of space, housing close to 1,500 people in a "country club" setting (and according to the business unit people, in a country club style of behavior, as well), I was immediately immersed in a new and fascinating world. Although I had the proper credentials and related technical background, I was unprepared for the breadth and depth of technical activities I was to oversee.

How do you tackle such a tremendous task? Where do you start? How do you get the needed support from people with diverse interests without resorting to "brute force"? There are, of course, no text books and few experts (there are many consulting companies who will offer you their services, but few who can really help). Because there are no maps for this sort of creative activity, I would like to use our case to show how we adjusted the work of our R&D lab to the redefined corporate needs of the nineties and beyond.

The first and most obvious issue was not technical performance; it was the lack of a strategic plan—specifically, one that was coupled to business needs. Developing a strategic plan became a first priority. We enlisted the involvement of as many people from the Center as possible, introducing business strategic planning techniques into the lab for the first time. Somewhat surprisingly, these were embraced by the R&D lab members because of their immediate applicability and usefulness. One of the main issues discovered in the plan was the lack of synergism between the R&D Center and the business units, and the need to have a closer coupling between the business unit technology plans and needs and the R&D labs' efforts. That might seem self-evident, but in fact was not the way lab activities had been carried out before. As part of this effort, we streamlined the operation by reducing the number of operating divisions and, most importantly, appointing all senior managers to matrix positions (reporting to the operating divisions as well as to the head of the R&D Center). Although this arrangement introduced new issues associated with matrix management, which required some adjustment, the outcome has been excellent in terms of coordinating creative ideas with creative applications. That, of course, was our main goal.

Another sensitive issue, shared by many other corporations worldwide, is that the administrative head of such a Center is also usually the Chief Scientist—a paradoxical situation. We solved that problem by appointing a world-renowned scientist, already on the staff, as the Corporate Chief Scientist.

Last, and probably of greatest importance, was the issue of the applicability of the Total Quality concept to an R&D environment. Does doing the right thing right—the first time, on time, and on cost—apply to creative environments? Or are we putting undue constraints on creativity and innovation by asking—actually demanding and expecting—scientists and technologists to invent on a timetable? The usual thinking here is that creativity requires unbounded freedom to engage in trial and error. Could we instead get creativity by decree?

It is relatively easy to introduce the concept and practice of TQM on a factory floor. The manufacturing environment lends itself readily to such ideas: You can make specifications, establish parameters, readily measure the output (e.g., Motorola's widely known six-sigma program), and easily measure the cost of nonquality performance. But in a highly complex and sophisticated R&D operation in which advanced degrees and advanced egos abound, introducing the TQM concept was tantamount to heresy: "How can you suggest that we, some of the world's greatest minds, are not doing the best we can?!" On top of professional egos, there is also the issue of lack of familiarity and understanding of the TQM concept in general. The "devil" they did not know was intimidating.

After some predictable false starts, feather-smoothing, and adjustments, we were finally ready for the first ever Total Quality Fitness Review—a well-tested process with excellent results in a variety of business unit applications, but a first for our creative R&D enterprise. The TQFR process uses a senior team of "outsiders" who try to identify issues and suggest critical areas to be addressed by the operation under evaluation. In our case, this process even generated a numerical grade, the value of which is primarily in deciding the areas that need to be dealt with on a priority basis.

The results of the TQFR were clearly communicated to the scientific community in the lab, because their participation was essential for a successful implementation of proposed quality measures. After careful review we agreed on the following measures for TQ at the Science & Technology Center:

- Timeliness of technical and business reports
- Patent disclosures per technologist
- Average overrun on fixed price contracts
- Proposal yield

To enable the center personnel—in every function from the night janitor to the chief scientist—to improve their understanding of the Total Quality concept, however, it was necessary to provide them with the appropriate tools. After an extensive global search and contacts with more than 100 R&D centers, we acquired the rights to the process developed by the Corning Corporation—which, under the leadership of their chairman, Jamie Houghton, has a reputation for being truly "fanatic" about quality. The training modules were adapted to our needs, and for the next year all of the Center's employees attended a 12-hour quality awareness program.

Training is only a part of the process, however; it is more important to convince the workforce that they actually own the operation, whether they are in union-represented positions or are clerical workers or senior technologists. The so-called ownership concept is difficult to introduce because of historical distrust between management and the workforce. Many organizations have experimented with different theories and techniques on this subject, and we again adopted and adapted some well-known concepts, such as QITs (Quality Improvement Teams) to get as many people as possible involved in defining the organizational and operational issues, and recommending to management appropriate implementation ideas. Another major effort encouraged every employee and every organization with whom we had business relationships to accept the "supplier-client concept." To do so meant that each person, unit, and organization needed to define the meaning of the concept for their work.

After 6 years of effort, what have we found? First, that a business-driven technology enterprise, as part of a major corporation, is a do-able and even mandatory approach to modern research and development. By becoming such an organization, both internal and external clients and customers recognize and benefit from the value added, which has led to increases in the amount of support and investment in technology. Second, that total quality is the only acceptable performance level and that in today's world no other behavior will do. And lastly, that the major asset was, is, and always will be the human resources in the organization. That resource is slow to change; but in the end people, even creative people, can adapt and accept new directions, but only if they are an integral part of the change.

Finally, to the most critical question: Can creativity be decreed? Put differently, and more appropriately: Can you expect scientists and engineers to be creative in a business-like environment, such as a corporate science and technology center—as opposed to a university or a national lab? The answer is unequivocally YES, but with the proper caveats, as summarized above. By decreeing creativity, we can add a new dimension to the technological wealth and well-being of the world. ▧

32 Creativity and Innovation
Keys for Preventing Environmental Gridlock

PHILIP X. MASCIANTONIO *Vice President, Environmental Affairs (Retired), United States Steel*

In domains involving the interaction of industry, government, and community, a number of different types of creativity are required. First, there is technological creativity. Second, there is an unfortunate, but nonetheless real, need for corporations to develop political creativity to deal with standards on industry. Lastly, because public image has so much to do with perceived success, industries also need to develop creative public relations and marketing approaches (i.e., perceptual creativity). The scope of required creativity is now much broader than the historical focus on technology.

$\mathcal{T}$here has been a large amount of attention devoted to environmental issues in the past several years, and we can expect this trend to continue through the decade of the nineties. Domestic and global environmental concerns have become deeply ingrained in our culture and, unfortunately, industrial activity continues to be viewed by the public either directly or indirectly as the main polluter of the environment. The trade-offs between the conduct of business and the preservation of the environment constitute a truly difficult problem to balance and indeed require some innovative thought and action to solve. As currently approached, some of the main players in the debate have essentially adopted intransigent positions that threaten to create a kind of environmental gridlock that poses some serious concerns for actually reaching a viable solution. I would like to deal with some of the issues here and at least point out some of the potential arenas for creative action.

ACCOMPLISHMENTS, COSTS, AND CONFLICTS

The steel industry to date has invested almost $10 billion in pollution abatement equipment and facilities. US Steel plants alone have about $1 billion of facilities in place to control air, water, and solid waste contaminants that result from manufacturing operations. Direct operating costs for these environmental facilities involve about $150 million per year, so our investments and costs are substantial. They are also successful, resulting in a 95% reduction of most pollutants from our facilities since the nation's major environmental laws were passed in the 1970s. We have all but eliminated hazardous waste disposal operations on our properties and have either closed previous sites or are negotiating approved closure programs. Residual solid waste disposal has been significantly decreased through facility modernization, pollution prevention programs, and recycle/reuse projects at each plant. Yet, the public perception of our performance does not seem to match our documented progress and activities.

One of the most controversial and poorly understood environmental concerns involves annual reporting requirements under Superfund—the community right-to-know provisions. Each year, we report our total discharge of certain EPA-listed chemical substances into the environment on a corporate-wide and plant-specific basis. Because the report requires the listing of total quantities of chemical substances discharged, irrespective of their concentration or environmental impact, these are perceived by the public to be enormous quantities that pose severe health threats to the community. Media and environmental groups have emphasized these data to gain political and public support for more stringent legislation and regulation. Such tactics have not contributed to actually solving problems of real concern to everybody, but instead have created adversarial relationships.

The Clean Air Act is symbolic of the demands being made on industry for further environmental improvement. In our view, there will be a very high cost in money and other corporate resources to achieve unmeasurable or relatively small environmental or health benefits. These resources also will be diverted from creativity and productivity as a consequence. For example, limited financial and manpower resources for developing new technology for modernization will be unavailable because new Clean Air requirements introduce uncertainty on future needs for compliance.

THE CREATIVITY REQUIRED

The Clean Air Act signals a new era of major environmental activities for the nineties. It will not be sufficient for manufacturing industries merely to attain marginal or substantial compliance with the law. The public is demanding virtual elimination of environmental health risk from industrial emissions even though it is clear that we cannot have a risk-free society. Manufacturers can expect a new wave of environmental legislation with more stringent provisions regulating emissions and discharges, and also demanding waste minimization, extreme energy efficiency, facility modernization, recycling, and theoretical "health risk"-based decisions. Given all these changes, as well as the current atmosphere surrounding the negotiation of environmental expectations, a creative effort will be demanded on all fronts.

In this sort of environment involving the interaction of industry, government and community, a number of different types of creativity are required on the part of our industry. First, there is the obvious creativity involved in coming up with the necessary technology and procedures to handle the more stringent provisions of additional legislation (i.e., technological creativity). This is just a new form of perhaps the oldest creativity issue—the invention of new technologies for dealing with a difficult problem. Second, there is an unfortunate, but nonetheless real, need for corporations to develop the political creativity required to deal with efforts to impose ever more strict and potentially unreasonable standards on the industry. We seldom discuss this side of creativity publicly, but because dealing with environmental issues is by nature an interactive process of negotiation, it is also by nature a political process. If politics is the "art of the possible," it is necessary to find creative ways for industry to negotiate on this playing field. If we do not, we will not be able to maintain our industrial health. Lastly, because public image has so much to do with the perceived success of environmental action by industry, industries also need to develop creative public relations and marketing approaches (i.e., perceptual creativity). That type of creativity is not just PR; if perception is reality, and it often is, then having the public recognize and appreciate the industry's activities might spell the difference between success and failure.

To prepare for this environmental "Third Wave," moving beyond command, control, and compliance, U.S. Steel initiated several years ago an ambitious program not only to achieve and maintain compliance but to make a positive improvement in the public perception of our environmental commitment. There can be no doubt that continued efficient and cost-effective operation of our facilities will require cooperation, understanding, and support from all employees, neighboring communities, government agencies, and political officials. Our environmental programs include many items that involve total environmental quality management (TEQM) and voluntary activities beyond normal regulatory requirements. These include:

1. Employee environmental training programs to encourage innovative and creative ways for employees to think about and act upon environmentally related issues.

2. Community partnership efforts. No industry solves environmental pollution problems alone. It requires collaboration with affected parties.

3. Solid waste management plans for each of our steel plant facilities to develop landfill sites for residual waste disposal. We are examining the potential for partnerships to enable us to employ the best technology for management of wastes.

4. Greenbelt and wildlife habitat programs to enhance plant appearance and to utilize surrounding properties in an environmentally attractive way.

5. Programs to reduce the generation of wastes, and for their disposal.

6. Installation of new technologies to improve yield and energy efficiency, and to reduce pollutants.

All of these initiatives constitute innovative approaches to dealing with the environmental issues in their own right. Yet, this effort will demand even more innovation and creativity, not only on the part of management and employees, but also on the part of communities, government agencies, and even our traditional opponents. The scope of required creativity is now much broader than the historical focus only on technology.

CREATIVITY AS A CONSENSUAL EFFORT

In a time when demands for new facilities and modernization strain the capital availability of our operations, it is difficult to allocate our resources for all of the environmental projects that appear necessary to fulfill our objectives. We must encourage creativity on everyone's part to develop cost-effective approaches, because the rapidly escalating cost for environmental action could easily erase the margin of profit in steelmaking. Environmental issues imply that the future will not be business-as-usual. The old ways of doing things no longer apply. That means that innovations are required not only in technology, but in techniques and systems as well. That can only be achieved by instilling a sense of the need for creative thinking in management, employees, and the community of people and organizations affected by our operations. We need the cooperation of government, communities, and political activist groups in seeking balanced, creative solutions to multifaceted issues if we are to be successful.

Environmental gridlock is unacceptable to industry and the public alike. Economic growth and environmental progress will require combining elements of technological, political, and perceptual creativity to provide the keys to free us from gridlock. ☒

33 Creativity in Government

WELLINGTON E. WEBB *Mayor,*
City and County of Denver, CO

Government creativity is not an oxymoron. Creative people in government can overcome the odds and be creative in any situation or environment. Our challenge in government is to create an atmosphere where people don't have to use up their creativity fighting the system. They need to be encouraged to use their creativity to do their jobs and serve their residents the best they can.

⊶⊷

As people's trust in and respect for their government continues to diminish, creativity to provide the goods and services our constituents demand becomes absolutely necessary. Unfortunately, this also often leads to further alienation of the public as government officials use their creativity to get around requirements that have been put into place to force uniformity and to attempt to separate politics from professional governance.

I have a number of friends and associates in the private sector who believe *government creativity* is an oxymoron. They are convinced that government either attracts people who inherently are not creative, or that governmental systems beat the creativity out of creative people. I disagree. I have worked through the years with many thoughtful and creative government employees. Unfortunately, government systems often encourage creativity more to get around the spirit of rules and regulations than to provide innovative product or service delivery. The systems that are cited as villains most often include government personnel systems and government procurement systems.

Civil service was established to stop patronage hiring and to ensure that only people with the qualifications to do government jobs were hired. Unfortunately, from those lofty goals emerged systems that, in many cases, have proven to be slow and unresponsive to the needs of their clients' (the government agencies that operate within their rules) needs. Any bureaucrat worth his or her salt knows many ways to circumvent the personnel system to hire who he or she wants in a much more timely fashion than strict adherence to the personnel rules would allow.

Similarly, governments installed elaborate purchasing systems to stop real and perceived abuses of buying goods and services at inflated prices without giving opportunities to the business community at large. In practice, however, the system became cumbersome and unworkable in many cases and ended up freezing out some of the people it was intended to benefit, because the cost and complexity of working within the framework of government purchasing made it impractical for smaller vendors to even try to participate. Much as with personnel, the historical lore of creative bureaucrats finding ways to push the envelope of purchasing rules is quite enlightening. Whether by breaking contracts into smaller pieces or finding ways to get someone else to pay for something, people in government have used their creativity to get around procurement rules.

These and other instances illustrate how and where government employees have creatively usurped the spirit of rules while clinging to the letter of them. I firmly believe that their motives have overwhelmingly been positive. In my 20-plus years of experience as an elected official and political appointee, however, I have always been struck by how much effort and creativity employees have had to utilize just to try to get their work done. I have marveled at how creative people have been at every level of government getting around requirements that probably didn't make sense in the first place. I've often reflected on how much more value we would receive for our tax dollars if we could find ways to eliminate onerous operating restrictions on government officials and unleash their creative genius. Unfortunately, that brainpower typically focuses on how to work within the letter of unwieldy but well-intentioned requirements rather than on how to meet the needs of our real customers in the most efficient and cost-effective ways possible.

The challenge for governments and the people who run them is to reestablish the trust of the people who pay their salaries so that flexibility is returned to government managers. Without enough flexibility to be able to operate programs in the most efficient ways possible, we will continue to see government use its best creative instincts to get around red tape instead of solving problems.

The other most significant barrier to creativity functioning positively in government is not restricted to government, but is a function of size. My experiences have shown me that in large bureaucracies, be they public or private, organizational culture is often not conducive to creativity. If the culture of an organization is to take the safe path and to avoid risk at any cost, creativity will be stifled. Similarly, when big organizations maintain their present systems and procedures because they have always done it that way, creativity will be discouraged instead of encouraged.

My creativity is driven by two things. First, an inherent belief that you can accomplish anything if you work hard enough. And second, an intellectual desire to be able to solve problems and create solutions regardless of how difficult they may be. Sometimes my most creative solutions are in response to being told no.

The fact that being creative in government, outside of working the system, is difficult doesn't mean that it doesn't happen. In my own career I have always tried to use creative thoughts and ideas to turn any situation into a positive that is in my favor. When I was elected Mayor of Denver in 1991, I was overwhelmingly an underdog who was having trouble raising money and being taken seriously by the media. Instead of looking at the things that are traditionally done in campaigns, I did the opposite. For 21 straight days, I put on a pair of running shoes and walked everywhere. Citizens of Denver put me up in their homes. I met and talked to the people of this city and ignored the events that were tailored for campaigns. I snuck up from behind and eventually won the election with 58% of the vote. A traditional response would have gotten me nowhere. A creative response helped me to realize my dream.

Similarly, from a program standpoint, I have looked for creative ways to accomplish my goals. I have always believed that job creation and economic development are accomplished through a steady sustained effort in which government is a partner to business instead of an adversary. Rather than approaching economic development from the standpoint of luring companies to Denver and Colorado with tax incentives or cash payments, I have taken a different and more creative approach. I've worked to accomplish my economic development objectives by streamlining government requirements and creating an atmosphere where businesses feel welcome. Similar to the sayings, "You catch more flies with honey than vinegar," and "Actions speak louder than words," my philosophy has been to create partnerships for economic development and give all businesses the same economic opportunities. It's a different way of looking at things, but one that has worked well for me both at a state and city level.

Creative people can overcome the odds and be creative in any situation or environment. Our challenge in government is to create an atmosphere where people don't have to use up their creativity fighting the system. They need to be encouraged to use their creativity to do their jobs and serve their residents the best they can. ▧

The Challenge of
Reinventing State Government

JOHN ENGLER *The Governor of Michigan*

*Business and government alike learned to tighten their belts and do
more with less. Successful business people understand the bottom
line. They do not let spending get out of control. They rightsize and
reorganize where necessary. They exercise restraint and give the
bottom line the grudging but necessary respect it deserves. Such
restraint does not stifle creativity; it encourages it. Even in a
prodigal age such as our own, necessity remains, as ever, the
mother of invention.*

If Michigan's state government were a corporation, it would rank
24th in the *Fortune* 500. A colossal organization, its revenue totals
almost $21 billion, putting it ahead of such corporate giants as
PepsiCo, Eastman Kodak, and Dow Chemical. In effect, as Governor
of Michigan I am the chief executive officer of one of the largest
human enterprises ever created. Creativity is an important component of any attempt to reform such a huge organization. Unfortunately, creativity is often limited in state government because organizational inertia and publicly sanctioned opposition make it almost
impossible to reach consensus over significant changes. In Michigan's case, however, a fiscal crisis created a climate in which state
government could be "reinvented."

CRISIS GIVES BIRTH
TO OPPORTUNITY

When I was elected as Michigan's 46th governor in November
1990, a massive fiscal crisis existed. The problem had been long in
the making. During the 1980s, Michigan's population remained

relatively stable, yet state government spending rose at twice the rate of inflation. State employees were paid at a rate 11% higher than inflation. Government employment increased by 5.6%, until there were some 66,000 individuals on the payroll. The results were predictable. Despite Michigan's constitutional requirement to maintain a balanced budget, 1990 ended with a projected $1.8 billion budget deficit and a debilitated economy.

By the time I took office in 1991, the handwriting was on the wall. State government in Michigan was too large and was beset with serious management problems. We had to devise an action plan that would bring people with different vested interests to the table. We had to present a vision of Michigan in a highly competitive global marketplace and cultivate a spirit of give-and-take, of compromise. For as Edmund Burke said, "All government—indeed, every human benefit and enjoyment, every virtue and every prudent act—is founded on compromise and barter."

It was time to revisit the very purpose and functions of the state government. To open the channels for discussing creative action, we went through a simple, three-step process:

1. If a government service or regulation is no longer necessary, it should be eliminated.

2. If a particular service is necessary but can be performed more efficiently and effectively at the local level or in the private sector, it should be privatized. To this end, artificial barriers to contracting out state services had to be eliminated; but state employees should, where appropriate, be given the opportunity to "bid" against private contractors.

3. When the function is necessary and can only be performed at the state level, then we must be absolutely intent on eliminating duplication and functional overlap to assure that taxpayers receive the maximum value for their dollars.

Creativity is filled with ambivalence. It is ironic that to create one thing, another must pass away. A new plant cannot sprout without "destroying" the seed. The birth of the new entails the passing of the old. In politics this occurs when a new administration is voted in to undo or redo what its predecessors had attempted. When I took office my mandate was to challenge the status quo, streamline government, and restore people's trust in their government. The most visible way to address this mandate was to find a way to rein in runaway spending. Consistent with a vision of a leaner, more efficient government, we trimmed 17% of our Executive Office staff positions and decreased total expenditures for salaries by 29%. In addition, we abolished an entire department whose functions could be incorporated by other departments. From these initial steps we were ultimately able to reduce the total number of state employees from 66,000 to 61,000.

The results? As of this writing, the Great Lakes State is experiencing an impressive economic rebound. There are more people working in Michigan than ever before, more than 4.3 million. In 1993 our unemployment rate was at or below the national average—the first time that has happened since 1966. Over the past 12 months, Michigan's job growth has been three times the national average, and our workers' income is rising at a faster rate than the nation's.

These numbers have translated into real savings. For the first time since 1978, we are debt free and owe the federal government nothing on our unemployment insurance. Also, the financial world has responded extremely favorably to our rightsizing and reorganization, and has put our state on firmer financial footing than had been the case for many years. To cite just one example, *City and State* magazine's eighth annual financial report saw Michigan improve from 43rd to 28th in its rankings, a gain of 15 states. The changes that led to these results were not easy to accomplish. They required a clear vision: to rightsize state government, lower taxes, and reduce burdensome regulations. We also needed to make tough decisions and significant sacrifices to realize this vision. But Michigan is in better shape today as a result. We have sent an unequivocal message that we are serious about improving our state's economic climate.

CREATIVITY THROUGH
SHARED VISION AND ACTION

The creative reorganization of a colossal enterprise like Michigan's state government requires a focused vision. As we examined our situation, we saw that it was time to stop viewing state government as a series of quasi-independent fiefdoms. Rather, we had to reconceive state government as an organic whole—view it as one government with one unified management system. The pursuit of this end required many creative acts.

For example, the state employees' labor unions presented a particular set of challenges and opportunities. The Office of State Employer has bargained voluntary agreements that are creative in the public sector and unique in the nation. We have placed an emphasis on superior performance by state employees by relating compensation, and to a certain extent seniority, to outstanding work. Furthermore, we abandoned the "entitlement" theory of compensation for state employees. It was necessary to relinquish the notion that state employees' compensation increases should meet or exceed increases in the Consumer Price Index, regardless of performance, the labor market, or the state's financial condition.

The State of Michigan and a coalition of state employee unions affiliated with the Service Employees International Union (SEIU) reached a 3-year wage agreement that provided for modest direct wage increases and for "incentive" wage increases tied to controlling the costs of group insurance. This landmark agreement has been a major step forward in building a new labor-management partnership. Rather than arguing over the rising cost of benefits for state employees, we have agree upon mutual incentives for labor and management to control these costs. Where public service is concerned, that's creativity at its best.

The SEIU agreement is particularly significant because it shows how an atmosphere of crisis helped us discover creative means for reinventing state government. Maintaining the status quo in our state was not an option. We faced an unprecedented fiscal crisis. The SEIU locals understood this. They were willing to accept change and to take risks. As a result of this spirit of cooperation, we have been able to begin a new chapter in management-labor relations.

Frightened by the pending fiscal crisis on the one hand, and encouraged by our vision for the state's future on the other, agencies were motivated to seek creative avenues for change. One of the most fruitful solutions to emerge has been government partnerships. In particular, several notable partnerships have been formed to address one of our most pressing problems, welfare reform. As of January

1991, 1 million of Michigan's 9 million residents were on welfare. Michigan taxpayers were paying almost $200 million per month to people in need. Pause for a moment and reflect on how much money $200 million is—that's real money with real consequences. The time had come for reform: Michigan was caught in a vicious circle. With a poorer business climate there would be even higher unemployment, which would make even more people dependent on welfare in the future, which would make our business climate poorer still.

The first step toward improving our situation was to reduce the state's role in the welfare system. Applying the same three-step decision process described previously, my administration decided to eliminate Michigan's General Assistance program. By doing so, the state began weaning 83,000 able-bodied adults who were without children from government support. They were still eligible for food stamps and other forms of assistance, but they were no longer going to live exclusively off Michigan taxpayers. Many of these individuals have taken advantage of Michigan's dramatically improved jobs climate and are now self-sustaining members of society.

In order to replace, and hopefully enhance, the level of support previously provided by the state, we enacted other changes by looking beyond government and finding partners to help us carry out our reforms. We used the governor's office as a bully pulpit and initiated programs to empower local groups, neighborhoods, and communities to do more for the needy. In Michigan, we have forged partnerships in three areas. The first is in the nonprofit sector. To help the homeless, one of our most successful partnerships to date has been with the Salvation Army. Because of this partnership, no one in Michigan need spend the night without shelter. We have also forged partnerships in the private sector. One pioneering example is a joint venture with a pharmaceutical company, enabling the state to provide free vaccines for every child in Michigan. In addition, our efforts to involve the news media, including the Detroit Newspaper Agency, as a broker between government and the private sector is giving communities across the state access to new ideas and resources to help individuals and families in need.

A third partnership has been forged with the clients themselves. This joint effort is the highlight of our new "Social Contract"—a pledge on the part of aid recipients that they will take steps to become independent and strengthen their families. These steps include finding work, taking classes, participating in job training, and volunteering in their community. The system can change and must change because everyone in our society can contribute to our society.

GOVERNMENT'S BOTTOM LINE

In the early 1990s, America came through a recession that taught organizations tough lessons. Business and government alike learned to tighten their belts and do more with less. State governments are finally learning what they should have known all along, that our citizens are customers; our taxpayers are clients. For all the sacrifice made by tax-paying working people, our citizens have the right to demand that government deliver the highest quality, most efficient services possible. This is not only a fiscal, but a moral, imperative.

Successful business people understand the bottom line. They do not let spending get out of control. They rightsize and reorganize where necessary. They exercise restraint and give the bottom line the grudging but necessary respect it deserves. Such restraint does not stifle creativity; it encourages it. Even in a prodigal age such as our own, necessity remains, as ever, the mother of invention.

When dealing with an organization as colossal as state government, there is no question that creative reform is difficult, both for clients and for government agencies. Yet Michigan's recent experience shows that it is possible. Not that "the system" can be transformed overnight; there will always be defenders of the status quo, and they will resist change at every step. Public servants can, however, work together in a spirit of good will. They can share a clear vision through all the twists and turns and frustrations of debate. They can be open to ideas that unexpectedly surface in the heat of the moment. In the search for good ideas to implement, we are doing nothing less than living up to our end of the bargain in one of the most significant contracts of all—the contract between citizens and their elected representatives. ▧

35 Creativity Today

GEORGE HEARD *Vice President, Engineering and Construction, Coors Brewing Company*

Creativity in business is the domain of groups rather than individuals. The major management challenges associated with improving creativity in organizations center on group leadership, group dynamics, and group rewards. The combined efforts of management and employees leading, organizing, and rewarding team effort can provide the opportunity for people to experience the emotional reward of creative task completion.

◆━━━◆○◆━━━◆

*T*hinking about creativity in business often brings forth images of the early pioneers of American industry, working in solitude in their laboratories with a lightbulb or a crude telephone on their workbench. Of course, many important inventions are occurring today, but they may not be as visible as were the inventions of transformational household items like the lightbulb or telephone. Many inventions that improve our lives are obscure and seldom encountered by the general public. Take, for example, the aluminum can currently used to package soft drinks or beer. Several hundred patented inventions are employed in the process of making an aluminum can. Coors pioneered many of these innovations in the late 1950s and continues to work on perfecting them.

For the most part, I believe that the image of the heroic individual inventor has outlived its usefulness in modern organizations. It should come as no surprise to managers if I suggest that creativity in business is the product of a group rather than the domain of the individual. In organizations, groups accomplish the majority of tasks. Therefore, the primary challenge facing managers who are interested in creative business solutions is to provide leadership that inspires creativity in a group context. Managing interactions and motivations among group members is central to this challenge. Relying on the

239

metaphor of the lonely inventor makes consideration of these processes a moot point and may help explain the difficulties many firms have encouraging creativity.

The major management challenges associated with improving creativity in organizations center on group leadership, group dynamics, and rewards. Managers of sports teams share many of these same challenges. The fact that winning coaches can go from team to team and constantly produce winners is testimony that leadership has a great effect on the performance of a team. Also, a proper team atmosphere fostered by productive interaction can greatly improve individual performance. Rewards are perhaps easier to administer in sports settings because there are comprehensive sets of statistics available for study. There is also a scoreboard. The teams and fans always know the score and the time remaining (if only appraisal systems could be this simple!). Pursuing this analogy a bit further, it is crucial for a team to possess a balance of skills if it is to succeed. Putting together a baseball team with nine people specialized as catchers will, of course, not produce a winning team. The various members of a team need to possess the range of skills necessary to play the game. In business settings, too many experts from a particular discipline may be detrimental to a group's interactions when coalitions develop advocating different solutions. This conflict often bogs the team down in details and dispute. A balanced team of focused individuals will outperform a collection of brilliant individuals whose skills do not complement each other and who are uncommitted to the end result. These analogies provide an interesting point of departure for discussing the challenges managers face when they search for creativity.

The first challenge I mentioned was leadership. Within a group there will usually be an official leader selected by either an informal or formal process. Aside from coordinating the activities of the group, the function of this leader is to communicate with outside influences. The group's task is likely to be assigned by one of these external influences through their official leader or project manager. The management structure above the project manager is likely to influence the outcome of the group indirectly by providing assignments and funding, rather than through individual behavior modification. Influencing individual behavior is a major challenge facing the group's leader. The group leader, with the help of others, must provide the necessary motivation to keep the overall effort on a positive course. The best motivator is positive reinforcement. One way a leader can improve the reinforcement dynamics within a group is to avoid having members intermingle with others outside the group who may provide conflicting reinforcements. This can be accomplished by keeping the group closer together physically, thus facilitating communication and mutual reinforcement among group members. Of course, when individuals play a part-time role in the group's efforts the management of the overall effort becomes more complex.

Managing both the complexity of the group's task and the complexity of the group's interactions is likely to require some measure of creativity. Dynamics among groups can also become an issue when a problem requires a complex solution composed of the products of several independent creative groups. In this case, a Project Manager is often necessary to serve as a superordinate leader who coordinates and facilitates multiple groups working on a single project.

I believe that group dynamics provide the greatest motivation to creativity. Individuals respond to attention from others and to the general atmosphere of the group. For a group to accomplish a task, there are usually several individual steps to complete, each of which requires a solution. The group may choose to struggle with each step of the solution as a whole (by brainstorming, for example) or delegate individual tasks on a volunteer or assignment basis. Obviously, there is a higher probability of success when the diversity of skills and abilities possessed by groups members closely matches the complexity of the task at hand.

Some people tout compensation as a prime consideration for motivation. Yet, in the hierarchy of motivators, money has a rather ineffectual influence on creativity. Adequate compensation is a requirement to obtain individuals with certain skills, and the free market system determines the rate at which each individual will provide services. Bonus, profit sharing, and other incentives for successful completion of tasks provide additional means of compensating employees. In the team concept, however, reward systems need to avoid the competitive orientations fostered by individual rewards and emphasize the collective behaviors demanded by group rewards.

To foster creativity, a reward system must endeavor to make *group members* feel like winners, rather than separate the "winners" from the "losers." In the industrial setting the win/lose determination is somewhat more difficult to figure and the rules of the game are infinitely more complicated.

A final consideration for managers is time. Teams should have life cycles. The initial rush of enthusiasm and dedication to purpose is important. Celebrations associated with the progress of the project can help establish an emphasis on success. Periodic team reviews regarding progress on the overall project can help highlight the accomplishments and deficiencies of the team. However, assignments must have definite time constraints. Otherwise, projects will drift with no sense of urgency. Just as there is great excitement at the beginning and at the end of a big game, the same excitement can exist at the beginning and end of the team life cycle. There is an emotional reward waiting at the end of a successful project that makes all the extra effort, long hours, sacrifice, and conflict worth what went into making it happen. The stimulus experienced from creativity is very powerful. Society could solve many of its chemical stimulus problems using these techniques.

The challenges of managing creativity associated with building, leading, and rewarding groups are necessary for companies, and indeed industries, to face. As we have seen, companies and industries that fail to provide services over the long term ultimately vanish. Creativity can be associated with improvements and efficiencies within a particular technology, or creativity can produce new technology that completely replaces another. Especially when seeking a radically new, transformational technology, a company needs visionary leadership to make task assignments that will ultimately merge to provide ideas that ensure the continuation of the business. The creative solution that saves the company will reflect the skills of the people, but it is management's responsibility to lead and to organize this talent into creative and effective teams. When the continuation of the business is at stake, the flexibility and creativity of all concerned during this transition is vital. After all, a new technology could produce product lines in other industries, completely new customer bases, and may even make your current offerings obsolete.

Of course, not all of the onus for creative production falls on management's shoulders. Each member of a team has an obligation to the other members and a commitment to his or her own assignment. There is a measure of creativity in each segment of the overall task. It is ultimately the individual's responsibility to complete the portions assigned in a creative and thorough manner. An unpleasant but necessary task of the team leader is to eliminate uncommitted members as early as possible. One rotten apple spoils the barrel.

The combined efforts of management and employees leading, organizing, and rewarding team effort can provide the opportunity for people to experience the emotional reward of creative task completion. The challenge of management is to initiate this. 〽

36 Are You Creating Solutions or Problems?

R. LARRY WUENCH *Director of Marketing,
Mitsubishi Caterpillar Forklift America Inc.*

Creativity has two faces. One is when we succeed in achieving the results we want; the other, ugly face manifests itself in chaos, confusion, and losses of money, market share, and talent. When a company creates a flexible organization where people can grow, products that customers want, and customer preferences that match its unique strengths, it can unleash creativity that causes big problems for its competitors.

---

*We're in a hostile industry; a dilemma quite perverse.
Too many sell; too few will buy, I can't imagine worse.
And we who would survive this hell, we dwell outside the box.
For those within, like roosting hens, are dinner for the fox.*

The trip began early in 1966 when my wife of only 2 years informed me that she thought being a career military officer was a dumb way to make a living. She was right. The ensuing quarter century in marketing at Caterpillar has been filled with success, failure, adventure, and, occasionally, sheer terror. Our biggest gains have usually come when the stakes were highest and the risks of failure were greatest; when someone or some group felt empowered to find a solution and get on with it. We've suffered when we've sat on the fruits of our success until they rotted; when we've lacked creativity!

I've worked with almost every race and religious group on the planet. Our cultural differences are enormous, but the desire to create things of value in our business exists everywhere. We've created flexible organizations that fit the talents and strengths of our employees, products that do exactly what the customer expects, a customer preference for doing business with us, growth opportunities for our people, big problems for our competitors, and above average profits. When we at Caterpillar have been at our creative best, the steps in the process have inevitably been the same, and, more important, in the same order.

Creativity, though, has two faces. One is when we succeed in achieving the kinds of results I just mentioned. The other, ugly, face of creativity manifests itself in chaos, confusion, and losses of money, market share, and talent. Let me talk a bit more about the five steps we try to follow when we seek creative solutions. On the positive side, these steps begin with organizational flexibility and end with profits.

Twenty-five years ago most major corporations were organized around centralized functions: manufacturing, engineering, finance, and sales. Individuals were hired and trained to conform to this fairly rigid structure. They were expected to spend their career within their organizational discipline. When I joined Caterpillar this was the norm, and the company had a respected position of industry leadership. There appeared to be no reason to "mess with success."

But at one point my Peoria office window gave me a view of the faded remains of an old Packard automobile sign. "What happened to Packard? My dad used to tell me they were great cars. Why aren't they still around?" About that same time I began to realize, too, that

244

there might be something lacking, organizationally at least, in Cat's approach to the market. I was the Small Products Marketing Manager, but it had been more than a year since I'd actually seen a small tractor at work or talked to a real customer about what he expected one to do. That simply wasn't how my job was done!

Fortunately, stronger competitors and a fundamental shift in demand from larger to smaller earthmoving vehicles began to push the company toward creating a new decentralized operating environment; one where the head of each product group could fit the organization to people's strengths to get the job done. It was at this point that I joined our Towmotor division, an acquisition we'd made in 1966 and unsuccessfully remodeled to fit our old functional lines. We were known as the "leading edge of the corporate dilemma," but we were free to experiment; to create something better.

In the 12 years since I joined our Towmotor division, not only have we redesigned products and found lower cost sources, we've reorganized and downsized at least six times. Each time we've tried to make the new organizational structure fit our remaining talent and give people more freedom to innovate. We've only been in our current structure for a year and we're already working on other major refinements. Because we have made change such a normal part of our routine, people are no longer "waiting for the other shoe to fall." They have learned that Caterpillars have a lot of feet!

One example of creating organizational change successfully is our lift truck replacement parts business. Previously it had been a division of marketing, then a part of our finance department (I think because they wanted to have something that made money), and now it's a separate profit center. Each change moved us in the direction of providing the freedom to grow in the business and be more efficient. We've created a parts organization that has protected our own machine repair base while we exploited that same base of our competitors. It's been our most profitable and highest growth area.

If creating a flexible organizational approach is the first, most critical step toward creativity, creating products that do just what the customer expects is a close second. It sounds basic. Our customers tell us they want a reliable, durable lift truck—delivered on time at a fair price. Too often in the past, we've been late delivering a truck that leaked, squeaked, and broke down. And we expected the customer to pay a premium for our brand! The only good thing for the customer was that, when it broke, we always had parts to fix it.

Now we've created a new organization with a new culture. We exist to serve the customer. And we've begun to involve customers and dealers at critical steps of the product development process. We have a new, lean U.S. production plant. "Customer satisfaction" is being institutionalized in processes that repetitively collect and analyze our delivery, product reliability, and price relative to our competitors. Our new products still aren't being delivered as fast as we'd like, but their cost is lower and they don't leak, squeak, and break down any more (too bad for the parts business).

A flexible structure that produces quality products is of little use if customers do not perceive our competitive edge. My third step therefore revolves around the notion of creating customer preferences. Companies like ours spend untold time and money trying to convince the customer that somehow we're better than our competitors. The question is: "How can we create a preference that causes the customer to do business with us?" Creative people find real customer needs that fit our company's unique strengths, then focus customer attention on those strengths. For example, our studies had shown that lift truck customers want replacement parts delivered within 24 hours. We knew we could deliver Cat parts, as well as those of our competitors, faster and better than anybody—95% of the time we could deliver a part in less than 24 hours. Unfortunately, customer perception was that "everybody delivers most parts in about one day." Certainly that's what everybody told them. Thus we had no advantage, based on customer perceptions, from what we knew to be one of our unique strengths.

Our solution was to have our advertising people create "Parts Fast—Parts Free," a no-hassle, national awareness campaign with teeth. Our pledge was, "If you order parts for your Cat, or any other brand of lift truck, and we don't deliver in 24 hours, the parts are free!" Some of our more nervous dealers asked us to make the program "valid at participating dealers only." We told them that their ability to meet this standard with our support was a condition of continuing as Cat lift truck dealers. A million-dollar contingency fund was set up for the first year. We paid out less than $50,000 in claims. Parts sales went up and numerous first-time, new truck sales have been attributed to this guarantee. Perhaps the most satisfying thing about our success is that our competitors hate it because they're not able to match our performance.

The fourth step on the road to creativity is to enhance your peoples' skills and motivation by providing challenging developmental assignments. People want to work in roles that match their strengths and where they can contribute and grow. They feel more involved. They see more chances to get ahead, and they accept more accountability for results. That's not just perception, it's fact! When a company adapts its structure to fit employee strengths, it creates more personal growth opportunities. For example, our dealer finance manager, who once reported to my position of marketing director, now works for our chief financial officer. Why? He's a whiz at currency translation and exchange. They needed his background (which wasn't being used when he reported to me). We all agreed his talent could be better used in our corporate finance group and that he could continue to work with dealers. I get a motivated financial assistant with improved skills, the foreign currency job is being done well and, because the job was expanded, he was promoted.

When a company creates a flexible organization where people can grow, products that customers want, and customer preferences that match its unique strengths, it creates big problems for its competitors. Recall the parts guarantee I described earlier and the problems it created for our competitors. We hope they'll find our approach too difficult, too risky, or too expensive to try themselves. They may not go out of business, but they will gradually cease to be a major factor in our market. It's going on right now in our industry.

The message in my fifth creativity step is that once you have an effective organization that serves real customer needs, you have to consciously want to make life difficult for your competitors. Create a relationship with customers that they can't match. Keep the pressure on. Instilling a desire to beat the competition can inspire creativity from unexpected sources.

The result of this step-by-step creative process is the ultimate business creation: profit! Without profits a company dies. With adequate profits, anything is possible. But be forewarned; focusing on generating profit as your first step toward creativity, rather than the last, will lead to ruin. When the creative steps are followed in their proper order, the financial rewards, even in a hostile industry like lift trucks, can be exceptional.

For much of my career at Cat we operated on the old principle, "If it ain't broke, don't fix it!" Today we've turned that principle into a question, "It may not be broke, but how can we improve it?"

37 Organizing for Innovation
From Individual Creativity to Learning Networks

THORALF ULRIK QVALE *Research Director,*
Work Research Institute, Oslo, Norway

Creativity is better construed as an ongoing group, organizational, and interorganizational process that is either facilitated or inhibited by structural relationships. The main enemy of organizational learning and creativity lies in the traditional, bureaucratic organizational paradigm. A participative, "empowerment" strategy that starts in the core production process with the redesign of jobs and technology based on the autonomous work group concept can disarm this enemy.

Creativity is seen mainly as an individual ability that occurs sporadically and unpredictably. Modern competence-based organizations, especially those that compete internationally, must find ways of organizing and managing resources so that creativity and innovation become part of "business as usual." In business organizations today, creativity and innovation are less often the product of individual genius and more often the outcome of proper organizing so that innovation can occur. Innovation should more appropriately be viewed not as an infrequent occurrence implemented through top management action, but instead as a normal, continuous process in which the whole organization as well as selected parts of the external environment are treated as a "learning network." A major issue in this discussion, therefore, is implementing a strategy for developing organizational forms that have the ability to innovate by using both internal and external human resources on a continuous basis. Two key steps are involved.

THE FIRST STEP: INVOLVING INDIVIDUALS AND STARTING AT THE BOTTOM

It is a rather trivial observation that personal involvement and commitment in work are important for helping a person utilize his or her abilities and capacities. Furthermore, the increasing complexity of the challenges and the interdependencies of tasks demand close cooperation between individuals and departments with different competencies and roles. Business innovations often derive from cross-disciplinary teamwork; consequently, R&D departments frequently have been organized as project teams or matrix structures in an effort to mimic key characteristics of innovative organizations. Problems typically occur, however, because other departments or functions still are organized according to the classic bureaucratic paradigm.

The implication of bureaucratic organization is that the individual person and the single, specialized task are assumed to be the primary building blocks of activity, and that coordination is assumed to take place through hierarchical control, vertical communication, centralized decision making, and so forth. In this common paradigm, it is management's job to ensure that new ideas from an R&D team are implemented in the rest of the organization. The usual consequence is that other functions—such as purchasing, production, marketing, and more—are unable to influence, adjust to, and use the innovation without loss of time and money.

Through a series of projects in Norway spanning three decades, we have found that a viable strategy for supplanting bureaucratic forms and implementing continuous innovation is to start in the production function with participative change planning and participative forms of work organization, such as autonomous work groups (this direct link to line management from the start gives a better chance for success than beginning, for example, with a redesigned R&D department). Such changes normally cannot be sustained unless top management gives continuous support to the introduction of new forms as the start of more general change processes in the company. Once new work design ideas have been developed and implemented, the (empowered) employees assume responsibility for management of the work, often coming back to management with problems, ideas, and support from adjacent departments, levels, and functions to further improve production performance and quality of the work environment. A hundred ideas a month is not uncommon in this sort of program. Such ideas can be used as a basis for developing new, collaborative relations across traditional functional and hierarchical boundaries. With sustained top management support a new participative, open, and innovative organizational paradigm encompassing the whole organization develops—in other words, it becomes a learning organization.

THE SECOND STEP: DEVELOPING INTERORGANIZATIONAL LEARNING NETWORKS

In the modern era, a successful, competitive enterprise must develop mechanisms for utilizing external resources (e.g., by learning to work with educational and R&D organizations, working closer with customers, making strategic alliances with other enterprises, etc.). In Norway, for instance, as a way of meeting rising international competition, organizations have for some years tried to take advantage of their flexibility and low overhead costs while looking for ways to compensate for their limited resources and capacities. Although such organizations can go a long way by better utilizing their internal resources, they still need to link up with other organizations in "enterprise networks" to survive.

Enterprise networks tend to develop from one of two starting points: either they start as "business networks" (i.e., joint business ventures sharing contracts), or they start as "learning networks" (i.e., joint training programs stemming from a common felt need for competence development). Regardless of starting point, however, it is necessary to develop the characteristics of both types of networks to survive as a viable network. Business networks must progress toward joint learning networks; learning networks must develop toward business networks.

An example case started as a learning network. A group of innovative, internationally oriented, electronics companies agreed to work together with a local engineering college to develop a better education system for electronics engineers. The companies wanted to help the college improve its program quality because they needed better basic technical education for their prospective engineers. They felt that not only did the curriculum need updating and enhanced quality, but the teaching methods ideally ought to reflect the participative, team-based way of working that was becoming common inside the companies.

Individually these companies had little chance of changing the college to fulfill their needs. As a learning network involving the college, however, their influence was magnified. The desired change was facilitated by the president of the college and a group of action researchers, who saw that more closely linking the school to industry would provide a permanent mechanism for competence/quality development and innovation in the college. A new "sandwich" course was developed; students participated as "apprentices" who worked on corporate projects half the time and attended college the other half.

The enterprises found that the students provided valuable links to the school's teachers, laboratories, library, and external professional contacts. New technology (e.g., a CAD/CAM system) was transferred from the school to industry through the students. In another case, a subset of the companies purchased an expensive electronic instrument and located it at the college where they could share it while also making it available for teaching. The network arrangements were so successful that the new teaching method spread to the other departments in the college, which made similar contracts with other businesses. A more general shift toward problem-based learning (PBL) in the college will take this development even further. It will, if successful, represent a major shift in the school's organization and also considerably enhance the school's ability to learn from its students and their business projects.

To make this interorganizational joint learning network succeed it was necessary for the individual enterprise to learn in practice that it actually was possible to get something useful out of interaction with a public education institution. It was also necessary for the teachers in question to come in direct collaboration on concrete issues with work life in order to see new possibilities that also could serve their own professional interests.

Another effect of this innovation, however, was that some enterprises that got in touch through this project, started to work together in other areas where they discovered joint interests. Some of these were linked to training schemes developed together with other schools, others were business oriented; for instance, a set of small enterprises introducing a joint production scheduling system so that they could use each others' machine tools for their own production.

The joint learning across companies that results from trying out new solutions together tends to emphasize common values and interests. These can be expressed and directed toward the enterprises' infrastructures and processes to further improve internal effectiveness and innovation ability. These examples point out not only the importance of joining external organizations and public education institutions as a means of resource spreading, but more broadly the necessity of engaging in wider interorganizational networks in general in order to set the stage for making innovation an ongoing process.

THE GENERAL LESSONS

These ideas, experiences, and observations suggest that it is misleading to continue to think of creativity in organizations in terms of discrete occasions of individual invention. Creativity is now better construed as an ongoing group, organizational, and interorganizational process that is either facilitated or inhibited by structural relationships. Organizations must organize for innovation. Systematic, continuous innovation in industry is a modern necessity because of rising internationalization and rapid technological development.

The main enemy of organizational learning and creativity (which is rooted in the effective development and use of human resources) lies in the traditional, bureaucratic organizational paradigm. A participative, "empowerment" strategy that starts in the core production process with the redesigning of jobs and with technology based on the autonomous work group concept can disarm this enemy. Continuous top management support gives a basis for changing the relationships between production and all other functions of the enterprise so that a more general, deep-going change in the organization takes place. A next necessary stage needs to be outwardly oriented, however, and aimed at creating alliances and collaborative relationships with other organizations in the external environment. Internal changes toward flexible, participative forms ("lean organization") is a prerequisite for successful participation in interorganizational learning and business networks, which are characterized by a common value basis, trust that is developed through interaction over time, and mutuality in the exchange of resources.

Finally, our experience also suggests that starting with a common felt need for enhanced competence and doing something together creates a basis for more effective later collaborations. Enterprises that enter directly into business collaborations frequently fail, because the conditions for success have not been sorted out. Therefore a business network needs to develop into a learning network rather quickly to remain stable. When it does, however, creativity and innovation become part of the normal conduct of work life. ▧

38 Principle-Based Creativity
Prompting Individual Initiative in Large Organizations

TIMOTHY F. PRICE *Group President,*
MCI Communications Services Group

MCI's culture, based on customer service and individual initiative, provides direction and encourages taking creative action beyond the shackles of traditional roles. Trust fuels the initiative necessary for creativity. A clear, well-communicated mission channels those energies to productive ends. Focused within a principled environment, freedom can foster the creative actions needed to sustain a growing business.

⁂

I have a fairly straightforward thesis regarding creativity in organizations: Creativity occurs when talented people are given a clear goal and freedom to pursue that goal as they see fit. Sound simple? Guess again. Unfortunately, three complexities inherent in modern bureaucracies preclude most companies from following this course: Poor communication of strategic priorities and company performance leads to ignorance and confusion regarding organizational goals; employee talents become outdated as market changes outpace narrowly focused job-related skill sets; and hierarchies, job descriptions, and other legitimate bureaucratic devises combine to diminish personal discretion and individual initiative.

I believe that my experiences at MCI have provided me with several insights that may be useful to managers who wish to avoid these common bureaucratic maladies. Before I present these ideas, however, I feel that I should say a few words about the unique situation that has shaped my experiences. MCI, in part because of fortunate circumstances and as a result of forward-looking management, has been able to create a strong culture that, so far, has allowed us to reduce the severity of the bureaucratic maladies I just mentioned. As a recent start-up company, we had the luxury of establishing an organizational culture essentially from scratch. We took advantage of this rare opportunity by emphasizing core values that facilitated our strategic mission—to provide outstanding customer service in what had previously been a commodity market for long distance communications. I like to think of our culture as a "principle-centered environment" that helps us reduce the bureaucratic "drag" that so often stifles creative endeavors.

Our culture emphasizes two core values, one ends-oriented and the other means-oriented. When MCI was founded with no customer base and no free market pool of uncommitted clients, we knew that each customer had to be earned. Recognizing that, we decided to differentiate ourselves through customer service. Therefore, our guiding strategy, our "golden rule," at all times, in all circumstances, is to provide excellent customer service. Our second principle can be summed up as "how we treat our people." We try to make it clear to every employee, formally through recognition programs and informally through the empowerment they are given, to exercise individual initiative. Taken together this principle-centered culture, based on customer service and individual initiative, provides direction and encourages taking creative action beyond the shackles of traditional roles. It should be obvious that neither principle can be served independent of the other. A strong goal with little discretion produces rigid behavior that cannot serve diverse customer needs, and ambiguous goals with broad discretion suggests anarchy.

Based largely on my exposure to this environment, I have come to believe that creativity emerges when deep-rooted principles meet opportunity to create action. Thus the primary challenge facing management is to impart a single strategic objective—customer service, in our case—through the socialization process and reward system. The subsequent, related challenge, then, is to select and train people with the skills and predispositions necessary to identify and take advantage of opportunities that utilize their creative talent. Limiting the growth of our structure and maintaining our employees' skills provides a context that allows the fruits of our selection, training, and socialization processes to be realized.

Of course, this principle-based approach is based on properly channeled employee discretion. But, discretion requires trust. One must be able to trust the motives and capabilities of others in order to utilize empowerment confidently. My experiences at MCI have shown me that effective communication produces the trust that serves as the basis for empowering employees. Without trust neither of our core values are viable. We must trust that our employees are willing and able to act in the best interests of our customers.

One would think that communication would be less problematic in the "communications" industry. It isn't. We face many of the same problems confronting other large companies. We have, however, employed our own technologies to help overcome some of these problems. We provide every employee, from administrative assistants to the Chairman, with access to a network of electronic mail that puts them in touch with every other employee. I believe that e-mail provides a much more interactive media than suggestion box-type systems. As a result, it can serve as a useful means of building trust and mutual respect. It provides an avenue of direct interpersonal contact—beyond the usual open-door policy—that further stimulates communication, which stimulates thought and unleashes creativity.

Of course, encouraging employees to offer their ideas is nothing new. Interventions akin to a "suggestion box" remain a staple of many shops. The one-way nature of such gimmicks, however, smacks of a bureaucratic, "management knows best" ideology that is ultimately self-defeating because employees quickly come to realize that few actions are taken as a result of their suggestions. These methods do not provide discretion; instead, they tend to breed a cynical, mistrusting culture that serves to insulate and block communications, decisively defeating its own purpose of encouraging individual creative thought. Our internal communication systems have helped us avoid these pitfalls, while at the same time reinforcing our principle of encouraging individual initiative.

Another way of facilitating the communication necessary for coupling our customer service orientation with employee initiative is an absence of bureaucratic layers. At MCI, for example, our customers are no further than six steps away from the President. A flat structure supported by effective communication channels facilitates extensive empowerment. Employees can be given as much power and responsibility to manage their portion of a business as the communication channels can support. Again, responsibility and discretion are underpinned by mutual trust. Trust that allows employees to take initiative and solve problems without fear of retribution for errors. Trust that communicates that the only intolerable action is no action. Trust that exuberantly encourages creativity.

By emphasizing core principles and faith in people, one can rely less on organizational charts and job descriptions, management tools that commonly and unintentionally serve both to cut off interaction and to deter creative action. In a principle-based environment engineers should be able to move easily to sales, finance people to marketing, and so forth, each bringing a varied perspective (but a common goal) to problem solving. Employees and functional areas should be regularly challenged to "think outside the box," to blur the lines of distinction between themselves and others, and to show interdisciplinary motion. Fresh viewpoints coming from nontraditional sources are a powerful and underutilized source of creativity. One saying that we have at MCI that reflects this type of thinking is, "Sales people service, and service people sell." This idea serves us well only because our employees are focused on serving the customer.

One example of how these principles are reflected in action, a particularly harrowing one, occurred when the children of a prominent business executive were kidnapped. To deliver their ransom demand, the kidnappers called the company's 800 number, believing they'd find the protection of anonymity among the flood of calls the company received daily on their toll-free 800 line. The company and authorities contacted MCI for help. The Customer Service representative who received the call had no idea if she could identify the originating phone number among the call records but immediately dove into the task. Working with the company that had taken the call, as well as local and federal officials, the representative identified the originating phone number and its location, resulting in the apprehension of the kidnappers and safe return of the children within a matter of hours.

One thought shaped this employee's action—"the customer comes first." Creative solutions to extraordinary circumstances are much more likely in a principle-centered environment. They are pure examples of a freedom of action that can only be achieved in an environment where the company's underlying values and course are clear. This was not the kind of initiative a company could teach. It was not the kind of responsibility that a company could write into a job description or include in a training program. Instead, it was the kind of personal creative problem solving that can only occur in an environment where the principle "the customer comes first" influences and shapes the actions of all employees.

To sum up: Based on my experience, I have identified five keys to successfully fostering creativity: Hire the best people possible. Trust your people and treat them with respect (trust and respect are reciprocal, you have to give to receive). Flatten the organization and push responsibility and discretion down to the lowest possible level. Provide all employees with easy, constant access to communication channels that ignore traditional bureaucratic structures (e.g., e-mail). Encourage, or require, cross-pollination of functional areas.

If there is an ultimate lesson to be learned from my experiences it is this—trust fuels the initiative necessary for creativity. A clear, well-communicated mission channels those energies to productive ends. Trust is also easier to nurture in an environment where everyone shares an understanding of the organization's goals. I also believe that empowerment makes people more trustworthy because they will tend to reciprocate your good faith. I also realize that trust is easier when you are fortunate enough, as MCI has been, to have a brief and successful history devoid of significant labor disputes, restructurings, downsizings, and the like. Nevertheless, trust gives employees the freedom to try and the freedom to change things for the better. Focused within a principled environment, this freedom can foster the creative actions needed to sustain a growing business. ▨

39 Membranes for Gas Separation
A Case Study in Creativity

WALTER L. ROBB *Senior Vice President (Retired),*
Corporate Research and Development, General Electric Company

A key aspect of creativity is the unpredictability of its paths.
Creativity is often not just a single event or episode; it is sometimes
an unplanned sequence of fortuitous events. Creative success leads
to further creativity, which helps to generate corporate funding to
continue work that initially did not appear to have potential—and
frequently leads to business opportunities. Creative advances might
be as important for providing the impetus for keeping going as they
are for providing the final answer.

⬤━━━━◆◆◆━━━━⬤

$\mathscr{C}$orporate research lab directors are called on more often to judge
the creativity of others than to exercise it themselves. Usually before
becoming an evaluator of creativity, however, a director has experienced for him- or herself the "high" of creative events or episodes that
demonstrate some of the essential features of creativity. Personal
experience with creativity lets you know it when you see it in other
people. One occasion when I felt I was really involved in a creative
act was in the invention of immobilized liquid membranes for gas
separation. I would like to recount that story as a way of making a
few points about creativity in organizations.

As is often the case, this invention was not a single event, but
rather a sort of relay race. It might even be appropriate to call it a
marathon because of its duration; or perhaps an even more appropriate image is the high jump, where reaching one goal simply inspires
stretching the limits and going even further, just to see what would
be achieved.

When the story begins in the late 1950s, I was trying to make pure
boron. Some of the solid-state electronics experts at the GE R&D
Center believed that boron would be the next semiconductor, sup-

259

planting silicon, just as silicon had supplanted germanium. So there I was, a chemical engineer decomposing borane over a hot filament trying to make pure boron, about which the other physicists were getting less and less excited. Just then a world-renowned physicist, Ken Kingdon, happened by and offered a very different proposition. He had heard that the Navy was looking for ways to separate carbon dioxide from oxygen by using membranes to recycle the oxygen in submarines. Kingdon's idea was to make a sort of molecular sieve for separating gases by using alpha particles or beta rays (accelerated electrons) to make holes in polymer.

Kingdon touted this idea to the head of chemistry, who passed it to my branch manager, who turned it over to me. It did not sound to me like a very promising approach, but it did not seem wise to argue with someone as eminent as Kingdon. I decided that the best course of action was simply to do a few experiments. I took a sampling of polymeric films and irradiated them with gamma and beta radiation and then tested their permeability. As I suspected, the permeability was not increased by the treatment. All it did was cross-link and embrittle them. Nonetheless, these results piqued my interest in working with membranes. I did some reading of the work in the area and discovered a paper by Karl Kammermyer, who reported that silicone rubber was 10 times more permeable to gases than any other polymer. It was 5 times more permeable to carbon dioxide than to oxygen, and obviously the thinner the membrane, the more gas would pass through for a given pressure gradient. Unfortunately, silicone rubber, although resisting high temperatures, had poor tensile strength and made lousy membranes.

Some of my colleagues at the R&D Center were among the pioneers in developing silicones and their applications, and I got a great deal of help from them in making thin silicone membranes. No matter how hard we tried, though, we could not make a hole-free sheet thinner than 10 mils, which was too thick for useful separation of carbon dioxide from oxygen. For that, we needed a sheet only about 1 mil thick. We could make sheets that thin—in fact, even thinner—but they always had lots of minute holes in them. So, there was my dilemma in a nutshell. I needed to make a very thin membrane without holes. I could make a membrane with no holes, but it was too thick; or, I could make a membrane that was thin enough, but had holes in it. What to do?

At that point the proverbial lightbulb went on over my head. Why not make two half-mil sheets and bond them together? Each would have holes, but it was very unlikely that the holes would line up with each other. Actually the two membranes could be chemically bonded to each other simply by heating. We tried it and it worked. The resulting membrane was about 5 times as permeable to carbon dioxide as to oxygen, which meant that it could be used in some interesting demonstrations. For example, we used the membranes to build an "artificial gill" around a hamster cage, which when put under water could maintain a concentration of oxygen inside the cage high enough for the hamster to breathe. That little demo brought us a lot of publicity (and the motivation to continue working in the area). Such membranes have been used ever since to cover electrodes in blood gas analysis, a small but profitable business for GE. Nevertheless, the 5 to 1 separation factor for carbon dioxide to oxygen was still not high enough for practical use in air purification.

Seeking a higher separation factor, we tested more than 100 polymers but achieved little improvement. At least we came to understand what was needed: a polymer with high solubility for carbon dioxide. We didn't find one among existing polymers, but we remained optimistic enough to continue the effort. I realized that I could not easily synthesize entirely new polymers. Why not try something simpler? Why not liquid layers, such as monomers, without worrying right away whether a polymer could be made from them or not. I first tried several organic liquids, making thin layers and measuring the permeability through them. This approach did not result in any striking improvement, but it did force me to face the question of how to make thin membranes of materials that were not polymers. We accomplished that by putting the liquid in a porous cellulose sheet; the combination of filter or sheet and the liquid behaved as if only the very thin liquid layer were present.

At this point I had another creative burst. Why not simplify things even further and try pure water? After all, it had good solubility for carbon dioxide, which was the property we needed. We tried it, and a pure water "membrane" gave about the same permeability as silicone rubber. Then I added a little caustic to increase carbon dioxide solubility and got some marked improvement. One of my colleagues, Herman Liebhafsky, knew from research on fuel cells that a cesium hydroxide solution dissolved a lot of carbon dioxide, so he recommended that I try that. It made a big difference, giving separation factors as high as 1,000 to 1.

About this time I became a branch manager. A chemical engineer in my branch, Bill Ward, took over the work. He studied the permeation of carbon dioxide and oxygen through bicarbonate solutions and the results were even more startling. Separation factors were now a few thousand to one. At this point I suggested that Bill talk to a physicist, Charlie Bean, who had an encyclopedic knowledge of both the life and physical sciences. Bill described his results to Charlie, who mused on the problem and said, "That sounds like facilitated transport," which is the carrier transport mechanism operative in the transport of oxygen in aqueous hemoglobin solutions. The process was well known to biologists—but not to chemical engineers!

From here Bill Ward saw the huge potential of the process and created a new research area for chemical engineering: facilitated transport in membranes. He learned that the carbon dioxide transport was reaction-rate limited and could be increased by the addition of catalysts to the liquid film. He developed an immobilized film of an aqueous bicarbonate-carbonate solution that was 4,100 times more permeable to carbon dioxide than to oxygen. His work marked the beginning of an extensive area of research and invention that continues to be very active to this day, and that has provided the impetus for several companies around the world to develop practical membrane-based oxygen enrichment systems.

So my "aha!" insight of gluing the two membranes together turned out to be only a footnote to the membrane story, rather than the final product. But perhaps the entire story does underline one aspect of creativity: the unpredictability of its paths. It would have been impossible for even the best research manager to plan the sequence of events that occurred. If I had not responded to Kingdon's original suggestion about making holes using radiation, I might never have looked up Kammermyer's article. If I had not read that article I might not have tried silicone membranes. If I had not achieved success with the laminated silicone membranes I might never have tried liquid membranes. If liquid membranes had not succeeded, Bill Ward might never have gotten started on his ultimately successful research. All this suggests that creative advances might be as important for providing the impetus for keeping going as they are for providing the final answer.

There is a final twist to this creativity story. It turned out that there was a very interesting way to make fine polymeric filters using holes made by radiation. It was invented in our laboratory by a group of physicists not very long after my unsuccessful experiments. It makes use of the phenomenon of particle track etching and is widely used today in applications ranging from medical research to brewing beer (it is not, however, used for gas separation; the holes are not small enough). Although it came at about the same time as my result, its inception had nothing at all to do with my work or Kingdon's suggestion. The inventors of particle track etching did not even know about these, even though we were all in the same laboratory. Particle track etching grew out of an independent, and erroneous, idea for studying the age of meteorites!

My own case leads to several conclusions about creativity in organizations. First, creativity is often not just a single event or episode; it is sometimes an unplanned sequence of fortuitous events. Second, creativity usually involves other people directly or indirectly, and sometimes they come from other departments or even outside the company; they bring divergent insights to bear on problems that converge on the interests of the company. Third, creative success leads to further creativity, which helps to generate corporate funding to continue work that initially did not appear to have potential—and frequently leads to business opportunities. I would like my last words about creativity to be these, however: Working toward a goal can help creativity, but trying to predict or control the paths that link creative acts to useful results may do more harm than good. ▧

NORMAN P. FINDLEY *Vice President, Domestic
and International Marketing, Coca-Cola Enterprises*

*On Job Creativity (OJC) has many advantages over retreats and
the like. For one thing, it is more timely. OJC can be tapped any
time a problem arises. It doesn't need to wait until the next
off-campus meeting. OJC also is more plentiful. It isn't produced
only during the 1 or 2 weeks allocated for strategic planning
meetings. OJC can be obtained from any member of the
organization, not just from those invited to the off-campus session.*

Every year, thousands of executives travel hundreds of thousands of miles to remote or exotic locations. They go for strategic planning meetings or for experiences such as Outward Bound, to help break down the barriers to creativity that have been successfully built back at the office. These sessions have their place, but to really stimulate creativity we also need to break down those barriers at the office.

"OFF-CAMPUS" SESSIONS CAN WORK

During 1984, word was spreading through the soft drink industry that Pepsi Cola was preparing to reformulate diet Pepsi by changing its sweetener to 100% Nutrasweet. The senior marketing team of Coca-Cola USA was at a strategic planning meeting in Tempe, AZ. The group quickly agreed that because of the market leadership of diet Coke over diet Pepsi, diet Coke should also switch. The problem, given the huge volume of diet Coke, was that it would be months before enough Nutrasweet would be available to make the change.

The Sprite brand director (who was not responsible for diet Coke) said that it was too bad that we could not get a small quantity of diet

Coke with 100% Nutrasweet to every retailer in America, to let them know it would be arriving shortly. The marketing operations manager suggested a barter arrangement with Federal Express in which diet Coke would produce an ad that said Federal Express was the choice of diet Coke to get its new taste to retailers "Absolutely, Positively, Overnight." The diet Coke brand director felt he could develop the ad in a way that would also tell consumers that an improved diet Coke was on its way. The project was tasked out and groups were dispatched to ensure that enough Nutrasweet was available, that Federal Express was a willing partner, and that all the other details to make the campaign successful were worked out. Roger Enrico, who at that time was President of Pepsi Cola USA, later complained that "100% aspartame diet Coke was 4 miles wide and an inch deep." In other words, the idea worked.

The off-campus strategic meeting environment helped it work. Were it not for that meeting, all the players who contributed to the idea would not have been together and could not have built upon one another's ideas. It is likely that the Sprite brand director would have been too absorbed in his own business to develop the original idea. He also might have felt that he was "butting in" on someone else's turf. Implementation was sped up by the fact that everyone at the meeting was asked to forgo their normal responsibilities and focus on this one problem.

Two things that made this particular meeting work were an open and cooperative attitude among all the players, and the emergence of a real issue to address. The biggest problem with off-campus creativity sessions is timing. Had there not been a strategic planning meeting going on, the problem might not have been addressed. Had there not been a problem, however, the meeting might have been a colossal waste of time. Telling people to "go away for 3 days and be creative" is more likely to succeed if they have something to direct their creative efforts toward.

ON JOB CREATIVITY IS PREFERABLE

On Job Creativity (OJC) has many advantages. For one thing, it is more timely. OJC can be tapped any time a problem arises. It doesn't need to wait until the next off-campus meeting. OJC also is more plentiful. It isn't produced only during the 1 or 2 weeks allocated for strategic planning meetings. OJC can be obtained from any member of the organization, not just from those invited to off-campus sessions. The objective in developing OJC must be to remove the barriers, as the Arizona strategic meeting did. It can be done. Here are a few ideas about how to crumble a few common organizational barriers to creative action:

Have an Open-Door Policy . . . Not Your Door, Theirs. Executives at many companies have open-door policies. The main problem is that you have to ride the elevator eight stories and get by three administrative assistants before you can get to their door. What can happen once you go through the door is even scarier. The best executives I have met do it differently; they spend a lot of time in other people's offices. People are more at home and more relaxed once they get used to the idea that management cares enough about them and what they are doing to stop in. Creativity flows more easily in the relaxed environment of one's own office than after having been summoned to the boss's digs.

React Well to Bad Ideas. Shooting down a new idea is easy to do, and often very fulfilling. The way we react to bad ideas, however, may be more important than how we respond to good ones. Creativity-building executives find something to build upon in almost every idea. That little bit of positive feedback keeps people thinking, trying to come up with better ideas. On the other hand, the best way I have seen to handle good ideas is to give people credit. It works better than any suggestion box or incentive plan. The president of our company often says, "I've been in the business forty years and I've never had an original idea, but here's one I stole from Joe Smith." The impact is immeasurable. Giving credit becomes contagious. Once people realize it is characteristic of senior management, they begin the same practice with their peers and subordinates. Because most people like receiving credit, they begin thinking of more ideas and sharing them generously. After the meeting in Tempe, the diet Coke brand director never hesitated to give the Sprite director and marketing operations manager credit for developing the Federal Express idea. The same atmosphere should exist at the office.

Close the Executive Dining Room. How does closing a dining room stimulate creativity? It forces executives to mingle with front-line employees rather than breathing the rarefied air of their own exhaust. People relax once they get used to it. They begin to open up and express their creative ideas. The executives get more front-line input, which improves their own creativity. Not every company has an executive dining room to close, but if executives travel in a pack to the same place to gather together, the end result is the same. Our company closed its executive dining room this year. The idea works.

Leave the Mahogany Behind. Executive floors and office suites are no different than executive dining rooms. Any department head with employees in the same building will gain more by being officed with his or her group than from the "status" of the executive floor. One senior vice president I know did this about 3 months ago. He left the executive floor and moved his office downstairs. He has been delighted with the results. Rather than scheduling meetings with his people, he has conversations with them. He is better able to implement his open-door policy as the doors he must open are closer to his own.

Go for a Swim. Organizational barriers to creativity are more likely to break down when people communicate in a nontraditional environment. This is one of the benefits of off-campus meetings. The same effect can be captured more frequently and closer to home. Coca-Cola, and many other corporations, sponsor employee fitness centers. Smaller firms negotiate group rates at nearby health clubs. Johnson Wax, listed as one of the 100 best places to work in the United States, even has an employee aquatic center. Such investments might reduce health care costs over the long term. In the shorter term, they provide an atmosphere for relaxed discussion of work-related issues. They allow interface among people who might not normally communicate. Companies that sponsor softball or bowling teams, group trips, or nights out realize the same benefits.

Close the Home Office. Although closing the home office might seem to be the most radical proposal yet, it really is not. Our company increased overall manpower this year, but reduced home office staffing by almost 40%. Every function that could be moved to the field was moved. Being physically closer to the customer and to our own front-line employees is very conducive to creativity. Moving out reduces formalized meetings and the bureaucracy that stifles creativity. Those few executives who cannot totally vacate the home office spend as little time there as possible. In an era of voice mail, fax, e-mail, and frequent flyer points, a good executive can be effective anywhere. Getting out enables him or her to implement the ultimate open-door policy by walking through customers' doors.

There is a role for off-campus, change-of-pace strategic or team-building meetings. It is important that they be an extension of the on-going creative process, however. These meetings should take creativity to the next level. Therefore the more conducive the organization is to OJC, the more effective off-campus meetings will be. We will no longer have to go "off-campus" to get creative. We will also get better results when we do elect to head for the mountains, the desert, or the beach. ▨

41 The Pro-Team
Solving the Dilemma of Organized Creativity in Production

KARL-ERIK SVEIBY, *Researcher and Consultant*

In business, creative problem solving and routine production must coexist side by side. The typical creative individual is in many ways a nightmare to a manager. This presents a bit of a conundrum. Managers, especially those who supervise knowledge workers, absolutely rely on the creative talents of their employees, yet approach the task of managing creativity with fear and disdain. We must learn how to manage a milieu encompassing both standardization and creativity.

Creativity is not necessarily good for business. On the contrary, business success is often firmly attached to the ability to repeat successful patterns over and over again. The founding father of McDonald's, Ray Kroc, may have been considered creative when his concept was introduced, but the ongoing success of McDonald's depends on consistent service that provides few surprises. And let us not forget what happened when Coca-Cola decided to turn its creative energies toward changing the taste of its cornerstone product.

I do not wish to belittle the importance of creativity so much as to emphasize the point that, in business, creative problem solving and routine production must coexist side by side. Publishing, my business, is a case in point. Readers want to enjoy creative stories presented in the familiar format of their morning paper. A publishing company is a strange blend of an academy (the editorial staff), a used-car dealership (the advertising sales department), and a steel-works (the printing plant). All are involved in the production process and must cooperate under extraordinary time pressure. In this essay I try to address the question, "How does top management organize a firm to allow maximum creative liberty to coexist within the limits of production standards and routines?"

My Swedish publishing company is the biggest trade press publisher in Sweden. The company publishes seven journals and has a total staff of 150 people—90 on the editorial staff, 40 in sales and marketing, and 20 in administration/service. The journals cover business, engineering, computers, electronics, chemistry, and medicine. The company has contracted out all the printing. Almost all the journalists have an academic degree in a technological field, in economics, or in business administration.

Our way of coping with the tensions between creativity and consistency has been to organize the company into seven editorial "pro-teams," a marketing department, and an administration department. I use the label "pro-team" to describe teams of professionals, lacking marketing or administrative knowledge, exemplified by a research team or an editorial department. A pro-team functions as an "adhocracy," to use the expression coined by Henry Mintzberg. It has a creative climate, a flat hierarchy, and is run by and for the professionals. It is not simply a project team, however, because the task is ongoing rather than limited. In what respect is a pro-team different from our functional departments? In this case the "function" of the pro-teams depends on the unfettered interaction of a team of creative professionals. This requires a distinctively different management style than other, more "normal" departments in the company. Our marketing department is thus not a pro-team and is run in a more traditional fashion.

Each unit possesses its own distinct professional knowledge, skills, and know-how. Creativity is clearly the domain of the pro-teams, however; the task of maintaining the enterprise falls on the departments. All of the editors have an academic degree within the respective professional field represented by their magazine. Each is also an experienced writer and often contributes to the texts. The editor has to be a professional with an action bias but is seldom the one with the deepest knowledge regarding a specific topic. The writers are expected to provide extensive expertise within their fields. As experts in their fields, the writers often exhibit the personality traits one typically associates with the creative individual. The editors allow them a large amount of freedom to pursue topics that are of interest to them. Although the editors are responsible for motivating the individual writers and encouraging the flow of ideas, they are also responsible for keeping the product "on track" so that the contributions are ready when needed and meet the requirements imposed by the marketing and administration departments.

The pro-team editors and the marketing and administration department managers are allowed maximum freedom to develop their own formulas for success, a freedom that encourages very different management styles. As a result, the company has distinct subcultures, remuneration systems, motivation methods, and working hours, none of which are determined by top management. It is more like a network of independent teams, albeit sitting in the same building. Is this confusing? Yes, to anyone using a traditional industrial perspective on management. This structure dictates that top management devote most of its time to issues other than those emphasized by conventional management wisdom. In particular, top management's primary mission is to facilitate the effective transfer of knowledge among various teams and among teams and the depart-ments. This open sharing of knowledge enhances trust among mem-bers of the organization, which serves to provide a sense of unity and continuity across the different groups. Top managers function as the "glue" in this fuzzy organization. They initiate and encourage the flow of information and knowledge among the pro-teams and facili-tate the coordination of each unit's idiosyncratic work processes.

A publishing company organized in this way is an attempt to link *organization* and *creativity*, which in many ways are contradictory in nature. It is widely noted that creative individuals find organizations, especially large bureaucracies, stifling to their creativity. From a traditional manager's point of view, the creative person causes com-plications. Creative people tend to be more loyal to their task, ideas, or profession than to the organization. Another problem is that creative people often take a dim view of working in teams. The typical creative individual is almost the polar opposite of what one thinks of in a loyal subordinate. In many ways they are a nightmare to a manager in a large industrial organization. This presents a bit of a conundrum. Managers, especially those who supervise knowledge workers, absolutely rely on the creative talents of their employees, yet approach the task of managing creativity with fear and disdain. This need not be the case, however.

THE LEADER'S TASKS:
MANAGING THE MILIEU

Because of the contradictory elements inherent among the person-alities of creative knowledge workers and the managerial know-how needed to run knowledge-based organizations, it is useful to make a distinction between professional knowledge and managerial knowl-edge. Figure 41.1 presents a useful matrix for understanding the interactions of these two types of knowledge. The prototypical crea-tive professional is represented by the upper left corner of the matrix and the traditional manager by the lower right corner. Producing an effective balance between these two sources of expertise becomes the leadership mandate facing top management. The insight I hope to

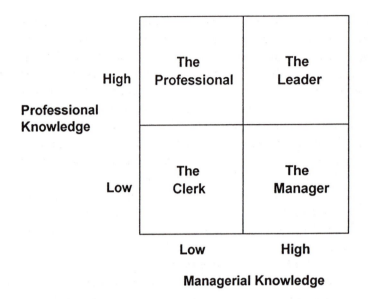

Figure 41.1. The Four Categories of Personnel in a "Know-How Company"

offer is that leadership in this context is akin to "managing the milieu" and that all four categories of employees are probably necessary to a successful knowledge company. It follows that to be successful, top managers need to know the profession, otherwise they are forever limited to "managing" rather than "leading." I like to call knowledge intensive companies that are able to handle this balance successfully "Know-How Companies." Peter Drucker (1991) has provided a similar description of management orientations in knowledge companies that is based on the extent to which a company must customize its output to satisfy customer requirements.

1. *Know-How Companies:* In know-how organizations productivity is measured in terms of quality and customer satisfaction, like scientific work in a research lab. Quantity of output is clearly secondary to quality. Management's orientation focuses on ends rather than means. To raise productivity, the manager can only ask: "What works?"

2. *Neither-Nor Companies:* Neither-nor companies include the majority of knowledge and service organizations where quantity and quality are

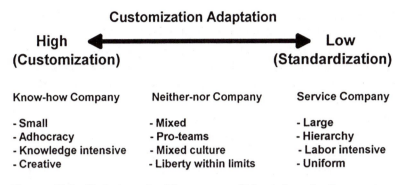

Figure 41.2. Variations in Management Orientations in Response to Customization Demands

utilized jointly to judge performance. Professional examples include architectural draftsmen, reporters, nurses, engineers. In my company, the quality of a journalist's work is important, but so is the number of articles produced. Raising productivity in these jobs requires attending to "what works," while maintaining accountability for following established work processes.

3. *Industrialized Service Companies:* Finally, there are many service jobs (filing, making hospital beds, etc.) in which performance is defined in terms of output quantity. This orientation is justified to the extent that customer satisfaction is based on service consistency. McDonald's is an exemplar of this category.

Know-how companies and industrial service companies represent two extremes in their distributions of workers across the four role classifications described in Figure 41.1. Obviously, these companies require different management approaches. Joining these different approaches is a challenge faced in a company like mine, which reflects a bit of both extremes. In this respect, my publishing company is probably similar to the majority of large organizations today. It is a "neither-nor" company. I believe that one of the sources of productivity problems in large organizations is that top management has not recognized the differences between these two approaches.

To return to the three categories described previously, companies that need to address diverse requirements from their customers would benefit the most from utilizing pro-teams. A Know-How Management orientation, as depicted in Figure 41.2, provides a means for utilizing the creative talents of an organization's employees and is therefore more likely to yield success for companies facing varied customer demands. However, this approach may lead to disaster in circumstances that require uniformity of service and, thus, general adherence to established procedures.

Fairly clear guidance can be given to firms at either of these two extremes; it more difficult to advise the majority of firms that lie between these extremes. I suggest that a balance must be created by finding ways of accommodating pro-teams within more traditional organization structures. My publishing company represents an attempt to strike such a balance. The concept of Know-How Management and the utilization of creative pro-teams within a large organization allows both chaos and structure to exist side by side. I believe that this is a positive and practical approach to utilizing the creative resources of human beings toward the goals of the organization.

I hope I have made it clear that I do not think creativity can be "managed" in organizations. According to my experience, "management" always harms creativity. Therefore, we must learn how to manage a milieu encompassing both standardization and creativity. ▨

REFERENCE

Drucker, P. (1991, November-December). The new productivity challenge. *Harvard Business Review*, pp. 69-79.

42 Fostering Creativity in Large Organizations

CAROLE F. ST. MARK *President and CEO,*
Pitney Bowes Business Services

There are always lots of reasons why a creative idea should fail, and large organizations, by their nature, like to protect the status quo. The key to success, in my experience, has been the patient understanding of this fact and the willingness to work with the organization to gain endorsement and understanding. A manager must strive for simplicity, measurability, and organizational accountability, if creative ideas are to become business realities. Don't try to change the organization, just work with it so that it doesn't kill a good idea.

⊶⊷

ℐhave spent my entire career in multi-billion-dollar, multinational corporations, and my experience is that few organizations of such size generate, let alone foster, creativity in their employees. The very nature of major corporations is such that structure, control, and multiple levels of analysis are essential for their success. They reward consistency and predictability, and have complex structures and processes designed to realize these aims. These structures are self-perpetuating and hard to change. Their very nature tends to stifle ill-defined or broad, conceptual ideas. Impact on the bottom line today and in the near term is paramount.

A notable area of exception to this assessment is the technical R&D centers of many large corporations, where creativity and ingenuity flourish. This is because companies that are successful in technical creativity have recognized the need to invest "seed money" to stimulate creativity without requiring a specific return on their investments. They view it as a necessary expense for their success.

Most large organizations recognize that the ability to change, to not get stuck in the past, to be flexible, and to try new things is essential to their futures. My experience, however, is that most creative ideas that emerge in large organizations are not sufficiently rooted in practicality for the organization to embrace the idea and run with it. Implementing the creative idea too often involves taking big risks, either financial or emotional. Also, the measurements and controls appropriate to foster the success of the creative idea do not exist or are poorly defined.

I believe that creativity is only valuable to an organization if it is implemented in a way that adapts to the organization's culture, values, and processes. The implementation is what takes great creativity. It is the creativity that asks, "How can we achieve the end result without disrupting or alienating the enterprise?"

I have seen many examples of innovative and creative new product ideas for which there is no market and highly creative advertising campaigns that fail to sell the product. Business leaders are looking for actionable ideas that have a direct impact on the bottom line. Getting from the creative idea to the actionable plan is difficult to do in organizations that are highly structured and control driven.

It is certainly possible to stimulate creativity within large organizations, but it takes certain specific and intentional initiatives to do so. The "skunkworks" that is formed to address a product or project is often successful if it is set apart from the bureaucracy, yet held accountable for results. This also suggests unique reward and recognition systems that would be inappropriate for the organization at large. The keys to producing creative solutions in large organizations are really rather traditional. A manager must strive for simplicity, measurability, and organizational accountability if creative ideas are to become business realities.

I was, at one point in my career, responsible for creating new business growth opportunities for my corporation. We are a highly successful company with multiple, mature product lines where we enjoy strong market share and excellent returns. At the time, stimulating new revenue growth was a necessity for future success. I formed a small group of bright, creative people who considered many opportunities. We looked at several acquisitions, but none were sufficiently attractive from financial points of view. We considered new products. We considered totally unrelated new businesses but were concerned about how we would nurture, grow, and manage businesses we had never been involved in before. Finally, we concluded that the best way to grow new businesses was to leverage some unique strength we already had. We produced numerous business plans, did market research, and formed some internal venture groups to test markets.

Out of all of the ideas and concepts that we pursued, one resulted in a major new business opportunity. It was far from the most interesting idea. In a way, it was fairly mundane. It was the simplest concept of all. The idea came from the sales organization of one of our larger divisions. Our customers identified it for us. They suggested that, because our equipment was increasingly complex and because the processes that our equipment automated were becoming increasingly difficult to manage, we form a business to run the operations for our customers. The problem was that this was a business that did not exist, in a market that was yet to emerge. There was no competition, because no one had yet tried to offer this service. So we could not analyze an industry to evaluate potential returns. But it was appealing and palatable to the organization because it was in a marketplace that we understood, with a customer base that was readily available to us. With this in mind, we set about pursuing the idea in a way that made sense to the organization. We talked to our customers, we studied their operations and their problems, and we defined a concept for a service business that many of our customers said they would consider buying. We had outside research firms survey multiple, vertical markets to determine if this concept might be of broad interest. It seemed to be.

We formed a small group, a venture team, to develop a business plan and to get the funding from the corporation to establish a new business. This group acted as though we were an entrepreneurial start-up company (within the corporation). We had to justify our request for funding to the Board of Directors, and we had to meet stringent milestones with respect to spending and plan implementation. We also formulated our own unique processes and reward and measurement systems because those in place for the corporation-at-large were inappropriate for a small start-up. Once we got our funding, we went about trying to sell the service and landed a major customer within a few months.

Forming this new business and getting it off the ground worked because it was a simple and pragmatic idea. We were meticulous in identifying the investments required, and we focused on generating positive financial results early in the process. We were allowed to continue because we were not a "drag" on the organization, even though our concept was totally unproven.

There were many junctures during the early days of this business where the idea could have perished. Because it was new and different, and because we were not operating according to the same rules and regulations as the rest of the organization, we were subject to great skepticism and severe criticism. Rather than ignore it or engage in turf wars, we spent a tremendous amount of time explaining the strategic viability of the business. This was time consuming and frustrating, and yet I believe that it was perhaps the most critical aspect of nurturing this new concept and fostering its success.

After we landed our first big account, our customer wanted to begin our service operations immediately. Up to this point, we had formulated the concept but had never actually performed the service! In addition, the entire human resources dedicated to our venture amounted to about five people. The start-up for this first customer required about 50 fully trained people, ready to provide the service. Once again, the venture team took a creative approach to what was a very practical problem. We just didn't have the people, so we borrowed them. We went around the company and asked for volunteers. We hired secretaries, security guards, administrators, and others and back-filled them with temporary employees that we paid for. In effect, we generated an entire volunteer workforce, fully trained and experienced in our company, within a couple of days. There was a tremendous feeling of excitement, esprit de corps, and enthusiasm among those who volunteered. They were creating something new, and they were determined to make this first customer very satisfied with our service. As a result, the start-up was smooth and the customer was very pleased and served as a ready reference for us for multiple new accounts. Once again, this creative approach worked because it was simple and pragmatic.

In the 6 years since that first contract, the business has grown exponentially to 8,000 employees serving hundreds of customers in every major city in the United States. We have also entered the international market. This did not happen without growing pains, mind-boggling problems, financial setbacks, and moments of utter frustration. However, it has succeeded because we kept the idea simple and focused, explained it thoroughly, related it to our core expertise, and committed to making our financial targets.

Creativity was demanded at every step of the way because this is the first service business our company has ever been in. Employee practices, benefit plans, work rules, communications systems, and reward systems all needed to be created specifically for this business.

There are always lots of reasons why a creative idea should fail, and large organizations, by their nature, like to protect the status quo. The key to success, in my experience, has been the patient understanding of this fact and the willingness to work with the organization, to gain endorsement and understanding, even though it may take four times as long as you would like. Corporations, especially publicly traded corporations, need consistent financial results. Setting aggressive targets and making them is the demonstration of success, which is the only acceptable measurement in a profit-making organization.

The bottom line is to keep the idea simple and explain it over and over again. Identify what the corporation needs to achieve and then achieve it—whether it is growth, diversification, profitability, return on investment, or cash flow—but be clear about what the goal is and then make it happen. Don't try to change the organization, just work with it so that it doesn't kill a good idea. ▧

43 Creativity at Woolworth Corporation

C. JACKSON GRAY *Senior Vice President of Corporate Planning and Development, Woolworth Corporation*

Some say that hitting a baseball is the most difficult act in all of sports. Perhaps introducing a new venture is the most difficult act in all of business. Because we are willing to take risks, we sometimes fail. In recent years, we have introduced several formats that no longer exist. However, we try to cope with the inevitable failures associated with creativity by managing our businesses so that discontinued new ventures do not result in material loss. The only guarantee against failing is not trying—but this is an alternative we reject.

At Woolworth Corporation, creativity includes improving current activities, as well as undertaking totally new activities. New ways of doing things typically lead to improved efficiencies; new activities generally involve new business ventures.

At Woolworth, much of my involvement in creativity is tied to developing new business. Therefore, my essay will focus on how those of us at the corporate level capitalize on the creative talents of the people in our various divisions.

Woolworth is a highly diversified retailer organized into several operating divisions that manage their own strategic and day-to-day activities. As is the case in most diversified firms, the corporate office is responsible for directing and allocating resources across different divisions. The typical choices made at this level include deciding on the mix of businesses the corporation will have, allocating capital among divisions, and determining the overall strategic thrust of the corporation. In 1983, Woolworth developed and prioritized a set of corporate strategic objectives:

1. To revitalize and renovate existing stores that seem able to meet our financial objectives within a reasonable time, and to redeploy those that cannot

280

2. To accelerate the expansion of existing specialty store formats with proven performance

3. To pursue internal development and expansion of new specialty store formats, and to acquire specialty stores that would expand the depth and breadth of our participation in the retail marketplace

Much of our creative energies at the corporate level are directed toward working jointly with our divisions in new venture development. Our progress on this objective has been crucial to the corporation's success over the past decade. Before I explain the process and environment behind the creation of our new ventures, I want to describe briefly some of our more prominent and creative new ventures.

The first business that we developed internally is now one of our most prominent divisions. We introduced Foot Locker in 1974 and have developed the business into a major international retailer with more than 2,000 stores in 13 countries. Our experience with Foot Locker convinced us that we could develop new ventures internally, with our existing talent, provided that we gave the ventures time to work. This success gave us the impetus and confidence to utilize our creativity as a strategic resource.

We have subsequently realized this strategic objective through the introduction of several other new businesses. Lady Foot Locker, originally developed by Kinney in Canada as a spin-off of Foot Locker and "exported" to the United States in a different form, sells women's brand name athletic footwear and apparel. This is probably our most outstanding recent example of a successful new venture. The first U.S. Lady Foot Locker unit opened in 1982. In 1987, we had fewer than 200 stores. At the end of 1993, we had 583 units. In its first 12 years, Lady Foot Locker has grown even faster than its big brother, Foot Locker.

A second internally developed and rapidly expanded concept is After Thoughts, developed by our U.S. Woolworth division in 1985. After Thoughts operates costume jewelry, handbag, and accessory boutiques, many in 800 square feet spaces carved out of existing Woolworth stores. Almost immediately, the After Thoughts concept was successfully exported to Canada where it is called Reflexions and, more recently to West Germany, where it is called Rubin, and Mexico, where it is called Carimar. At the end of 1993, we had 1,280 costume jewelry units.

One of our newest specialty store formats is Northern Reflections. It is an upscale casual sportswear store targeted to women. The store design simulates an outdoor feeling by using a lakeside decor. The selection of quality, casual, classic sportswear is narrow, providing for long selling seasons. We opened, as a new venture, our first 11 Northern Reflections in Canada in 1987, and had 42 at the end of 1988. The first 4 U.S. Northern Reflections opened in 1989, 5 more opened in 1990, and 21 opened in 1991. In 1992 and 1993, we opened 214 units in the United States. We now operate 178 in Canada and 244 in the United States. We plan very rapid expansion of Northern Reflections U.S. in 1994 and beyond. In the past 9 years, the total number of units in just these three of our most important internally generated formats has grown from only 17 in 1983 to almost 2,300 in 1993. I believe that the creative ideas we introduced with these new ventures has been critical to their explosive growth.

The process we use to develop new ventures relies on encouraging creativity from our operating divisions, coupled with a selection process that allows the best ideas to be tested and implemented in relatively short order. The three ventures just described are excellent examples of the new formats developed at Woolworth employing this process. Each operating division of Woolworth is encouraged to be creative, venturesome, and entrepreneurial in developing new specialty formats. At the corporate level, we view our operating companies as our "R&D laboratories," in which new formats are developed, tested, and, if warranted, rapidly expanded. Our new-product development function is thus a "bottom-up" rather than "top-down" function. We believe that operating units are clearly in the best position to evaluate their own operational and organizational strengths and have a much better grip on market and customer requirements.

As a result of encouraging the implementation of creative ideas from the bottom up, Woolworth now operates over 25 more specialty formats than it did in 1983. We view this as a measure of the productivity of our "R&D Labs." Of course, because we are willing to take risks, we sometimes fail. In recent years, we have introduced several formats that no longer exist. However, we try to cope with the inevitable failures associated with creativity by managing our businesses so that discontinued new ventures do not result in material loss. With dozens of small-store, mall-oriented specialty formats, space can easily be recycled from underperforming formats into either brand-new experimental formats or proven-successful ones. The only guarantee against failing is not trying—but this is an alternative we reject.

What are the key elements that allow us to nurture and develop creative ideas for new business ventures? The most important elements are:

1. *Vision From the Top:* A chairman, and a chairman's group, who are totally committed to new venture development.
2. *Freedom to Act:* We have a process that makes initial start-up easy. We require little research and rely heavily on our intuition and judgment when deciding on whether or not to fund a test.
3. *Freedom to Fail:* Some say that hitting a baseball is the most difficult act in all of sports. Perhaps introducing a new venture is the most difficult act in all of business. As is the case in baseball, we recognize that if we bat .300 we are doing very well indeed.
4. *Limited Risk:* We only fund 5 to 10 stores to test new ideas, and these stores can be quickly changed, so the initial risk is small.
5. *Talented People:* We have highly experienced, creative operating executives who are capable of and willing to start new ventures. Idea generation is totally in the hands of divisions. Division executives must serve as sponsors from day one.

We continue to foster creativity at the division level by emphasizing these factors at the corporate level. This style of strategic management continues to produce. In fact, we have several other promising new formats that are currently emerging from our new venture "labs." For example, Northern Getaway is an internally developed format, introduced recently in Canada, that serves as a good example of our enduring commitment to developing internal new ventures. It was started by Woolworth Canada in 1991 and has already grown to 36 stores in Canada and 11 in the United States. Northern Getaway is a children's version of Northern Reflections. Also in Canada, we are testing Northern Traditions, a dressier version of Northern Reflections. We now have 26 units. Finally, Going to the Game was developed by Kinney U.S. as a specialty store geared to the sports-minded mall shopper. With a unique store design, it features licensed or team-imprinted items, such as apparel collectibles and memorabilia. The creative edge of this format is its in-house imprinting capability that often allows Going to the Game to stock winning championship-team product less than 24 hours after a finals victory. Consequently, much of the store's product is not available from competitors. We now have 60 units open, up from 6 in 1990.

I believe that creativity is a core strategic capability that has allowed our corporation to be successful across a variety of retail markets. In this essay I have tried to describe how Woolworth seeks, and perhaps demands, new ideas from our operating divisions. The processes I described have encouraged our divisions to try out creative formats and have allowed our corporation to utilize these new ideas to produce competitive advantage in the marketplace. Our commitment to creativity is well demonstrated by the development of our new ventures. From these seeds will grow the opportunities facing our corporation in the years to come. ☒

44 Acquiring and Managing Creative Talent

NORMAN E. JOHNSON, *Senior Vice President, Technology, Weyerhaeuser Company*

A common belief among product development leaders is that if you expose ideas too soon, "corporate antibodies" will concentrate their efforts to "cleanse the organism" of the new threat. I still think that covert "skunkworks" are important at the beginning stages of product development. It is a lot easier to sell a prototype than an idea on paper. However, a new project may not get the support it needs without the business units feeling some sense of ownership and participation.

My Myers-Briggs Type Indicator is ENTP (Extraversion, Intuition, Thinking, Perceiving), briefly described as: "Quick, ingenious, good at many things. May argue either side of a question for fun. Resourceful in solving challenging problems, but may neglect routine assignments." I'm an intuitive, thinking extrovert. Unfortunately for me, most of the other members of Weyerhaeuser's Senior Management Team are more "serious, orderly, logical, quiet, practical and realistic," according to Myers-Briggs type descriptions. I've been variously described by my colleagues as an "idea man," a "hip-shooter," a "challenger of the system," a "change agent," and a "tightwad," among others. Of all the descriptors, the one that perhaps fits best is "idea man." With this revelation of myself, let me outline what I think it takes to have a creative organization.

A creative person, in my mind, is one who effectively uses information from diverse sources to solve problems or create new things. There are those who are creative at selling, others at solving complex people problems, devising new systems, or developing new products. An unresponsive organization, however, can almost certainly thwart the efforts of a creative individual. I believe, therefore, that managers must take responsibility for nurturing the creative talent of their employees. With this in mind, I would like to offer the following suggestions to managers who are interested in realizing the creative potential of their people.

Select Based on Creative Ability. Consultants say, and I agree to a point, that a person's ability to create can be improved. But, I'm of the opinion that creative ability is as innate as are abilities in math and music. No matter how much I might try I could not be a good mathematician or musician. Therefore, if you want a creative organization you should select persons who can demonstrate that they have this capability. These are what I think make up the key attributes of a creative person:

- An ability to see things and situations in different ways
- A high level of curiosity
- An insatiable appetite for knowledge

- A contrarian style and a dislike of the status quo
- A certain boldness to try things before they are proven
- A great deal of tenacity
- A willingness to learn from one's own and others' mistakes
- A tolerance for appearing to be a fool at times
- A serendipitous capability

Actually, these attributes probably have more to do with a person's practical intelligence and willingness to take risks than with specific creativity skills. Nevertheless, these are qualities that I look for when trying to judge the creative potential of an individual.

Improve Creative Ability. Having said that I think that creativity is innate, let me hasten to add that I think that this ability can be improved in many ways. For example, establishing participative problem-solving teams, providing creativity classes, asking questions that lead toward creative solutions, and helping people develop creative solutions through coaching, planting ideas, and more, are all simple, effective means of encouraging creativity. Perhaps more powerful, and often more difficult to implement effectively, is to establish high expectations regarding creativity and reward those who come up with innovative solutions.

Join Together for Creativity. Time and again I've witnessed teams coming up with solutions that are better than those of an individual, creative person. A team composed of a diverse set of talents, experiences, cultures, and attitudes can accomplish amazing things. A key reason for this is that in a diverse team someone inevitably asks the "unaskable" or "dumb" question that will force specialists outside of their "functional foxholes." Einstein reportedly said; "No problem can be solved by the same consciousness that created it." The solution to making the cotton gin work came to Eli Whitney when he was visiting friends. He was discussing the problem he was having with his idea when the wife of his friend showed him the solution using her hairbrush and comb. We can all cite examples of where a technician rather than a scientist asked the question that led to the creative solution. Or having one's children or grandchildren come up with an idea that would never have occurred to one's self. Creating intellectual synergy by coupling diverse talents is one of the most exciting experiences a manager can enjoy.

Nourish Creativity. Once a creative person, always a creative person. But where will this creativity be manifested? If the work environment hinders creativity, a creative person may leave or find other outlets for this creativity. I've observed a number of things that management can do to help nourish creativity. For example, establishing a shared belief that the organization values and rewards doing new things is crucial. This may include allowing creative people to wander around within the company's structure and giving them discretionary time and money to pursue their own ideas. It is also helpful to encourage creators to search for users of their innovation. If their ideas are good, this can provide valuable feedback that can serve to improve the idea and to motivate further effort. Finally, it is crucial, for many reasons, to develop a company culture that supports the betterment of the total organization rather than its separate parts.

Unfortunately, it is easier to hinder creativity than to help it. Gary Davis, author of "Blocks and Barriers" in a 1992 issue of *R&D Innovator*, listed several common squelchers, including:

- "We've never done that before."
- "We did all right without it."
- "It's too early."
- "It's too late."
- "We're too big (small) for that."
- "Don't rock the boat."
- "Don't step on any toes."
- "We can't do it under the regulations."
- "That's not your job."
- "It's not in the plan." (1992, p. 5; reprinted by permission)

Direct Creativity. It may sound paradoxical to talk about directing creative activity, but most companies cannot afford undirected creativity. There are two ideas in this regard that I have come to rely on. First, there is no need to have a corporate lab if it doesn't produce several times more business value than it costs. Second, the basis of competition is well defined in most industries. Failure to align R&D effort with an appropriate business strategy produces risky and usually futile expenditures of corporate funds.

The first step in directing creativity is for the company or business to set a clear vision and supporting strategies. Lacking this, creativity will likely be directed toward things that may not create value. A second important ingredient is to include creative people on those teams that deal with customers. A few years ago on an Industrial Research Institute-sponsored trip to Japan, I asked several companies where their new product ideas originated. They were astonished that I asked this question, but quickly answered that most new ideas came from their technical and not their marketing people. With a little more probing I learned that many Japanese companies went to special efforts to get scientists into the marketplace so that they could better understand the customers' present needs and therefore be in a better position to anticipate the customers' future needs as well.

A third thing that I've lately begun to appreciate is that it is helpful to utilize a product development process that involves the businesses at the early stages of the development cycle. Previously, I had been of the opinion that it was best to keep new product development well hidden until after market testing was well started and a business case could be defended. A common belief among product development leaders is that if you expose ideas too soon, "corporate antibodies" will concentrate their efforts to "cleanse the organism" of the new threat. I still think that covert "skunkworks" are important at the beginning stages of product development. It is a lot easier to sell a prototype than an idea on paper. However, a new project may not get the support it needs without the business units feeling some sense of ownership and participation.

Clearly, this is a fine line to walk. At Weyerhaeuser, a technology strategy council—led by me, the chief technology officer—manages this process and determines whether or not to recommend to the company's senior management team that a project be funded. The corporation will fund the early stages of the project with more and more funding shifted to the appropriate business as the process of commercialization progresses.

Sell the Products of Creativity. Nicolo Machiavelli once cautioned:

> It must be remembered that there is nothing more difficult to plan, more doubtful of success, nor more dangerous to manage than the creation of a new system. For the initiator has the enmity of all who would profit by the preservation of the old institution and merely lukewarm defenders in those who would gain by the new one.

Even in those companies that depend heavily on technology, change comes only with a great deal of effort. Here are my final suggestions for improving the chances of selling the products of creativity to a business:

- Have a process in place that establishes a framework for product development.
- Give the creator time, money, and shelter from the "nay sayers" early in the process.
- Find a respected person in the business who will help sponsor the new product.
- Build credibility by putting together a team consisting of business managers, scientists, and engineers and persons with marketing, finance, and operations experience.
- Remember that respected consultants in the product area can also be useful here.
- Use a flexible business plan that can capitalize on emergent attributes of the product.

Perhaps the most powerful piece of advice I can offer is to simply hang in there. William Feather said, "Success seems to be largely a matter of hanging on after others have let go." Literature is filled with stories of innovators who took years to sell such successful products as xerography, the 2-liter soft drink bottle, asphalt roofing, bar codes, cellular phones, Post-it Notes, thin disposable diapers, and many more. Henry R. Lace noted that, "Business more than any other occupation is a continual dealing with the future; it is a continual calculation, an instinctive exercise in foresight." I'd add that it takes creative people to keep any business healthy, young, and growing.

REFERENCE

Davis, G. (1992). Blocks and barriers: Are they squelching your creativity? *R&D Innovator*, 1(5), 4-6.

45 Creativity Through Self-Appraisal

F. E. BAILEY, *President and CEO,*
Bailey Financial Group, Inc.

JAMES R. BAILEY, *Assistant Professor of Management,*
Rutgers University

We have used self-appraisal primarily as a tool or hook to
overcome the inertia and skepticism that is endemic to the
corporate mind-set. When entering organizations with ideas that
appear radical, it is wise to step gingerly around the interests and
deeply worn habits that dwell within. Peering inside one's self can
be a disconcerting exercise, to be sure. Self-appraisal has allowed
us delicately to lead naturally defensive individuals to recognize,
by their own hand, needs and potential courses of action.

⎯⎯⎯⎯⎯◦◦◦◦⎯⎯⎯⎯⎯

$\mathcal{O}$bserving the vicissitudes of the American corporate vista, we are struck with a nagging sense of dissatisfaction. Promising talent unfulfilled and squandered opportunities of all variety appear more the rule than the exception. We believe the roots of these problems lie squarely at the intersection where individual ability meets environmental contingencies. As complex as the meeting between individual and organization may be, it does not require a high priest of popular management fashion to see that a desire for creativity is a common theme melding the interests of both halves of this whole.

The lack of creativity apparent in organizations has been especially striking to us. As change agents—that is, dealmakers and consultants—in the financial services industry, we have trained our eyes to detect creative potential in the production, marketing, and delivery of financial instruments. Any special insight we possess, however, is due in large measure to the removed perspective we enjoy. We are not embroiled in the trials and tribulations of everyday management of the companies we work with, and as a result we can see possibilities that are not apparent to them. Over the years, our unique position as outsiders on the inside has led us to formulate a notion of creativity that has facilitated our efforts and benefited the individuals and companies that have enlisted our services.

The hope for this essay is to communicate this notion. We believe that "insiders" need to develop their abilities to see their own circumstances as an outsider would. This can be accomplished by introspectively examining one's self-concept so as to understand better the collage of influences, experiences, priorities, assumptions, needs, aspirations, and competencies that define and distinguish one's core identity and potential. Individuals and organizations possess, at some level, an awareness of who they are and how they act. Our central point is that reflecting on one's own makeup can enable one to recognize and capitalize on current and future circumstances. We call this process *self-appraisal,* and we believe it is important for individuals as well as organizations.

UNCERTAINTY AND
THE SELF-APPRAISAL PROCESS

Philosophers, historians, theologians, and behavioral scientists are in rare agreement that much human striving is directed toward rendering the unknown known. Stated differently, people develop various means to alleviate uncertainty in an effort to gain some sense of stability, security, and predictability in the midst of a threatening and chaotic world. One need not look far to find convincing evidence of this principle. For instance, individuals often turn to religion to provide a framework of meaning for their lives. Similarly, societies construct official institutions to ensure the orderly operation of necessary duties and transactions. In the business domain, organizations apply scientific techniques to forecast market trends so as to adjust production, inventories, financing, and advertising appropriately.

The reduction of uncertainty, then, is a powerful and pervasive motive because it allows people to take action, even in complex, ever-shifting environments. But this motive is especially important in relation to one's self-concept, because this identity is the fulcrum on which beliefs about talent and expectations of situational demands are balanced. The need to engage in self-appraisal has been recognized for a long time. The Greek adage that an "unexamined life is not worth living" and the Shakespearean advice, "to thine own self be true" attest to the enduring nature of this process, and research in psychology has further explored the particulars of self-appraisal. Specifically, *self-appraisal* refers to how people and organizations learn about their abilities in relation to their circumstances, and how they integrate these understandings. We should note, however, that self-appraisal often runs counter to another powerful motive: the desire for self-regard. In much the same way that individuals want to hold a positive view of themselves—to think of themselves as proper, smart, and kind—organizations often engage in activities and rhetoric aimed at enhancing their identities as upstanding, worthy corporate citizens.

Thus, the notion of the self-concept refers to an individual's or organization's view of their core identity and potential in all its complexity, contradiction, and coherence. Self-appraisal refers to the process through which an understanding of these elements is developed. Realistic self-appraisal provides two very powerful benefits to practicing managers. First, it can allow the selection and construction of work environments where abilities, limitations, and situational demands are well matched. By capitalizing on strengths and avoiding, overcoming, or compensating for limitations, people can enhance their effectiveness. Second, developing self-appraisal skills may improve one's ability to empathize with others. This is a crucial talent for those who wish to introduce change within an organization. Similarly, organizations can benefit through a better understanding of their core competencies and through greater sensitivity toward consumer and competitor responses. Even though the initial pain of recognizing one's faults can be significant, positive regard can be maintained or enhanced if the insights gained lead to improved competence and performance.

THE SAVINGS AND LOAN INDUSTRY

To make this rather abstract discussion a bit more concrete, let's consider the case of a large corporation. Its self-concept reflects its charter, board philosophy, CEO personality, industry standards and practices, financial profile, personnel, economic circumstance, tangible and intangible resources, and so on. Regardless of this corporation's past performance, however, the marketplace it faces inevitably changes. In the face of such change, a corporation's self-concept can be blinding. The firm will survive and prosper only so long as it holds realistic expectations of its abilities and competencies as they relate to the new challenges in the business environment.

The savings and loan debacle stands as a prime example. The charter of a savings and loan (S&L) is simple: to make and collect loans, and to profit by the margin between interest paid on deposits and interest collected on loans. The smooth operation of this cycle had, in the past, been as simple as the charter: Maintain a broad deposit base, and ensure collateral on loans. However, deregulation and competitive infiltration by large banks combined to thin profit margins. S&Ls responded to these changes with a singular strategy that was well understood within their self-concept: Increase loan volume. That is, to compensate for the thinner margins, more loans were made. This mentality, however, led S&Ls to make loans that, although in accord with regulatory requirements, were not in accord with good banking practice. In fact, the regulatory presence was so dominant that the goal of good loans was subordinated to the goal of conforming to government directives. When the smoke cleared, S&Ls were extended beyond their means, lacking the capital and surplus to cover undersecured loans. What the S&Ls missed, because they were bound by a static sense of self, was the opportunity afforded by deregulation. Margins between interest paid and interest collected were not and are not the sole means to profit, but their self-concept didn't include other prospects. The environment eventually ruptured the self-concept of the S&Ls, but had they been thinking creatively about what they were and what they needed to become—that is, if they had been actively engaged in self-appraisal— they might have been better equipped to adjust and in a better position to thrive.

Our analysis of the S&L crisis helps to illustrate a critical feature of self-appraisal: People and organizations don't exist in isolation. Rather, they exist within a complex and intricate environment that includes competitors, suppliers, and regulatory bodies, as well as the prevailing social climate. This means that no matter how intimate a firm is with its self-concept, no matter how comprehensive its accounting of resources and competencies, it is doomed to stagnation at best, abject failure at worst, unless it also attends to the creative potentials inherent in the environment. This is why it is a paramount priority to engage in self-appraisal in relation to one's environment, what is often known as environmentally sensitive management. "Know thyself" is sound advice, but it is only half of successful business: Self-appraisal requires a dialectical relationship between an individual's or an organization's capabilities and the demands of its environment. One must analyze talents against the backdrop of circumstances, and consciously coordinate the two.

The self-appraisal concept has been helpful to us in a number of ways. As change agents in the financial service industry, we are often called on to introduce innovations to businesses that, despite the best intentions, are reluctant to change. For instance, just prior to and during the collapse of the S&L industry, we approached dozens of individual institutions with a radical innovation that would circumvent the problems caused by thinner margins and overvalued collateral. Up to that point, the only significant change in S&L practice was the introduction of NOW accounts. Our market research had confirmed a trend already in progress, however: People wanted to diversify their assets further. Given that S&Ls were among society's most trusted institutions, and that they already had a built-in client base, they served as a natural springboard for launching a multifaceted financial program. Banks and other big players like Sears had already profited by diversifying their financial offerings some time earlier, but S&Ls seemed reluctant to respond to the threats and opportunities of the new regulatory environment. Specifically, we proposed to implement a broad array of financial services through the S&Ls, including securities (e.g., stocks, bonds, mutual funds), all variety of flexible insurance instruments (e.g., variable life and annuities), and comprehensive financial planning. Our plan included assisting in all licensing efforts, retraining their employees, and shepherding them through the entire process. The ultimate goal was to convince these institutions that they were in the money business, not just the savings and loan business, and that it was in their best interest to expand their self-concepts. Our ideas were fiercely resisted by some and cautiously accepted by others. We have met with more success in banks where, mindful of the lessons of the S&L fallout, the atmosphere is bolder and more open to creativity and change.

SELF-REGARD AND
THE INTRODUCTION OF CHANGE

Through all our travels and travails in the financial world, the self-appraisal concept has served us well. We have used it primarily as a tool or hook to overcome the inertia and skepticism that is endemic to the corporate mind-set. When entering organizations as we do, with ideas that appear radical, it is wise to step gingerly around the interests and deeply worn habits that dwell within, lest we menace their self-regard. Peering inside one's self can be a disconcerting exercise, to be sure. As agents that initiate such examination, we run the risk of alienating the very entities we set out to assist—akin to "killing the messenger." Still, to maintain viability and encourage vitality, this painful process is necessary. Self-appraisal has allowed us delicately to lead naturally defensive individuals to recognize, by their own hand, needs and potential courses of action. Our role, then, is perceived as one of helpful facilitators as opposed to threatening instigators. For us, self-appraisal is not just a way of thinking, it is also a port of entry.

CONCLUSION

As our own company grows, we have found new uses for the self-appraisal process. New employees are introduced to the idea first thing and are challenged to examine their own self-concepts to identify better their strengths, weaknesses, and biases. This better prepares them to focus on facets of their new responsibilities that may need some fine tuning, and others where they can hit the ground running. We ask them to begin to think of ways to introduce the self-appraisal concept to our clients so they can more effectively identify problems and propose solutions.

Our notion of self-appraisal suggests a dynamic interplay between special abilities and situational vagaries, and in this way resembles the evolutionary process by which species are selected by environmental demands. Although there are parallels between these two processes, it would be a mistake to equate them. In pure evolutionary terms, survival depends on the fit between a species' idiosyncratic characteristics and the existence of an appropriate niche; hence the term "survival of the fittest." The curiously long neck of the giraffe, for instance, was selected because there was digestible foliage in the forest canopy. It would seem, though, that the giraffe was merely acted upon by outside forces—an unwitting pawn in destiny's game. In contrast, we maintain that individuals and organizations are not so passive. Self-appraisal is critical because a realistic awareness of one's capabilities and talents can help one select or create a more hospitable niche. In our opinion, creativity is necessary to align competencies and circumstances effectively. ⬧

46 Organizing for Creativity

TERRY O'CONNOR *Director, Marketing Services, BASF Corporation*

The creative environment is not always comfortable. For comfort join a club. To organize for creativity, prepare for life without certainty. You enjoy less order, you institutionalize more uncertainty, you share leadership, you run what others see as an untidy ship, and to top it all, you have no guarantee of success. Why do it? The presence of this climate, it is true, is no guarantee of success. Its absence, however, does in time guarantee failure.

Let's define Creative Organizations as those that are consistently able to develop or utilize original ideas, products, processes, or relationships in such a way that they contribute to the organization's success. The key words originality + consistency = success. Having defined the terms, let me quickly add that any organization in any field can be either creative or stultifyingly conventional. The seeds of both exist everywhere.

Euclid tells us that "the whole is equal to the sum of all its parts." What's true of mathematical principles is not, however, true of organizations. An organization is equal to the sum of all its parts plus the way they are organized. One hundred disorganized men are a rabble. Organized they become an army. My point is that truly creative organizations have not simply stumbled into their positions, they have planned for creativity, and they have organized themselves so as to achieve it. It can be done in organizations large and small. Let me postulate a few simple rules for creating the appropriate climate for those interested in organizing for creativity.

MANY DISCIPLINES, NO DISCIPLES

Some of the most comfortable working environments I have seen are the least creative or productive. Communication and rapport stemming from shared beliefs, background, and skills are wonderful. Then what is wrong with this picture? What's wrong is that every member of the group is a mirror image of every other member. They were hired in their supervisor's image, and each makes the other redundant. Never hire anyone to echo your opinions. Rather, hire those who will challenge your convictions. Hire what you don't have. Fill the gaps and you will have a broad base for truly informed decision making. The creative environment is not always comfortable. For comfort, join a club. To organize for creativity, prepare for life without certainty. The results can be well worth it.

FIND CRAFTSMEN—
ARTISTS NEED NOT APPLY

Here's a problem. Those who consider themselves artists don't feel they need to apply themselves. They wait for divine inspiration, they commune with their muse. They do everything but the basics.

Craftsmen, on the other hand, approach tasks in a totally different fashion. They role up their sleeves, get their hands dirty, and learn the details of every task from the ground up. They believe that God is in the details, not in the clouds. A true craftsman rarely sinks below highly professional work and on good days achieves art. Self-styled "artists" usually blame the world for not being refined enough to recognize their achievement. It's a "the problem is not mine but thine" approach. Surround yourself with craftsmen of energy, and inspiration will follow. Let the dilettantes, no matter how gifted, grace some other organization.

AVOID SHARKS, TRAINED OR OTHERWISE

The presence of sharks in an organization is usually explained away with the phrase, "Yeah but he's/she's my shark." The manager who employs a shark feels he has a hired gun, a paladin to enter the lists and fight his fights. Pretty soon I've got my gun up against your gun and we're enfeebling not only our departments, but our entire organization.

Avoid hiring sharks, shun them, boycott them, get them out. They create little and destroy much. The social fabric of the group can't take the strain. Their only creation is confusion. They obscure the ownership of ideas, they drive out contributors, they eat their own.

LEADERSHIP ON LOAN

Leadership, we have all heard, is an obligation, not a reward, an activity rather than a position. In a healthy department in the course of a day or week, leadership will be shared, traded, bartered, and exchanged with or among those with the best talents for the task at hand. When the tank breaks down in combat, the wise commander quickly moves into a subservient role and willingly becomes the gofer for the best mechanic in the unit, no matter how low his or her rank. Real leaders have learned the art of following. After all, it is the total effort of the entire group that elevates everyone. That is the leader's only objective. Leadership shared can be leadership squared. Treat it casually and it expands, cling to it as yours alone and you diminish it, your group's ability, and finally yourself.

ALL WINDOWS, FEW WALLS

Communication isn't everything—but it's damn near. The value of the free flow of ideas is much like fresh air and sunlight; our bodies crave it, it makes growth possible. Managers must become experts at climate control, or rather the lack thereof. Let ideas circulate, share information, let it rain on everyone. We don't know which seed will germinate first or bear best. In all job descriptions and assigned tasks, allow for considerable overlap. Frequently the breakthrough comes from the outside. It literally breaks through by entering what was previously a closed system and leads to a quantum leap. Soldiers for centuries had to dismount to fight. Then the stirrup was invented. For the first time a mounted warrior had sufficient traction to wield a sword from horseback without overbalancing himself. It was the harness maker and blacksmith who changed the face of war.

Open the windows and blur the distinctions between crafts. Let's focus intently, but focus more broadly. Our tool chest is often better stocked then we allow.

GO FOR GOALS—MINIMIZE MEANS

Going for goals and minimizing means sounds so simple, but in practice, we are all slaves to our paradigms. When the bell goes off, we either come out fighting or simply salivate like Pavlov's dog. We are conditioned by our past successes to repeat familiar means even in those areas where they guarantee our failures. Emphasizing goals rather then means sounds simple but so too does "do good and avoid evil."

One method of approach is to begin by disallowing past solutions and force new patterns into existence. Past practices carry the halo of "proof," untried solutions are suspect. Spend time—and a fair amount of it—defining the problem or describing the opportunity. Keep pushing it back to its most basic roots. Remember that the customer wants a one-quarter inch hole, not necessarily a one-quarter inch drill bit.

LOTS OF LADDERS

When it is obvious in the organization that there is but one well-worn path to the pinnacle, it becomes equally obvious to all those laboring in other crafts that you "ain't gonna get there from here." The best leave, thus weakening the organization. Those of lesser talent linger, weakening it ever further. What may have started out as an accident becomes a self-fulfilling prophesy or self-perpetuating necessity. In this case, the only ones fit to take over the top spot are Manufacturing VPs, or Chemists, or whatever, because all the truly adequate others have been driven out. A predisposition can become a practice, which can become a policy without a line having ever been written in a company manual.

Look at your company's/department's history. Check hiring practices, track compensation across departments. Has it happened in your organization?

PERFORMANCE—THE ONLY PROOF

It looks great in the lab. In a document it's dynamite, and the executive committee has endorsed it. The only problem is that customers and prospects lack enthusiasm. All solutions that are put into play differ in results from what is intended—sometimes superior, frequently flawed. The only proof that should be acceptable is empirical.

Tinker continually, especially with your successes. We frequently devote man-years of attention to weak products, processes, and markets showing little clear opportunity for breakthroughs. At the same time we starve and neglect areas where we already enjoy dominance.

The theoretical model of the bell-shaped curve for a product life cycle has led to the abandonment of many winners far short of the finish line. If the curve were always true, Ivory Soap and numerous other products would have been off the shelf ages ago. The theoretician has a place. It is not, however, above that of the tinkerer. Cherish the people who are able to work nearest the heat, who are geniuses of practicality and experience. There are fewer of them than we realize.

ALLOWABLE LEVELS OF DISORDER

A military platoon or regiment is characterized by discipline, but then its task or charter is not to create radically new methods or procedures. A marketing department or research lab is another entity altogether. There the emphasis is always centered on the new, the better, the more efficient. The comfort and certainty that is right for one organization has a dramatically limited role in the unit organized and charged with creating the new. It's not chaos, certainly, but to the outsider the logic may not seem apparent. *Ferment* is not a term often found in management or organizational tomes. It is, nevertheless, exactly what the creative organization requires. The ability to jettison long-cherished ideas, products, or practices is not a naturally occurring one. Creation brings with it confusion, disruption, and pain. Something is always lost along the way.

People like us and organizations like ours must develop cultures that welcome and embrace change. It's easy to see resistance to change in others. When we do it, it's called experience or wisdom. We must learn to be less wise and become more childishly enthusiastic.

SUMMARY

If you choose to follow these few precepts, you will create a climate that may appear to cost you dearly. You enjoy less order, you institutionalize more uncertainty, you share leadership, you run what others see as an untidy ship, and to top it all—you have no guarantee of success. Why do it? The presence of this climate, it is true, is no guarantee of success. Its absence, however, does in time guarantee failure. The choice is not between anarchy versus order. The choice is between leading rather than losing. Creative organizations don't develop new game plans, they develop entirely new games with new rules that they write. Guess who wins? ▨

47 Ideas Dancing in the Human Being

ROBERT MICHAEL BURNSIDE *Senior Research and Applications Associate, Center for Creative Leadership*

One of our greatest limitations to fostering creativity in organizations is this current crippled thinking about creativity. We are focused only on the parts of creativity, rather than the whole. We can greatly enhance our ability to improve organizational creativity when we think of it as the uniting of cognitive (thinking), affective (feeling), and intentional (willing) aspects that come together to be carried out in deeds (doing).

Come then, dancing sprite of my imagination, thought-form idea so clear and alive—Drink from the well of my feelings— brew, quickening thyself to life, shaping thy body from my warmth— delight, then Quickly! Quickly! Dive down into the limbs of my willful desire, my hands of hope, my feet of fire, then GO! GO! Shape the outer world, human-enlivened thought-being of idea-warmth-fire, GO I SAY, I am thy vehicle, thy birth-bed, life, and death-bed, I, thy maker, the Human Being, Am.

R. M. Burnside, March 1993

"*Help* us do 'out-of-the-box' thinking! We're so stuck in the same old ways of looking at things, we need your help to see our problems and opportunities in new ways!" So says the Marketing Director for a consumer products firm. "Okay," I say, wondering if this might be another time when I help a group form exciting boundary-spanning ideas that will come to nothing when planted in the meager soil of institutional languor and scarce resources.

"Can you just give us a high energy inspirational talk on creativity? You know—get everyone laughing, loosened up, and in a good mood for the rest of the conference?" So asks the Conference Director for an upcoming Human Resource Professional conference. "Okay," I say, wondering if this will be one of those feel-good-in-the-moment and soon-forgotten presentations that nowhere leads to real impact.

"Help our organization be more creative and innovative. We used to be a really creative group. Somewhere along the way we lost our enthusiasm and creativity—we're more dead than alive." So says the Vice President of Research and Engineering for a chemical products firm. "Okay," I say, wondering if I'm about to embark on another "irritate the prisoners" exercise, where we quicken a group's enthusiasm for alternative realities to the one they are living in, only to find that the institutional will to keep the status quo is stronger than the Vice President's will for change.

"I've got a million creative ideas here! We don't need any more ideas! Just help us figure out how to implement the ones we've got!" So says John, the R&D Director of a tire-components manufacturer, to me, the creativity expert from the Center for Creative Leadership. "Okay," I say, not surprised, as every one of my clients says this same thing. I discover here as elsewhere, however, that when we study the situation those "million creative ideas" are all in a small box labeled "how to make a stronger tire" and no one's thinking about defining the problem in different ways, such as "how to help things move over the ground."

What these four examples have in common—from my experience—is that each identifies only one aspect of creativity as the problem, rather than seeing creativity as a holistic process that involves four aspects:

1. Thinking—"Just help us have out-of-the-box thinking"
2. Feeling—"Just help us feel good about our creative potential"
3. Willing—"Just help us build our motivation for creativity"
4. Doing—"Just help us implement our ideas"

In my experience, one of our greatest limitations to fostering creativity in organizations is this current crippled thinking about creativity. We are focused only on the parts of creativity, rather than the whole. The current, most popular crippled conceptions of creativity are:

Creativity Is Mental Gymnastics: This approach takes a "head only" approach to creativity, believing that if we just teach the mind agility in forming notions, and how to overcome internal blocks to creative thinking, we'll have solved the problem. Most creative problem-solving courses focus here. This conception's motto is, "She who thinks different, is different."

Creativity Is Innovation: This approach emphasizes finding a formula for product or process improvement across groups in the organization. It focuses on cross-functional teams and dealing with the real politics of resource allocation. Its motto is, "It ain't creative unless it sells."

Creativity Is Mystical Insight: This approach emphasizes intuition, use of other ways of knowing, poetry, music, and the arts. It sees creativity as something new and different that feeds the soul. This creativity, however, doesn't like to be asked for results. Its motto is, "It's creative if it's beautiful to me."

Creativity Is Intrinsic Motivation: This approach emphasizes the necessity of the individual's personal values and interests to the creative task. Its motto is, "It's creative if I want to do it."

These four notions recall the ancient story from India of the Blind Men and the Elephant: Four blind men went to discover what an elephant is. The first grabbed the tail and said, "An elephant is like a rope." The second grabbed a leg and said, "An elephant is like a tree." The third grabbed a tusk and said, "An elephant is like a thorn." The fourth grabbed the trunk and said, "An elephant is like a snake." Who was right and who was wrong? All were right and all were wrong! It's the same with our current notions of creativity: All are right and all are wrong.

What can unite our four crippled conceptions of creativity? From my experience, the four aspects of creativity mentioned above come together as the four aspects of the human being; thinking-feeling-willing-doing. Other words for these same four aspects of the human are:

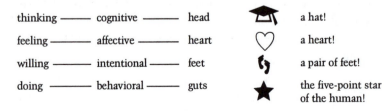

thinking	cognitive	head	🎓	a hat!
feeling	affective	heart	♡	a heart!
willing	intentional	feet	👣	a pair of feet!
doing	behavioral	guts	★	the five-point star of the human!

It is my belief that we can greatly enhance our ability to improve organizational creativity when we think of it as the uniting of cognitive (thinking), affective (feeling), and intentional (willing) aspects that come together to be carried out in deeds (doing). Therefore, any act of creativity, whether by individuals or groups, needs to consider the following:

> *thinking*—have we blue-skyed all the alternative problem definitions and solutions?
>
> *feeling*—have we considered our own feelings and life experiences in relationship to this problem and solution?
>
> *willing*—have we considered our intrinsic and extrinsic motivations in relationship to this problem?
>
> *doing*—do the above three add up to a deed we can do? Are resources available? Who/what/when will do it?

So, you ask, impatient reader, much like my other clients, "Help me make sense out of your ideas here—help me use this so my organization can be more creative." "Okay," I say, wondering if this new idea will really work . . .

WHAT YOUR GROUP CAN DO

Take the imaginative image at the beginning of this essay and work with it as follows with your group:

1. Clarify your thinking.

"Come then, dancing sprite of my imagination, thought-form idea so clear and alive—"
How clear are we on what this idea is that will solve our problem? Is the problem itself clear? Is our idea imaginative or dull? Is it alive—is it well rounded, interesting, workable (i.e., can it be further worked)? Do we all share the same picture of this idea? Is it a good idea? What is the ideal behind our idea?

2. Warm the idea with your feelings.   ♡

*"Drink from the well of my feelings-brew, quickening thyself to life,
shaping thy body from my warmth-delight."*

How do we feel about this idea? Do we like it? Is it beautiful,
elegant? Does it delight us? Do we want to play with it? Do we want
to spend time with it, dress it up, flesh it out? Does it feed our soul,
bring us energy? Would others like it? Does it feel good? What's
blocking us from doing this idea?

3. Seek to know your will.   ☙

*"Quickly, Quickly! Dive down into the limbs of my willful desire,
my hands of hope, my feet of fire."*

So, what will we do with this idea? What does the situation demand
of us? Will we do it? Will this bring about a good end? Is it good for
us, the organization, the world? Whose wills are opposed to this? Do
we really care about doing this? Do I care if it happens or not? Does
the organization really care? What are the consequences of failure?
Of success?

4. Don't just stand there, do something!   ★

*"GO! GO! Shape the outer world human-enlivened thought-being
of idea-warmth-fire, GO I SAY, I am thy vehicle, thy birth-bed, life,
and death-bed, I thy maker, the Human Being, Am."*

So, who will do what? How much money is there? Do we make it
out of nickel or aluminum? Who has time? When will we promise
results? What will the tangible result of our efforts be—what good will
it do? How will we measure our success or failure?

Thus, by following the above four steps with your group, you will
have fleshed out the whole act of creativity—from the idea into its
manifestation in the world—the act of creation. If your role is to
support the group that will be doing the creative act, you can do the
following, which is based on CCL's research on organizational cultures for creativity.

WHAT THE ORGANIZATION
CAN DO TO HELP GROUPS BE CREATIVE

1. PROVIDE FREEDOM (Thinking): Give a clear goal to the group, and then give as much freedom as possible to them to allow them to entertain any and every possible way to attain the goal. Don't constrain them, don't tell them how to attain it.

2. GIVE WARM ENCOURAGEMENT (Feeling): Let them feel how much you appreciate their efforts. Bake them cakes. Ask them how they are doing. Show interest. Give them constant warm psychological support.

3. CLARIFY THE ORGANIZATION'S WILL IN REGARD TO THEIR TASK (Willing): Tell them why the organization needs this done. Tell them the ideal outcome the organization is striving toward. Tell them why the organization's situation requires this to be done. Give historical context for the purpose of the activity. Deliberate who wants it and who supports it and who will stick by it for the long haul. Arrange bonuses, reward system, recognition.

4. PROVIDE RESOURCES (Doing): Give them a budget, people, things, access to what they need to accomplish their task. Carry out their wishes as soon as possible. Get stuff done for them. Take their spouses out to dinner. Send for pizza.

Ready to begin the creative journey? Searching for that good idea? Try this: Close your eyes, relax, and let your heart's longing carry you along the river of your imagination to the palace of your dreams . . . you've only just begun, but you'll get there if you'll see it all the way through all four steps: Good luck!

48 Gee Whiz!—So What?

ALAN G. CHYNOWETH *Vice President,*
Applied Research (Retired), Bellcore

The technical advance or breakthrough is only the beginning of what may be a long and uphill trail to the marketplace. A rough rule of thumb is that research results take about a decade before a commercial component is achieved. This, in turn, may take another decade to be incorporated into a system. This often puts researchers in the difficult position of having to "sell" their work at a stage where its eventual benefits can be articulated only in rather broad, vague terms. This approach is rather unconvincing to managers primarily concerned with relatively near-term financial results.

"Gee Whiz! What a beautiful result," exclaimed the researchers as they reflected on its wide-ranging implications. "So What?" grumped the business manager sitting at the back of the room, who had paid for the research. There, in a nutshell, is the essence, the two prime aspects to technological creativity, the Yin and the Yang. *Cognoscere et uti.* Discover and Apply. The synergy between these is fundamental to the successful introduction into the marketplace of a new product or technology. When it is working smoothly this synergy is beautiful to behold. But how does it get started?

Nearly always it starts with an idea, a moment of inspiration when a light switches on in someone's brain. But what preconditions lead to the birth of a creative idea? Nearly always the genesis arises from a problem, either one generated from the unknown, or, more often, by a known or anticipated problem. Although the unknown may inspire curiosity-driven research in scientific fields, in technological and industrial fields, foreseen business needs and opportunities determine the priorities among technological problems to be solved.

Obvious problems with short-term consequences are usually associated with pressure to find solutions quickly, especially if the problems are salient to the business managers. Researchers, on the other

308

hand, bear the added responsibility of looking beyond the horizons of business managers and anticipating future problems and needs. This often puts researchers in the difficult position of having to "sell" their work at a stage where its eventual benefits can be articulated only in rather broad, vague terms. This approach is rather unconvincing to managers primarily concerned with relatively near-term financial results. In retrospect, developing creative research may often seem easy compared to the task of managing the total innovation process, from the research laboratories to the marketplace.

GETTING TO "GEE WHIZ!"

Given all the hurdles that have to be surmounted before a researcher's achievements can bear business fruit—particularly in industries based on a highly complex systems technology—what induces the researcher to try for something new and original in the first place? Why not simply leave it to the business manager to decide what technical work needs to be done in order to meet management's marketplace agenda?

The short answer is that top quality researchers "know in their bones" that pandering to short-term perspectives leads inevitably and inexorably along a downward spiral path. True, the future must be met by taking a series of short-term steps; but without a long-term vision based on a sound understanding of what business the company is in, progress is more likely to take place inefficiently in a semi-purposeful, haphazard fashion.

The importance of having a steady, long-term vision of the mission of the organization cannot be overstated. The vision is of even greater value if researchers feel that it has broad social value and is not seen only in crass profit-making terms. For example, Bellcore adopted this vision early in its existence: "People and their machines will be able to communicate easily and securely with each other, anywhere in the world, at any time, in any medium—voice, data, image, video—and at acceptable cost." This vision serves not only to inspire, but to help both managers and researchers in their daily decision making. Defining the mission of the organization in these terms can be a valuable means of reducing the differences in managers' and researchers' perspectives regarding how they must operate within their respective business areas. Also, the direction provided by an inspiring vision can help reduce conflicts and focus efforts on developing "Gee Whiz" breakthroughs.

Although contributing to a significant societal goal is a strong motivator for researchers, it would be foolish to believe that personal and tangible rewards are of secondary importance. The possibilities of fame, fortune, peer recognition, and monetary rewards are tremendous incentives to individual researchers just as they are to those in other walks of life. These factors provide an important means of focusing effort on creative projects.

Another consideration is that research is a highly competitive "sport," with its own "rule book," in which researchers pit themselves against professional peers all around the world. This competition gets played out externally at technical conferences and in professional publications. Within large organizations, competitions among different technical approaches get played out at innumerable meetings, informal as well as formal. Whichever way, the key to channeling these competitive forces into creative technical progress is a tremendous amount of communication. Of course, communication is a two-way street. In the external professional world, the best way to gain access to the results and perspectives offered by others is to share your own technical research results. By doing so, researchers become members of the worldwide research club, gaining early technological intelligence on behalf of their company.

Internally, meetings serve to achieve the cross-fertilization and synergies among different research efforts. By listening to colleagues and "customers" in other parts of the organization, researchers often pick up ideas vital for focusing their work, making it more effective, and increasing the chances of producing a successful "Gee Whiz!"

Another positive consequence of a high degree of extra-organizational communication among researchers is the phenomenon of virtually simultaneous invention or discovery. It's as if, through almost constant communication, the research world is everywhere at the same technical state of the art, primed to take the next, usually incremental, advance. Thus, more or less the same creative advance can occur almost simultaneously and "independently" in various parts of the world, like bubbles rising in different parts of a simmering cauldron of brew.

Nowadays, it is more difficult than ever for researchers and labs to "go it alone," especially when time and funds are scarce. Researchers have always been adept at balancing competition and cooperation, exercising control over what they give away in order to get something they need in return. Now, whole companies are having to acquire analogous skills—of cooperating in technology even while competing in the marketplace.

Management has an important responsibility in helping the researchers achieve their "Gee Whiz" results. Besides the vital role of providing vision and focus, management must see to it that researchers have the funds and the facilities necessary to give them a fighting chance in worldwide research competition. Without this support, a company's research staff may not be able to spawn the critical mass of creative production necessary to be a player in the global research environment. Furthermore, and particularly critical, management must understand the need for—and provide—adequate freedom for researchers to manage their own programs as much as possible. Given this freedom, top quality researchers will usually act responsibly and often provide extraordinary returns on the sponsor's investment.

OBVIATING "SO WHAT?"

The technical advance or breakthrough is only the beginning of what may be a long and uphill trail to the marketplace. This is true even when the breakthrough is in response to a client's request, and is worse when it is the researcher who initiated the project. The more complex the system into which the technical breakthrough must fit, the longer the trail and the greater the number of obstacles that have to be surmounted. A rough rule of thumb is that research results, whether in the mathematical or the physical sciences, take about a decade (7 to 15 years) before a commercial component is achieved. This, in turn, may take another decade to be incorporated into a system. A total innovation period of 20 years or more is not unusual when complex systems, such as telecommunications, are involved.

Of course, once a major breakthrough has occurred, variations on the theme often follow thick and fast, giving rise to the perception that the pace of innovation is quickening. However, bringing about major, original innovations seems to take as long as ever despite all competitive pressures to speed up. There seems to be a natural law at work—that researchers tend to aim at innovations on a 7- to 15-year timescale. If it is shorter than that, the project is mainly development, making use of largely known technologies. Anything longer than that will probably exhaust the patience of even the most knowing of sponsors.

In today's world there are many hurdles that may lie across the innovation trail, and not just technical ones. They can involve the problems of technology transfer at each stage, the acquisition or training of experienced personnel, and the challenges of investing in and mounting a production effort. Market trials, problems of standards, federal and state regulatory matters, and legal maneuverings by other companies can also obstruct or delay innovation. When an innovation finally reaches the market, the real-time challenges of competition, demand (or disinterest), performance, and customer service are encountered.

How does a company maximize its chances of traversing the innovation trail successfully? Many books have been written on this subject, often under the title of managing technology. Many schemes with various degrees of analytical sophistication or bureaucratic detail have been proposed or used to achieve technology transfer. One scheme that has assumed much greater importance and recognition in recent years is the forming of interdisciplinary innovation teams. The time it takes to produce an innovation sequentially, one function at a time, is a luxury that can no longer be afforded. Instead, it makes more sense to pull a whole, interdisciplinary "innovation team" together at a relatively early point in the research phase, with representatives from each of the steps likely to be critical along the innovation trail. Representative end-customers can also be brought into the early technology development and trial stages. Early end-customer input can often spell the difference between success and failure.

Pulling an innovation team together can go a long way toward "greasing the skids" as a new technology, product, or service is launched. These teams help communicate the relevance of a new technology throughout the organization and help improve understanding regarding details of the project. The same principle applies, but in more concentrated form, in any hand-off from one group to another—from research to development and production, for example, or from a university or national laboratory to industry. Involving some production engineers upstream with the researchers early on can pay off handsomely in achieving a smooth and quick transition to production. Likewise, researchers following downstream into production can help immeasurably with overcoming the inevitable glitches that occur. No wonder that effective technology transfer has been aptly described as a "contact sport" where "it takes two to tango."

Finally, one other major lesson from experience is that—particularly with technologically complex enterprises—new technologies, products, or services are usually easier to introduce when they bring about cost reduction in existing operations or services. An innovation of this sort can serve the masters of both managers and researchers. Cost reductions are obviously pleasing to managers because they make immediate positive contributions to the bottom line. In contrast, elegant new technologies, products, or services that require major new investments to be made before they produce new revenues need a lot more "selling" to hard-bitten business managers. Mindful of this dichotomy, wily researchers may find (realistic) ways to position their new advances first as heralding cost reductions in the short run, even though they know full well that the technology has far greater potential as a revenue creator in the long run. By effectively employing cross-functional, and perhaps cross-organizational, innovation teams, and by placing greater emphasis on generating cost savings, researchers can go a long way toward obviating the "So what?" question.

LOOKING AHEAD

The current trend toward the breakup of big business into specialized fragments poses entirely new challenges for those responsible for managing innovation. How meaningful will a long-range vision for the enterprise now be? Can a single-minded focus on the customer's needs, whoever the customer is, fully take its place? Will a fragmented, constantly churning industrial environment be able to provide the relative stability that research needs if it is to tackle ambitious objectives rather than only modest, incremental ones? Can a counterbalance be retained to the otherwise inevitable downward spiral engendered by obsessive attention to the customers' understandably short-term interests?

Although the business and research environment is changing rapidly, almost violently, creativity still has to be carried out by humans. Managers must realize that the fundamental attitudes and emotions of humans change very, very slowly, as any reading of history confirms. Thus, managers intent on maximizing technological creativity must still cater to the human needs for support, recognition, fair rewards, and a degree of security. Managers must still go all out to attract and keep the most imaginative, inventive, and technically sound researchers available. And then, they must see that these researchers not only understand the business environment that they are in but are excited by it. The old formula still holds: Acquire the best people, communicate the business interests to them, and then trust them to optimize their performance as they respond to a free market of ideas and objectives.

On the other hand, today's outstandingly creative researcher must be a "Complete Technologist"—one who has business savvy as well as technical skills, who happily accepts constant change as the natural state, and who enthusiastically engages in teamwork in order to achieve successful innovations. Being able to work the worldwide research network—with professional peers, with business colleagues, with non-technologists, and politicians—is also necessary. This should keep the "Gee Whizzes" coming and the "So Whats?" at bay.

Ultimately, if a company is guided by a widely shared vision and practices the total quality management techniques that are available to all, it is the quality, skill, resourcefulness, originality, and—above all—the morale of the researchers and developers that can give a company its competitive, creative edge. ▨

Understanding and Influencing Creativity in Organizations

PART IV

49 Contrasts and Convergences in Creativity

Themes in Academic and Practitioner Views

DENNIS A. GIOIA *The Pennsylvania State University*

*F*orty-six essays. Quite a kaleidoscopic trip through the world of creativity in organizations as seen by academicians who think, research, and write about creativity and as seen by practicing executives who contemplate, encourage, and try to manage creativity in organizations. A varied anthology if there ever was one. What might we make of these multiple voices and multiple views, all of which consider creativity in one form or another? If we treat these essays as evidence of the current state of thought and application concerning organizational creativity, what distinctive patterns emerge? In particular, are there telling differences and/or similarities in the ways that academicians and practitioners construe this world of creativity in organizations? In a word, yes.

I readily admit that my own way of seeing inevitably colors the identification of patterns in the writings; I also confess that our cleaving of the world into academic and practitioner categories is itself probably an artificial distinction. Nonetheless, I believe it can be informative to look at differences and similarities in the way these two groups consider creativity in organizations. In many ways an enthusiastic reading of these essays alters the definition or conception of creativity, especially as it applies to organizations. It certainly has altered mine.

AN EVOLVING PERSONAL
DEFINITION OF CREATIVITY

I have been a long-time dabbler in creativity. Although I don't consider myself to be a particularly creative person in any grand sense, I nonetheless have maintained a fascination with the topic. I have even had the frustrating experience of trying to teach it on occasion. As a result of my dabbling, I have tried to articulate my sense of what creativity is in some pithy phrase that captures its essence for me. Now, any reasonable person who has sampled this book will recognize the folly of this attempt. Still, it is informative to me to look at how my own thinking has changed, particularly as a result of editing this book.

Early on, I just thought of creativity as "thinking differently." Pretty simple, really, because it focused my sights only on individual processes and the novelty of ideas. Over the years, I elaborated this view only in small ways. I adopted the observation that creativity is "the ability to hold two competing thoughts in mind simultaneously." An advance, perhaps, in complexity of the concept (and number of words), but still not much progress beyond the same, inherent confinements. Similarly, I also saw creativity as the process of "making the familiar strange." And so on—a successive litany of witty phrases but inadequate conceptualizations. These notions perhaps offer some insight, but I have since deemed them to be incomplete, especially for the task of considering creativity in organizations, and especially since reading these essays.

In the process of editing this volume, I arrived at a way station that saw creativity as "escaping the taken-for-granted," but soon settled on a mode of understanding in which I see creativity as "effective rebellion against prior learning." I like this one better for the moment because, while it still retains its pithiness (and therefore memorability), it is notably more encompassing. It connotes both thought and action; it presumes value as well as novelty; it is extendible beyond the individual level to the organizational level; and it suggests the kinds of constraints from which creativity must escape.

Nevertheless, to try to capture the essence of creativity in organizations in an incisive little phrase is a bit too much to expect. To see why, it is useful to look with a different lens at the essays—to look for a kind of deep structure that considers the contrasts, complexities, and convergences displayed in their form and content. In that spirit, I would first like to note some impressionistic contrasts in the ways that academics and practitioners conceived of creativity. This broadbrush view shows that there are some intriguing differences in tone between the two groups. Then I would like to take a short narrative tour through the identifiable themes that emerged from each group. Summarizing these themes captures many of the essential insights available in the book and highlights many of the key observations. Although this little tour is again arranged by group, it not only points up the differences, but also begins to show the many themes around which the representatives of the ivory tower and the real world converge with each other. Finally, I would like to provide a brief display of the common ground our diverse authors share.

CONTRASTS IN ACADEMIC AND PRACTITIONER CREATIVITY THEMES

1. Academics dwell on the novelty dimension of creativity.
   Practitioners dwell on the value dimension.
2. Academics seek novel solutions and look for value.
   Practitioners seek value and look for novel solutions.
3. Academics emphasize the divergent thinking and acting involved in creativity.
   Practitioners emphasize the convergent thinking and acting involved.
4. Academics think of creativity as thinking differently.
   Practitioners think of creativity as doing differently.
5. Academics seek the impetus for creativity within the organization.
   Practitioners seek the impetus for creativity outside the organization.
6. Academics focus on producing diverse ideas.
   Practitioners focus on satisfying diverse interests.

7. Academics make more general, global statements about creativity.
   Practitioners make specific, local statements about creativity.
8. Academics treat creativity as an unbounded enterprise.
   Practitioners treat creativity as a pragmatically bounded enterprise.
9. Academics talk about creativity as an aesthetic accomplishment.
   Practitioners talk about creativity as a practical prelude to innovation.
10. Academics are more dispassionate and removed in their discussions of creativity.
    Practitioners are more passionate and personally involved in their discussions of creativity.

Admittedly, these contrasts are overdrawn; one could easily cite disconfirming examples. Nonetheless, this coarse-grained analysis serves to point up some intriguing distinctions in the ways that the two groups think and act concerning creativity. Academics lean more toward novelty and divergence, are more conceptually oriented, and like more extensive, analytical observations. Practitioners emphasize value, convergence, and effectiveness, are more action oriented, recognize more constraints on creativity, and treat it in a more personal, close-to-the-bone fashion. A more fine-grained theme analysis of the essays can help to lend some insight into the specifics of these differences in academic and practitioner conceptions of creativity in organizations.

ACADEMIC THEMES

In the academics' essays there is frequent homage paid to the role of chance and serendipity in the discovery and production of creative products and services. The unpredictability of possibilities and the spontaneity of ideas, as well as an orientation toward aggressive opportunism in the context of ambiguity emerge as well-springs for both creativity and innovation. This recurring theme echoes a feature associated with creativity in other contexts.

Similarly, creativity in organizations is also aligned with traditional portrayals in that it is variously characterized as divergent thinking that results in "seeing in new ways," as "breaking out of existing ways of thinking and acting," as the "shazzam!" or flash of insight that leads to novel and valuable products and services, as the synthesizing of diverse information or possibilities into new opportunities, as the production of variation and variety that provide new solutions to sticky old problems, and as the happy accident or surprise that creates opportunities or markets where none were envisioned before.

The nature of the creative process continues to be cast often as intuitive, nonrational, and nonlinear—as tacit knowledge or perceptions of significant patterns in information or events that are out of conscious awareness. This characterization continues a long-standing belief that there is something almost "mystical" about creative processes; this also is a description that fits nicely with views of creativity in other settings.

But, contrary to this common view, there is a strong undercurrent in these pages that creativity in the specific context of organizations also is often decidedly not nonlinear—that the structuring of organizations and the typically instrumental nature of their activities in fact implies that creativity occurs in an often purposeful, sometimes even sequential, goal-oriented fashion. It occurs among people who are paying close attention to the possibilities for surfacing solutions to identified problems in which they have an intense interest and an intrinsic motivation to find or invent a solution.

Prior knowledge, skill, or experience in a relevant domain and a reasonably focused organizational agenda imply that creative processes are not necessarily scattered or haphazard. Indeed, they can be quite methodical. Actually, creativity in organizations might often be most aptly described as some combination of nonrational and rational processes—processes that allow fluidity and flexibility, but also structure and closure. Creativity also applies to the post-processing of information. That is to say that creativity need not be only a front-end-loaded process designed to generate creative outcomes, but also can be an after-the-fact process that makes sense of events or outcomes in a creative way after events have occurred.

Taken together, the above observations imply that the domain of creativity in organizational settings is quite expansive. They also have a related implication: that the potential for creativity is actually widely distributed; it is not merely the playground of only a few geniuses or special individuals, but in principle resides in many organizational members (not everybody, but certainly a wider possible circle of contributors than hero stories would imply). There is a further implication in these essays that organizational creativity should be construed as "normal." People, and especially people working together on shared conundrums, have natural creative tendencies. Given the potential for creativity, organizations should expect that their members can and will produce creative solutions to significant problems or market opportunities.

From this line of thought also emerges one of the strongest themes in the book: that, especially in organizations, creativity emerges not from the work of isolated creators, but from those immersed in group or team efforts. This view comes up repeatedly in either direct or indirect fashion and tends to undermine the traditional caricature of creativity as a lonely pursuit. Although the authors do not dismiss the potential for individuals to produce creative outcomes on their own, the overwhelming emphasis is on the facilitating potential of teams. In some ways this observation might simply be seen as a manifestation of the old adage that two heads are better than one. But it calls into question the common mythology that we need to identify and isolate the individual genius who will come up with a creative solution. Not so. What we need to do is to encourage the natural creativity that emerges when people collaborate in interactive, team-oriented settings.

This focus on creativity as a social process suggests a significant change from the traditional concentration on individuals in the creativity literature and distinguishes creativity in organizations from, for instance, creativity in the fine arts. Thinking of creativity as a collective enterprise amounts to a substantial reorientation and puts the spotlight on an essential hallmark of organizations—that they are organized collectivities. Teams bring diversity and a range of skills, views, and experience to bear on problems. Individuals working in teams often thrive on cooperative and collaborative ventures, and they gain the trust and support necessary to foster off-beat solutions. Paradoxically, team members also provide the doubt necessary to forge worthwhile solutions (i.e., occasionally, everyone needs an opponent . . . and frequently the most constructive opponents come from within the creator's own team).

The organizational context supplies many of the sources of inspiration and motivation for creators. These can come from many directions—from inside or outside the team or from loose networks of professional acquaintances. Extra-departmental network links often provide the kind of heterogeneity that sparks the solution to a problem that homogeneous teams frequently do not see. Of course, networks, too, are a hallmark of organizational life, one that provides a distinct advantage over creative individuals working alone.

The focus on the organizational context also emphasizes some of the dynamic processes required to shepherd creative solutions through a not-necessarily-receptive system. Creative ideas are often resisted simply because they challenge a comfortable status quo. New solutions often have implications for the powers-that-be—a fact of organizational life that calls attention to the political dimensions of creativity. Ideas need to be promoted, often with champions or sponsors who can navigate them through existing power structures with the aid of insiders' knowledge and political skill. Otherwise, creative solutions die young.

That observation calls forth another strong theme from the academic authors: Creativity can be a risky business. First, attempting a new approach usually implies a lower probability of success than sticking with an old approach. Second, as noted, producing new solutions means taking the chance of precipitating controversy or conflict with powerful players who might disagree with the idea or its implications. For both reasons, creativity requires courage—and *courage* really is not too strong a word here. Rather than courage in the physical sense, this is courage in the psychological sense. For those who experience the disappointment of expensive or expansive ideas not working out, or who must endure the disapproval of peers and superiors, courage is a requisite. There are two strong implications for practice here: First, creators should be able to fail creatively, yet persist in the face of failure and not be penalized for either failure or persistence; second, creative failure should be treated mainly as a learning opportunity.

Overall, there is a strong collective voice among these essays that touts the need for creative organizational cultures—cultures that supply: (a) managerial support for creative effort in general and risk taking in particular; (b) collegial, collaborative support; (c) rewards and recognition for creativity; and (d) freedom, flexibility, and autonomy to get on with the creative work. Creative cultures also emphasize challenge, technological leadership, and trust. In addition, they imply flexible organizational structures. Many writers pointed to the classic bureaucratic hierarchy as an impediment to creativity and argued that the hierarchy needs to be managed so that it does not stifle creativity. In that sense, structural change itself can be a creative act.

Lastly, the academic writers often saw creativity as an evolving, changing phenomenon, implying that organizations need to be oriented toward change to feed the creativity and innovation necessary to cope with external shifts. Creativity, then, is a form of organizational learning, perhaps a key reason for promoting its development.

PRACTITIONER THEMES

Practitioners first of all are not particularly romantic about creativity. They tend to think and operate within a pragmatically bounded conception of creativity, mainly because they are more finely attuned to the business or organizational environment. Within that environment the dominant focus is on a pronounced customer orientation (broadly defined), with an eye toward the practicalities of delivering a product or service and the returns on doing so.

Practitioners take very seriously the notion that creative products are those that are novel and valuable. The "So What?!" question is ever present and tempers the basic fascination with discovery or invention. If new technology is the initial focus of organizational creativity efforts, then the feasibility of transferring technology to practical application is a close second. Practicality represents a high hurdle that must be cleared before technological novelty demonstrates the kind of value that earns the label of "creative." Good ideas must progress from *discovery* to *development* to *deployment*. A stopper anywhere in that chain damns the idea or prototype to oblivion. Even if it is an undeniably original idea, it is nonetheless stamped as an uncreative solution if it can not be developed and implemented in a cost-effective manner.

Practitioners view creativity as customer- and market-driven. The necessity to be sensitive to the organizational environment raises a number of issues not usually considered in traditional treatments of creativity. These include issues relating to the structuring of ambiguity, negotiating among multiple constituencies with multiple preferences, and trying to deal with loosely coupled (yet influential) interconnections among organizations and their multiple stakeholders and environments.

Overall, the practitioner approach to organizational creativity is more concerned with the production of value, particularly value that addresses some societal need. Satisfaction of such needs is typically operationalized in terms of commercial value and is measured by commercial success. Indeed, several of these writers view creativity predominantly in terms of commercial success. There is a strong value for value, so to speak. Yes, originality matters, but only insofar as it translates into a usable product, service, or program.

Again, there is little romanticism here. Divergence, originality, unconventional thinking, inventiveness, imagination, and asking non-obvious questions are all honored, welcomed, and encouraged, in principle. But all must pass tough standards for the marriage-of-necessity with usefulness. In general, that means ideas and solutions must have a foreseeable relevance and practicality about them, which implies that they must converge with applications. Ideas must display technology-market connections, which means that R&D labs cannot be anarchies. Solutions must be capable of implementation, and they must have quality, however defined by the end user.

This sort of practical creativity needs to be guided by a clearly expressed organizational vision, by leadership that espouses and acts in accordance with the vision, and by strategies and tactics that support it. Creative environments breed creativity. Visionary initiatives and an orientation toward new ventures establish that environment. The vision should be long term, should spring from the organization's values, and should be touted in unequivocal language by top management. Simultaneously, however, leadership needs to be shared in the sense that creative people should be permitted to manage their own efforts to achieve solutions that fit within a broadly defined strategic vision.

Strategic relevance is simply essential. In that light, strategic planning can facilitate creativity because it supplies a framework whereby R&D activities can be aligned with strategic vision. Properly done, planning need not stifle creativity, but instead can channel it.

Structure becomes facilitating rather than constraining. In an almost paradoxical sense, structure is freedom.

Within the context of a broad vision and overarching strategy, however, the practitioners believe that creativity is best facilitated by a clear focus on a given problem. Staying focused is an echoing theme in the essays. Organizational creativity almost never is construed as an undirected process. Even if a problem area is broadly defined, it is best defined as clearly as possible. Ideas and solutions are considered in terms of articulated project or corporate goals. The notion of "managing" creativity is assumed to be necessary; the notion of "directing" creativity is considered to be within the realm of possibility, but only so long as there is a well-defined problem and an intent focus.

To foster creativity in these terms, the practitioners make a compelling case for strong management support. That support comes in many forms, from simple encouragement to the provision of physical facilities. Most notably, however, it comes in the form of supplying resources—or more accurately, risking resources to pursue creative possibilities. The upshot of risking resources for several authors was an unequivocal recognition that creative enterprises sometimes fail, but that failure is tolerable within a concept of limited risk.

Many of the writers viewed bureaucratic organization as the prime barrier to an orientation toward risk, seeing it mainly as an obstacle to good work. They noted the influential role of organizational culture as well. Although acknowledging culture's potential for encouraging creativity, there also was an undertone of wariness toward culture's potential for inhibiting creativity. Resistance to the changes implied by many creative solutions often is in-bred in strong organizational cultures. Both the organizational hierarchy and the organizational culture need to encourage some form of freedom to set the stage for creativity. Whether described as autonomy, flexibility, discretion, venturesomeness, empowerment, or entrepreneurship, it was deemed necessary to the process of exploring interests that might generate creative organizational applications. Although goals should be organizational in nature, freedom to choose approaches to attaining goals should reside with the creators.

Perhaps in an even more pronounced fashion than the academic essays, the practitioners emphasize the team or group aspects of creativity in organizations. They noted once again that teams facilitate creativity by fostering cooperation and collaboration and by balancing diverse but complementary skills that synthesize possibilities into workable outcomes. These writers, however, conceived of the team approach to creativity more broadly than the academics. They spoke not only in terms of creativity within work groups, but often as it related to task forces, networks of groups, divisions, other organizations, partnerships, and even communities and governments. The conception here was notably cross-disciplinary, with a forthright and widespread willingness to argue the permeability of assumed boundaries. Linking up with others, it seems, does not need to recognize traditional boundaries.

Overall, there was a strong sense that creating the context for creativity requires conscious attention to the structures and processes of organizations. Therefore, organizations that want creativity and innovation must be designed to facilitate it. Steps range from the obvious encouragement of curiosity, to attempts to decentralize decision making, to restructuring reward and recognition systems, to designing systems that facilitate more rapid movement from discovery to development to deployment.

Taken together, it is clear that there are some informative contrasts between the views of the academics and practitioners. Yet, in many ways those contrasts reveal something about shared similarities as well as differences. The themes in the previous sections suggest that both groups of writers also converge around similar notions, despite the sometimes subtle contrasts within a given theme. Thus a different set of lenses, focused this time on convergence, allows us to see that these authors are not talking past each other.

CONVERGENCES IN CREATIVITY THEMES

There are a number of interesting and useful commonalities among the academic and practitioner writings, especially at the level of more general themes. Because each of these themes has been discussed above, rather than belabor the points, we can quickly summarize the convergences with a set of compact observations.

1. Creativity in organizations is typically a team enterprise, not an individual phenomenon. Creativity seldom emerges as the work of solitary geniuses, but as the collective work of collaborative groups and networks. It is in this realization that creativity in organizations most notably differs from traditional and popular conceptions.

2. Creativity is, by its nature, a risky business. Creative enterprises sometimes fail, but creators should be able to fail without undue jeopardy. The hallmark of creative organizations is the commitment to risking resources to pursue creative possibilities.

3. In organizations, new ideas alone do not constitute creativity. Ultimately, ideas must progress from the discovery of novel solutions with practical relevance, to development of the value potential of those solutions, to their successful deployment in the marketplace. In other words, the elemental components of creativity in organizations are novelty, value, and effectiveness.

4. Creativity in the context of organizations contains strong doses of rational as well as nonrational processes. Contrary to folk wisdom, creativity involves deliberation and consideration as well as flexibility and fluidity. Creativity is almost never construed as an undirected process, but rather as a goal-directed process.

5. Managerial leadership and support are critical to creative effort. A guiding vision helps to provide creativity goals, but support also comes in the provision of resources, rewards, and recognition within a facilitating culture of freedom and autonomy. Creative environments breed creativity, which in turn, breeds more creativity.

6. Traditional bureaucratic hierarchies are impediments to creativity. Organizational creativity often takes the form of creatively transforming the organization structure in ways that facilitate the activities of people looking for an opportunity to be creative.

7. Creativity should be seen as a *normal* part of organizational life. People at work can be expected to produce creative solutions as a matter of course, not as a cause for surprise. Expecting creativity leads to the realization of creativity.

So there we have it: a look at some of the themes, contrasts, and convergences that characterize the essays of our academic and practitioner contributors. We have chosen to symbolize one of these overarching themes on the cover of this volume: that creativity in organizations involves both divergent and convergent thought and action before it is effective. The stylized diverging/converging arrows capture this key observation. As enlightening and informative as these thematic analyses might be, however, they are nonetheless somewhat limited in that they are a small universe unto themselves. But, what would happen if we joined these insights with the findings presented by the existing research literature on organizational creativity (as articulated in Chapter 2)? What sort of revised framework for understanding creativity in organizations might emerge by simultaneously considering ideas from more than 40 years of research and from state-of-the-art organizational practice? That question constitutes the heart of our exploration in the next chapter. Finally, what guidelines might we offer to interested researchers and practitioners on the basis of this revised framework? That question is the driving concern addressed by our concluding chapter in the volume.

50 Striking Inspirational Sparks and Fanning Creative Flames

A Multi-Domain Model of Creative Action Taking

CAMERON M. FORD *Rutgers University*

*R*eaders of this volume have been blitzed with ideas about how to influence creativity in organizational settings. Some of these ideas are based on accumulated empirical evidence, others are rooted in years of scholarly theorizing, and still others derive from the reflections of practicing managers. Chapter 2 organized and presented findings drawn from more than 45 years of empirical research on creativity in organizational contexts. The preceding chapter uncovered themes among the voices of the contributors about influences on organizational creativity in modern organizations. This chapter attempts to integrate, or at least reconcile, the varied conclusions drawn from the existing creativity literature and from our contributors.

It begins by noting some of the qualities that distinguish professional and organizational creativity from creativity in other domains. I make these observations in the spirit of cautioning readers to be wary of popular conceptualizations of creativity that have their roots in non-organizational domains. Next, the concept of "behavior episodes" is introduced as a way of thinking about the configuration of forces that combine to give rise to creative acts. The chapter then presents a revised framework for understanding and influencing creativity in organizational contexts. The framework first emphasizes one of the main distinctive features of creativity in organizations: the multiple domains that facilitate and constrain the actions of individual creators. It then presents a depiction of individual creativity embedded within these multiple domains. After this framework is articulated, the final chapter specifies a number of guidelines that can improve the ability of organizational actors to enhance their own creativity and the creativity of others.

The framework described here offers several distinctive contributions to our understanding of creative action in organizational contexts. It uses the systems view of creativity proposed by Csikszentmihalyi (1988, 1990) as a point of departure, proposing that creativity is best thought of as the result of an interaction among a domain (a body of knowledge that is transmitted to individuals), a person (who takes action based in part on domain knowledge), and gatekeepers (loosely organized institutions and individuals that reject or retain creative actions for future inclusion in the domain). This perspective is especially well suited for the purpose of understanding creativity in organizations because it recognizes the reciprocal influence processes between creators and domains.

The framework presented here, however, extends this systems view in several ways that make it more useful for organizational researchers and practitioners. First, it points out that creative actions in organizations often face *simultaneously overlapping, multiple domains* rather than single domains. The discussion continues by identifying the most significant domains that influence organizational action, and exploring the complex implications that follow from attempting to please multiple audiences, with different tastes, perhaps on multiple occasions. Next, it provides a comprehensive description of the motivational and cognitive processes that influence the nature and persistence of an individual's actions. An important characteristic of this portrayal is that it can be used to describe influences on both habitual and creative actions. A final contribution is that it illustrates more specifically than previous portrayals the nature of the interactions between individuals and organizationally relevant domains that lead to creative action. Specifying these interactions helps to develop organizationally-wise guidelines for creative organizational actors and their managers (the subject of the final chapter).

WHAT'S DIFFERENT ABOUT ORGANIZATIONAL
AND PROFESSIONAL CREATIVITY?

A common view of creativity holds that great works spring forth from the efforts of individuals working in isolation. So many of Western culture's powerful popular images, from Dr. Frankenstein in *Frankenstein* to Dr. Brown in *Back to the Future*, present an image of misfit geniuses laboring to solve a tantalizing problem (e.g., creating life, solving time travel). These images support a widely held belief that creative talent is a rare commodity so compelling that it virtually forces those who are blessed with it to pursue creative ends doggedly in all of their endeavors. If they subject themselves to the stifling influences imposed by outsiders or organizations, it is cast as a tragic case of extraordinary talent wasted on pedestrian undertakings.

This person-centered view is consistent with a widely held tendency of people to use oversimplified explanations for events, and to attribute the cause of great achievements to individuals (what is known in some circles as the "fundamental attribution error"). This romance with creative heroes, however, has unwittingly led even practitioners and researchers to focus their attention too narrowly on identifying individual differences that elicit creative performance. This person-centered view has outlived its usefulness. No other theme so unites the contributors to this volume. What is worse is that this dominant myth continues to distract us from a more useful focus on the higher potential source of creativity: the modern organization as a collective of talented people working together.

The next major step forward in understanding creativity generally, and organizational creativity specifically, is in accounting for the influence of *context* on the origination, evaluation, and realization of creative actions. Organizations possess distinct qualities that present challenges and opportunities to those interested in creativity. Three overwhelming meta-themes that distinguish the study and practice of creativity in organizations have been voiced throughout this volume: (a) organizational creativity places a greater burden on value production and subjects a creator to a broader array of evaluations than creativity in other domains, (b) creative action in organizational settings requires more perseverance and social savvy than is typical in other contexts, and (c) creative acts in organizations emerge within a highly interactive social milieu.

The first of these meta-themes relates to the definition of creativity within organizational and professional contexts. Creativity in this setting clearly refers to novel acts that produce value relative to an organization's mission and markets. Academics can quibble over criteria and measures all they want, but as a practical matter novel ideas that do not produce value relative to a firm's strategic thrust fail to make the grade as "creative" solutions in organizational contexts. In addition, novel proposals are typically subjected to multiple evaluations on multiple occasions from multiple judges representing multiple domains. One step toward closing the relevance gap between researchers and practitioners in this area would be to adopt a common language for creativity that reflects an emphasis on value as well as novelty. For researchers and consultants, this means pursuing a more balanced agenda that supplements popular approaches aimed at facilitating the production of novel ideas (e.g., brainstorming, synectics) with methodologies aimed at developing and justifying the worth of novel ideas.

The second meta-theme points out that, more so than in domains such as art or education, creative action in organizations typically requires sustained efforts that may take weeks, months, often years or even decades to be realized. Organizations demand both working and waiting—a paradoxical combination of intense activity and studied patience. The birth of a creative idea may be the easy part; bringing ideas to fruition within a context that demands a touch of moxie provides additional challenges that give organizational creativity its distinctive character. Given this observation, one wonders if such old creativity training tricks as asking for many different, possible uses for a brick or a ping-pong ball, or for solutions to brainteasers like the "nine-dot problem," have any relevance at all for engaging creativity in organizational contexts. Fun? Yes. Transference of skill to the job? Doubtful. For these reasons, one could speculate that in organizations, creativity is more likely to whither because of problems related to attention and motivation rather than an absence of creative talent.

The third meta-theme suggests that traditional conceptions of creativity need to be expanded to account for the quintessentially social nature of creative action in organizational settings. Interpersonal and intergroup interactions increase the likelihood that novel ideas and associations can emerge within and across domains. They also help to sustain and develop novel ideas to the point where they are able to contribute value. Simultaneously, trying to conform to implicit conventions and explicit evaluations imposed by multiple gatekeepers can quickly snuff creative ideas. Thus, a more realistic and refined view of creativity must be able to account for the multiple and varied influences of social contexts.

There is one additional distinction that has been underplayed in prior discussions of creativity that is particularly relevant to organizational settings. It probably will come as little surprise that organizational contexts are typified by their common frames of "habitual" thought and action that lead to the production and reproduction of established patterns of behavior. Shared interpretive frames lead organization members to see issues in a similar light (Daft & Weick, 1984) and to enact "tried and true" procedures and solutions without generating or considering alternative options (see March & Simon, 1958; Nutt, 1984). Organizations that attempt to build strong cultures through aggressive socialization, training, and retention strategies are especially likely to engender consistent interpretations and actions that lead to the "exploitation of old certainties" as opposed to the "exploration of new possibilities" (March, 1991). This final distinction is key: Creative actions in organizations are especially likely to compete with well-established responses to particular circumstances.

Traditional approaches to thinking about, researching, and influencing creativity are based primarily on identifying factors that either facilitate or constrain creative behaviors. The implicit assumption is that if one can somehow remove the "blocks" to creativity, then the natural talents that most people possess will blossom. The focus on overcoming "creative blocks" is so ingrained in our thinking that its logic is seldom questioned. This orientation, however, focuses on only half of what we need to know in order to encourage creative acts. In response to a particular occasion, a person could undertake an almost limitless variety of potential behaviors. Yet, the range of *likely* behaviors is usually very restricted, especially in familiar settings. Put simply, people typically respond habitually to situations they have encountered before. Furthermore, we have a talent for interpreting unfamiliar situations in familiar terms that allow us to enact habitual behaviors regardless of their relevance to novel circumstances. Thus, we usually observe a "perseverance effect" in most peoples' behavior. Behavior has a predictable regularity to it, rather than a creative adaptiveness. In this light, it is easy to understand how seeing the world though a child's eyes can open up a world of creative opportunities, because a child does not possess the cognitive and behavioral baggage that comes with experience.

These observations about normal human fallibilities lead us to suggest that it is shortsighted to assume that one can elicit creative behavior simply by concentrating on factors that facilitate or constrain its occurrence. Such an approach ignores the probability that, even in the most favorable circumstances, there are likely to be familiar behavioral options available that are relatively more attractive based on their past success, ease, and certainty. Therefore, creative actions are not likely to emerge unless they present consequences that are more desirable than existing behavioral options. This point is so important that we have chosen to give it a label: "*The Competitive Advantage Principle of Creativity*": *Creative actions must hold a competitive advantage over old, familiar actions before they will be undertaken.*

This suddenly complicates an already difficult task. We not only must try to engage creativity, but we must simultaneously attempt to circumvent comfortable behavior patterns. Prior conceptualizations of creativity have not emphasized the competing behavioral options that exist at every turn in organizations or the management challenges associated with them.

This statement is not a manifesto for indiscriminately subverting established behavior patterns. Such patterns provide efficiency, continuity, and comfort. They embody learned skills and are the basis of high reliability and quality. At their best, they constitute what we commonly refer to as wisdom. However, to the extent that they make new problems difficult to apprehend, outdated or inappropriate solutions easy to fall back on, and novel alternatives difficult to imagine, this entrenched "wisdom" can derail creativity. Ingrained behavior patterns need to be recognized and temporarily put on the shelf when creative actions are sought.

Just as routinized behavior has advantages and disadvantages, so do creative acts. On the plus side, creative acts provide potential sources of differentiation that can help a firm improve its market status. They are also likely to produce improved service levels, especially in contexts where high levels of customization of end products is required. Creative acts are also immensely satisfying for most people, and are generally seen as the pinnacle of fulfillment of personal potential and are a measure of organizational prestige. On the downside, creative acts can be disruptive and expensive because of false starts and steep learning curves. They create uncertainty and can lead to low reliability. They are often effortful, uncomfortable, and at odds with the social systems in which they are embedded. As a result, the risks of creative actions frequently defy capture via traditional cost-benefit calculations.

Overall, creativity, especially in organizational settings, involves two simultaneous challenges: facilitating creative acts on the one hand, and bypassing tacit, routinized behaviors on the other. In practical terms, a manager trying to encourage creative action must attempt to understand and arrest standard interpretations and actions while simultaneously directing attention and effort toward creative alternatives. The framework to be presented addresses this challenge by depicting creativity as a process in which individuals produce creative actions while inextricably embedded and intertwined within organizational contexts and domains that constrain and facilitate both customary and creative behaviors.

THE PIECES OF THE PUZZLE:
CREATIVE PEOPLE, PROCESSES,
PLACES, AND PRODUCTS

Creativity researchers have argued for decades about the relative merits of studying creative persons, creative processes, and creative places. Although these arguments have helped to refine research approaches to creativity, they have also highlighted limitations to practical relevance that arise from narrow research orientations based within solitary scholarly disciplines. More recent views have moved from these tired debates toward the notion that creative products should be the predominant benchmark for judging creativity (see Amabile, 1982). However, this evolution has provided little guidance for reconciling the different approaches utilized by scholars of different stripes, or the recommendations for practice gleaned from past research.

One promising approach has been to view creativity as an interaction between a person, a domain (a context characterized by shared notions regarding thought and action), and judges within the domain (who ultimately evaluate and select creative acts for future inclusion in the domain) (see Csikszentmihalyi, 1988, 1990; see also Gardner, 1993). From this perspective, individuals provide variations (i.e., new ideas, products, services, etc.) within a domain, judges select and retain high-potential outcomes that they favor, and the domain becomes more elaborate as it adopts new outcomes. This interaction is continuous and reflects the gradual elaboration of a domain by creative actions over time. This perspective echoes the evolutionary variation-selection-retention processes used to explain natural selection. All three components are necessary for a complete description and definition of a creative act.

However, one important limitation of this framework is that it ignores the influence of variation, retention, and selection processes arising from outside a particular domain. In organizational terms, this would be like orienting oneself toward a single interest group rather than considering the multiple and often competing interests of multiple interests within and beyond an organization's boundaries. In organizational contexts it is necessary to consider the influence of multiple stakeholders (representing multiple domains), to develop a comprehensive understanding of the variation-selection-retention processes at play in a particular instance of creative action. Therefore, to develop a more practical understanding of creativity, I extend this framework by *depicting creative actions that are simultaneously influenced and assessed across multiple domains.*

Central to this focus is the notion that creative acts occur during definable episodes of behavior and are characterized by the development of a product deemed creative by interested stakeholders. These episodes may take only a few seconds, or they may unfold over years. They always include a person and a process and a place (domains and accompanying judges), however, that together give life to the creative product. Consequently, our framework for understanding creative action attempts to describe how both commonplace and creative behaviors are simultaneously facilitated and constrained by dynamics within and across multiple domains.

BEHAVIOR EPISODES:
WHERE IT ALL COMES TOGETHER

The potential variety of facilitators and inhibitors on creative and routine action can be represented within a "unit of analysis" called a behavior episode (Ford, 1987). Behavior episodes are "slices of life." In a nutshell, they are our "experiences." They are directed toward some goal(s), occur in a particular context, and have a beginning and an end. Such experiences are the building blocks of learning and memory; they include ourselves, our actions, the context of those actions, and the outcomes produced by those actions. The concept of behavior episodes thus represents an ideal means toward our end of considering the joint influences of people, processes, places, and products on creativity.

Actions, and memories of those actions that guide behavior episodes, are organized by goals and contexts. As our experiences accumulate over time, repetitive elements of these experiences are retained in memory as structures of knowledge known as *schemas*. Schemas reflect consistencies and commonalities across the behavior episodes that make up a person's experiences. Some schemas are anchored within particular settings and specify appropriate actions one normally would take within that context. These types of schemas are known as *scripts*, so named because of their resemblance to the directions in a play. They enable common actions with minimal mental effort (Gioia & Poole, 1984). In fact, on previous occasions in this book when I referred to habits or habitual behavior, the more "technically" accurate terms would be *scripts* and *scripted behavior*.

Schemas and scripts often lead people to undertake repetitive behaviors automatically, without "active" thought. They are wonderful cognitive structures that allow people cognitive efficiency. They also allow people to impose plausible interpretations on difficult-to-understand or ambiguous situations (Gioia, 1986), thus making action possible. Obviously, gaining a lot of experience (i.e., many behavior episodes) in one domain enables the development of increasingly elaborate and sophisticated schemas reflective of that domain. Yet, there is a cost for this marvelous cognitive efficiency. Schemas fill gaps in knowledge with "default" information already retained in memory. Although scripts make performing repetitive tasks, even enormously complex ones, increasingly easy over time, they make noticing novel features within and beyond a particular domain increasingly difficult. Schemas also resist change; they lead people to respond in standardized ways to nonstandard situations. As a result, rote behavior becomes more likely as experiences within a particular domain accumulate, especially if that domain is narrowly defined.

In a nutshell, then, our experiences (behavior episodes) define our memories (schemas), which guide our interpretations and actions, which produce new experiences and outcomes, which further define our memories, which further guide our interpretations and actions, . . . and so on. This is the ongoing, recursive cycle of action-outcome-interpretation that defines our efforts to make sense of, and act on, ambiguous circumstances. It is this cycle that is the basis of our depiction of creative action in organizations. This cycle emphasizes the inseparability of action from the context of an action and subsequent interpretation of the outcomes of that action. The nexus of the multiple domains that make up the context wherein subsequent interpretation and action occurs helps us further explain creative action.

THE MULTIPLE SOCIAL DOMAINS OF CREATIVE ORGANIZATIONAL ACTION

People interpret their experiences, and they take action based on these interpretations. Those actions have effects on their relevant domains, which serve to influence subsequent interpretations, actions, and the nature of the domain itself. This interplay is necessary to consider because of the relationship among domain, interpretation, and action. To better illustrate this interaction, one must first understand how various domains influence an individual's experiences and related schemas. Recall that a domain is defined as any social system with shared rules for representing thought and action. A number of different domains could be considered as sources of conformity and regularity, and thus as sources of habitual interpretations and behaviors. Given our focus on organizational action, we will confine ourselves to a series of overlapping social domains that encompass organizational experience. An individual's interactions within and between domains are typically social in nature. Therefore, this multi-domain model reflects both past and current social influences on a particular individual that may facilitate and constrain creative action taking in a particular instance.

The broadest, least organized, and arguably most important domain is markets for products and services. Markets present their own selection processes that determine the viability of creative offerings (e.g., "The four Ps" of product, price, promotion, and placement). Another important, far-reaching social domain presents experiences that reflect the influence of various institutions. These institutions include those that provide formal education and professional training, government agencies, labor unions, professional associations, and more. Although each of these institutional influences could be considered as a separate social domain, we will consider them as a single class of domains for our current purposes. An explicit or implicit mission of institutions is to legitimize and regulate practices and standards within a particular task domain (e.g., standard accounting principles, real estate licenses, election procedures). An institution seeks to instill uniformity in the thoughts and behaviors of those under the institution's jurisdiction (DiMaggio & Powell, 1983), and is therefore a critical domain in regard to organizational creativity. A particular organization provides yet another domain for creative action. Job procedures, political dynamics, and corporate culture all reflect the conformity-inducing influences of a specific organization on an individual's behavior. Even within an organization, subunits and groups can further facilitate routinized behavior via group norms, member roles, and status relationships.

Although all of these domains can simultaneously influence creative action taking, it may be that the preeminence of particular domains varies during the evolution of a creative idea. For example, a creative idea for a new service may first have to survive the selection processes within subunit and organizational domains before progressing to institutional and market domains. Because each of these domains is guided by its own set of "rules" and values, it is likely that the selection criteria imposed on the new service will change as the target domain shifts. A proponent of this service would be wise to articulate the proposed action in the "native tongue" of each domain as it progresses. This may improve its odds of surviving (i.e., being selected by the judges of the domain) because the idea will not sound as foreign as it might otherwise.

Another implication that follows from considering multiple domains, each with its own standards and judges, is that different domains may disagree about whether a particular act is creative. It is fairly easy to see how an action deemed to be creative within a work group could be seen as fairly routine in organizational, institutional, and market domains. There is, however, no reason why disagreements couldn't emerge among any combination of domains, or why acceptance by one domain couldn't influence acceptance by other domains. This reinforces the importance of considering the intended audience for one's creative actions.

CREATIVE ACTION TAKING WITHIN MULTIPLE SOCIAL DOMAINS

The discussion to this point has described the basic attributes of a behavior episode, the way schemas develop, the way schemas impose interpretations on ambiguous stimuli and link habitual behaviors to those interpretations, and the embedded nature of the various fields within which creative actions are deployed and judged. Now that the stage is set, a cycle of creative action and interpretation within multiple social domains can be illustrated by Figure 50.1. This framework depicts the continuous, developmental processes that facilitate and constrain habitual and creative behaviors in organizational settings. Overall it represents two roads of behavior: one that proceeds over well-traveled avenues that are familiar, comfortable, and easily navigated with scripted knowledge, and another that blazes new trails in the face of ambiguity. This second road represents the challenge of creating meaning through action taking in ambiguous organizational environments. There is a sense of sequence to the processes to be described. However, it is fairly arbitrary to select a starting point and to argue a strict causal sequence among these processes, because events in one behavior episode are likely to influence processes that occur in subsequent episodes. The following discussion will attempt to describe each of the component processes represented in the model.

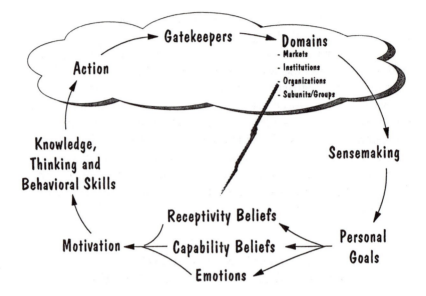

Figure 50.1. A Multi-Domain Model of Creative Action Taking

Social Domains Influence Sense Making. In psychological terms, social domains represents a field of "cues" that are continuously interpreted and subsequently acted upon by individuals. As described previously, experiences within and across domains (e.g., upbringing, education, work experiences, etc.) lead people to develop preferred interpretive frameworks (schemas) that they often employ unknowingly to facilitate quick interpretations and routinized action. This is a historical model of behavior in that future interpretations and actions replicate those developed and utilized in the past. However, some individuals may be more susceptible to imposing familiar interpretations than others. Those who possess the ability to view situations from multiple angles, "find" problems, or ask novel questions may be able to develop novel interpretations that require novel solutions.

Overall, pessimism is warranted when people are faced with familiar circumstances, based on the likelihood that standard interpretations will be enacted over novel ones. Yet, novel interpretations gain some measure of competitive advantage when a person is faced with making an interpretation of an unfamiliar, ambiguous situation (less ambiguous situations are likely to be rendered "certain" when routine interpretations are imposed on them). For instance, structured domains, or paradigms, characterized by "hard and fast" procedures, norms, and rules lead to uniform interpretations and actions (e.g., accounting), but less developed domains characterized by ambiguity evoke greater creativity (e.g., new product development) (Levitt & Nass, 1989). Ambiguity may be amplified intentionally, even in well-established domains, when overlaps among domains are considered. For example, businesses that function in multiple market domains may find new, creative outlets for established services. Multifunctional teams are typically advocated under the premise that representing views from multiple domains should broaden the potential interpretations and responses available to the group. The ambiguity associated with underdeveloped domains, or with varied perspectives from overlapping domains, can serve to invalidate scripted behavior and, in turn, facilitate creativity.

The Primacy of Personal Goals. Personal goals organize interpretations, actions, and experiences. Interests guide people's attention, lead them to engage in particular activities rather than others, and lead them to participate in domains that reflect their interests. Given the chance, individuals will tend to focus their efforts on a few core goals across a wide variety of situations. They will attempt to select situations that give them the best chance to pursue their most salient interests. Also, because interpretive schemas serve to link goals to specific contexts, it is likely that episodes in familiar settings will elicit personal goals that have been previously associated with that context.

Previous creativity research has identified several personal goals that seem especially important to creative individuals. These include interests in creativity, variety, independence, achievement, and superiority. Individuals with these interests could be expected to seek opportunities to organize their behavior toward creative actions if given the chance. Unfortunately, the episodes that make up day-to-day experience for most organizational members offer few opportunities for creative, varied, independent action. More ominously, aside from not being sanctioned, creativity is often deemed inappropriate at work for a variety of reasons.

In the vast majority of behavior episodes that take place in organizational domains, creativity is, at best, a marginal goal from both the individual's and the organization's point of view. Although it might make for nice frosting on the cake, creativity customarily ranks far behind more expedient goals. These more pervasive and salient goals tend to facilitate habitual action. To the extent that organizational creativity involves more perspiration than inspiration, creativity needs to become a more compelling personal goal that is facilitated rather than constrained by relevant social domains.

Organizations that are truly interested in taking creative action can facilitate the enactment of creativity goals by linking creativity to the strategic mission and reward system of the organization and by communicating how individuals' day-to-day activities fit into this "big picture." The burden on management is to develop ways of communicating this link. Exhortations that cannot be understood in the context of an individual's behavior episodes are unlikely to influence behavior. Also, coming up with ways to legitimize creative action within the organizational domain can help link creativity goals to organizationally based schemas. For example, Edwin Land, the founder of Polaroid, maintained a garden atrium within the corporation's headquarters and encouraged employees to tend the garden during work hours. To the extent that gardening reflects a common behavior episode where individuals enact their creativity goals, this garden provided a means of linking a popular creative outlet to the organizational domain. Obviously, subsequent efforts would need to be undertaken to link these rather trivial gardening episodes to more consequential actions. However, such symbolic methods can allow creativity to gain a toehold within the organizational domain. As an aside, efforts to achieve these links through off-site training are usually doomed to failure because the episodes they entail are not well grounded in the organizational domain.

As was mentioned earlier, creativity in organizations is distinctive in part because it refers to acts that produce value relative to an organization's mission and markets. Given this, it is misguided to focus creativity intervention efforts on single acts of inspiration. Consultants almost exclusively offer variations on brainstorming, synectics, nominal group technique, and the like, as the road to organizational creativity. These methods are tried and true and can be useful for generating ideas. But this narrow focus ignores the big picture—creative actions in organizations typically require sustained efforts that may take months, years, or decades to be realized. People may carry creative ideas around with them for years, looking for opportunities to garner the support, resources, and so on, necessary to bring an idea to life (Cohen, March, & Olsen, 1972). Organizations have creative ideas percolating inside of them all the time. Timing is therefore critical to realizing a creative solution. An organization's political landscape can add further challenges as those who favor stability and the status quo advocate decision criteria that favor familiar solutions and work to keep novel ideas off meeting agendas.

Personal goals serve as a primary influence on the motivation necessary to initiate creative action. Other motivation processes, however, play a central role in sustaining these creative actions. It is important to understand that *unless people are intentionally trying to take creative action, the following motivational processes related to creativity will be inactive, and therefore irrelevant.* Even in the case where commonplace actions lead to unanticipated creative consequences, an interest in creativity will be necessary to sustain further creative action.

Positive Capability and Receptivity Beliefs: "The Power of Positive Thinking." Even when people hold strong desires for certain outcomes, they will not be motivated to pursue those dreams unless they believe that they are personally capable of achieving the outcome and that the domain will be receptive to their efforts (Ford, 1992; Locke & Latham, 1990; Vroom, 1964). A person who is full of self-doubt is difficult to motivate. The same can be said of those who believe that their efforts will be ignored, shot down, or punished. These beliefs develop through experience and are important components of a person's schemas. They are often ingrained early in a person's life and reflect a significant role played by a person's upbringing. Collectively, these beliefs have been described as a person's "voice of judgment," or VOJ for short (Goleman, Kaufman, & Ray, 1992). The VOJ reflects the combined influences of the domains included in a person's experiences that have been internalized and integrated within a person's schemas. It is as if the judges from all of the relevant domains of a person's life are sitting on his or her shoulder whispering encouraging and/or discouraging words that will lead to further effort or to quitting altogether.

Because negative beliefs (i.e., self-doubt and a "cynical" outlook) tend to preclude action, they make it difficult for people to accumulate new experiences that might make their expectations more positive. Positive beliefs, on the other hand, encourage actions that may bring rewards that reinforce optimistic expectations. These tendencies give these beliefs a self-fulfilling quality. As a result, over time the correspondence of these beliefs to "reality" may grow more distant. Nevertheless, it is crucial for managers to understand that expectations, rather than realities, produce motivation. This is why poorly communicated programs seldom work and why managers with low credibility are virtually powerless to influence motivation.

Capability beliefs are people's expectations regarding their ability to accomplish a particular action. At a higher level of abstraction these beliefs are often referred to as self-efficacy (Bandura, 1986) or self-esteem. More specific capability beliefs are linked to particular goals, such as playing a musical instrument. Capability beliefs related to successful habits are likely to be quite high and robust, making habitual actions very attractive, self-confirmatory behavioral options. Capability beliefs related to creativity, on the other hand, are likely to be relatively fragile for the majority of people who only rarely dabble in creative endeavors. Previous research has shown that creative actions are associated with people who possess creative self-images and self-confidence. An organization may have to cajole people quite a bit to enhance these beliefs because they are rooted in a lifetime of experiences reflecting a person's real level of creative talent. Building on small successes may be an important means for getting people to engage in significant creative ventures. Confident people who possess a thick skin where their capability beliefs are concerned may be better able to focus on learning from their mistakes (improving skills), rather than dwelling on the personal implications of failure to their own capability beliefs.

Receptivity beliefs are expectations regarding the response that a domain (or multiple domains) will have to one's actions. These beliefs are the individual's mapping of the selection and retention processes at work in various domains. As with capability beliefs, these expectations are developed through experiences and are reflected in a person's schemas. When previous experiences have established favorable receptivity beliefs for a particular behavior, then that behavior is likely to be repeated based on the probability that it will produce rewards. Obviously, this process facilitates routine actions. When a person believes that a relevant domain(s) will reject a creative act, then motivation to persevere will be severely diminished. Legends of creative heroes who overcome rejection from their immediate domain (e.g., the organization) describe courageous perseverence based on the belief that others outside the domain will respond favorably at some point (e.g., markets). In most cases where resistance is expected, however, creative interests will likely be dropped in favor of easier, more reliable pursuits that offer more immediate and certain reinforcement.

There is an important correspondence between *reality* and *perception* here that is represented by the link connecting social domains to an individual's receptivity beliefs noted in Figure 50.1. Experiences during behavior episodes shape these expectations, but once established these expectations can shape the way behavior episodes are interpreted. This is one of the key ways in which the environment and an individual interact (see Woodman, Sawyer, & Griffin, 1993). Those with strongly positive expectations, even if they are delusional in nature, have a striking advantage in terms of producing sustained effort in the face of negative responses from the environment. Self-confidence that permits overlooking the judgments of others can help sustain creative action. For those who are less taken with themselves, however, another strategy could be described as "take it one domain at a time." In organizations, this typically means attending to the demands of judges from the most immediate domains first until approval can be won, and then retooling efforts to satisfy other domains as may be necessary. Simultaneously considering the demands of judges from across the entire spectrum of relevant domains may prove so intimidating that creative action will be thwarted before it has begun.

In most cases, however, the difficult challenge facing managers is to get employees to believe that creative actions are desired and will be rewarded. An organization cannot simply enhance its creativity-related characteristics, it must aggressively publicize them if employees' receptivity beliefs are to be affected. Within the cynicism that characterizes much of our society, organizations need to work fever-ishly to publicize support for creativity in highly visible and symboli-cally important ways. The environment should reward, or at least not punish, creative acts within the range of desired variation specified by the organization's mission. Managerial rhetoric and action can have a powerful impact, but it must be reinforced by a chorus of feedback from co-workers, work experiences, performance reviews, and more, that sends the same message regarding creative efforts.

Charismatic, visionary leaders can often enhance their employees' motivation to attempt challenging, risky courses of action by describ-ing the environment in terms that favor the leaders' vision. Powerful leaders affect the way their followers interpret the world around them, and can feed peoples' desire to feel that they can "handle" things. A leader's credibility also plays an important role in his or her ability to establish and modify receptivity beliefs. Trust and credibility imply that a leader's statements can be taken at face value as a meaningful appraisal of a domain. Encouraging words can be an invaluable means for influencing people's receptivity beliefs, but the danger of hypocrisy is high if management fails to "walk the talk." Half-hearted imple-mentations of creativity programs that are abandoned after the first bad business cycle or after the first failure are likely to do more harm than good by further eroding people's beliefs regarding the organiza-tions receptivity to creative action.

Emotions Provide Energy and Passion. Emotions provide a person with evaluative information and supply energy for behavior. They are typically elicited by expectations of future events. Therefore, they tend to reinforce the dry, cognitive expectations regarding individual capabilities or domain receptivity with gut level feelings of excitement, fear, interest, resentment, and so on. Creative indi-viduals have been found to be especially open to emotional experi-ence and expression. They also have been noted for their produc-tivity and generally high level of energy. This implies that creative individuals find their work interesting, enjoyable, and relatively nonthreatening. On the other hand, a person with negative recep-tivity and capability beliefs related to creativity would probably be anxious or fearful if assigned a creative task.

The overall emotional climate of a domain may provide a "comfort zone" that can help sustain creative actions even in the face of discouraging setbacks. Furthermore, overlapping domains may be able to provide "motivational insurance" to the extent that they reinforce the same actions. For example, professors are typically rewarded for publishing within their departments, by their schools, and by their discipline. Discouraging aspects of one domain may be compensated for by more encouraging aspects of other domains, thus keeping negative emotions at bay.

In summary, interpretive schemas developed through prior interaction with various social domains are elicited during particular behavior episodes. Familiar interpretations evoke personal goals habitually pursued during previous similar behavior episodes. Positive capability beliefs, receptivity beliefs, and emotions developed through previously successful episodes that involved pursuing these goals in a particular setting are enacted. The strong motivation produced by the interaction of salient goals, positive expectations, and pleasant emotions (or absence of negative emotions) engages habitual behavioral scripts that ultimately produce common actions. But, when interpretations are ambiguous, familiar schemas become less salient. Personal goals associated with creativity can gain prominence, and capability beliefs, receptivity beliefs, and emotions specifically related to creative action are evoked. If these processes reinforce each other, then motivation to take creative action should be high. However, motivation cannot be converted to creative action without requisite knowledge and skill.

Skills Translate Motivation Into Action. Now that the pieces are in place to provide an individual with a strong desire to engage in a creative act, the talents necessary to commit such an act must be addressed. Without real skills, a motivated person's actions would likely be fruitless (it is important to keep in mind that *expectations* influence motivation, and that *talent* influences performance). The vast majority of creativity interventions are aimed at enhancing skills. Yet, skills are irrelevant without motivation.

Knowledge, thinking, and behavioral skills can all be important contributors to creative action. Prior knowledge of a domain is critical to, and may even be a prerequisite for, creative performance (Amabile, 1988; Simon, 1986). The argument goes that you can't intentionally build new ideas without knowledge of the construction materials offered by a domain, or the rules used by the building inspectors who judge the creativity of an end product. Prior learning, especially when it produces diverse knowledge, provides "absorptive capacity," which allows new knowledge to be utilized in creative ways (Cohen & Levinthal, 1990). Not investing in diverse learning experiences can serve to foreclose future learning and development opportunities, thus thwarting creative possibilities that might arise through new experiences.

Thinking skills related to utilizing knowledge to produce creative ideas have been the primary focus of research on creative processes. Most frequently noted are divergent thinking and associational thinking skills (Barron & Harrington, 1981). *Divergent thinking* refers to the ability to generate a wide range of ideas, and *associational thinking* focuses on identifying useful links among independent elements. It is important to note that by focusing almost exclusively on cognitive processes related to problem interpretation and divergent thinking, most creativity research has failed to represent the important roles that motivation, emotion, and the influence of social domains play in creative action taking.

Several popular creative problem-solving techniques have been utilized in organizational settings, although their impact on action is suspect. Techniques such as "lateral thinking" (deBono, 1970), "brainstorming" (Osborn, 1963), and "synectics" (Gordon, 1961) have become widely known and utilized techniques when creativity is a salient goal. In the terms used here, lateral thinking requires looking across multiple domains for novel problem interpretations, rather than digging deeper for an interpretation within a singular domain. Alternatively, brainstorming attempts to render the influence of negative capability and receptivity beliefs impotent until a substantial number of alternative ideas are introduced. Synectics has an aim similar to lateral thinking in that it seeks to produce alternative interpretations of a problem by "making the strange familiar" and "making the familiar strange."

Teaching and utilizing these methods is grounded in an assumption that creativity can be taught. Although undoubtedly true, the expected impact of learning these techniques on the process of creative action taking depicted in Figure 50.1 is rather limited. It is probably best to think of creative thinking abilities as only loosely coupled to creative action taking. Linking creativity goals to specific organizational behavior episodes, improving creativity-related capability and receptivity beliefs, enhancing the emotional climate, and exploring the implications of multiple domains are also important aspects of training that are ignored in most cases. Creativity training should aim to enhance motivation through skill enhancement by providing opportunities to test new skills and build more positive capability beliefs.

Behavioral skills are seldom mentioned in treatises on creativity, but they are certainly important, especially in domains where performance is important (e.g., dancing, singing, sports). In the social domains under consideration here, the most important instrumental skills involve a person's ability to communicate within and across domains. Verbal fluency, an ability related to creativity in some studies, may be particularly useful for creative action in social domains. Social networking and effective communication are critical to developing novel ideas and garnering support and sponsorship as an idea moves forward to realization. Thus, knowledge regarding the content and structure of different domains, trustworthy social contacts from multiple domains, and communication skills that facilitate exchanges within and across domains can be seen as capabilities that are perhaps uniquely important to organizational creativity.

Creative Actions Premier Before an Audience of Gatekeepers. Creative variations arise from individuals. However, gatekeepers within the social domains described previously select and retain these variations (Csikszentmihalyi, 1990). Creative acts that are retained in a domain modify the frame of reference used by judges so that what was once considered creative may later be considered commonplace. Recognizing these dynamics raises many interesting possibilities. For example, it implies that opinions regarding creativity can be influenced just like other opinions. Particular individuals are likely to be trusted as opinion leaders who help shape consensus regarding creativity within a domain. These people may hold tremendous power as sponsors, champions, and gatekeepers for creative actions. Spin doctoring, marketing, and campaigning can all be employed to influence creativity judgments. Also, habitual actions may produce unintended consequences that can be subsequently judged to be creative.

Understanding that creative actions occur within overlapping social domains, and that the relative importance of different domains may evolve as a creative idea moves through a series of behavior episodes toward realization, highlights the importance of playing to the appropriate audience as a creative action evolves. Creative ideas in social domains should probably be articulated as clearly and as simply as possible in the preferred language of the target domain. As the evaluative frame changes with other domains' involvements, the methods and terminology used to generate support for a creative action may need to change as well. Packaging and framing creative actions in simple terms reduces uncertainty for judges within a target domain and allows other domain members to analyze and interpret the idea on their own. Within the organizational domain, it is critical that significant creative actions, intentional or otherwise, be articulated in terms of the organization's mission so that the value of those acts within the organizational domain can be more easily assessed. Moreover, those with experience and contacts across a continuum of relevant domains will give their creative acts a significant survival advantage.

EPILOGUE: SO WHAT'S NEW HERE?

The presentation of this multi-domain model of creative action taking has attempted to represent a broad array of ideas and insights in relatively few pages. Therefore, before progressing to a discussion of guidelines for enhancing creativity in organizations in the final chapter, I would like to highlight some of the more noteworthy contributions offered by this work. In no particular order, they are as follows:

1. Thinking about creative behavior episodes provides a means for simultaneously considering the contributions and interactions of people, processes, products, and places. It is also useful for orienting thinking toward creative *action* and the relationships among action, gatekeepers, and domains.

2. Creativity is not an inherent quality of a person, process, product, or place. Rather, it is a domain-specific social construction legitimized by judges who serve as gatekeepers for a particular domain.
3. The fascination we have for creative heroes is probably driven in part by a common tendency people have to attribute the cause of complex, ambiguous events to individuals. This tendency results in a "romance with creativity" that is ill suited for facilitating creativity in organizational settings.
4. A particular creative action may be relevant to, and influenced by, multiple domains. In organizational settings, the influence of relevant domains is especially likely to be social in nature. Also, there may be differences in the importance and timing of evaluations across domains that can serve to shape influence strategies necessary for the survival and development of a particular creative action.
5. Organizationally relevant domains present special challenges for creative action. Specifically, they place more emphasis on value production, require more perseverance, and are more heavily influenced by social processes than in domains such as art or education. These characteristics may limit the usefulness of creativity research and interventions established in non-organizational domains.
6. Creative actions are especially likely to compete with well-established, scripted behaviors in organizational settings. This leads to the *Competitive Advantage Principle of Creativity*.
7. Creative actions are necessary to create meaning in ambiguous circumstances. Therefore, creative actions may be worth taking based solely on their contribution to organizational knowledge production.
8. Based on the overall perspective depicted in Figure 50.1, one should expect creative talent to be only loosely coupled to creative action taking. Also, one would be well served to consider a broad array of creativity-related skills in organizational settings such as creative thinking skills, verbal skills, and leadership/influence skills, to name a few.

REFERENCES

Amabile, T. M. (1982). Social psychology of creativity: A consensual assessment technique. *Journal of Personality and Social Psychology, 43*, 997-1013.
Amabile, T. M. (1988). A model of creativity and innovation in organizations. *Research in Organizational Behavior, 10*, 123-167.

Bandura, A. (1986). *Social foundations of thought and action: A social cognitive theory.* Englewood Cliffs, NJ: Prentice Hall.

Barron, F., & Harrington, D. M. (1981). Creativity, intelligence, and personality. *Annual Review of Psychology, 32,* 439-476.

Cohen, M. D., March, J. G., & Olsen, J. P. (1972). A garbage can model of organizational choice. *Administrative Science Quarterly, 17,* 1-25.

Cohen, W. M., & Levinthal, D. A. (1990). Absorptive capacity: A new perspective on learning and innovation. *Administrative Science Quarterly, 35,* 128-152.

Csikszentmihalyi, M. (1988). Society, culture, and person: A systems view of creativity. In R. J. Sternberg (Ed.), *The nature of creativity: Contemporary psychological perspectives* (pp. 325-339). New York: Cambridge University Press.

Csikszentmihalyi, M. (1990). The domain of creativity. In M. A. Runco & R. S. Albert (Eds.), *Theories of creativity* (pp. 190-212). Newbury Park, CA: Sage.

Daft, R. L., & Weick, K. E. (1984). Toward a model of organizations as interpretive systems. *Academy of Management Review, 9,* 284-295.

deBono, E. (1970). *Lateral thinking: Creativity step by step.* New York: Harper & Row.

DiMaggio, P. J., & Powell, W. W. (1983). The iron cage revisited: Institutional isomorphism and collective rationality in organizational fields. *American Sociological Review, 48,* 147-160.

Ford, D. E. (1987). *Humans as self-constructing living systems.* Hillsdale, NJ: Lawrence Erlbaum.

Ford, M. E. (1992). *Motivating humans.* Newbury Park, CA: Sage.

Gardner, H. (1993). *Creating minds.* New York: Basic Books.

Gioia, D. A. (1986). Symbols, scripts, and sensemaking: Creating meaning in the organizational experience. In H. P. Sims & D. A. Gioia (Eds.), *The thinking organization: Dynamics of organizational social cognition* (pp. 49-74). San Francisco: Jossey-Bass.

Gioia, D. A., & Poole, P. P. (1984). Scripts in organizational behavior. *Academy of Management Review, 9,* 449-459.

Goleman, D., Kaufman, P., & Ray, M. (1992). *The creative spirit.* New York: Penguin Books.

Gordon, W. J. J. (1961). *Synectics: The development of creative capacity.* New York: Harper & Row.

Levitt, B., & Nass, C. (1989). The lid on the garbage can: Institutional constraints on decision making in the technical core of college text publishers. *Administrative Science Quarterly, 34,* 190-207.

Locke, E. A., & Latham, G. P. (1990). Work motivation and satisfaction: Light at the end of the tunnel. *Psychological Science, 1,* 240-246.

March, J. G. (1991). Exploration and exploitation in organizational learning. *Organizational Science, 2,* 71-87.

March, J. G., & Simon, H. A. (1958). *Organizations.* New York: John Wiley.

Nutt, P. C. (1984). Types of organizational decision processes. *Administrative Science Quarterly, 29,* 414-450.

Osborn, A. F. (1963). *Applied imagination.* New York: Scribner's.

Simon, H. A. (1986, March). How managers express their creativity. *Across the Board,* pp. 11-16.

Vroom, V. H. (1964). *Work and motivation.* New York: John Wiley.

Woodman, R. W., Sawyer, J. E., & Griffin, R. W. (1993). Toward a theory of organizational creativity. *Academy of Management Review, 18,* 293-321.

51 Guidelines for Creative Action Taking in Organizations

CAMERON M. FORD *Rutgers University*

DENNIS A. GIOIA *The Pennsylvania State University*

The framework presented in the previous chapter offers a number of insights that can be easily translated into practical guidelines for nurturing and managing creativity in organizations. Throughout the process of producing this book and devising our multi-domain model of creative action taking we have tracked and thought about the implications for practice that follow from the observations made in these pages. To draw out and summarize some guidelines for practicing creative managers, we again use Figure 50.1 as a useful map. As a coda to this volume we offer a series of: (a) key observations, (b) guidelines in a (we hope) memorable form that derive from those observations, (c) focused commentary supplying rationales for the guidelines, and (d) suggestions for interventions that can facilitate creative action taking.

Observation: People create certainty by imposing familiar interpretations on ambiguous or unfamiliar situations.

Guideline #1: Doubt what you think you know.

Rationale: Adherence to favored interpretations prevents consideration of alternative interpretations and alternative actions. Embracing multiple alternatives and multiple interpretations from multiple sources is a key to creativity. Continued adherence to preferred ways of seeing also makes learning from experience difficult because new information is either ignored (because it does not conform to an existing worldview) or else is unconsciously and insidiously "force fit" into a standard interpretation. Explicitly acknowledging doubt and ambiguity makes entertaining alternative interpretations a central concern of creators and creativity managers. It also circumvents the "perseverance effect" that results in people who depend on scripted or habituated patterns of understanding and action. Creative doubt is especially crucial for top managers whose interpretations become the "certain" premises upon which other organization members base their thoughts and actions. Cultivating an appreciation for ambiguity at all levels legitimizes the pursuit of "different" action and accentuates the creation of meaning through action.

We recognize that this first guideline might be seen as running counter to an important observation about leadership: Leaders lead by imposing order on ambiguity. Does this apparent contradiction imply that leadership and creativity are mutually exclusive? No. The paradox of leadership and doubt is that wise leadership often first depends on creative doubt. Doubt opens up a spectrum of options, from which can be chosen those options that can be managed with assurance and certainty. Leadership is often a matter of deciding what is a good decision (in the face of multiple possible interpretations). Doubt should temper the key choice of the "good decision," but once taken, faith and firmness should prevail—at least until the next opportunity for creative doubt.

Interventions: There are a number of interventions that can help to broaden one's interpretive scope; some are personal and others are social in nature. Becoming a more reflective manager encourages people to be more aware of their own worldviews. Self-awareness is the first step in making interpretations more of an active choice than a passive, automatic process. Other personal processes involve problem-finding activities such as lateral thinking, synectics, and so on. (Of course, these processes can be undertaken in groups as well.)

Social methods include actively maintaining a network of diverse, respected, and trusted colleagues. Creative networking can be done in the context of multifunctional teams, task groups, social contacts, professional organizations, consulting, and the like. Such people serve both as resources for new viewpoints and as "reality checkers."

Observation: Creative actions occur mainly as a response to ambiguity.

Guideline #2: Treat ambiguity as opportunity.

Rationale: As noted in the first observation, the initial response of most people to ambiguity is to reach for cognitive stability—to try to make the strange familiar. Such responses serve the purposes of day-to-day life well, but they are a saboteur of creativity. We are looking for a provocateur, and ambiguity is that provocateur. Necessity might be the mother of invention, and it is usually some sort of odd conundrum that produces the necessity for a creative solution. Creativity begins with the non-usual, so its breeding ground lies in the very ambiguity that so many seek to avoid. In fact, ambiguity is an impetus for creativity, but only if it is viewed as opportunity rather than threat.

Interventions: On a rather mundane level, it is management's role to provide a greater appreciation of the ambiguity inherent in even the most commonplace activities. Even in situations that do not appear ambiguous, a creative act is to call attention to the hidden ambiguities, dilemmas, ironies, and contradictions that infuse organizational life. On a more strategic level, ambiguity is also an impetus for organizational change. A complacent organization is not one that is likely to change, even where change might be necessary. Therefore, a catalyst for initiating change is the occasional but intentional creation of ambiguity by top management. Destabilizing existing interpretations by suggesting such things as new visions, products, services, and markets, cognitively readies people for a shift in orientation and prepares them for change. We acknowledge that creating such ambiguity-by-design can amount to playing with fire. If improperly handled, organization members end up confused and demoralized, but if necessary change is the issue, then injecting ambiguity into the interpretive world facilitates creative change.

Observation: Creative actions in organizational settings are usually judged according to the standards of multiple social domains.

Guideline #3: Tailor creative acts and products to key evaluative domains.

Rationale: For an individual considering a creative undertaking, it is important to anticipate the potential reactions of the sponsors, gatekeepers, and audiences within each relevant domain (e.g., department, division, top management, competitive market, etc.). A form of "stakeholder analysis" can provide a useful means for identifying the domains that might take an interest in a creative act, as well as those that might prove resistant. Such an analysis also serves as a means for recognizing the different languages, values, and rules employed within each domain, for prioritizing the relative importance of various domains, and for suggesting a tactical timetable for presenting the creative act to each domain. The results of this sort of stakeholder analysis can help people package creative acts so that they appeal to the sensibilities of each domain.

Interventions: Creators who might be technically astute are not necessarily politically astute. In organizations, especially, where there are multiple "turfs" with their own arcane rules and preferences, creativity needs to be shepherded along. Creators and their managers might require focused training in the politics of creativity and innovation and the organizational skills necessary to keep a creative idea alive. On the one hand, this may sound rather Machiavellian, and it is. But, it provides those within a domain with their best chance of fairly evaluating the merits of a creative action within their own interpretive frameworks and then designing the tactics likely to have the idea succeed in a highly competitive and perhaps even hostile environment.

Observation: Goals for creativity are rarely articulated in organizations.

Guideline #4: Establish explicit creativity goals for tasks, projects, and programs.

Rationale: Typically, the work that people do, even on special assignments, seldom includes creativity as a focal concern. Consequently, there is little opportunity for organization members to build the interpretive frameworks that lead toward the natural taking of creative action. It is hypocritical to bemoan the lack of creativity in the workplace if one never mentions creativity before assigning work. On balance, people do not lack creative potential. But, experience too often has a way of teaching people that creative actions will not be rewarded, and might even be punished, thereby making creativity an avoidance goal much of the time. Because people seldom think of creativity in their day-to-day work activities, or else view it as potentially threatening, they too seldom view organizations as appropriate and intentional outlets for their creative interests. Without intentions, creative talents and other motivation processes are irrelevant. Therefore, organizations should not waste money on skill-based creativity training unless they are committed to making creativity a salient goal in employees' daily worklife. We know by now that many people can be wonderfully creative when called upon; the problem is that they are almost never called upon to be creative.

People more often seem to think of work-relevant creative ideas while they drive, shower, or mow the lawn. Creativity emerges in these mundane settings mainly because other goals and behavioral options are not salient, and because the behaviors in which they are engaged are largely automatic, thus requiring no conscious thought. Therefore, if a person has a relevant goal at hand (e.g., ways to improve customer service) the mind wanders toward that goal and spins happily away on creative possibilities. This is the force behind the "incubation" of ideas. People once pondered in this fashion in front of the fire, but in today's hectic, multimedia, information-filled organizational world, occasions for such musing are increasingly rare.

Interventions: There are several ways that organizations can make creativity a more salient personal goal, despite the character of the modern world of work. Obviously, one can hire people who already have a keen interest in creativity. However, the simple expedient of merely asking people to "be creative!" on specific projects has been shown to be surprisingly effective. Including the request to be creative into formal work assignments is a cost-free benefit. If the organizational domain is seen as stifling, retreating to a remote location (to remove cues that trigger usual thinking and behavior) can be useful in generating different solutions; it also makes it easier for people to develop creative intentions. This tactic, however, should mainly be used as an intervention to solve specific problems, not as a means for enhancing general creativity back at the home office. To enhance creativity within the usual work setting requires linking creative intentions to the organizational context through repeated creative behavior in a given domain. For example, Edwin Land's company garden provided an opportunity for people to be playful within the walls of Polaroid's headquarters. Periodic brainstorming sessions (where creativity is the primary purpose of the meeting) can also help. However, events like this in isolation will fail to enact change unless other events reinforce the message that creativity is a legitimate pursuit. Mixed signals in this regard will always favor a perseverance effect, and a reversion to previously successful behavior patterns.

The best way to send a consistent message is to link creativity to other salient goals that guide work behavior. For example, rewards and promotions can be partially determined by assessments of the creativity of a person's work. (Be careful with this one, though, because it will tend to focus a person's attention on a single domain— the one inhabited by the evaluator. Broader evaluations that represent multiple domains might be necessary.) If people enjoy working with the other members of their network or team, attempts to develop creative actions can be turned into social occasions. The entertainment value of creative action can serve as a powerful means of linking creativity to a number of social and task-related goals. It may even make people enjoy coming to work more.

Observation: People often have fragile beliefs in their own creative capability because of inexperience with creative action in organizationally relevant domains.

Guideline #5: Enhance creative capability beliefs with a small-wins strategy.

Rationale: The organizational experience tends in many ways to be essentially a repetitive experience. The most common message from the work environment is that things are as they were before; there are actually only infrequent opportunities to exercise creativity. Even when such occasions arise, they tend to be constrained by organizational rules, policies, and culture so creativity seldom ranges very far from the norm. People consequently have little experience testing out creative ideas, actions, and products; therefore, they typically do not develop robust beliefs about their own creative abilities. They need both the opportunity to engage in creativity and the encouragement that bolsters self-confidence in their capabilities. What to do?

One approach is simply to hire people with self-confidence (especially in their creative abilities), but even those people often do not have experience in domains relevant to organizations. However, even this straightforward tactic of hiring for self-confidence has its problems in the complex world of creative action. If a person is especially self-confident in his or her worldviews, inflexibility in the way she or he views problems can arise. On the other hand, if creative interpretations occur, then self-confidence can help a person speak with the conviction necessary to convince others in the domain.

Interventions: Managerial strategies for enhancing on-the-job capability beliefs center around empowerment. The most potent method is to provide people with new skills (or identify under-used, existing skills) and give them an opportunity to be successful in using those skills. Like learning to ride a bicycle, people need to learn some basics first and try easy tasks that produce confidence-building success. Once they begin to rise on the learning curve, creativity confidence and capability both escalate. The key, therefore, is in acknowledging, building on, and celebrating small wins that can grow into continuing creative capability beliefs that result in success.

Observation: Confidently held beliefs that an organization (or other domain) is receptive to creative actions are key. Negative beliefs strongly favor familiar actions over creative actions.

Guideline #6: Remember the Relative Advantage Principle of Creativity: People undertake creative actions only to the extent that they expect them to confer advantages relative to other available behavioral options.

Rationale: Negative receptivity beliefs may represent the most intractable restraint on creative action taking. They also represent perhaps the most significant interaction between a person and the environment because these beliefs are a direct reflection of individuals' attempts to make sense of the domains around them. A critical underlying characteristic of this interaction is trustworthiness. In settings characterized by consistency, credibility, and trust, people can be confident that they know the "rules of the game" and can be forthright with their intentions and their actions. In contexts where about-faces, hypocrisy, and deception are common, however, people cannot develop reliable expectations about the consequences of their actions. In the face of mixed signals, people often become skeptical and cynical—neither of which is conducive to creativity.

Intervention: Underlying any suggestion we might offer to convince people that a particular domain is receptive to creative actions is the caveat that consistency and credibility are crucial. Established receptivity beliefs (e.g., "Our company rewards creative actions") can be quickly fractured by a single disconfirming instance (e.g., "The latest promotions list is full of 'Yea-sayers'!"). Similarly, managers who have low credibility are impotent when attempting to change others' beliefs in the receptivity of the organization to creativity. Thus, efforts to enhance creativity-related receptivity beliefs should not be undertaken lightly: They require commitment. Organizations prone to backsliding on this issue are better off simply not touting receptivity in the first place. Being caught in a contradiction is worse than being perceived with relatively low receptivity to creative action.

This caveat aside, our simplest advice is to hire optimists. They tend to persist in creative actions, whereas more cynical types would revert to actions with a more proven track record. We also suggest that articulating assumptions about the nature of various domains can help alleviate unwarranted concerns and highlight real obstacles for creators. Visionary leadership is often characterized by attempts to communicate (perhaps unreasonably) positive beliefs about how the world will respond to the organizational mission. Yet, mission awareness helps people to channel their creative energies on a limited range of strategically important products or services where their efforts will be best received. Symbolic behaviors—presenting humorous awards for creative actions or hanging inspirational posters promoting creativity, for example—may also send or reinforce a message regarding the selection processes at work in the domain. Talk, however, tends to be cheap; receptivity beliefs can be best influenced by direct experience. Therefore, putting people in circumstances where they can test the domain and receive positive feedback can be invaluable.

Observation: Negative emotions favor habitual action; positive emotions favor, and are favored by, creative action.

Guideline #7: Ambiguity leads to anxiety as well as creativity. Creativity is served by dispelling fears and engendering positive emotions.

Rationale: It is hard to overstate the importance of a nonthreatening, consistent, supportive culture to creative action. Negative emotions like anxiety lead people to withdraw to their most reliable patterns of established behavior. Positive emotions like interest, enthusiasm, satisfaction, and liking create an atmosphere of security and comfort that encourages exploring new ideas and actions. This is not to say that the world needs to be viewed through rose-colored glasses. For example, disagreements over interpretations can help to facilitate creative action. Indeed, disagreements in a setting where status is not salient and where "anything goes" are likely to be interesting and fun. But disagreement in a domain characterized by status differences and possible retribution is almost invariably threatening.

Intervention: No intervention necessary, really, so long as there is a culture of support. If there is not a supportive culture (or if it is seen as untrustworthy), negative emotions prevail and subvert the positive emotions associated with creative intentions and actions.

Observation: Talent matters, but knowledge and skills can be developed that facilitate creative action.

Guideline #8: Creativity is trainable, to the extent that creativity training is domain-relevant.

Rationale: The dubious results produced by creativity training programs that focus solely on skill enhancement are not too surprising given the number of other considerations described up to this point. This may actually be good news for advocates of these programs, however, because their frequent ineffectiveness may be caused more by motivational deficits or unresponsive domains than by flaws in the training per se. It is probably sensible to practice the traditional creative problem-solving tasks that typically are the focus of creativity training programs only if they bear a likeness to relevant domains for intended creative actions. Many of the previous nuggets of advice in this book could be interpreted as creativity skill development (e.g., entertain alternative interpretations, explore analogies, make creativity a goal, explore assumptions about the receptivity of various domains, articulate the interests and demands of stakeholder from different domains, etc.).

Interventions: Of course one should hire creatively talented people, but we suggest that this talent be thought of more broadly in organizational domains. Aside from divergent and convergent thinking skills, communication-related skills (e.g., verbal fluency, writing skills, credibility, charisma) should be sought after and developed. In addition to these talents, diverse knowledge and experience provide useful "input" to the creative thought processes a person might employ. Overspecialization and narrow experience make it difficult for people to address ambiguity with novel responses. Training programs need to be designed for domain relevance. General creativity training might be a lot of fun in the classroom, but it does not produce the kind of skills that are needed in a specific domain of application.

Observation: Creative actions produce meaning out of ambiguity.

Guideline #9: Don't just sit there thinking . . . Do something creative!

Rationale: This is an important point with which to conclude. Without getting into an esoteric discussion about how we know what we know, we can note that people often overestimate the level of certainty in the organizational world. Social domains are fraught with ambiguity. People socially construct order out of ambiguity, often without being aware that their cognitive processes and actions serve to produce order where order is actually in doubt. The danger of believing in certainty is that it implies that the consequences of actions can be predicted accurately if enough data and analyses are developed. In a certain world, feedback can be safely ignored because of the assumption that it would only confirm the results of the prior analyses. An alternative view is that more and more homework will not help to predict the outcomes of actions in ambiguous situations. In circumstances such as these, action requires a leap of faith. Analysis is ineffectual. Therefore, action taking gains priority over analyses. More to the point, creative action replaces analysis as the key method for making sense of the environment.

Interventions: Organizational selection criteria and management methodologies that are based on a reliance on learning-through-action need to be legitimized. Organizations must weigh the relative cost of analyzing while delaying action versus acting, failing, and learning. This trade-off can be tipped to favor creative action by reducing the downside risks associated with creative action and by documenting and communicating the understandings developed based on the responses various domains had to a creative act. Organizations need to make it as easy and inexpensive as possible to shift activities and resources from one action to another. Also, creating information systems that document and communicate the lessons from failures (even those that are not terribly flattering) as well as successes can facilitate the development of a common organizational understanding based on creative action taking.

Obviously, these recommendations need to be considered as part of a comprehensive commitment to stimulating creative action. Creativity skill training will fail unless creativity is a legitimate, salient goal in the organizational domain. Intentions to produce creative action will go unfulfilled if individuals feel that they are not up to the challenge. Telling people that the organization is supportive of creativity and innovation is useless if creative actions fail to gain serious consideration. Diverse work teams will fail to live up to their creative potential if members feel frustrated and anxious around each other.

Each point in the cycle of creativity we have described represents a potential exit off the road to creative action. Managers are the primary guides along this road. But managing creativity requires its own brand of creativity. The guidelines above serve as a set of guideposts that can help make creative action a regular event in organizations.

Index

 Editor Profiles

CAMERON M. FORD, Assistant Professor of Organization Management, Rutgers University, Faculty of Management. I'm not really sure why I am interested in a topic as elusive and maddening as creativity. I've been told it's a bad career move. I can't profess to having a lifelong, burning interest in the topic. In fact, as a kid I envisioned myself as a corporate working stiff. Nevertheless, I think I have concocted a fairly reasonable tale. My father, Donald, is an eminent psychologist who created and was Dean of The College of Human Development at The Pennsylvania State University. I never thought much of the prattlings of my dad's psychologist friends, but I thought it was amazing that he, in effect, started his own business and was "the boss" of a college. My mother, Carol, also ran a charitable arts and crafts business for 25 years. I guess I felt that being a boss was my destiny, so I decided to go to business school. One day, a wacky professor walked into class, jumped on his desk, and asked us what we thought about him: enter Denny Gioia. The lasting impression he made on my life was cemented when he presented the biggest fork I'll probably ever face in my career; enter Penn State's Doctoral program versus pursue a corporate career. Perhaps subconsciously thinking that it would be fun to jump on desks at work, and seeing the fulfillment that an academic career had brought my father, I decided to return to school after a brief stint in the corporate world. I subsequently became fascinated with research indicating that most decisions involve consideration of only one alternative, thus serving more as justification exercises than as rational choice making occasions. This interest utltimately led me to study creativity in organizations. In retrospect, I feel fortunate to be pursing interests rooted in my upbringing with a scholarly, administrator father and a creative, humanitarian mother. It is also important to me that creativity is a pragmatic concern that captures the interests of practitioners. I am proud that we have been able to join the forces of top-flight academics and practitioners in this unusual volume. I must admit that, as a fledgling scholar beginning his career, I am a bit star-struck by the collection of contributors we have assembled here. However, Denny always encouraged me to pursue big ideas that can make a difference. I hope this book is a start in that direction.

DENNIS A. GIOIA, Professor of Organizational Behavior, The Pennsylvania State University. The truth is that I have been intrigued by creativity for as long as I can remember. As a kid, raised without a lot of worldly possessions, I lived an imaginative mental life with many vivid alter egos. In school I gravitated toward science because, having been raised not too far from Cape Canaveral, FL, the idea of space travel captured me. It struck me as the ultimate high-tech adventure, so I looked to engineering and physics to feed my imagination. I had the dream fulfilled; I actually worked at the Kennedy Space Center on the Apollo 11 and 12 lunar launch teams. It remains the great drama and great accomplishment of my life. But the Apollo program had its own demise designed into it, so I turned to my other passion, which (in this, my first public admission) was sports car racing. To me racing car design and driving both were sublime creative skills. At that time Ford Motor Company was involved in racing, so I joined them in the fanciful hope of winning a place on the racing team. Life apparently went a bit awry at this point, though; I instead found myself acting as Ford's vehicle recall coordinator and somehow got involved in the infamous Pinto fires debacle. That episode constitutes the one great skeleton rattling around my personal closet (the only big one, honest). The experience with Ford, however, instilled in me a fascination with organizational behavior, so I decided to study that. Been doing it ever since. In my academic career I have especially concentrated on understanding the ins and outs of cognition in organizations. It is an intriguing field. Yet, I have often looked for an important practical topic that might benefit from some of the marvelous, if esoteric cognitive theories that dot the academic mindscape. That little quest led me to creativity, which resulted in the closing of a personal circle for me because it rejuvenated a lifelong interest in the subject. One outcome of that process, thanks in great part to Cameron Ford, is this book on creativity in organizations.

Research Contributor Profiles

TERESA M. AMABILE, Professor of Business Administration at Harvard University, has been studying creativity since 1975. Her major accomplishments provide a good historical trace of her own professional development: from traditional experimental social psychology (having published her book *The Social Psychology of Creativity* in 1983) to a purer focus on a theory of creativity and innovation (having published her "Model of Creativity and Innovation in Organizations" in 1988) to field-based creativity research and consulting (in organizations such as Hughes Aircraft, J.C. Penney, DuPont, and Procter & Gamble), with forays along the way into children's creativity (doing federally funded research on "Development and Maintenance of Creativity in Children" from 1983-1986, and publishing her book *Growing Up Creative* in 1989), and public television stardom (serving as host/instructor of "Against All Odds: Inside Statistics" on PBS). She recently joined the Harvard Business School, where she became even better acquainted with the real world of organizations.

JAMES R. BAILEY is a fledgling academic at Rutgers University, spoiled by all the privileges his father's hard work afforded. He received his doctorate in psychology from Washington University (St. Louis), where he supported his bad habits by consulting widely in the financial services arena. He has published papers on varied topics, some of which his father thinks are ivory-tower banter, others of which his father approves. In the spirit of this volume, this unique authorship represents an attempt by father and son, practitioner and academic, wisdom and youth, to forge a useful bond from their sharply different life experiences.

DAG BJÖRKEGREN is Associate Professor in Organization and Management Theory at the Stockholm School of Economics. In 1974, during his undergraduate days, he discovered that pop music was something more than music when the Swedish pop group ABBA won the annual European song contest. This impression was reinforced in the beginning of the 1980s, when he spent one year as a visiting scholar at Harvard University and was given the opportunity to experience American popular culture. Since 1988 it has been possible for him to combine his fascination for the commercial potential of the clothes ABBA wore with his professional interests. He is doing his research and teaching in the field of arts management. Currently he is studying the Swedish film and TV industries.

DANIEL J. BRASS maintains a multiplexity of network ties with his colleagues at The Pennsylvania State University where he is Associate Professor of Organization Behavior in the Smeal College of Business Administration. He has strong ties to the faculty and former students at the University of Illinois-Urbana where he received his doctorate. His research interests can be structurally modeled as a network of these ties in combination with his social network research friends and acquaintances. He studies the relationship between organizational technology and structure (viewed from a social network perspective) and individual jobs, attitudes, behaviors, and power. Among his strong ties, he is best known for his addictions to golf, cigarettes, and landscape gardening. His most creative accomplishment is a life-sized topiary train, sculpted from a privet hedge.

JAY A. CONGER started his career as an anthropologist in South America and Turkey, unearthing Peruvian mummies and Greek theaters. With so many baby boomers filling all the available anthropology positions, he decided on an MBA and entered the world of business. He spent 5 years as the international marketing manager of the world's leading manufacturer of photovoltaics—a complicated word for solar cells. Determined to one day become a teacher, he moved on to a doctorate at the Harvard Business School to study organizational behavior—or as he sometimes says, organizational misbehavior. Long fascinated by leadership, his dissertation was a study of charismatic business leaders—the charisma part reflecting his tendency to do things a little out of the ordinary. Finding his true love in teaching others, his classrooms and his writings have become his greatest sources of creativity. These inspired him so far to author three books, *Learning to Lead* (1992), *The Charismatic Leader* (1989), and *Charismatic Leadership* (1988), as well as more than 60 articles, papers, and chapters on leadership, empowerment, and management education.

MIHALY CSIKSZENTMIHALYI is Professor of Psychology at the University of Chicago. He is the author of more than 140 scholarly articles and 10 books. *Beyond Boredom and Anxiety* is still in print after five editions. His last book, *Flow: The Psychology of Optimal Experience*, has brought him wide acclaim and has been translated into eight languages. Substantial articles on his work have appeared in most major newspapers and magazines. His 1965 doctoral thesis analyzed artistic creativity, and his interest in creativity has continued throughout the past three decades. He is currently directing several major research efforts at the University of Chicago, including the "Creativity in Later Life" study of 100 eminent creative individuals in the second half of life.

FARIBORZ DAMANPOUR started his career as a chemical engineer but was quick to go back to school and get a graduate degree in industrial and systems engineering, majoring in operations research. This degree got him a job as an operations analyst, which soon turned into a designer of information systems, where an attempt to implement one helped him stumble into organizational development consulting. Several years of this job were enough to send him back to school again, this time to get a doctorate from the Wharton School at the University of Pennsylvania. He is now Associate Professor of Organization Management on the Faculty of Management at Rutgers University. His specialty is in the management of innovation and technology, and organizational change and redesign. He also is interested in issues related to corporate ownership and has studied the role of institutional investors and the CEO's power on firm performance. His most recent research project focuses on organizational evolution in the U.S. banking industry.

JAMES L. FARR is Professor of Psychology at The Pennsylvania State University, where he has been for more than 20 years. Exposure to novel environments, however, has greatly contributed to his thinking about creativity and innovation in organizations. This includes his sabbatical leave at the University of Sheffield (U.K.), Social and Applied Psychology Unit, with Michael West and Nigel Nicholson, which spawned *Innovation and Creativity at Work* (1990), edited by West and Farr, and a recent sabbatical at the University of Western Australia, Department of Management, with Robert Wood and John Cordery, where the ideas in this volume's essay coalesced. His normal work environment at Penn State has provided the certainty and stability necessary to implement these ideas in the form of written products. He is the author of more than 60 professional publications and an editorial board member of four scholarly journals, as well as a member of the Executive Committee of the Society for Industrial and Organizational Psychology and a member of the Council of Representatives of the American Psychological Association.

PETER J. FROST is the Edgar Kaiser Chair of Organizational Behavior on the Faculty of Commerce and Administration at the University of British Columbia. His research interests focus on organizational culture and political processes. He has authored or edited 10 books, most recently *Doing Exemplary Research* (Sage, 1992) and *Reframing Organizational Culture* (Sage, 1992). A former Executive Director of the Academy of Management, he has won several awards for his teaching skills, including the David L. Bradford Outstanding Educator Award, a 3M Fellowship for Teaching Excellence, and the CASE Canadian Professor of the Year Award for Teaching. When not directing his creative energies on scholarly pursuits, he enjoys movies, birding, hiking, and most recently Scottish country dancing.

CONNIE J. G. GERSICK is Associate Professor at the Graduate School of Management, University of California, Los Angeles. She has been interested in social change since high school, and was Director of Yale's Office on the Education of Women before earning her doctorate in organizational behavior there. "Time and Transition in Work Teams," her first publication, won the 1988 award for outstanding contribution to organizational behavior from the OB division of the Academy of Management. Her subsequent laboratory study of project groups was named Best Paper of 1989 in the *Academy of Management Journal*. She has continued exploring change in human systems through research on theories of punctuated equilibrium, start-up companies, and athletic teams.

NIGEL KING is Lecturer in Psychology at the University of Huddersfield. His interest in creativity can be traced back to reading Liam Hudson's "Contrary Imaginations" as a senior at the University of Kent, and subsequently writing an essay on whether scientific creativity and artistic creativity are "the same thing" (he can't remember his conclusion). Next, he obtained a doctorate at the Social and Applied Psychology Unit, Sheffield, where through a mixture of personal interest and serendipity his research focused on innovation in elderly care institutions. His research interests currently are in the areas of decision making and patient-practitioner relationships in primary care. He has, however, maintained an interest in creativity throughout his reading and writing, and is currently exploring ideas for new research on the subject.

SHELLEY A. KIRKPATRICK is a Research Analyst at the Pelavin Research Institute. She holds a doctorate from the University of Maryland, College of Business Administration. She is interested in creativity as a leadership trait, specifically the role of the leader's creativity in the formulating of a vision.

KRISTIAN KREINER is Associate Professor of Organization Management on the faculty of the Copenhagen Business School, where he also received his M.Sc. He received his doctorate from the Technical University of Denmark. He has published work on leadership in radical free schools, on construction management, corporate architecture, scientific networks, and international collaborative projects. His thinking has been formed by attending to abstract, theoretical schools of thought such as garbage can decision processes, loosely coupled systems, existential paradoxes, organizational symbolism, and management of innovation. Because he continues to collect piles of empirical data, however, his interests must lie with the real world.

EDWIN A. LOCKE is Chair of the Management Faculty at the University of Maryland. He last studied the creativity literature in depth when he was a doctoral student at Cornell in the early 1960s, but he has had a continuing interest in the subject ever since. He has been especially impressed with Tom Peters's observations to the effect that you can get innovation simply by asking for it. However, he believes that asking for innovation will be more effective if the organization does other things too—these "other things" are the subject of the essay in this book. He is a Fellow of the Academy of Management and of the Society of Industrial and Organizational Psychology (SIOP) and was recently given the Distinguished Scientific Contribution award by SIOP.

TODD I. LUBART received his doctorate in psychology from Yale University. He is co-author with Robert J. Sternberg of an investment theory of creativity which is described in a 1995 book, *Defying the Crowd: Cultivating Creativity in a Culture of Conformity*. His research centers on creativity and innovation. He is currently a visiting scholar at the Ecole Supérieure de Commerce de Paris (Paris School of Management). He is also affiliated with the University of Paris V.

CRAIG C. LUNDBERG is the Blanchard Professor of Human Resource Management in the School of Hotel Administration at Cornell University, Ithaca, NY. He has been associated with higher education for more than 30 years, alternating his professional persona in business schools between teacher, researcher, administrator, editor, and intellectual gadfly. His academic pedigree, however, masks who he really is—a would-be poet, a serious though inept fly fisherman, a pretty fair skier, an overly romantic cattle rancher, and a gentle reformer of all systems of which he is a member. Although he consults to a wide variety of client organizations, he actually does the same thing with each—helping them surface and examine their assumptions and values. His written work regularly vacillates between the pragmatic and the scholarly, between the empirical and the conceptual. His interest in creativity stems from his early and continuing identification with two mentors, one personally creative because of his authentic humanness, the other creative because of his willingness to be intellectually risky and playful.

HARRY NYSTROM received his doctorate from the Stockholm School of Economics in 1970. After spending 5 years as Professor of Business Administration at Uppsala University, he has since settled in as Professor of Marketing and Organization at the Institute of Economics in Uppsala. In the 1970s he became fascinated with creativity as a research topic and has since tried to study management problems from a creativity point of view. He published his book *Creativity and Innovation* in 1979 as a revised English version of a Swedish book from 1974. His most recent book, *Technological and Market Innovation—Strategies for Product and Company Development*, was first published in 1990; it presents a framework for studying product and company development based on a large number of empirical studies he has carried out since 1975. It covers a wide range of industries and technologies and summarizes his research on company creativity and innovation.

MAJKEN SCHULTZ is Associate Professor of Organization Management at the Copenhagen Business School. Her primary interest in creativity derives from her own work on organizational culture. Although her thinking on creativity was originally based on an artistic tradition, her later experience and persistent questioning led her to view creativity in organizational settings as an ability to confront and pursue the unknown. The ability to pursue unpredictable and emergent opportunities in a disciplined manner is a distinct characteristic of the researchers working in the cross-national high-tech collaborations of the EUREKA program in which she is involved. Here, creativity is especially needed so that unpredictable and emergent opportunities can be linked to an overall business vision.

NIRMAL K. SETHIA is Associate Professor of Management and Human Resources in the College of Business Administration at California State Polytechnic University, Pomona. He also serves as Faculty Director of the American Business Center of Design. The Center, which is jointly supported by the Colleges of Business,

Engineering, and Environmental Design at Cal Poly Pomona, is dedicated to multidisciplinary education and research focusing on the business and social implications of design (industrial/product design, graphics/communication, design, and architectural/enviromental design). In his current work, he is studying the dynamics of creative collaboration in design projects, and the role of design creativity in creating customer valued quality. Recently, he has been awarded a grant from the National Endowment for the Arts to develop an interdisciplinary course in applied creativity titled "Design, Quality, and Entrepeneurship." He earned his B. Tech and doctorate from the Indian Institute of Technology, Bombay, and also holds an M.S. in electrical engineering from the University of Wisconsin.

DEAN KEITH SIMONTON is Professor of Psychology at the University of California at Davis. Since earning his doctorate from Harvard in 1975, he has published more than 100 journal articles on various aspects of genius, creativity, leadership, and aesthetics. A distinctive characteristic of his research program is the integration of scientific methods, especially in the context of biography and history. Because his research is emphatically interdisciplinary, he has published in four dozen different journals. He has also published more than 20 book chapters and five books, most recently *Greatness: Who Makes History and Why* (1994). He is a fellow of the American Psychological Association, the American Psychological Society, and the American Association of Applied and Preventative Psychology. A highly dedicated teacher, he received the 1994 UC Davis Prize for Teaching and Scholarly Achievement.

WILLIAM H. STARBUCK is ITT Professor of Creative Management at New York University. He applies the modest creativity he possesses to avoiding work, but with disappointing results. He has edited *Administrative Science Quarterly*, directed the doctoral program in business at New York University, serves on the Board of Governors of the Academy of Management, and passionately advocates the use of active verbs. Fickle interests have led him to publish articles on accounting, bargaining, business strategy, computer programming, computer simulation, decision making, forecasting, human-computer interaction, learning, organization design, organizational growth and development, perception, scientific methods, and social revolutions. He has also edited four books, including the *Handbook of Organizational Design*, which won an award as the best book on management published in 1981.

BARRY M. STAW is the Lorraine T. Mitchell Professor of Leadership and Communication at Berkeley's Haas School of Business. He has written a number of articles relevant to creativity, although he is not part of the mainstream of creativity researchers. Some of his work has been on how people and organizations get hopelessly stuck in losing courses of action. Other work has been on why common motivational techniques can cause people to lose their own initiative, forcing them to follow the erroneous prescriptions of others. Finally, he has been broadly concerned with the trade-offs of conformity and innovation, how they play themselves out in both individuals and organizations alike. His essay in this volume, "Why No One Really Wants Creativity," should not be interpreted as a surrender in researching creativity, but rather as a tactical maneuver in the protracted effort to understand creativity in organizational life.

ROBERT J. STERNBERG is IBM Professor of Psychology and Education at Yale University. He was graduated summa cum laude, Phi Beta Kappa from Yale in 1972, and received his doctorate at Stanford in 1975. He is a Fellow of the American Psychological Association and the American Psychological Society, and currently is Editor of the *Psychological Bulletin* and is President, Division 1 of the APA. He is the author of more than 300 books, chapters, and articles in the field of psychology. He has received more than $5 million in government and foundation grants to study intelligence and related topics, and is currently involved in several projects in the schools. He has won numerous awards from various organizations, including the American Psychological Association, American Educational Research Association, Guggenheim Foundation, Society for Multivariate Experimental Psychology, and the National Association for Gifted Children.

KARL E. WEICK is the Rensis Likert Collegiate Professor of Organizational Behavior and Psychology at the University of Michigan. He studies such topics as how people make sense of confusing events, the social psychology of improvisation, high reliability systems, the effects of stress on thinking and imagination, indeterminacy social systems, social commitment, small wins as the embodiment of wisdom, and the linkage between theory and practice. He was trained in psychology at Ohio State University, where he received his doctorate in 1962. Since graduating from Ohio State, he has been associated with faculties at Purdue University, the University of Minnesota, Cornell University, and the University of Texas. In 1990, he received the highest honor awarded by the Academy of Management, the Irwin Award for Distinguished Lifetime Scholarly Achievement. In the same year, he also received an award for the Best Article of the Year in the *Academy of Management Review*. He is also the former Editor of *Administrative Science Quarterly*, the leading research journal in the field of organizational studies. He has also written 60 journal articles, 55 chapters in edited books, 74 book reviews, and has presented 203 speeches to academic and practitioner audiences. His interests, aside from writing and editing, include jazz bands, railroading, and photography.

ROBERT W. WEISBERG is Professor of Psychology at Temple University. His research career began with the study of problem solving in the laboratory, but gradually shifted to broader areas of creativity, since one could argue that problem solving, even when exhibited by lowly undergrads in the lab, involves creative thinking. The literature in creativity at that time was dominated by such ideas as incubation and divergent thinking, and spontaneous leaps of insight, and it was almost universally agreed that some sort of extraordinary thought processes were involved. But his research has been concerned with trying to understand creative thinking through the mechanisms of "ordinary thinking" that cognitive psychologists study, such as memory. His research has led him to believe that the thought processes involved in even the most exalted acts of creative thinking are the same as those that we all use all the time, as when we decide what we will have for dinner.

MICHAEL A. WEST is Professor of Work and Organizational Psychology, University of Sheffield, United Kingdom. His interest in psychology developed initially from a passion for the plays of Shakespeare. His own study of human behavior initially focused on the psychology of meditation, the subject of his doctoral thesis. Meditation (or individual reflexivity) is an alternative means of exploring human experience and is, at one level, a research methodology as valid as the surveys and laboratory studies of psychologists in the West. His interest in the psychology of creativity developed in parallel over many years. He balances his focus on individual creativity and individual experience in meditation with a commitment to social action. These two strands of thought come together in the idea that reflexivity is fundamental to value-driven creativity in a social context.

RICHARD W. WOODMAN is the Clayton Professor of Business Administration and Professor of Management at Texas A&M University. He has a B.S. in industrial engineering and an MBA from Oklahoma State University. His doctorate in organizational behavior was granted by Purdue University and, to date, has not been recalled. At Texas A&M, he teaches organizational behavior, organizational change, and research methodology. By the time this appears in print, he will be, God help him, the Head of the Department of Management at Texas A&M University. Not being particularly creative himself, he has long been fascinated by creativity.

Management Contributor Profiles

F. E. BAILEY was born in 1925 in a Colorado lumber camp, and rose from the Depression by enlisting as a Navy pilot during World War II. Like so many of his contemporaries, he used the G.I. Bill to fund his college education, eventually winding up with a B.A. in mathematics and an M.A in education. After a stint as a public school administrator, he began a long career in the insurance industry, first as an agent, later as a manager. Increasingly discontent with corporate folly and lethargy, he struck out in 1984 and founded Bailey Financial Group, Inc. His firm has gained a national reputation for bringing together providers, marketers, and consumers of financial products in an innovative, entrepreneurial fashion. Despite his considerable successes, he considers his greatest achievement his children, which is a good thing, because his co-author is his son.

ISAAC (ITZIK) R. BARPAL, Ph.D., joined AlliedSignal Inc. in August 1993 as Senior Vice President and Chief Technology Officer overseeing the Corporation's technology efforts and administering its central, multi-disciplinary Research and Technology Center. He earned his B.S. degree in electrical engineering and applied mathematics from California State Polytechnic University and his M.S. and doctorate in electrical engineering from the University of California at Santa Barbara. He also attended the Advanced Management Program at Harvard Business School. Before joining AlliedSignal, he had a 22-year distinguished career at the Westinghouse Electric Corporation, which included engineering, projects, operations, and general management assignments. He has written numerous technical articles and holds several patents. Active in a number of engineering and professional societies, he is a registered engineer in California, Florida, Pennsylvania, and Brazil. Born in Argentina, he has lived in seven countries and now resides in Morristown, NJ.

ROBERT MICHAEL BURNSIDE is Senior Research and Applications Associate for the Center for Creative Leadership (CCL). He joined CCL in 1985. His work there has lead to innovative methods for leadership development and to a better understanding of how organizational cultures stimulate creativity. Prior to joining CCL, he spent 12 years with Wrangler Jeans in various marketing and merchandising positions in which he experienced the joys and difficulties of leadership and innovation. Before that he was in the Peace Corps in India, and he has a B.A. in political science that has certainly been of use to him throughout his career. His two sons, 14 and 12 years old, and his mate of 18 years, are constant reminders to him to not define himself solely by his work.

ALAN G. CHYNOWETH has recently retired after having spent 40 years at the R&D heart of the Bell companies—a career that took him from the early days of transistors through to laying the technological groundwork for the nation's information superhighways. He was schooled in England, receiving his doctorate in nuclear physics from London University, King's College in 1950. Over the years, he has published research papers, received 11 patents, participated in countless internal management and corporate meetings, had numerous external talks, contributed to committee activities of the National Research Council and of the North Atlantic Treaty Organization, received awards for his research and research management, served on professional society and university advisory committees, and enjoyed it all.

PEDRO CUATRECASAS has been Vice President of Warner-Lambert and President of the Pharmaceutical Research Division, Parke-Davis, since October 1989. Prior to joining Warner-Lambert, he served as Vice President of Research and Development at Burroughs

Wellcome Co. (1975-1986) and Senior Vice President of Research and Development for Glaxo, Inc. (1986-1989). Before joining Burroughs Wellcome, he served as a researcher at the National Institutes of Health, as Professor of Biochemistry at George Washington University, and as Professor of Pharmacology at The Johns Hopkins University School of Medicine. He has also held adjunct professorships at Duke and the University of North Carolina since 1975. Since 1990, he has held adjunct professorships in the Departments of Pharmacology and Pharmacy at the University of Michigan. He received his B.A. (1958) and M.D. (1962, magna cum laude) from Washington University, St. Louis. He has been elected to membership to the U.S. National Academy of Sciences (1982), the Institute of Medicine (1981), and American Academy of Arts & Sciences (1988), and he is a recipient of the Wolf Prize in Medicine (1988); he has more than 400 publications.

JOHN ENGLER was elected as the 46th Governor of Michigan in 1990. Born in 1948 in Mount Pleasant and raised in Beal City, MI, he earned a bachelor's degree in agricultural economics from Michigan State University and a J.D. from the Thomas M. Cooley Law School. In 1970, at the age of 22, he was elected to the Michigan House of Representatives and advanced to the Senate in 1978, where he served as Majority Leader from 1983 through 1990. Upon taking office in 1991, he launched the "Taxpayers' Agenda," a strategy to cut taxes, limit the size of government, create jobs, and improve the quality of public schools. His actions transformed a $1.8 billion budget deficit into a $312 million surplus, even though 11 tax cuts spared taxpayers $1 billion annually. As of 1994, Michigan's economic recovery led all industrial states, income growth was first in the Midwest and second among the nation's 10 largest states, and the unemployment rate was at a 20-year low. Michigan created one out of every three jobs in the nation, and created more manufacturing jobs than the other 49 states combined during this period. Leading business publications have described him as America's "most consequential" Governor, and said that the passage of Proposal A, which cut property taxes while guaranteeing school funding and reducing inequities among school districts, was the most dramatic change in public school financing in the past 100 years.

NORMAN P. FINDLEY is Vice President, Domestic and International Marketing for Coca-Cola Enterprises. He began his career in soft drink marketing in 1970 as a bottling company distribution analyst and joined Coca-Cola USA in 1976 as a District Manager. After holding positions including Area Marketing Manager, Vice-President, Marketing and Bottler Services, and Vice-President, Marketing Operations, he joined Coca-Cola Enterprises as Vice-President, Marketing in June 1989. In 1993, he was promoted to Vice-President, Domestic and International Marketing where, in addition to his domestic marketing responsibilities, he became responsible for managing Coca-Cola's first international bottling operation in the Netherlands. He notes that "When most people think about creativity and soft drinks, they think about advertising. But, creativity is more widely utilized for less glamorous activities such as developing new points of availability; synergistic opportunities with other companies, new packaging, etc. Organizations and corporate cultures which grow these kinds of ideas provide substainable competive advantage." He earned a BBA in marketing management from the University of Notre Dame, holds an MBA from the University of Southern California, and is a graduate of the Strategic Marketing Mangement program of the Harvard Business School. He is also a member of Beta Gamma Sigma, the national business honorary fraternity.

RUSSELL C. FORD is Senior Vice President for the Harristown Development Corporation in Harrisburg, PA. He holds bachelor's degrees in Community Development and Park and Recreation Administration from Penn State University and a master's in Regional Planning from the University of North Carolina at Chapel Hill. He began working as a city planner and urban planning consultant, but has spent the past decade planning, financing, developing, and operating complex multi-million dollar real estate projects. These projects, which include hotel, retail, office, transportation, and public improvement facilities, form the core of the downtown revitalization program for Pennsylvania's capital city. He also serves as president of several real estate partnerships related to this work, and is currently Chairman of the Hershey, PA, Planning Commission. He coaches Little League with his creative eye peeled, appreciating the value of difference in making a difference.

C. JACKSON GRAY is Senior Vice President of Corporate Planning and Development of Woolworth Corporation, and is a member of the six-person Chairman's Group. This group is responsible for strategic planning, new venture development, and capital-allocation planning. The Chairman's Group creatively used strategy in the restructuring of Woolworth in the past few years through new ventures, acquisitions, and redeployment of stores throughout the United States and abroad. He also serves on boards of several of the corporation's retailing subsidiaries and advisory boards of other organizations, such as the Association for Corporate Growth. He has recently been appointed to the advisory board of Texas A&M's Center for Retailing Studies, which aims through the variety of programs to interest and better prepare college students for a retail career. In his work with college study groups, he challenges students to view the future of retailing, and pushes them to be creative as they prepare for the future.

GEORGE HEARD, Vice President of Coors Brewing Co., received a B.S. in chemical engineering from Texas Technological College in 1961. He later earned a master's of business administration from the University of Texas. He has spent the past 21 years working in a variety of positions, including management of operations and utilities, research and development, quality assurance, quality control, regulatory affairs, maintenance, and presently engineering and construction. Motivating people to obtain results has been a common thread throughout his 30 years of industrial experience. The techniques that solve complex technical problems are quite similar to those required to solve problems that require little if any formal training. It's so simple when you know how! It's illusive and frustrating when you can't figure it out. The challenges and rewards are to solve all the various problems, to end up with each piece of the puzzle in place. A jigsaw puzzle with three missing pieces just doesn't cut it!

DELBERT H. JACOBS is Vice President and Center Manager, Northrop Advanced Technology and Design Center. The Northrop Advanced Technology and Design Center is responsible for originating, co-ordinating, and directing all Northrop research, technology development, and design efforts in future manned and unmanned aircraft systems, as well as other advanced applications. His mixed history related to creativity includes inventing a fracture-reducing ski binding in 1948 (which he failed to patent), winning the Eisenhower Award at Westpoint (1955) presented by President Eisenhower, serving as a professor and co-author of the first Astronautics textbooks at the USAF Academy (1961-1964), serving as a USAF creator-engineer-advocate-implementor and test pilot of a telescope system that produced a tenfold resolution improvement for fighter pilot target identification (a national award winner that is still in production 25 years later!), and serving as the Design Team Leader and Dem/Val competition winner of YF-23 Advanced Tactical Fighter Prototype (1986). He also owns *F-9A*, the fastest 31-foot sailing trimaran on the West Coast (1993).

NORMAN E. JOHNSON, Ph.D., is Senior Vice President, Technology with Weyerhaeuser Company. He has worked there since 1956 with the exception of 2 years on the faculty at Cornell University. He has worked in most of the timbered regions of the United States and spent 5½ years in Southeast Asia. He has been a scientist, research manager, operating vice president, and senior vice president. He has served on U.S. presidential task forces to Honduras and Zaire. He is also a member of the board of directors of the Pacific Science Center in Seattle. His career has led him through both practical and academic pursuits. While he was a forest entomologist he published more than 100 research and general scientific papers.

F. BEN JONES was born in Minnesota, reared in Columbus, OH, and graduated from Ohio State University with a degree in organic chemistry in 1954. After working 10 years as a polymer research chemist and research supervisor, he joined Phillips Petroleum Company in 1964 as a research supervisor in adhesives science. He continued to progress through the company until he finally retired in 1992 as the sixth R&D Vice President in Phillips' history. He is also a member of the American Chemical Society, past member of the Society of Plastic Engineers, The Adhesion Society, the Industrial Research Institute, and is member-emeritus of the Directors of Industrial Research. He is author of more than 20 technical publications and 26 U.S. patents. He also owned and operated a ranch where he raised beef cattle and hogs. Currently his creative energies are directed toward his six children, 12 grandchildren, two dogs, beautiful flower gardens, and high golf handicap. Life is good!

ALEXANDER MacLACHLAN accepted an appointment as Deputy Undersecretary for Technology Partnerships in the Department of Energy after retiring as Senior Vice President, DuPont Research & Development after a 35-year career. Whatever creativity he has he correlates with a clear definition of an important need. His earliest creative solutions involved caring for a dilapidated 1933 Chevrolet. At DuPont, his earliest days were merely an extension of his childhood: people depending on him with important needs to satisfy. There is no more exhilarating feeling than coming up with a solution to what initially had looked hopeless. His experience at DuPont included mostly research management in a variety of businesses, a wonderful year in Germany as a research director, several years running a good business, and a few years resurrecting one in really tough shape. In all these assignments, problems abounded and there were long periods of stress and uncertainly. Every once in a while he helped creatively and saw success. The wait for those moments was worth it.

PHILIP X. MASCIANTONIO, Ph.D., has worked to develop positive and innovative approaches to the resolution of environmental concerns through non-confrontational partnerships among industry, government, and environmental groups. He recently retired as Vice President of Environmental Affairs from U.S. Steel Group (USX Corp.) and is now President of PMX Global Ecology Partners, an entrepreneurial consulting firm. His work has included research management, project development, and encouragement of creative techniques to resolve environmental problems. He has published broadly, lectured extensively, and patented several coal and chemical products and processes. He continues to serve on a number of advisory committees and organizational boards of research and environmental groups. His academic training came from St. Vincent College (B.S.) and Carnegie Mellon University (M.S. and doctorate).

TERRY O'CONNOR notes that an essayist like Charles Lamb would begin his bio with a subtle and thoroughly engaging presentation of credentials that would draw you toward his mind and mood. O'Connor says he can't do that. He won't even try. Instead (trusting in the statute of limitations), he admits that he spent his childhood in the Midwest, his adolescence in the sixties, and the past 6 years at BASF as Director, Marketing Services. Apart from that, he chooses to take the advise of his wife, which is, "In your case, the less said the better."

TIMOTHY F. PRICE is Group President of MCI Communications Services Group, a role encompassing responsibility for MCI's business and consumer markets, operating alliances, and new emerging markets, such as information services and wireless communications. Formerly, as President of MCI Business Markets, he was the architect of the industry's first national brand for business, Proof Positive. He also led MCI's entry into the software business with networkMCI business. As Senior Vice President of Sales and Marketing for MCI Consumer Markets, he engineered the development and launch of Friends & Family, the industry's first and most recognized long distance brand and winner of the prestigious Gold Edison Award from the American Marketing Association. In 1994, he was named Outstanding Corporate Strategist by Frohlinger's Marketing Report, Marketer of the Year by *Media Week* magazine, and Marketing Executive of the Year by the National Accounts Management Association.

THORALF ULRIK QVALE has focused his activities for 25 years around the question of how to design processes that cut across organizational levels and institutional borders so that local organizational innovations can grow and be sustained. He believes that democratic work organizations and direct, trusting participation between people and organizational units are preconditions for the success of such innovations. He continues to be impressed with how well-organized groups can accomplish complex tasks if you take away bureaucratic, structural obstacles to innovation. He is currently research director at the Work Research Institute in Oslo, a position that allows frequent, hands-on, and deep-going exploration of innovations that address the problems of work life.

WALTER L. ROBB recently retired as Senior Vice President—Corporate Research and Development after 41 years at GE. He is finding that life after GE, as President of Vantage Management, a consulting and investor service business, can be every bit as fun, exciting, and profitable as his career at GE. From having his photo in *Life Magazine*, demonstrating his artificial gill, to receiving the National Medal of Technology at the White House for his management of major CT and MR scanner projects, he has been well recognized for his entrepreneurial, risk-taking work. He is especially happy now, encouraging young people interested in math and science, a small repayment for the mentoring he was given by his high school science teacher.

KEITH SAWYER received his doctorate from the University of Chicago in 1994. His dissertation focused on how children learn creativity and social skills through social pretend play. In addition to his academic research, he has worked for 10 years as a new technology consultant to large organizations, including Citicorp, USWest, and the U.S. Postal Service. He is currently a consultant in New York City with the Culpeper Consulting Group and is continuing with his research projects in children's play and improvisational theater.

CAROLE F. ST. MARK is President of Pitney Bowes Business Services and an officer of Pitney Bowes, Inc. She got to this position via a circuitous route, however. After receiving an A.B. in Russian language from Douglas College, Rutgers University she couldn't get a job. She eventually worked for an employment agency on straight commission and then placed herself in a recruiting job with General Mills. Realizing she knew nothing about business, she got an MBA from Pace University. She worked for 18 years in various human resource jobs with General Foods, St. Regis Paper, General Electric, and Pitney Bowes before getting a chance to switch fields as the Vice President of Strategic Planning. Since she didn't know anything about strategic planning, she hired consultants to teach her, but then became intrigued by the possibility of new business development. With the growth and success of one of the ventures she created, she was given responsibility for several operating units in 1988, and was promoted to her current position in 1990. She also trains horses and is the proud owner of a big American Quarter Horse named Luke and a Hunter Show Horse named Leonardo.

KARL-ERIK SVEIBY believes, in retrospect, that he has spent all his working life unlearning! First he spent 6 years as a manager in Unilever unlearning what he had learned in the university. Then he spent 15 years unlearning the Unilever experience as senior partner and manager of a publishing company. During that period he was also the co-founder and editor of Sweden's first management magazine, in which he tried to unlearn what American management gurus had taught him. He recently left the line operation of his company. Today he is primarily a researcher, author, and board member/consultant to knowledge-intensive organizations, mainly in Scandinavia and Europe. Thus he is currently busy unlearning what he has previously been actively doing in management and strategy. Still, he has at least one ongoing learning experience; the relationship with his wife and his daughter, now 15 years old. This is how he defines creativity: Creativity is the ability to transcend the taken-for-granted.

WELLINGTON E. WEBB became the Mayor of Denver, CO, on July 1, 1991. It was just the latest step in a distinguished 20-year career of public service. In addition to being elected Mayor of Denver, he previously served a 4-year term as the elected Auditor of Denver and was elected to the Colorado House of Representatives three times beginning in 1972. He was appointed by President Jimmy Carter to be the Regional Administrator of the Department of Health, Education and Welfare and was a member of former Colorado Governor Richard Lamm's Cabinet as Executive Director of the Department of Regulatory Agencies. He is married to Wilma J. Webb, also a former state legislator, and has four grown children. A former college basketball player, he presently plays on the Mayor's Office team in the City of Denver employee league.

R. LARRY WUENCH is Director of Marketing for Mitsubishi Caterpillar Forklift America Inc. He was born in Memphis, TN, a long time ago and graduated (barely) from the University of Tennessee as a civil engineer in 1962. After spending four years as an officer in an Army tank unit, he joined Caterpillar as a sales trainee in 1966, because he had grown to love anything that ran on tracks—as long as there were no guns mounted on it. For 15 years he worked with

Caterpillar dealers and customers in North and Central America, Europe, Africa, and the Middle East to increase sales of Cat earth-moving products. In all that time he learned there are never any simple solutions to business problems, but there are always several intelligent, creative choices. Sometimes he picked the right one! Since 1982, he has been helping Caterpillar survive in the "hostile world of fork lift trucks."